# $12 BILLION OF INSIDE MARKETING SECRETS DISCOVERED THROUGH DIRECT RESPONSE TELEVISION SALES

And how you can profitably apply them to your business.

## By Steven Dworman
Publisher of the *Infomercial Marketing Report*

**$12 Billion of Inside Marketing Secrets Discovered Through Direct Response Television Sales**
**And how you can profitably apply them to your business.**
**By Steven Dworman**

Published by
**SDE Publishing, Inc.**
12254 Montana Avenue, Suite A
Los Angeles, CA 90049
(310) 826-8810
steve@itreallyworks.tv
www.drtvsecrets.com

Cover & Book Design: Hugh M. Aoki for Design Warriors, a division of Marketing Warriors

Dworman, Steven.
$12 billion of inside marketing secrets discovered through direct response television sales: And how you can profitably apply them to your business / by Steven Dworman.

Library of Congress Catalog Card Number: 2003098738

ISBN: 0-9726438-0-X

1. Marketing.
2. Business.
3. Interviews.
4. Infomercials.
5. Direct marketing.   I. Title.

Printed in the United States of America
10 9 8 7 6 5 4 3 2 1

# TABLE OF CONTENTS

# TABLE OF CONTENTS
## (CONTINUED)

## *Bonus!*

# ACKNOWLEDGMENTS

First, I'd like to thank Greg Renker, who endorsed the *Infomercial Marketing Report* with the very first issue and helped to launch it. Greg and his company, Guthy-Renker Corporation, have saved every copy of the newsletter and often refer back to it for specific information. It was Greg's idea to turn these interviews into a book.

Second, I'd like to thank all of the subjects of my interviews over the past 12 years who answered some very inside questions in a very open and honest manner. This is a very competitive industry. They knew all along that their competitors would read every single word, and yet they were nonetheless forthcoming with very inside information.

I'd also like to thank my associate and friend Clare Jacoby for being a bright light I looked forward to seeing every single day. Thanks also goes to Michelle Hafle, who kept the office running as smoothly as a fine Swiss watch. My deepest appeciation goes to my friend and assistant Dana Chaney, whose friendship and caring puts a daily smile on my face.

And finally, I'd like to thank all the truly good, lifelong friends I've made over the past 15 years in this industry. I appreciate your faith, confidence and trust in giving me an insider view of what truly goes on behind closed doors.

# INTRODUCTION

꧁✿꧂

*T*he infomercial business began in the mid-1980s when the Reagan administration deregulated the amount of advertising time allowed per hour on television. Cable television stations were in their infancy and they were hungry for revenue. A few smart entrepreneurs realized that they could purchase this suddenly abundant cable airtime for literally a few hundred dollars per half hour and run their own programming—selling products, investment courses and business opportunities. In the late 1980s, several companies formed to take advantage of this new marketing medium. Among these were the Synchronal Corporation, Twin Star, Media Arts and Guthy-Renker. American Telecast, a company that already amassed a strong sales record in direct response television, decided to venture into the "infomercial" realm. In 1989, two key infomercials hit the airwaves and they changed the industry forever. American Telecast launched Victoria Jackson Cosmetics featuring a then unknown Victoria Jackson, a Hollywood make-up artist with her own cosmetic line. Her infomercial starred Ali MacGraw and Lisa Hartman, two celebrities the likes of whom had never before been seen in an infomercial. Meanwhile, Guthy-Renker launched their Tony Robbins *Personal Power* infomercial with Fran Tarkenton as the host and a slew of well know endorsers from the worlds of entertainment, sports and government. Over the years, Tony Robbins' infomercials have grossed over $300 million. Victoria Jackson's series of shows have gone on to gross even more.

In August of 1991, I published the first issue of the *Infomercial Marketing Report*. The industry was hot. Entrepreneurs believed that infomercials were the next gold rush. Huge amounts of money were being made through a combination of a winning product, a winning offer and a winning show. In 1991, one out of seven infomercials were financially successful, meaning that they were turning a profit. Today, only **one out of sixty** infomercials turns a profit. Why the tremendous difference? There are two primary reasons. First, during the early days, an average consumer had less than nine stations to choose from on their television. Today, with cable and satellite television, they now have several hundred viewing options. So obviously there are far fewer people watching each individual station. This is why the audience for the major networks has shrunk to such a staggering degree. Second, even though the number of eyeballs watching has decreased, the media rates have gone up by as much as 500% over the past 14 years. Still, major corporations like Salton-Maxim are using infomercials to launch new consumer products into major department stores. At a conference I sponsored at the Waldorf Astoria in 1993, Marvin Traub, the former Chairman of Bloomingdale's, stood up and remarked that he'd never seen anything move product at retail in such tremendous quantities as a successful infomercial.

The *Infomercial Marketing Report* took off like a rocket from the moment it was launched. Read by thousands of people in 20 countries around the world, this inside report broke many newsworthy stories that were picked up by The Wall Street Journal, The New York Times, The Washington Post and hundreds of other notable media entities. Each month, the entire industry waited for their copy of this vital news source to arrive in the mail. If an issue was even a day late, the phones in our publishing offices would ring off the hook with readers wondering where their issue was. And sometimes people didn't like what they read. For a period of three months, the heads of three major infomercial companies refused to talk to us because they were unhappy with some of the inside information we printed. Often that included actual copies of lawsuits recently filed that contained hard sales numbers and the ever important deal points for major infomercial campaigns. We certainly stirred the pot a number of times. On the other hand, the newsletter was also responsible for helping many inventors to sell their products. This included one of the top grossing infomercial products of all time, The Total Gym, which showcased Chuck Norris and Christie Brinkley in the show. That product alone has grossed just under one billion dollars.

Companies subscribing to the *Infomercial Marketing Report* paid a total of $4,740 to receive it over the course of the 12 years of its publication. What you hold in your hands represents a goldmine of information culled from those 12 years of inside information. The exclusive interviews in this book represent some of the most important marketing information ever divulged from the world of direct marketing and television infomercial sales. Since the *Infomercial Marketing Report* was an "insider" newsletter, no one from outside the industry ever had the opportunity to view this wealth of carefully guarded secrets…until now.

These interviews not only give you insightful, inside marketing data, but they also serve as a history of the industry itself. Since the inception of the direct marketing infomercial industry in 1991, the industry has gone through a rapid maturation process. Only two of the major companies that started the infomercial revolution are still in business today. Those two pioneers/veterans are American Telecast and the Guthy-Renker Corporation.

Why did some companies succeed while the others failed? What secrets did they learn that the others didn't, or failed to heed? You'll uncover the answers to these questions within the covers of this book.

Unlike the Internet boom, the infomercial business is based on three major elements: 1) Selling a product or service profitably; 2) Purchasing the media to advertise the product at the most economical price; and 3) When possible, creating an ongoing relationship with a customer and selling them more or additional products.

Every single one of these elements should be incorporated into all businesses. But unlike the infomercial industry, most outside businesses don't track their results. Advertising agencies can tell you how many people saw your ad, how many may have read your ad, what the demographics are of the people who may have read your ad, but they'll never tell you how many people picked up the phone or went down to their local retailer and actually purchased your product.

Direct response television companies test price, offer, and product configurations before rolling out. It has surprised many people throughout the years that often a consumer will be more likely to purchase a product at a higher price point than a low price point because the higher price increases the perceived value of the product. The wealth of information gathered over the years from this continuous consumer testing is a treasure chest of data.

A general rule of thumb is that an infomercial will not stay on the air if it isn't profitable, however, unless you're privy to what is going on behind the scenes you'll never really know whether a campaign is profitable or not. For example, one company created a low-priced exercise show selling three exercise videos for only $40.00. They didn't expect the show to be profitable; instead their intention was to get customers to sign on to a continuity program for vitamins. But when the show was tested it surprised everyone that the video offer worked on its own, was extremely profitable, and the vitamin sales became a highly profitable gravy that will pay a good chunk of their overhead for years to come.

Joe Sugarman, one of the interviewees in this book, made a fortune from his line of BluBlocker Sunglasses. Joe remarked to me once during a private conversation that he attributes his success to the fact that he failed more times than anyone else.

Marketing guru Jay Abraham said to me on several occasions, "I try a lot of stuff Stevie, more than anyone else I know. Some work and some don't. You don't know unless you try."

And that's what I'd like to impart to you. There is such a wealth of information contained within this book—information that is the result of 12 years of constant and continuous research. I urge you to take even the smallest bit of information and test it in your own marketing campaigns. You don't have to launch an entire direct response television campaign. You can start with a simple letter to your customer base making them an offer similar to the ones talked about in this book. Watch what happens. I think you'll be very surprised. Many of these techniques also work with print advertising. Maybe you didn't realize it, but when you run print ads that sell directly, you very often qualify for a substantial discount in the advertising rates. This too is discussed in this book. You can easily make back the cost of this book ten times over with your very first advertisement.

I hope you enjoy the treasure hunt you're about to begin.

Best of luck to you,

Steven Dworman

# JOSEPH SUGARMAN

*A* legendary direct marketing and infomercial pioneer, Joseph Sugarman became the first direct marketer of hand-held pocket calculators when he took out his first full-page ad in *The Wall Street Journal* in 1973. Soon afterward, he published the first electronic products catalogue, JS&A's *Products That Think*. Sugarman also led a number of highly influential seminars on how to break into the catalogue direct marketing business. Attendees included representatives from Victoria's Secret to direct marketing legends like Joe Karbo. In 1973, Sugarman's company became the first in the U.S. to use toll-free phone numbers to take credit card orders.

Sugarman also launched one of the longest-running and most profitable infomercial series ever for BluBlocker sunglasses. At the time of this extensive interview, Sugarman had sold between two and three million pairs of BluBlockers and ranked among the top five manufacturers of sunglasses. His innovative production and editing techniques and his unique sales strategies have helped set many standards for the infomercial industry.

**Steve Dworman:** Initially, you ran into some problems with the FTC and stopped the electronic catalogue.

**Joe Sugarman:** At that time, the FTC's bureaucracy was out of control. They were extremely aggressive and came down on us very heavy for no real good reason. And I believed that if you were right, and fought the government, you would win. So I fought the government.

**SD:** And did you win?

**JS:** We had to settle eventually—so the answer is no, I didn't win. On the other hand, I feel that I accomplished a great deal toward preventing what happened to me from happening to others.

**SD:** And after that trouble settled down, I believe you went into print with BluBlockers.

**JS:** After that settled down, we tried to get back into the business we were previously in, which was electronics, similar to what DAK and Sharper Image were doing. But they had already grown considerably in that year or two, so it was very difficult to capture the previous position that we had in the market. We tried, but soon realized that the market was changing and that we had other opportunities to direct our efforts toward. So we got out of electronics and more or less eased into health and fitness.

**SD:** What kind of products did you handle at that point?

**JS:** The two major ones were a vitamin continuity program and BluBlockers. We had a major print campaign for those two products and it firmly established our company in the health and fitness area. So now we were starting to grow once again and then we heard about infomercials and we created one infomercial for the vitamins and one for the sunglasses. Both of them took off and became quite successful.

We had a little problem with the FTC, part of being a pioneer in a new business. Although we announced at the beginning of our show that it was a commercial, and again very clearly at the end that it was a commercial, the program appeared to be regular programming. So the FTC insisted that we tag the show in the middle as well as at the beginning and the end, which we did. In fact we went overboard. To make absolutely sure there was no confusion whatsoever in our program, we changed the format and the name and called it *The Making of a Commercial*. The entire show revolved around how we were making this commercial to sell sunglasses, so there could never be any question about what we were doing.

**SD:** Wasn't the set up for the first show almost a consumer test, in which BluBlockers were rated best?

**JS:** It was called *Consumer Challenge*, and it wasn't that BluBlockers were rated best. We sent out a couple of reporters to interview a lot of people and almost everybody, of course, had glowing reports. But we also had a few reports from people who didn't like the sunglasses. So we tried to make it a balanced presentation. The problem was that it appeared to be regular programming and not an actual commercial. The show ran for a year and a half.

**SD:** What year was that?

**JS:** I believe that we started working on it in 1986 and started running it in the first part of 1987.

**SD:** So you had one of the first infomercials?

**JS:** One of the early ones, yeah.

*SD:* And at that time the CPOs were phenomenal.

*JS:* We couldn't believe it.

*SD:* Didn't the sunglasses sell for $59.95 initially?

*JS:* That was in print. When we went on TV, we sold them for $39.95. Our CPO (Cost Per Order) was $3.00 a pair.

*SD:* People will gag at this point.

*JS:* The people we were working with, who knew the industry, said that they had never heard of a CPO that low.

*SD:* Did you come up with the idea for BluBlockers, or did you license the product?

*JS:* BluBlockers have been around since World War II. A BluBlocker lens is a coating that filters out blue light. So we produced a pair of sunglasses that removed all of the ultraviolet rays and blue light, which wasn't unique. Our unique angle was to publicize the fact that ultraviolet rays and blue light are bad for your eyes and also a phenomenon that I learned in photography—which is that if you remove some of the blue light, you get greater clarity, because the blue has a tendency to scatter.

So to answer your question—and I'm sorry I can't answer it simply—the technology has been around for many, many years but nobody really knew how to sell it. In addition, we've added some recent technologies to the lenses to make them state-of-the-art.

*SD:* The glasses were manufactured initially in Los Angeles?

*JS:* Initially, but by the time we got on TV, we had them manufactured in Taiwan. When the sunglasses were made in Los Angeles, they cost us 4 to 5 times as much as they did to have them made in Taiwan. And we were selling them for $59.95. Then we dropped the price to $39.95 because we were able to buy the product for much less and hit a much broader TV market.

*SD:* What happened with the vitamin infomercial?

*JS:* We ran it for a couple of years and it was quite successful, but at the time I was rather naive, after having been in electronics where a 50% margin was terrific. We had that with vitamins and I was pleased. We were making money, but after a couple of years it started to peter out. I found out subsequently that a 10x mark-up on vitamins was normal, but we were succeeding with just a 2x mark up. But those were the early days of infomercials and everything worked.

*SD:* Did you buy the vitamins from a distributor?

*JS:* Right, and the distributor in turn bought them from the manufacturer. The distributor provided us with a few extra services—they did all the drop shipping and they did all the computer work and fulfillment, so there was a reason for that 50% margin. But as I learned later, margin is extremely important in infomercials and ours just wasn't enough to sustain a steady program with that product.

But I wasn't prepared to go behind my distributor's back and create another vitamin. So I decided at that particular point, even though it was successful, I would phase out of that program. Although we haven't advertised for years, the continuity program is still running. We still ship vitamins and the income covers some part of our overhead every month.

*SD:* I'll bet the back-end of the program was huge compared with the front-end.

*JS:* Well, the back-end was quite successful because it was a continuity program. Once we made the sale, and made the profit on the sale, then every couple of months all we had to do was ship out the next shipment, and it was all profit. Of course, we also worked the back-end strongly by offering other products to our customers.

*SD:* It seems that a lot of infomercial companies are starting to realize that they're not going to be very profitable unless they really work the back-end.

*JS:* It's where the action is today. That's really where the direct marketing expertise comes in, because making it on an infomercial isn't what it was several years ago. Like I said, you could slap anything on the air and still make a decent profit. Today, it's very marginal and you've got to have a strong back-end in order to make it work.

*SD:* We're seeing a glut of skin care products coming out, from Victoria Jackson and Victoria Principal, to Cher signing a deal for her own skin care line. Everyone is finally catching on to the potential of the back-end.

*JS:* Yep.

*SD:* You are also one of the premier direct marketing copywriters in the country. You wrote all the copy in your ads and catalogue yourself. Do you write your own television shows?

*JS:* Yes.

*SD:* They have a very spontaneous feel about them. Is most of that scripted?

*JS:* The only part that is scripted is when the hostess and I talk back and forth and we introduce the segments. But even though that is scripted, we do not pay attention to the script. We talk off the top of our heads. Sometimes we'll goof up, but often we'll still use that portion that we goofed up on. But, in the sense that we have to start somewhere, the show is scripted.

*SD:* The shows move very fast. Do you get involved in much tweaking after the show is tested?

*JS:* That's probably our secret. We'll produce a show and probably spend as much money editing after the show is finished and first tested as we do prior to running it. This has taught us an enormous amount. When you tweak, you try different experiments and run them on different stations and you keep doing it until you have the show that works the best that it can.

A good example is that for three or four years we've run our show without showing our clip-ons. Clip-ons are the pair of sunglasses that fit over a pair of prescription glasses. We've shown a pair in a still shot, but in our new commercial, we show them being put on somebody's glasses and we demonstrate how they are used. As a result, our clip-on sales in August were triple what they had been in the previous month.

That tells us a lot. It tells us that you've constantly got to test and learn from your tests. You test with focus groups and you test them on TV. It takes awhile, sometimes a month or two, before you're really ready—even after you think you're ready.

*SD:* I've heard mixed reactions about the value of focus groups. Some marketers believe that what people say in the focus group context isn't really trustworthy.

*JS:* I don't believe all the comments that people make in focus groups. I listen and then I filter the comments through my mind. People often say things they don't mean, and mean things they don't say. My perspective comes from a great deal of experience in direct mail copywriting, experience that has shown me what really works and what really doesn't work. I've had ad agencies plead with me not to do something and I've gone out and proved to them that my suggestions were right, even though they went against everything the advertising community taught.

*SD:* Can you give an example of that?

*JS:* There were a couple of instances, but they're rather confidential and they are keys to some of our successes. I didn't mind talking about the clip-ons because that was an obvious example, and clip-ons are a rather pronounced segment of our show now. But the other examples are very subtle.

*SD:* How many BluBlocker shows have you done now?

*JS:* Four shows over the last five years.

*SD:* Aside from maybe Dave Del Dotto, you've probably had one of the longest running products on the air. That leads to a whole series of questions. To what do you attribute your longevity? And do you think most infomercial marketers give up on their products too soon?

*JS:* Let's put it this way. When you've peaked with a product and the commercial wears out, the tendency is to say, "Well, the product is worn out. Let's go on to something else."

We're a one product company, so we've decided to tackle one of the most difficult problems—that is, keeping a single product in front of the television audience for as long as possible. That has meant constant testing and innovation so that every infomercial we come out with is better than the previous one. It gets harder and harder and harder, it really does. But we just keep refining the show.

The other factor is that we're not making as much money as we did in the beginning. In the beginning, this was just a wonderful business to be in. Now, there are some weeks we don't earn very much money at all. As a matter of fact, we have weeks where we lose money. But that mailing list that we've generated from our names is extremely valuable. We've tested, for example, the optimum length of time between the time of a sale and the time that we send the customer a new solicitation. We've also determined which solicitation draws the greatest response, and how frequently we should mail to our customers.

After a sale, we segment our list so we know which customers bought which products. Then we go back and hit them with similar or related products. Our back-end is so highly refined and so tweaked that it—and not the profitability of the infomercial itself—is the secret of our success now.

*SD:* What products are you selling on the back-end?

*JS:* We have a catalogue of about 20 to 25 types of sunglasses, with different approaches to the lens. For example, if customers really like BluBlockers, they might want a few different styles. So we have different styles. If they don't like the color enhancement of the BluBlocker sunglasses, we have other sunglasses that don't have that enhancement but that provide a slightly different view. We have lenses and sunglasses that you can hit with a hammer and they won't break, very much like safety glasses. We have polarized glasses. So we have a whole variety of choices that people can pick from. We use direct mail, solo mailings, package inserts, and a catalogue—a lot of different approaches.

*SD:* So you sell primarily sunglasses?

*JS:* We're looking at a few other products. We've focused on sunglasses and we've become somewhat experts in that field. So, why scatter yourself? As long as our strategy continues to work, we're going to continue doing it. Our banker has a philosophy, "If it keeps on working, keep doing it. If it stops working, then stop doing it."

*SD:* Have you ever been tempted to go retail?

*JS:* We've been tempted and we probably could do a pretty effective job at retail, but I can't imagine comparing retail with mail order or direct marketing. We have a fairly low overhead and we have a small staff now. To go retail, we'd have to double our staff and the profitability wouldn't be there. So we're not that anxious to go retail.

*SD:* There seems to be a trend to go retail after television sales have faded. But from my experience, when you sell retail you're wholesaling at a minimum of 50% off, and it takes just as much money, if not more, to get people in the stores.

*JS:* That's right, and then you've got money tied up for a long period of time. I've sat in my office and watched a couple of thousand orders arrive in the morning mail. We have a little retail place in our office where people can come to the front door and pick up a pair. I've seen people stand there and try on different pairs, unable to make a decision. They waste the time of an employee who could be processing a hundred orders during the time that they're taking just one order from a customer. So I'm not that crazy about retail, although it's always a possibility and we're certainly building a brand name out there. BluBlockers are being recognized, and a lot of people own them, and a lot of people are talking about them. So maybe that is a possibility. But I'm not that keen for us to do it.

*SD:* What about marketing the product in catalogues, such as Sharper Image?

*JS:* We do market the product in other catalogues. We're not in Sharper Image—and there are reasons we're not in Sharper Image—but we are in other catalogues. BluBlockers are syndicated throughout the oil companies and banks. We're in several different direct marketing venues primarily because the product is not available in retail and we have no retail competition.

*SD:* Are you still doing print advertising for the product?

*JS:* That's funny, I grew up with print in direct marketing, but I haven't done any for the last three or four years. You really can't compare print with TV. With TV, as you're probably aware, you can pull out of a time slot with only a couple of weeks notice if your show starts to fade.

But in print, you're committed, and you're committed two months in advance, sometimes three months in advance. If the show bombs, or if some major event takes place, there's no way you can get out of your commitment. You're stuck running the ad, at the full cost of the ad. So print is very difficult, and also, the response rate seems to be down in print. So we're very cautious about getting into print again.

*SD:* If I recall correctly, I remember seeing full-page ads several years ago in the airline in-flight magazines. I'd think that would be a perfect venue for your advertising.

*JS:* It was. But since that time, we've gone through a run-up of advertising rates to a level that's considerably more than we're willing to cover. Also, when you go into print, you invite knock-offs. We had been in print for about a year when all of a sudden, along came all these knock-offs offering supposedly the same pair of sunglasses for only $10.00. In fact, they were cheap lenses in a cheap frame, no comparison to ours. So we decided that print was a lot more trouble and a lot less fun than TV.

*SD:* In testing a show, how much money do you typically spend?

*JS:* Not that much, actually. It depends on a variety of factors. If we spend a month and a half testing different concepts for a new show, we may spend $100,000. I'll give you an example: For instance, as an experiment, we decided to a show entirely in San Francisco—that is, we did all the interviews in San Francisco and all the shooting—and then to run the show in San Francisco and in some other city to see if the fact that it was a local show had an impact on the program's success elsewhere.

We discovered that the show was strong in San Francisco, but didn't do that well elsewhere. As a result, we realized we had to go out to different cities and to put together a show that was more generic.

*SD:* But wasn't one of your shows shot primarily in Chicago and another shot at Venice Beach?

*JS:* You'll find that in every show, there's one portion that's more memorable then any other. Our Venice Beach show was very memorable. Then we did a good portion of another show in Chicago, but we also shot in Las Vegas, Fort Lauderdale, and a few other places.

*SD:* Bathing suits help?

*JS:* I don't know if they really help. We haven't really proven that they do. There's nothing in any of our testing that indicates that bathing suits add to anything in the show.

*SD:* One unique aspect of your testimonials is that you get a very spontaneous reaction to the project the first time someone tries them on. With most other products, or type of products, you don't see that kind of spontaneity.

*JS:* That's true. And now that there are literally millions of pairs out there, we're constantly running into people who go out of their way to come up to us do an interview. In our latest show, we walked into a restaurant and found a guy who was wearing a pair. So we did an interview with him, very spontaneously, and found out he'd had them for a year. Another time, we were walking along Venice Beach and a person came up to us and said, "I've got to talk to you. Your sunglasses are terrific."

*SD:* You've sold between two and three million BluBlockers?

*JS:* Yes.

*SD:* That would probably put you among the top five of sunglass manufacturers.

*JS:* It does.

*SD:* So much for retail.

*JS:* That's right. No retail.

*SD:* How much time does it take between when you start working on a show and when the show gets on the air?

*JS:* That varies from a couple of months to nine or ten months. It really depends on my schedule, on how the current show is doing and the urgency of coming up with a replacement, and on the testing. Many factors are involved. For our last show, we did an awful lot of testing and it took a couple of months.

*SD:* With sunglasses, do you find the response is seasonal?

*JS:* To some degree, but people use sunglasses all year round. Don't forget, there's sun in winter. There are skiing and other sports. Sunglasses really are used all year round. We really don't have an off-season per se.

*SD:* Do you tailor your media buys to specific areas, such as heavy ski areas, in the winter?

*JS:* Not at all. We go all over the country. We don't really look at whether it's a Sun Belt or snow zone because we look at the bottom line. Did the commercial pull? If it did, I don't care if the area is Siberia, we'll run the ad. If the commercial didn't pull, we will take it off the air.

*SD:* But have you seen any trends according to season with the stations that do work?

*JS:* Not really. We have sold sunglasses in the middle of winter. We've sold them in the summer. We've sold them in the South in the winter and the South in the summer. It really depends on the commercial. There are people watching TV all the time. A good example: When the Gulf War crisis hit, during the first weekend we were a little nervous because we thought people weren't going to buy sunglasses because they'd be too busy watching news coverage of the war. We thought viewers would be very uptight...

*SD:* That seemed to happen to almost everyone in the industry.

*JS:* It didn't happen to us. In fact, our sales took a dramatic leap upward. We suspect that there were a lot of people flipping through the channels who came across our show and found it gave them some relief.

*SD:* That's really interesting because a majority of companies in the industry took a tremendous hit during the first quarter of this year (1991).

*JS:* Really? Well, the Gulf War crisis did eventually hurt us a little, but the first weekend actually helped our response.

*SD:* Joe, aside from testing and working the back-end, are there any other elements from your direct marketing background that are specifically applicable to infomercials, and maybe are not used very often?

*JS:* I think the principles are all the same. I think the big mistake is that marketers think that viewers watch only a few minutes of an infomercial, just long enough to get the toll-free number and place the order. I believe that's wrong. I believe that people watch the entire show. Therefore, if marketers looked at the show as an entire entity, like they would look at a full-page ad, I think they'd find that their response rate would increase.

*SD:* Several shows on the air repeat several segments from the first half in the second half.

*JS:* Sure, and that's okay—but then they could probably get by with a ten-minute show. The problem is that stations don't have ten-minute slots. So, these marketers just take a ten-minute commercial and repeat it three times. The most effective way to sell a product in print is with a lot of copy—if you can convince people to keep reading. The same principle applies to an infomercial. The most effective way to sell a product is to convince people to start watching your show and stay with you for the whole show. You then have a hell of a good opportunity to sell your product.

*SD:* To follow up on your statement about copy, do you think people read as much as they used to? Does the wisdom on long copy ads still apply?

*JS:* I question that myself. I think we're getting into the MTV generation where people are more attuned to video. I would suspect that reading comprehension is down and television watching is up. That's just a gut feel. I think it's the national trend. The people who are now your big purchasers grew up with television and during the last 10 or 15 years, they've grown up with the MTV approach. All television commercials are now like MTV. Everything is so fast paced. That really says that your shows have to be fast paced. I still feel that there's very much a place for print advertising, but I think we're going through a cycle where it's less effective than it used to be.

*SD:* Is the most effective approach, in both print and in an infomercial, to present a problem and then offer a solution? Or do you think marketers are better off not presenting a negative at the beginning?

*JS:* There are some situations where if you have a problem, you want to raise that problem so that people recognize it. Then you can dramatically show that your product will solve the problem.

Unfortunately, every product is different. Every product has what I call a "nature." Some products require that you raise the problem and resolve it, and other products lend themselves more to demonstrations of their benefits.

For example, for an acne product, you'd want to show people with very bad acne, people who give very emotional, heart-rending and compassionate intros. So you would show the problem in a very emotional way. Then, once the audience identifies with the people on the show, you offer a solution. I don't know of any stronger way to sell this kind of product. You just can't show people who have beautiful faces and say, "If you use this, you'll have a beautiful face." That just isn't real. But if you show people with pockmarked faces, the target audience will identify with it.

*SD:* Are there any shows on the air that you particularly admire?

*JS:* I think Kevin Trudeau is a great pitchman. He could probably relate to a lot of other products if he wanted to. He's skilled and a likable guy. I'm impressed with Dave Del Dotto. He does a good show. It's fascinating, and if you're interested in making a lot of money, you're going to watch that show and get sucked in.

Richard Simmons really pulls those emotional strings. He does an excellent job. I saw his *Dancing to the Oldies* show—really clever the way he did that. It was a unique format in which he showed different people and their reactions to the video while he danced in the background. He covered so many emotional hot points. It was very, very clever and it was a different kind of format. There are a lot of very clever formats out there.

On the other hand, a lot of people send me their shows and ask for my assessment about why the shows didn't work, or for recommendations for improvement. I'm always amazed that some big infomercial producers turn out real dogs that totally miss the point of a product or totally miss the best way to sell the product. It's amazing how much garbage is out there! Everyone thinks that all you've got to do is produce a half-hour show, put it on the air and collect a lot of money.

*SD:* And put a celebrity on it.

**JS:** And put a celebrity on it. You'll notice in our shows, we don't use a single celebrity. We discovered that viewers remember the celebrities, but what good does that do? They've got to remember the product and write down that toll-free number. But I'm sure there are some shows that would definitely benefit from a celebrity.

**SD:** Apparently, some marketers believe that using a celebrity adds credibility to the product.

**JS:** There was an article in *The Wall Street Journal* that said people don't believe that the celebrities really use the product. They believe that the celebrities are getting paid. But viewers do remember celebrities. And celebrities are particularly important to many products targeted to women who like to identify with a beautiful person demonstrating or using a product.

**SD:** Do you have any new tricks up your sleeve?

**JS:** We've had a lot of competitors go after us and come out with half-hour commercials for their sunglasses. For the most part, these marketers haven't done very well. And as you know, one of them has literally copied our format. We have a couple of other formats that we're going to experiment with very shortly that I feel will be very effective. I think there are a lot of different ways to skin a cat. I think anyone who copies us is just asking for trouble.

**SD:** Your company is set up very differently from other infomercial companies. By comparison, Media Arts, which produces *Amazing Discoveries*, does two shows a month at this point.

**JS:** *Amazing Discoveries* is a cross between Home Shopping and a typical infomercial. Its format lends itself to throwing on various products and finding the ones that work and sticking with them if they do. It's a very clever concept and another example of how finding the right concept is just as important as finding the right product.

We'll continue to produce our shows, but before our shows are aired they're going to work and we'll have thoroughly tested them and spent a fortune on re-editing. But they'll be right.

**SD:** You certainly have longevity on your side.

**JS:** Well, we have momentum. I'm not saying that this thing will last forever. We've been fortunate enough that every time one of our shows dies, we have another show ready with certain enhancements that propel it to the top again. That's a hell of a job, I want you to know.

I love this process because it really is a challenge. If I can continue to succeed, then I will have accomplished something that most of the people in the infomercial industry have been unable to accomplish. Also, our success so far has given me the knowledge and experience to take any product and either duplicate it using the sunglass program, or at least produce another type of commercial with a lot more expertise than I would have had otherwise.

*SD:* Have you been able to discern the average effective lifespan of a show—the duration of time before you'll need a replacement show?

*JS:* Typically, we run our shows for a year-and-a-half.

*SD:* Which is longer than most infomercials out there.

*JS:* Yeah, a year-and-a-half. A lot of people really love our shows and watch them again and again. We develop fans. People write to us and tell us about their favorite segments.

*SD:* Do you maintain a fairly consistent level of media spending throughout the lifespan of a show?

*JS:* In general. We may spend a little more in the beginning, but generally it's pretty consistent.

*SD:* Joe, with your background in print, have you had success in testing a product in print before spending all the money on a show?

*JS:* I have found that products that work exceptionally well with print advertising will always work on TV. So one of the best ways to test a product before going into the expense of a commercial is to try it in print. If you can't make the product work in print, then I'd stay away from TV because you're not going to make it. There are exceptions. There obviously are products that are very demonstrable and TV lends itself well to the demonstration.

*SD:* One thing that marketers complain about all the time is that ad testing costs an absolute fortune.

*JS:* It does. I mean no matter how cheap a show you put out, it's still going to cost you $30,000 to $50,000, and if you do it right it's going to cost you some more to tweak the show. So it's a gamble.

People come to me all the time and say, "Joe should I go into this?" And I tell them, "It's just like the record business. When I was in print I had everyone and their brother copying what I was doing and very few made it, and it was the same in the record industry." But I never discourage anyone. You never know what little concept they'll come up with that will work.

*SD:* What's your average budget for a show?

*JS:* We spend about $100,000.

*SD:* And does that include the tweaking?

*JS:* Yes. We spend about $50,000 to produce the show and we could spend about $50,000 to tweak it.

*SD:* When you're taping in different cities, do you use the same crew or do you hire crews locally?

*JS:* We do both, depending on the circumstances. We have a favorite crew that we prefer to use. They're in tune with us and they know what opportunities we want them to capture. Sometimes we'll delay our shooting just to have this crew available. But other times, we've hired people locally and come up with some pretty good results.

*SD:* Is there anything you want to add?

*JS:* No. Just that it's getting rougher out there.

# VICTORIA JACKSON

❦

Victoria Jackson, a Hollywood make-up artist and American Telecast Corporation, created one of the fastest growing cosmetic companies in the country. They also did something else that had never been done before in the infomercial industry: They created a brand name with name recognition. Using celebrities Ali MacGraw and Lisa Hartman as endorsers this show took off like a rocket from the first moment it began airing in 1989. The cosmetic line grossed $450 million during its infomercial campaign on media time costing $150 million. During the height of the campaign, Victoria Jackson Cosmetics generated up to 10,000 new customers per week. Today Ms. Jackson is still promoting her line, and has created a brand new line called Lola, which is available at many high-end department stores.

**Steve Dworman:** You're one of the few people in the industry who has developed a product from scratch. You were a make-up artist...why don't you start from where the seeds of the idea came from?

**Victoria Jackson:** I was a make-up artist and seven years into my career, I had never found a base, a foundation, that I thought would be perfect for print work, photography, advertising and street make-up. I wanted one foundation that would just be perfect, that I could use for my work, yet that would also be a great base that women could wear every day and never look like they had make-up on, just perfect skin. Because I could not find this product, I became really motivated to try to create something.

So I mixed up a concoction of what I thought would be the perfect base. I knew the shades that I wanted, which at that time had a little more yellow undertones , and I knew the finish that I wanted. I tried to get the name of the best cosmetic chemist in town. I went to see this guy, who I didn't know at the time, was one of the best in the country. I told him what I wanted to do but that I had no money. I

15

said I really wanted to try to market this foundation.

At this point in my career, I was teaching make-up at UCLA. So I really had a great test market among all of my students. I taught every quarter and I had about 50 students a quarter. So not only could I test the makeup on the celebrities that I worked on, but my students as well. So I put the line together: 14 foundations in professional sizes. And because I had so many students I'd send them to stores around Los Angeles asking for my product. I followed up by asking the stores if they were going to carry my product. Otherwise, I said, I wouldn't send them my students anymore. And they said, "Okay."

The biggest stores carrying it were Frends Beauty Supply in the San Fernando Valley and Columbia Drug. These were the two sort of "Hollywood Stores" that catered to all the make-up people in the entertainment business. So it was great. My little following grew and became a little cult following for my foundation. Everybody had to have it. And that's when I knew I had a great product. From that point, I decided to put together a full color line and test buying habits of women and find out what colors they really seemed to go for.

By accumulating all this information, I continued to try very hard to raise the money to launch my cosmetics line. It was very difficult. I put together a limited partnership, and I tried to sell shares to everyone in my family and every other family I knew. I had 25 shares that I had to sell by a certain date and I sold only 18. In retrospect, it was probably the best thing in the world that the company didn't take off then.

Then I was in a "close encounter" with Tova. We were about to do a deal but it never went anywhere. Now, looking back, I can see that although these events were great disappointments, I was actually fortunate because had any of them actually come through, they would have changed the direction in which I ultimately went. Then I made a deal with some people from Texas who were involved with Beverly Sassoon. To make that long story short, they really didn't have the money to make the deal a reality.

I had to go through a real transition from make-up "artist" to "business" woman. But I really learned a lot about people. I learned that what people say and what's actually the truth are often two very different things. And a lot of the deals that I was very close to doing, the people didn't really have the money. I was starting to feel toward the end that I didn't really know how I was going to make my dream a reality—that is, how I could make this product succeed.

I'd have actresses call me in the middle of the night to say, "I'm shooting a film tomorrow and I have to have the base." So I knew I had a great product, and that's what kept me trying. My friends told me, "Hang in there, because people have to know how good this product is." Through all of this encouragement, a student of mine told me that she wanted me to meet a group of gentlemen who did infomercials. She asked if I would be interested. At that point I had so many "close encounters" that I said, "Yeah, sure, sure, yeah, okay, I'll meet them." I met with them, and they didn't really believe that you could sell cosmetics through television. I told them how I'd put together these color-coordinated kits and how it was really simple and if they put their money where my mouth was, I could make this succeed.

At that point I was really ready. I'd had all these disappointments. Because I'd been in so many business meetings, I was really primed and ready for this encounter. And two days later I had a 17-page contract and the go-ahead to do my thing completely—to develop the line, put in as many products as I wanted to. These men said they'd get back to me in three months and then we'd shoot the show. And that's exactly what happened. They completely let me go off and then I hit the books and found out who's the best of the best in town and who could help me find compacts, and I just put it all together. Three months later, we shot the show and it's been a success ever since. The end.

*SD:* Well that brings up a couple of questions. When you were teaching at UCLA and came up with the idea for the base and then the colors, did you try different versions of the base and get reactions from your students? Or did you have it completely formulated before showing it to them?

*VJ:* I pretty much knew what I wanted. That was one big plus of being a make-up artist. During the time I was teaching, I developed 14 shades. I started with two or three, and then developed more as I felt I needed to. And then I knew which ones were my biggest sellers. But I came up with something right away, I can't say by myself because I had an amazing chemist who really understood what I was trying to do and who created an incredible product. The product that was a hit back then is still the premier product of the line. It's the one product that every woman uses.

*SD:* So you used the students essentially to give you marketing feedback?

*VJ:* Absolutely. When you're working with 50 students every quarter, you've got every skin type and I'd had so much experience making my living as a make-up artist. Teaching was something I did because so many people wanted to learn how to do what I do. It was a good experience for me. Ultimately it was invaluable, because when I went to do my "How To" tape, those seven years of teaching at UCLA made it very easy. I knew at that point what colors were going to work and not work. That was easy. That's part of being a make-up artist.

*SD:* Did your sales volume grow much in the two stores?

*VJ:* I started to see that it was really growing in the two stores. I also started to see that it required a lot of time, energy, money, and up-keep. It became a whole other business in addition to my being a make-up artist. I also sold all the cosmetics to people who just had to have their emergency stash. I worked out of my garage. My garage was my office. It was, for a long time, my research and development department and art department also. Everything was in my garage. It was really my mom and some friends that kept it going by helping me with all the money that was required to go into this. They believed in me, and I kept telling them that I knew this was going to take off, so just hang in there.

**SD:** Before the infomercial deal came through, how did you plan to roll out your products?

**VJ:** Originally, I was focusing on retail, department stores, that type of thing. I know that when I was in business with Beverly Sassoon and the people from Texas, their plan was multi-level, which was a concept I never really understood. All I knew was that I didn't get a really good vibe on these Texas people. Something about them just didn't feel right. My vision had always been more like, "I really want to be in Bullocks!" Then when I started to see some of these infomercials and met with this group I thought that this was perfect because I've got this whole concept that would work perfectly for television.

**SD:** After you signed the contract and they left you alone for three months, you developed the products and the casings. How much did you have to do with the show?

**VJ:** I had a lot to do with the first show. Basically because I think they were looking to me in terms of the visuals. I did all the before-and-afters. I had a lot to do with the way we communicated to women.

I think you have to speak to women intelligently. We're selling make-up, we're not curing cancer here. We should be able to talk like three women just talking about make-up and being excited about a great product. At times, we had differences of opinion. They wanted a certain amount of information to come across in a little more structured way than I felt comfortable with, so we'd go back and forth a little bit.

But the first show, I have to say, I really had a lot of final say. I didn't do the editing, although I sat in the editing room and said, "Can't we do this?" And they'd say, "No!" But usually, I try to be as involved as possible because I have a whole vision and I try to see it through. I don't just say, "Here are these lovely little products with my name on it. Here's a nice little mascara I did." I see the whole way of not only creating the product, but also of translating it to women effectively.

**SD:** Were you surprised by how successful the first show was?

**VJ:** Yeah. I remember the scariest moments were on the day the showed aired and people around me were telling me, "Now Victoria, you've got to be prepared. This might not fly. Nobody's done this before." I was so nervous and I thought, "I don't know what I'll do now."

Then they called and told me that the show was a big hit. I felt so elated. I was on another planet. I had always tried to keep believing and having the faith and reading my own success story. As I was going through my stumbling blocks, I'd hoped that at some point, I'd be doing an interview and they would all be part of my success story. So I was glad it looked like it was going to turn out that way.

*SD:* Who was responsible for bringing the celebrities to the first show?

*VJ:* Ali McGraw was a friend of mine and she had used the products for a long time and had always been supportive. Like when she says on TV, "I wanted to help Victoria," that's the truth. She had helped me before when I was in the deal with the Texas people and Beverly Sassoon. She was never paid for that and she put in a lot of time and energy. When people believe in you in the beginning, you really want to bring them in when it finally looks like the project is going to pay off. At least I did, for her.

So I brought Ali to American Telecast, and they negotiated with her. She does now make a lot of money from this and it has kind of turned things around for her. Lisa Hartman was someone they felt would be a nice a balance. I can't tell you that I knew Lisa, or that she was my best friend, because she wasn't. But she's a lovely, lovely girl. She's just terrific and she's really professional and really good. It was important to me before we shot the show that I meet with all of them and that they really used the products and liked them, and it was important to them. They all had a sense of integrity when they did the show. No one wanted to do this if it didn't feel right because there wasn't any huge guarantee of money at that point. So they were, in their minds, taking a risk. But everyone genuinely liked the products.

*SD:* Meredith Baxter Birney did the second show. Why was she brought in?

*VJ:* Meredith was somebody I had worked on. As a make-up artist, I did a *Redbook* cover with her and she always liked my work and the products. American Telecast has always felt from the beginning that the celebrities are really key to selling the cosmetics—that they're the channel stoppers, or that they build credibility, or reinforce the credibility that I may have. They felt that for the second show, since no one had done two celebrities before, we'd get a new look with a very credible celebrity, which Meredith is. The show would therefore have the potential to become an even bigger success.

*SD:* Was the second show bigger?

*VJ:* I don't know if it was bigger. I think it's pretty much on par with the first show, although I've heard from a lot of people that Meredith did add to the response. I think she was very effective.

*SD:* How much did you have to do with the second show?

*VJ:* I didn't have as much to do with the second show as with the first. Businessmen came in and started making more decisions. Still, I had control over what I would say and not say. I'm not just somebody that you tell, "Here's your script, now read your lines." I know what I'm comfortable saying or not saying. Regarding the opening, which I really like, they came up with the idea of Meredith throwing out all of her make-up and I actually thought it was a very cute idea. So I was still involved, but more in the background.

*SD:* You're working on the third show now?

*VJ:* Yes. Our third show will be shot next month.

*SD:* With the same three celebrities?

*VJ:* Yes.

*SD:* Anything different with this show?

*VJ:* We're going to give it a whole different look. We have a lot of products that people don't even know about that are back-end once they've bought the initial products. But we'll keep the focus of the show the same, with the same peach, pink and red colors, and the same offer. I'm trying to get across to women that this is about timeless beauty. It's not a fad and it's not trendy. So it's not as if we brought out these colors two years ago and now they're out. These are classics and I really want to instill that in women because there are some out there who haven't bought yet. So I want to reinforce that message.

It's an easy offer to understand and comprehend and visualize, and it has worked so well in every show we've done. We get such a substantial response. The approach is still working. So I guess we'll give it a try and see if it works one more time with a whole new look. I don't think you'll be seeing the three of us just sitting in a living room again. I think that gets to be static after a while. You need to create a whole new sort of energy.

*SD:* Playing Frisbee maybe?

*VJ:* Yeah, playing Frisbee with mascara. That's what we'll do. Good idea, Steve. Thank you so much.

*SD:* You're welcome. To talk more about your success, an article in *The Los Angeles Times* mentioned that your show was generating 10,000 new customers a week.

*VJ:* Right. Which is pretty amazing! As Meredith says on the show, "That's like 10,000 new faces every week." The response we had was amazing, and it still amazes me now when I go through all the mail and I read how women really use the products and love them. It really affects how people see themselves because they feel so much better about themselves and how they look. That's why I spoke at the NIMA [National Infomercial Marketing Association] convention. I feel so strongly about how great the power of the infomercial is. In just two years, look at how quickly we've built this huge customer base and how the show has given me name recognition. It's pretty incredible.

*SD:* Do you have any idea what the re-order rate is from customers who initially buy the product through television?

*VJ:* I know we have a really high re-order rate. That is what our business is built on, the re-order. It's not built on front-end through television. Our cost of goods is very high. Our package is expensive because there are a lot of products in there.

We make our money on the back-end because of the re-orders, and through our catalogue, our continuity programs, and the programs we have set up with our operators. At one point, we did a survey and found we had over 50% worth of re-orders. The rate was very high—the highest of the industry because we also have a really high customer satisfaction rate.

*SD:* I've also heard that the way your in- and out-bound operators deal with your customers is phenomenal.

*VJ:* American Telecast did a very comprehensive job with the phone program installations and with training of the operators. The training process is really involved. I've done training tapes. We've put in a lot of time and energy, and at this point we've more or less worked out all the bugs. And I hear a lot of good things about our operators. They've done a great job.

*SD:* Now aside from American Telecast, you're branching out into a whole new realm with a jewelry line.

*VJ:* Yes, I'm going into jewelry now and I'm really excited about it. I can get excited about anything I'm doing as long as I'm creating it and feeling good that I'm not just putting my name on something that I can't relate to. Hopefully, you're not going to see me sell out even though I've had a lot of offers to do things that I just don't believe in. I'm not going to rip anyone off by putting my name out there on just anything. So I feel very excited about the jewelry. It's a little bit different and has a story to tell, and again it's about giving women a lot of different options.

*SD:* And though the deal isn't finalized, it looks like it's going to be done with Home Shopping Network Entertainment.

*VJ:* Right. And right now they've been very generous in listening to the things I have to say and they really like the product and are excited about it. Whenever you go into a new type of encounter, you hope for the best.

**SD:** Is this a different situation for you in that they'll be involved in producing the show and airing it, but you'll be totally responsible for the marketing of the product?

**VJ:** No, not really. They're manufacturing the product based on the ideas I've developed. They're not able to put my name on just any piece of jewelry and say it's Victoria Jackson's. But they'll be controlling the manufacturing and the creative will be jointly done. I think people want me associated with something because I'm not an actress who would just read lines. I think people want to hear what I have to say. Whether they'll ultimately agree with me, I don't know. There may be more of a give and take process, but I don't have a real problem with that. I try to think everything through and not fly off with stupid comments. I try to come up with things that I think will really help to make a difference.

**SD:** What's the timeframe on the jewelry show?

**VJ:** We're hoping to shoot the infomercial by December, and then it would roll out at the first of the year.

**SD:** So the new cosmetic show and the jewelry show will be rolling out at the same time?

**VJ:** Yeah. It's pretty exciting. We're on a roller coaster ride.

**SD:** Why do you think the American woman seems to relate to you so well?

**VJ:** Maybe because I'm not threatening. I really relate to women. I'm just trying to offer them a solution. I'm not telling them that this is the only way, or "You have to do this...." I'm just trying to help solve a problem and fulfill a need.

And, being a woman of the '90s, I think I have a good bead on where women are these days. I feel very lucky that I'm able to communicate fairly easily to women. I never want to abuse that. My cosmetics and jewelry both represent solutions and choices for women. Even with my cosmetics, I'm the first to tell women that whether they buy mine or someone else's, they should always buy what works for them. And I really mean it—because ultimately they will anyway. I'd like them to buy mine. I think mine are great, I think they're the best, but I'm just a firm believer in giving women choices. And I just want to help give them the best choices.

**SD:** Besides your actual makeup, one thing that is really unique about your line is the packaging. You come up with some ingenious ways to package your cosmetics. Is that all your doing?

**VJ:** I do all the packaging of all the products. I created things like my survival kit. To me, that's the fun part. I am the happiest when I go into the lab and start mixing up the powders, which I do for all my new color lines. I create all my own colors, but that's the result of 13 years of being a make-up artist.

And recently I just finished a bath care line and a hair care line that's coming out shortly.

*SD:* What advice would you give to people who have products and are looking to get into the infomercial business, but who are struggling and looking for financing.

*VJ:* More than anything, you have to believe in yourself and your idea. You have to really have thought it through and have all the answers for all the people who are going to tell you why it won't work. In that sense, you have to be really prepared.

I did that by knocking on as many doors as possible and talking to anyone who would listen. You have to keep persevering and completely believe in yourself and your ideas so that you'll find the way. I think that's what sorts out the true entrepreneur from the person who's going to give up. The true entrepreneur will find a way.

A good product will find its way out to the public if you really do your homework. I'm always encouraging people to stick with quality because, in my case, here it is all these years later, and my premier product is still the same one that I had seven years ago in my garage. So with all the marketing and all the hoopla, it's still basically the same product. If you've got a great product, I encourage people to hang in there and find a way to make it happen—'cause it will.

*SD:* How about some practical advice to someone about to make his or her first deal after struggling for years?

*VJ:* It is really, really important when you are going into your first deal—and I say this because when I came into my first deal I was really more of a make-up artist than a celebrity—I think you really have to do your homework. You can't trust just one person if there are things you're not sure about. You need to really feel comfortable with whomever you're signing your name with on that dotted line, because it could be something you'll live with for a very long time.

*SD:* That's good advice. Thank you.

# TONY ROBBINS

 ony Robbins was a very successful motivational speaker prior to his 1989 *Personal Power* infomercial. The show was produced by Lenny Lieberman for the Guthy-Renker Corp., setting a standard for documentary-style infomercials. The show featured Fran Tarkenton as host and numerous leaders from government, business and entertainment all raving about Tony and his course. Robbins is a communication expert. He uses very unique language patterns and marketing skills in his shows. They obviously work. His series of infomercials have generated over $300 million in sales. The latest show, featuring Leeza Gibbons, launched in early 2003.

**Steve Dworman:** If at any time you'd like to share some trade secrets that you've never before revealed, feel free to do so.

**Tony Robbins:** My personal belief system is that if everybody shares whatever their secrets are, we will just have to have more of them. One reason I am here is because I want to see this industry thrive.

**SD:** I'd like to talk about some of the interesting language patterns you use on your show, which I have never seen anybody discuss.

**TR:** Give me an example and we will talk about it.

**SD:** First of all, you seem to touch all representational systems. You seem to build feeling, create auditory excitement and paint pictures. I don't see a lot of that being done.

**TR:** My view of an infomercial is that we need to put together a show that informs people and entertains them to action. In my view, if we do a show that is strong enough in quality, then people will watch it just to watch it. We have something that is valuable as long as we can also create enough momentum so that someone really decides to take action.

I think that there are a lot of ways to do that. One of those ways is to understand the values of the people in the marketplace. I try to find out what this culture's values are, and about what I call psychic wounds, the things that we all have in our lives that we want desperately, but that our current lifestyle is not meeting.

A large number of people in our culture want very much to be unique. They will do anything to be unique, and they are the achievers of our culture. It is not about making money for them, it is really about finding a way to differentiate and demonstrate that they are individual. If you can show these people that what you are doing can help them not only to achieve, but also to create a more unique quality of life for themselves, you are immediately going to get their attention.

Another group of people want to be like these achievers. They are emulators. These people are constantly striving to develop more confidence. If you can show them that they can succeed by becoming more confident and more able to achieve as the achievers have—and many of them perceive me as an achiever—and I am, without a doubt—then they are going to be very excited about what you do.

Another group of people are the societal conscious. These are the people least likely to buy from an infomercial. These people are very conscious about society, they are very mission-oriented. They are not driven by money. They certainly wouldn't mind earning more, but that is not their drive. For them, the drive is quality of life, and they want to be intelligent. The thing that they are most concerned about, their wound, if you will, is this whole idea of being manipulated. So they are the people who attack infomercials the most, and I think that is good, because their attacks have caused a lot of people to pay attention. It's gotten the government's attention, and while that may be an inconvenience in the short term, it makes our industry better in the long term.

With all that attention, everybody has got to raise their standards. And I, along with my partners Guthy-Renker and Lieberman, have tried to do that with our infomercials. We try to always constantly demand more from ourselves than anybody else could possibly demand. So the answer to your question, specifically, is that everything I do on that infomercial is to try to meet the emotional needs of the people in our culture. And I try to reach as many of them as I think that product can reach, by talking in their language and talking in a way that gives them visual stimulation, auditory stimulation and emotional stimulation.

*SD:* You told a very interesting story on one of your *Power Talk* series of tapes concerning the focus group you did for the second show. Can you talk a little bit about that?

*TR:* What was interesting was that the first show was going very well. We were working on the second show knowing that eventually...basically we thought the first show should have died six months earlier just from the massive exposure we had.

We were in Hawaii, doing a program for two weeks there. We came in one night about midnight and turned on the television and there I was...turned the station, and it was not me...next station was me. In fact, out of 13 or 14 stations, we were on six.

*SD:* Simultaneously?

*TR:* That is overlap of media, number one, but that's pretty good market penetration. So we were on a roll. But my whole focus is always a discipline of CANI: Constant and Never-Ending Improvement.

So I said, "How can we improve this next show? Let's take a look at the first show and see what we can do better. "We did that. We set up a focus group. I sat behind the one-way glass expecting to hear these incredible comments about what a phenomenal program it was, and the moderator introduced everybody, and interviewed them all, and then he showed the show, and had them all write down their comments.

*SD:* This was your second show?

*TR:* Actually, it was our first show. And so, we knew it was already successful, but I wanted to get feedback because we wanted to work on the second show. While I sat behind the glass, the focus group participants all wrote down what they thought of the show. Then the moderator asked, "Okay, who would like to start out?"

One guy raised his hand and said, "I thought that was absolutely incredible. I really want that product." The minute he said that, three other people pounced on him. They just didn't say, "Don't be seduced." They said, "Are you crazy? Don't you know they are trying to rip you off and trying to take your money? They are a bunch of manipulators." And they went on and on and on. So much so, that the first guy had to defend himself for wanting to invest in a product that could improve his life.

I was struck by the amount of emotional intensity. These people were angry. They were not just telling the man, "You're being stupid." Pretty soon, you could see other people who would have been very positive just button up. It was interesting group dynamics.

To make a long story shorter, the moderators then interviewed the people. Some were very emotional. They were asked things like, "What do we have to lose? There is a money-back guarantee." People said things like, "Ah, you know, they won't give you your money back." So the moderator said, "Wait a second, all you have to do is call the FCC. Let them know what is going on. Call the station. These guys will be off the air in a minute." And people said, "Yes, well maybe you will get your money back, but it will be so hard, it will take you forever, and they will make it almost impossible."

And they were asked, "What evidence do you have that this would happen?" And they said, "Well, I once bought something, and they never sent it, or it was a lousy product." Almost all of them had negative experiences. But there was a bigger issue. These people were so skeptical, and they remained so, even after hours of going in circles. I couldn't believe it. Never seen anything like it. Then the moderators had the focus group evaluate Fran and me on sincerity quotients and all that kind of stuff, and I got 9s and 10s on sincerity. One person said, "He was sincere, but he was lying."

*SD:* How can you be sincere and lie?

*TR:* She said, "He was lying about where he lived. He never could have been that bad off." And the moderator asked, "What if the guy was here? What if he walked in and talked to you? Would that convince you?" And she said, "Nah."

So the group talked a little bit longer, and then the moderator said he'd be right back. He came into the back room and asked me if I wanted to talk to these people. And I said, "No, but I will."

So I walked back in with him. You could see an instant state change in the room. People reacted like, "Oh my gosh, it's him. He's real."

I walked up to the woman who'd said I was sincere but lying, and I said, "Ma'am, 2516 Pacific Avenue, Apt. 3A." We were doing the focus group in Marina Del Rey, maybe 10 minutes from where I used to live. And she looked at me and then kind of backed off.

I said, "Look, that glass is a two-way, mirror, and I have been here the whole time watching you guys, and I've got to tell you, I really appreciate your being here because you have taught me a lot. I had no idea society was this skeptical. I'm real, my product isn't perfect, but it works for hundreds of thousands of people, and that show you guys just destroyed is the most successful show of its type ever done. But you know what? I'm here to make myself better, so I want to put myself in your hands. Let's be a team here, and tell me, help me. I am a businessman. I do need to make money but I really want to do something that is quality and I believe my product will really change people's lives. So how can I reach you?"

So we went around and around, and the talk was all surface stuff. Finally it became obvious to me. I turned and I said, "I think the real problem here is that you guys are just afraid. You are afraid to get your hopes up. Because I am hearing you over and over again talk about how you once bought a product, or you once got involved in something, and your hopes were high, and then they were dashed. So in the beginning you got excited because you wanted to change your life, make things better, but then you were disappointed so many times, that now your brain is pained even when you get excited. So now you are trying to, at all costs, avoid getting excited because you don't want the letdown. If you don't get excited, and you are not willing to hope again, and not willing to have some belief that things will get better, that a product can help you, then you have already lost. So you can judge me all day long, or you can at least expose yourself. And there is no way you can lose with a money-back guarantee when you can call anybody and nail us."

We were running out of time so I said, "Look, our time with you is up. I would like to have another 20 minutes with you. I could pay you for that time, or if you want, trade you my tapes. They are worth $179. You guys got only $40 for your time being here. Would you be willing to trade, or get paid? I'll do either one." It was interesting. Every single person wanted the tapes—including all the people who had said no at first.

We pulled two lessons from this experience:

1) Our culture is much more skeptical and pessimistic than we realize. It comes from a whole variety of elements, everything from Iran Contra to Watergate, etc. People are afraid to get excited.

2) They want to be excited. If you can be sincere enough and communicate to people that what you're saying is true, if you can be real with them, then people may be willing to trust you and hope again. We really need to develop a relationship of trust. My goal in this industry, and my goal on our shows, is to develop such a quality product that even if viewers do not buy our product, they feel that the show has value.

Most shows, even those on broadcast television, are all commercials. They can not be on the air without somebody buying a product. And I think that not all of them do the three things we talked about. Not all of them inform and entertain and inspire. And most of them don't offer a solution.

We are not in the infomercial business. I don't even think we are in the direct marketing business, because we can directly market a lot of things, and have it be a lousy product, but we are not going to remain in business. I think we are in the solutions business. I think that as an industry, we have to say, "Look we want to do everything that a normal show does. We want to entertain, inform, and inspire. The difference is, when we are done, we want to give somebody a way to do something to make their life better."

So many of the talk shows on television are about problems but they do not offer a solution. So they may inform me, they may even entertain me, but very few of them inspire me to do something. Very few, if any, give me something I can physically do to make my life better. If we do that, we provide too much economic gain for the television stations for them not to use us, and we also provide quality programs. So I have no fear for our future if we raise our standards continually. I have a lot of fear for our industry if we have people who go out there and try to cut corners.

*SD:* How do you surmount the fear of the people at home watching the show? What do you actually do in the show to get through it?

*TR:* I want to say one more thing about the focus group, if I may. And that is, that if we had listened to that focus group, we would never have gone on the air. I told my partners, Greg, Bill, John Schulberg, and Len Lieberman, "You guys have all the wrong people in this room. These people don't buy anything on television. These people are already skeptical. None of them, virtually, are buying things on television. Maybe one or two. But they are not our market. Now if we want to expand our market, then we need to talk to these people, and I understand that. And I want to do that. But let us make sure that we don't take everything as gospel. We also have to know that we are paying these people to be critics. That's a whole different philosophy, and we need to take that balance in."

I have the privilege of having worked now with 300,000 people in seminars over a seven to eight year period of time—including people in the South Bronx to CEOs of major companies. At this point, I have so many references about what is real and what is not. I may not always be right, but I have enough references to make a better decision. So when I listen to what the focus group is saying, I ask myself, "Does that make sense? Does that hit me in the gut right here? Is it consistent?" Then I see if the ideas are worthwhile or not. I think if you listen to focus groups exclusively, you are going to be chasing your tail forever and you are never going to have an effective program. Now your original question was what, before I interrupted you?

*SD:* How do you overcome people's fear and skepticism? Because you are promising a lot on your show….

*TR:* You are right. You may think that this is incongruent, but I believe that as an industry, we have to under-promise and over-deliver. And you may say that doesn't seem like what you are doing. But among the people who stop me in the street—a dozen to three dozen, literally, a day—not one person in 2 1/2 years, not one person has said, "Your product is lousy." That doesn't mean there isn't anybody unhappy out there, but the law of averages says that if there were many of them, somebody would come up to me and tell me so.

I think that the best way to sell a product is to use some understatement while you're creating a desire for the product and showing the results. If you watch my show—for example, this third show with Martin Sheen—there is a point where Fran comes back to me and says, "What about these people who are broke and depressed? Can we help these people? Change their lives?" And I say, "They have to help themselves. The bottom line is that no one can do it for you, but we can be a good coach. I can be there for you and share with you strategies and techniques and hopefully inspire you a little bit, and I can be a friend, but I can't do it for you. Anybody who says they can do it for you is lying to you."

When I make a statement like that, I believe it makes our show go through the roof. Because other people are saying results, results, results, and making it sound like the product is perfect, and there is no way it can break down. You know as well as I do that most people who get a product won't even use it. So we have to challenge people to use our products to benefit from them. How we take care of the fear—in answer to your original question—is by developing a quality relationship, knowing that you have the privilege of being in somebody's home, maybe even in their bedroom, and you had better respect that relationship.

I mean this whole business is relationship. It is our relationship with the consumer. It is our relationship with the television station. It is our relationship with government and our relationship with each other. Those four relationships define our success or failure. And all those must be maintained. The way to do that is to have a quality show, a show that has value no matter what happens. My favorite thing is when people stop me in the street and say, "I watch your show every Sunday." And I say, "It's a commercial." And I tease them about it. And they laugh and then say, "But it's so good, I get inspired." That's the sign of a good show. We've been on continually since April 1989 because we have added value, because the show has value even if viewers don't buy.

You worry when people come up to you and say, "I am so upset because I missed last week's show and forgot to tape it. What happened?"

Then you know you have the wrong marketplace.

The second thing is to make sure you have an incredibly good quality product. I can't tell you how many products I used to buy in the early days, like a frying device that didn't use any oil—a piece of garbage. First of all, it came broken. Ordered the second one, it came screwed up with chipping aluminum. I looked at aluminum as unhealthy to cook something in. With experiences like that, people get burned.

In the focus groups, all we hear are the reflection of either those people who got burned, or the people they've talked to. That's why I'm here. I want to make sure our industry raises its standards continuously, that we commit to the constant never-ending improvements. And if we really do that, it benefits me, my partners, all of our associates, all of us in this industry together, because then viewers will trust us. And I think with compression television coming, and all the other elements that are involved in our business, we have to increase the quality of our relationship with all those viewers and with each other.

**SD:** I was happy to see Fran Tarkenton back. I know there was period of time when his return was up in the air.

**TR:** Yes, there was a time that we considered not using him, but part of that was because we wanted to create some differentiation. I think we succeeded in having differentiation and still keeping the best of what we had.

The other thing that pushed me over the edge was that Fran made a lot of personal changes, including developing a quality relationship and quitting chewing tobacco, which he had been doing for almost 20 years. When I first met Fran, he was chewing and spitting in a spittoon. I thought, "This is Fran Tarkenton? I don't get it." So I am very proud to be associated with him. I feel even more strongly about our relationship because he is really using the product. And using it at a level that would be more than what most people would expect. That really made a difference for me.

And of course, having Martin there reaches another group of people. Fran will reach the emulators and achievers, and maybe some of the belongers. People who are little America. And I think Martin will reach a lot of the society conscious people because they know Martin will not do anything he does not believe in 1,000%. He gets on the show and says, "My wife ordered the tapes, and I would not have done them because I was too skeptical, but I'm so glad I did. I am here for only one reason and that is to let you know that Tony Robbins is real, he is sincere, and this product absolutely works. It has worked for me and thousands of other people, and if you are wondering if I am being paid...not one thin dime." I think that is going to have some impact. Maybe I am wrong. Our third show may fall on its butt, who knows, but I am going to feel good about what we put out regardless. And that commitment to quality, I think, is the key to our success so far.

*SD:* I noticed in the second show that you state very clearly that nobody had been paid for his or her testimony.

*TR:* That's correct. And that came out of the focus group, by the way. Because one of the things people said was that they knew the celebrities were all millionaires and being paid. So we had to make it even more explicit in the commercial. We do that again in this show. And then we've got Martin saying right up front, "I am not paid to do this." I think that is pretty strong.

*SD:* Let's talk a little more about what you previously alluded to, that people buy tapes and then they don't use them.

*TR:* I think it's true of any product, but especially tapes. It's worse than books. I don't know who did the study, but approximately 10% of people who buy a book don't read past the first chapter. It just looks good, it feels good buying it, and then they put it on the shelf. I feel okay about that myself, because at least the resource is there for them. I buy a lot of books that I do not intend to read now. My schedule is too busy. But I know the books are there, so when I want a particular answer, wham, I can pull it off the shelf. I think the value of our products lies in offering people resources, not only for the present, but also for the future.

*SD:* What infomercials on the air, aside from your own, do you particularly like?

*TR:* I like any infomercial that I feel is honest, has integrity, and has no incongruency about it. There are so many shows where marketers make claims and everybody knows they are not true. I was involved recently with an organization that markets quite a few products. On one of their shows, after the woman who was selling the product came off the screen, she said, "You know this product isn't really very good. The rollers on this thing are sticking, and some of our customers are going to be unhappy."

And I watched one of the executives there say, "Well, yeah, yeah." And she said, "No, all they have to do is put on a little lever element to lift the back so it doesn't stick." How they are going to deal with that problem will determine if they are going to be here in five years.

Regarding specific shows, I didn't get to see the whole show, but I just recently saw little bits and pieces of *Hooked on Phonics*. I liked it primarily because I think the product is so valuable and I think it fills an important need in the culture. I respect the company for bringing it forth. I like *Where There is a Will, There's an A*. I think they have done a quality job through time, and I think that's why they have been successful. I like the people they have on screen, and the way they package what they are doing, and making it the right price point.

I have seen quality shows that unfortunately didn't sell on the air. I was involved at the very end on *Drug Free Kids* on PBS. I thought that was a quality show, but it didn't move me to action, and I didn't necessarily think the product was the right product. It also required parents to do something. They would much rather buy the tapes for their kids and say, "Listen to this. I've supported you, now you be successful."

*SD:* You touched on another interesting topic, which is, how do you move someone to action?

*TR:* Trust, respect and trust. Inspiration to see the possibility that there may be something more and greater for their life. A reinforcement of social proof. Social proof is a major part of my seminar's meaning. I can sit here all day long and tell you how great a product is, but I would rather have a peer tell you.

Most people think a peer is a someone from Oshkosh, Wisconsin who is overweight and saying this thing made me feel good. I think that is the market for some products, but I think our unique strength is that I've gone out there and talked to my friends and people who have an impact. So I get a Martin Sheen on the show, and when he speaks, more people listen. Fran Tarkenton, I think, helps in that area without a doubt. When a congresswoman gets up there...

*SD:* In my mind, she was the most effective testimonial on the second show. People expect actors and celebrities to do commercials—we think they can be bought. A congresswoman people still feel, despite everything that's happened in our government, can't be bought.

*TR:* I think the audience will see that also. I try to make sure we have a nice balance among different people representing the primary social groups. The other thing is absolute sincerity. I don't think you can fake that. When I'm looking at the camera, and I do what I call "state bite," where I am talking right to people—people really like that. The biggest feedback we get is that people want more of me, and want to hear more about what the product is and what we do.

So when I go to do that, I'm looking at that camera, and I'm looking like it's somebody I absolutely love and respect. I know I am entering somebody's bedroom. I want to be totally respectful and I also want to challenge them. I want to take care of them as if they were my best friends. I want to talk to them as if they were my children with whom I knew I wanted to share this information. I don't want to offend them or be too aggressive, but I also want to say, please, if you trust me at all, try this. You've got nothing to lose. I'll take care of it. I'll take it back if it doesn't work.

And I think those feelings come through in my face and my eyes. There is no way to manipulate that. And I think you've got to believe in your product. All the people in our show believe in our product. Every person there has been influenced by these tapes in a massive way and they want to give something back. A lot of them put their reputations on the line, and a lot of them get attacked for it. Even Fran. And Martin has already gotten it from a few people too. People say to him, "What are you doing on that show, are you crazy? You look like you are endorsing something. What if it doesn't work out?"

So these people took a big risk with me, and I could not be successful today if it weren't for the team. The team is all the people who commit their time, support and put their reputations on the line. I would not be anywhere near where I am without them. The team is Guthy-Renker, Lieberman Productions, and Tony Robbins Productions, but the three of us together are all committed to quality. I drive my partners a little crazy sometimes with quality, because my standards of quality are pretty intense, and that has cost us a lot more money. But I respect my partners so much because they may fight me a little bit, and maybe they are right in some places, maybe I should mellow my standards a little bit, but for the most part they are willing to roll with me on it. I think we have been paid back a thousand fold as a result.

# MARJORIE POORE

Long before infomercials had a name, Public Television was packaging books and videos to sell via 800 numbers as accompaniments to their shows. Marjorie Poore helped innovate these product tie-ins throughout the U.S. You'll also learn how a more traditional marketer uses television programming in a much subtler way to build a very successful ancillary business.

**Steve Dworman:** Tell us a little bit about yourself and your background.

**Marjorie Poore:** I have worked in public television for 19 years on the production side, and actually had been working primarily in production management positions until the early '80s when I started developing projects for KQED [in Northern California].

You'll notice my use of the word "projects" because that's how we view them. I think some people in my position would say they're developing "programs" or "productions," but I started looking at the properties that we were developing in a very comprehensive way. So if we were developing some information about cooking with a special host, one derivative of that might be a television series, but it also might be a book, or some other form of an outreach program.

We started looking at these productions as multi-level projects, in which we might have varying degrees of involvement. The area that actually leads you to me is what we did with cooking programs. Clearly after watching a great chef prepare a menu or some dishes, people wanted to further their involvement and get the book, get the recipes, so they could actually do the things they had just seen performed on television. In about 1983, we did our first project, which was a series called *Great Chefs of New Orleans*. Luckily, my predecessor had taken it a step further where KQED would also publish the book. Therefore we owned both the book and the TV series, and that was very beneficial.

Back in the early days, and we smile when we remember this, on the first show we had, the program would come to a close, and all the viewer would see would be a key of a phone number. There was no picture of the book, no description of the book, it would just say, "If you would like a copy of the book that contains all the recipes seen on this series, please call the toll-free number on your screen."

*SD:* The book probably wasn't even produced at that point.

*MP:* Exactly. It's pretty predictable I guess. In fact, I inherited this area about a week before that first program went on the air, and it took me two days to figure out where the toll-free house was that was managing this operation. And yet the toll-free number had been out on programs that were appearing all over the country.

We've been using the same toll-free number service ever since, which is now Neodata. They called me up that Monday and said we had 3,000 orders! I took it very matter-of-factly, I didn't know that was a good response. We then had to figure out where the books were, get them finished and bound and into cartons and all that. We eventually figured it out, and continued to sell books at a rate of 3,000 a week. Later that summer, I went to a book marketing conference, and a lecturer stood up and said that book telemarketing doesn't work. So I raised my hand and said that we had sold 30,000 books through tele-marketing, and he said, "Well, maybe there's an exception."

*SD:* Another expert...

*MP:* Right. It was working for us at that time because our audiences were really responding to our cooking shows—especially when the shows would break the mold of being in the studio and go out to restaurants to see different kinds of chefs. Really up until then, Julia Child had been it. Our first goal has always been to provide quality television shows to public television stations. The telemarketing of companion books is just part of the project, which has proven very successful.

*SD:* Let's back up for a minute. People might not be aware of how the PBS network system works. Do you develop your shows independently, or in conjunction with the PBS network?

*MP:* It actually works both ways. Sometimes we develop them in conjunction with the network, and in those cases PBS has provided us with funding for the shows. Often, station producers and independent producers provide the shows. So KCET or KQED may produce a show, or the show may come from an independent production company. There are people who are experienced in what makes a good public television show, and sometimes they will do it without any blessing from the network. To get funding, one has to be in communication with the powers that be in public television.

*SD:* The cooking show that you refer to, was that aired locally, or nationally on the network?

*MP:* It was aired on public television stations around the country. It was not actually the PBS network.

*SD:* So it's picked up, as in syndication?

*MP:* Yes.

*SD:* Do you have any idea what the viewership was?

*MP:* No, but our cooking shows tend to rate about a 2 rating point.

*SD:* We just did a seminar in which it was proved conclusively that ratings have nothing to do with responsiveness to direct marketing ads on television.

*MP:* That's right. I think that's something public television people inherently know. We try to give some weight to the impact a program has. It depends on the relationship of the program to the person. In fact, since these cookbooks got started, 85 to 90% of our business is still from cookbooks. We're working over 60 titles. It's still very heavily a cooking and how-to response that works. My theory on why other programs that get higher ratings don't work is that I don't think someone who has just spent an hour of their life watching a show about submarines wants to pursue that interest, whereas with cooking, they do. I think they've had it with submarines after an hour.

*SD:* After the cooking show, I would assume you made a profit on the cookbooks. What happens to the money then? Does it go into producing other shows?

*MP:* It depends. We have done some cooking shows where we've counted on the book sales to actually pay for the production itself. In other cases it goes to help support our station. One of the goals of KQED in particular has been to develop sources of revenue besides pledging on-air. It's a wonderful way to become self-supporting.

It also provides a viewer service. We feel pretty strongly that it helps change the relationship between the viewer and the station, and the relationship to public television. Say they watch *Cooking at the Academy* and they got so excited by what they saw that they ordered the book. They get the book and decide to have a dinner party, and they make this scrumptious meal, and what do they talk about that night? They talk about the cooking show. And that benefits us. It allows us to have a greater impact on our viewers, which is what public television loves to do.

We know we don't get the kind of ratings that commercial television does, but we like to believe we have a higher impact. And we like to believe that benefits our funders as well. The funder of *Cooking at the Academy* is Braun, a very savvy and smart company. The cookbook extends their association with the show, because the people who order the book see the Braun name and support in the book, and they associate Braun with fine cooking and high quality. So that's the total picture.

*SD:* What was the next step after the cooking show?

*MP:* We've probably developed and launched about 15 cooking series. We then started to talk this up to other PBS stations. By this time, we had set up the telemarketing and fulfillment operations to support all this. A lot of other stations were not interested in getting involved in this end of the business, and many of them only had one or two projects a year, or every two years. So we offered them the service of handling the telemarketing and fulfillment. That's how we ended up with so many titles. We've done a wide range of properties, from *Victory Garden* books, to *This Old House* books, some of the James Burke books, *The Civil War*, lesser-known how-to books like *How to Buy an Oriental Carpet*, and *How to Survive an Earthquake*.

*SD:* Where you involved in the *Cosmos* series or *The Astronomers*?

*MP:* No, we were not involved in *The Astronomers*. Some stations in the system are able to do their own fulfillment, and KCET in Los Angeles is one of them.

*SD:* Do you have your own facility for fulfillment?

*MP:* No, we subcontract. We use Neodata for telephone service and we use Motivational Packaging for fulfillment service.

*SD:* But you had all the computer software, everything in place with them?

*MP:* Yes, and also managing the service. We have quite a big role in tracking inventory, ordering inventory, handling customer service, managing the operation. A lot of stations in the system don't have a clue about how to negotiate with publishers, and there are huge minimums that these services have that the other stations couldn't afford. We do all the financial reports, and make sure that expenses are reasonable.

*SD:* Now do you have enough faith in the project that you have the books produced before the show is rolled out?

*MP:* On cooking shows, we do a lot of our own publishing, and yes, we gear up to produce a series and produce a book. We've published several of the books through KQED. In just over a year, we've had 70,000 viewers call in for *Cooking at the Academy*. And an equally phenomenal success with our recent Jacques Pepin series, *Today's Gourmet*.

*SD:* I'm not familiar with him.

*MP:* In the food world, he's a real god, and also a very attractive Frenchman and a wonderful on-air presence. We've had over 80,000 people call in for his book in 18 months.

*SD:* And what do the books generally sell for?

*MP:* Both of those books were selling for $12.95. Recently we raised *Cooking at the Academy* to $14.95.

*SD:* So you're about at the million-dollar range in terms of gross taken in.

*MP:* Yes. And that doesn't include bookstore sales.

*SD:* When you say you're at 70 to 80,000 in sales, over what period of time did that happen? How many airings of the show, how many weeks, how many times a week is that?

*MP:* It's pretty complex. The first factor is the number of shows in a series. *Today's Gourmet* has 26 programs, *Cooking at the Academy* had 13.

The other thing you need to look at, which is very difficult in public television, is the number of re-runs. Public television is a very loose network, and actually stations make their own decisions at the local level. So we have developed fairly sophisticated promotion programs just to get the stations to run our cooking shows and run them in good time slots. Right now there is enormous competition in public television for cooking shows. So you can't take for granted that your show will be run.

The next factor is the percentage of U.S. markets that the series reach. And that's fairly stable. KQED does have a reputation for producing high-quality cooking shows, so we usually get between 80 to 85% coverage. The really difficult question is how many times those shows are repeated. We usually get carried for the first run, but after that it's very difficult to track.

*SD:* And an episode in the first run can repeat two or three times in the same week.

*MP:* Exactly. Another factor is the market. For example, KCET in Los Angeles happens to be an excellent cookbook market. And by the way, we do not really study this religiously, that's where our public television side comes out. We're not really marketers at heart, so more sophisticated marketers would have a lot more information than we have.

We've spent more of our energies getting the books published and making this work than in tracking information. Last time we checked, Boston was not a great book-selling market. Chicago is excellent.

*SD:* I might be getting too specific, but is there a drop-off in orders from the first airing of a show on a first run to a second airing in the same week?

*MP:* I'm sort of amazed at how level it stays. The response seems to remain very level.

*SD:* And what about when the show goes into its second run?

*MP:* We just don't know. It would be fascinating to know, but we just don't.

*SD:* Let's talk about the bookstore sales. How do they compare with the direct response sales?

*MP:* It's been running about half.

*SD:* So when you mention selling 80,000 of the cookbooks, then you might have sold another 40,000 through retail?

*MP:* Yes.

*SD:* That's fascinating. You're selling a lot of books.

*MP:* Yes, we're selling a lot of books.

*SD:* Tell me about videotape sales. That's a relatively new development within the last couple of years?

*MP:* Yes. They have not worked at all for cooking. That's pretty common knowledge. They're starting to work in other areas, like the how-to areas. I think if you had a program like *How to Survive an Earthquake,* and you had it in book and video form, my guess is that you'd be running 50/50 between book and video. And it's very price sensitive. If you can get that video down to $14.95, you'll probably sell more videos than books.

*SD:* If a viewer were that interested in a show like *The Astronomers* or *Cosmos,* which were both released as video sets, why wouldn't they just tape the shows off the air?

*MP:* I'm not an expert in this area, but I think that people just don't get their act together to do that. They also like the packaging. We do a have a more affluent customer base that can afford to not go through the hassle. They may not realize until the end of the program that they want to keep a copy of it.

*SD:* That's true.

*MP:* People also say to me that if viewers see the recipe on the screen, they won't buy the book.

*SD:* The videos generally sell about as many as the books, but not in the cooking field?

*MP:* Right. There's just not a success story out there about a cooking video selling really well.

*SD:* To what do you attribute that?

*MP:* I think there's something very special about cookbooks, and the way one would use a cookbook just doesn't come close to the way one could use a cooking video. Plus the value, you get a cookbook with 100 or more recipes. There can't possibly be more than ten recipes on a cooking video—there are usually only four to six. And you have to take time to watch it. And it could be that there are so many cooking shows on public television that people think, why should they pay for something they can get for free?

*SD:* Do you find that the correlation extends to retail?

*MP:* Yes. There have been a couple that did okay, but there's no great story.

*SD:* You rank the success of book and video projects with the most successful category being cooking, and the second how-to. How do the others follow?

*MP:* Way, way behind. On a typical prime-time documentary-type series, you'll get between 100 and 500 responses. And that's a program that should theoretically have double the audience of a cooking show. So with a show like *Cooking at the Academy* we get 2,500 responses, and that's with half the audience of an average documentary program.

*SD:* That's fascinating.

*MP:* The only exception we've seen to that is if something is a collectible. If it's an art series and maybe people want to collect the art book, there might be a higher response. James Burke had a phenomenal response on his last series that we did.

*SD:* So the order of response is?

*MP:* First is cooking, second is other how-to, and third is something that is collectible or perhaps religious. Everything else is last place.

*SD:* Even though you didn't do it, how did shows like *The Astronomers* and *Cosmos* do?

*MP:* Through the grapevine, I heard they did poorly. Now *Cosmos*, you can't really compare because telemarketing wasn't really up and running at that point in public television. We really pioneered this with our cooking shows.

*SD:* What about *The Civil War*?

*MP:* It did poorly.

*SD:* The book did well at the retail level.

*MP:* Over the air, it did not do well. I have to tell you some other factors I didn't mention before. Another factor is where the offer is placed. There's been a dispute about that in public television. Some powerful forces, like the PBS network in Washington, feel very firmly that these offers may be viewed as clutter by our viewers. They feel very strongly that the offers should appear after the PBS logo. So in other words, there's the question of how many people tune out after the credits and never see the offer. Because of that, KQED has taken all of its programs through another distribution service that allows us to put the offer on right after the program.

*SD:* What do you mean by another distribution service?

*MP:* It's a second distribution service in public television called the American Program Service.

*SD:* And they get the shows on educational television as well? Like another syndicator?

*MP:* Same sort of system. We respect the view of PBS, because these programs don't generate the kind of revenue that underwriting and corporate grants do. So it's one of the inherent pulls and tugs in public television. On a program like *The Astronomers*, the offer would definitely run after the logo. But again, there's just really never been a prime-time show that gets a huge response.

*SD:* But I thought that *The Civil War* was on the retail best-seller list for a while.

*MP:* Yes, it did much better in the stores than over the air. Of course the other factor is price. Our cookbooks sell for $12.95 or $14.95.

*SD:* And that was a $50.00 book.

*MP:* I have personally avoided any high priced items. We like to stay under $30.00.

*SD:* Do you expect less response in the $20.00 to $30.00 range compared to the under $20.00 price point?

*MP:* Yes. Considerable. There have been a few exceptions. Unfortunately, we are not able to experiment with pricing. We can't produce a different commercial and see how people respond. PBS just isn't set up like that. So we have to do a lot by gut, or by the, "If it ain't broke, don't fix it," motto.

*SD:* Has PBS ever put more than one announcement in the course of the show to sell the product?

*MP:* No, that's absolutely off limits. We do not interrupt our programming.

*SD:* Not even a crawl half-way?

*MP:* No.

*SD:* So it's always at the end of the program, hopefully before the logo.

*MP:* Yes.

*SD:* Have there been any cases aside from *The Civil War* where the retail sales have accounted for as much or more than the television sales?

*MP:* No. But again, understand that our strength is in over-the-air.

*SD:* You've been doing this for a very long time, longer than the new breed of infomercial makers. What have you learned that we haven't really discussed that would be of interest to people in this industry?

*MP:* One more thing we've learned, which I think would interest the people in your industry, is that when products were offered around programs other than the one they were associated with, we got almost no response. That was fascinating to us.

For example, we produced a beautiful spot for *Miracle of Life*, and granted it was not hard sell, but it was beautifully done, very tasteful. *Miracle of Life* is, I think, the number one selling video of any program ever offered on public television. We produced this direct response spot and we would get like two orders across the country. Viewers were just not in the mood to order something unless they had already been involved in what was going on. That emotional involvement seems all-important.

*SD:* Where did you run those spots?

*MP:* Around other prime-time shows. Between shows, maybe after a *Masterpiece Theater.*

*SD:* *Miracle of Life* is the kind of program you want to own a copy of when you see it.

*MP:* And nobody called in. There could have been other things going on. I guess everyone is familiar now with the success of Time-Life's *The Trials of Life*. Clearly, they produced an incredible infomercial. Maybe if we'd had a similar one...And it was at a very low price. So that's one thing we've noticed.

Another thing is that people love to watch an interesting process.

*SD:* For example?

*MP:* Well, cooking. That's why we've never produced, despite many proposals, any series on wine. I got involved in one, and I kept it two minutes long, because there's no process there. There's nothing to show people except different labels, and that's not a process.

*SD:* How many times can you swirl it around the glass and spit it out?

*MP:* The more interesting the process, chances are the more successful you'll be.

*SD:* Was there a show that you thought was going to really do well in terms of sales that surprised you and didn't?

*MP:* Yes. In fact, it was probably the only show that surprised us, and it goes back to my point about process. We geared up for a show in 1986 called *Dining in France.* We had been toying around in the cooking area, and we thought, "Oh, this one is really going to be big."

It was shot on film, in France, Pierre Salinger hosted. We thought this was going to be the ultimate cooking show, because we spent more money and the show was more highly produced. Well, we got almost no orders. It generated about an eighth of the response of what we thought it would do.

But the show was so highly produced, they left out the process. They were more intrigued with, you know, a dolly through a forest in France picking truffles, than actually being in the kitchen with the camera on the process. And quite frankly, I think that had a lot to do with the low response.

They also made it inaccessible. A show has to be accessible for people to get involved. It has to look do-able. This show was clearly not do-able. I mean, they'd go into this area of France, and they'd say, "Okay, here's this area where they raise this special kind of chicken, and it's only raised in these ten square miles." And then give them the recipe for making this chicken. Well, nobody in the audience thought they could do that, and the response was down.

*SD:* Have you ever tried to take some of the spots made for your cooking shows and air them on commercial television?

*MP:* No.

*SD:* Any reason?

*MP:* No, in fact we'd be interested in trying that. Again, it's our public television side, where there are certain areas we have not been aggressive in.

*SD:* You might get some calls based on this interview from people wanting to help you do just that.

*MP:* We'd welcome it.

*SD:* How does the sharing of the revenue work with the other stations?

*MP:* There is a fund where we deposit 20% of our profits. KQED manages the fund for the rest of the stations. We distribute the fund back to all the local stations as a way of acknowledging their participation in all this.

*SD:* How do you pro-rate what each station gets?

*MP:* We set this up at KQED. There's a formula that PBS uses to divide up costs among the stations, and we use that formula to divvy up the money. The stations have been pretty happy with us because we're sending them a check four times a year.

*SD:* There's been a lot of talk lately about incorporating the sale of products into commercial television shows. For example, if there's an author on *Oprah Winfrey*, putting an 800 number at the end for people to order the book directly. So there's almost no selling involved; it's almost done as a service. You were absolutely the pioneers in doing things that way.

*MP:* Yes, we have a lot of experience. That could be an enormous thing, if they started doing it. But it takes something away. I'll put my public television hat on again now. You have to think through the rules. Remember, we're producing information, trying to disseminate information, and we choose to do it by publishing a book and producing a television series. I think that shows like *Oprah Winfrey* could start to lose some credibility if they did that because it would appear that they were on the take, and they would lose some of their editorial status. Inevitably, they'd collect some of the money, and then what happens if somebody refuses to sell their book? Do they not get on the show?

*SD:* Right. Well, the talks that I've heard, it would not be done all the time, it would just be done occasionally. It would sure be a boon to the small publishers out there.

*MP:* I'm just bringing it up as something that needs to be thought through. Did you hear the story about Marianne Williamson?

*SD:* No.

**MP:** She's one of the New Age inspirational speakers, and she went on *Oprah Winfrey* and the next day, you may want to check this with the publishers, but I think they had over 100,000 orders for the book in one day.

**SD:** Did your mouth start salivating?

**MP:** Yes, in fact I met with her. We also produced the John Bradshaw series. That's a very high impact property as well.

**SD:** That created a whole industry. You can't go into a bookstore now without seeing a dysfunctional section.

**MP:** Well, we helped get that one launched! We got involved with John Bradshaw in 1989. The show was low ratings, high impact. A phenomenal response. People got emotionally involved.

**SD:** Did you sell books?

**MP:** Books, audio, video.

**SD:** How did that series do for you?

**MP:** Extraordinary. And he's extraordinary. He really touches a chord with people.

**SD:** Was that in the 70,000 to 80,000 range?

**MP:** Oh, more than that. John Bradshaw's programs in public television have become pledge programs, so stations run them to get people to join. So a lot of people join because they want to get the tapes. So this is a little different from infomercials. But still, it's putting something on television and getting people to want the product, so we're still in the same area.

**SD:** Thank you very much.

# MICHAEL LEVY

s the producer and host of 110 episodes of *Amazing Discoveries*, Mike Levy has earned one of the most successful track records in the infomercial industry. In this rare interview, which first appeared in *IMR*'s September and October 1992 issues, Mike reveals many of his pioneering secrets. On a personal note, I worked with Mike very closely on a project in 1994. His innate ability to structure a sales proposition—an offer—is one of the most remarkable I've ever come across. He knows how to sell and how to make the telephones ring. Heed his advice and it will pay off for you.

**Steve Dworman:** Let's start at the beginning. How did you get into this business?

**Michael Levy:** Well, I was born with a big mouth. At least that's what my parents say. They remind me of the times I used to connect a tinker toy to a piece of string and talk into it like a microphone.

And then I went to school and became an electronics engineer. I got out of school and went to work for a consumer electronics company designing high-end audio equipment, and quickly noticed that electronic engineers are never going to be the wealthiest people in the world. I then hooked up with a recording company in Hollywood called Custom Fidelity records, which is no longer in existence. This was back when I was 22. They were one of the very first full-service independent record companies.

Then I saw K-Tel emerge, selling all the oldies records with this strange telephone number that began with 1-800. Back then it wasn't too common. So my partners, who were college buddies, and I decided, "Hey, we've got a pressing plant here, we've got all the facilities, why don't we go out and make deals with the artists and put them on a royalty basis and compete with K-Tel?" Which we did, with success.

That was the first time that I created a direct response television ad. At the time there wasn't such a thing as videotape. When you did a commercial, you did it on 16mm film, which now is the flavor of the month, but back then the equipment was very primitive. I wrote the commercial, I was the camera operator, the audio man, the lighting guy, everything. We did the :60, :30, and 1:20 second commercials and sold a lot of record albums.

*SD:* What was the first album you did?

*ML:* The *25 All Time Golden Greats*. For $9.95.

*SD:* You actually produced the spot.

*ML:* I did everything. Put the record together. I even took the picture that was on the album cover.

*SD:* What gave you the background to be able to do that?

*ML:* Well, I was watching television, and beginning to see a new medium evolve called direct response, and people were getting excited about it. I've always been the kind of person to study what other people enjoy. I began to ask questions to friends and neighbors and associates, asking them if they'd seen the thing on TV where you could order records from K-Tel, and they'd say, "Yeah, and you can actually get some good merchandise sometimes." So it was a very intriguing opportunity to be able to reach so many people without having to own a franchise like a Wal-Mart. That was the very beginning of my interest in direct response.

*SD:* What did you learn about direct response from selling the records?

*ML:* Well, there's been a real genesis since then. The interesting point is that we were 22 years old, and selling 10,000 to 18,000 records a week. Yes, they were $9.95 apiece, but you have to weigh it for the dollar value 20 years ago. I then went into the management consulting business, which required a lot of advertising.

*SD:* And you were 22?

*ML:* I was 24 at that point, when I got out of the record business. And then after that I went into the management consulting business, and I began to write print advertising for that company. I was watching newspaper ads, and backs of magazines, and I would notice print ads that would repeat themselves. Obviously, if an ad repeats itself it must be working. I saw an ad on the front page of *The Los Angeles Times* classifieds that said, "Lazy man's way to riches." Remember that one?

*SD:* Joe Karbo.

*ML:* Right. The style of writing was brilliant, to say the least, which was my first awareness of the advertorial form of direct response. I began to put together a campaign for a series of things from craft items to vitamins, and I tried a few more record albums—all in direct mail and statement stuffers.

The next thing was that my son was growing up and he was playing with a kid down the street, and the kid's father was the make-up artist for "Dynasty." I met the father, and I said to myself, there has got to be a mail order campaign here. So we put together a cosmetic company utilizing a lab and this guy's talent, based specifically on the cosmetics he used on Joan Collins in "Dynasty." I wrote a head-line: "Dynasty's make-up artist reveals Hollywood's best-kept secrets." We ran this ad in about 300 major newspapers, full page, and generated about 10,000 to 15,000 orders for these skin care kits per month.

*SD:* Was it skin care or make-up?

*ML:* Skin care. Our intent was to back-end it, which did very well. This was when infomercials were in their early inception in 1984. Then the people from Twinstar called me, and identified themselves as being in the infomercial business, and they were interested in my full-page ad. They thought it was something that could be a great television half-hour story, especially since we had already done one- and two-minute spots that were effective. Our CPO was good because the product line had a terrific back-end.

*SD:* What was the back-end?

*ML:* Two more parts of the skin care system, plus make-up. The name of the company was California Cosmetics. It's still in business and doing great. My ex-wife bought me out. The show has not been on the air for about three years. Altogether I think we did about 500,000 orders and she still has a tremen-dous amount of those orders on a continuity program.

*SD:* What did the kits sell for?

*ML:* They sold for $39.95. And that was 1984-5. Steve Weber was our outside accountant at that company. He had the job of untangling a large company that was totally creative driven.

I watched some of the infomercials that were out then, which seemed to have that sleazy element, so I told them I didn't really want to be involved in that genre. The California Cosmetic product line is very legitimate, and we're concerned about our client base, so they said, "We'll give you creative con-trol." At first I was flattered, but then I found out the reason they gave me creative control was because no one at the company had ever produced an infomercial before.

So I produced an infomercial on the California Cosmetics Silk Skin System. The host was Lauren

Sydney, who was a CNN newscaster. It was a very good experience. We had an audience, some testi-monials...it was a very emotional show, and we didn't have one before-and-after. The emotion drove the show because the stories were all true and they were virtually unrehearsed.

We shot the show at KSCI. That's when I first met Steve Moore, our director, who's now been with me seven years. Steve and I physically built the set. We went out in the back of KSCI and found old doors and Venetian blinds, went out and got tempera paint, and painted everything. We brought chairs from home for the audience, our own pictures from home to hang on the wall.

There was so much emotion and excitement about doing the show that it was contagious. I'm still proud to look at that show. It went on the air with very limited media. You weren't able to buy that many half-hour slots back then. We generated between 25,000 and 40,000 orders a month, which was phenomenal at $39.95 back then.

I began to have a lot of respect for the half-hour format. Twinstar went from a company with three employees in a small rental office to eventually becoming a public company of which, at one point, I owned 20%. They approached me to buy into the company because of my creative contribution. Steve Moore and I then produced a flock of shows for the company, utilizing celebrities as hosts. Our con-cern about having it look good resulted in great production value. We went the extra mile. My elec-tronics background enabled me to actually get into the trenches and do the editing with Steve.

*SD:* Were you here or in Arizona then?

*ML:* I moved to Arizona for a year and commuted. I formed Positive Response Television when I joined Twinstar in order to be able to do creative work for other companies on projects that would not compete with Twinstar.

Eventually, the demise of Twinstar was imminent. They began to wonder if it was really necessary for the creative team to be making as much money as they were. They felt that their tremendous media buying power was the key. They started making shows that didn't have the high production values and they wound up producing one flop after another. So I initiated an invitation to buy me out, which was a mutual desire. They were beginning to get greedy and felt that I was participating too much in the company. Greed has been the poison that has killed many people in the direct response business. People begin to think they're omnipotent. This business is very good for you—if you do your homework.

*SD:* What do you mean by that?

*ML:* We do a lot of research here. Research that most people don't do. There are a lot of people in this business who have platinum American Express cards but not a library card. Before we do anything we do a lot of homework.

*SD:* Give me an example.

*ML:* We look at computer databases. We spend thousands of dollars a month on computer research. We read all the consumer and trade magazines and journals to measure the trends, which is how I came across the Juice Tiger.

*SD:* Were you doing that much research back in the Twinstar days?

*ML:* Back then I wasn't doing formal research. I used to go to this particular coffee shop back in my single days—it was a real working class kind of place where the truck drivers and women who worked at the grocery store would go. I used it as sort of a focus group. I would ask the people there which name they liked for a product. I learned a lot by interfacing with these people who actually buy the products.

Another way I did research was through my association with California Cosmetics. I became friends with the guy who started the Matrixx answering service, Seldon Young. He started Matrixx (formally NICE) in his living room to take incoming calls for the Mormon Church. He had four lines, and he built the company up to a staff of 3,000 people. He was bought out by Cincinnati Bell for $27 million. I used them to take my in-bound calls.

Seldon allowed me to go in and train the people who answered the phones in our product category. This was one of the first times that someone had gone to the trouble to fly up there and actually run the pre-shift meetings. This increased my upsell by 11%. Neil Powell once said to me, "If you want to learn this business, go put a headset on and start taking orders." So I went through the employee-training course and took orders. It was an eye-opening experience. It let me know what questions the consumer was asking. On our own shows, I'd see a pattern of questions that people had that were not answered in the infomercial.

*SD:* Give us an example.

*ML:* Well, at the time, the big issue was hypoallergenic cosmetics. And I began to hear questions asking how the products were tested. At the time I had no idea how cosmetics were tested, or that they used animals to test cosmetics. So I went back to Bob Sidell, who had developed the products, and he said there was no animal testing. So we put that in the show. And it's that kind of feedback that's so important. Throughout several campaigns, I made the journey to Ogden, Utah, rented a hotel room and stayed for a week to nurture the campaign as it was being born, to fine-tune it early in the game.

*SD:* Were there any cases where you shot a show, answered the phones, and ended up shooting new material?

**ML:** There were instances where we had changed the commercial, but not the body of the show. There were instances where we changed the script that the telemarketer was given.

Most direct marketing people pay very little attention to what's called "the information screen," the information that's given to the telephone operator. All of my campaigns have page after page of information on the information screen. This allows a lot of objections to be cleared up, so that a lot of calls that would have been inquiry calls become orders. When one of our products came up as an incoming call, the operators knew they were armed with information, so their attitude was different. They had a much more positive attitude.

**SD:** So, you left Twinstar at that point...

**ML:** Right. I left Twinstar and had Positive Response Television. I was then looking at various companies to do business with. I had an association with Nancy Langston when I was with Twinstar because they did a joint venture with Media Arts and I produced the show, a weight loss program.

I remember Nancy inviting me to Virginia. We met, we talked, she showed me all the shows she had on the air, all of which were doing fairly well, none of which she was personally proud of. She asked me if I'd be interested in becoming the creative force in the company, and I said absolutely. I didn't want to be an employee on a salary basis, and we worked out a commission royalty basis, and went to work on a show.

We began to analyze some products she had in house, and there weren't a lot of products that I was interested in. Nancy and Pam Daly and I were in New York, interviewing an actor who had a no-smoking program. I wasn't really sure if it was going to be a success because another smoking program had already run its course and was just going off the air.

I suggested that we take a different twist and create a show that would be a continuing series instead of a one shot deal like all the real estate and other infomercials. This works well in syndication and in the record business where you have one artist with several albums. I felt it would not only add legitimacy but also build a base audience. So they agreed.

I went home and thought about it, and being recently divorced I had plenty of time to think and type. It hit me one day that perhaps we were approaching this whole infomercial thing in the wrong way in getting celebrities to host the shows. The press was saying that the infomercial producers were getting celebrities to host the shows to deceive the public into thinking they were watching a regular show. So my thought was that if somebody came along and played it totally honest and totally straight, that we would dazzle them with our honesty.

I also felt that the customer should be watching the product anyway, not the celebrity. The human brain is able to function at such a rapid pace that is much faster than talking. When someone is watching a soap opera star, they may start thinking about what soap opera he or she is in and lose track of the product. I proposed that since I had to be there anyway to produce the show, why didn't I host the show? Nancy said to me, "We're a public company. Can you send us an audition tape?" I told her I had never done this before. But she had faith in me and told me to proceed.

Steve and I built the sets in Arizona, went shopping for paint, just like you would for your house, and then I got a call from Nancy. She said, "The board of directors said that if the show doesn't work, since you have no experience, we would like you to reimburse us for the production costs." I didn't know how to take it, but I believed so much in the concept that I said okay. The agreement was that if *Amazing Discoveries* didn't work, I would reimburse Media Arts for the first show. Production costs were not what they are now. I think we had budgeted about $43,000, but that would have been a tremendous amount of money for me to come up with. That was in 1989.

*SD:* What was the product?

*ML:* The Europainter. And that was an interesting story. I found the guy who brought Europainter to us when I was traveling in Australia looking for a distribution deal for the cosmetics. David Geller hooked me up with his people in Sydney to show me the possibilities of direct response over there.

I ran into the people who had successfully marketed the Europainter in Australia. They introduced me to Ian Long, whose father owned the molds that made the plastic, and had for years had been supporting his family by selling the Europainter out of the back of his station wagon throughout England and Germany. He passed this little enterprise on to Ian, who had been selling it everywhere from trade shows to carnivals, to fairs. Ian speaks three languages, but of course the only thing he speaks in these languages is his pitch. People really thought that he knew the language. He could pitch this product in any language across Europe and he sold hundreds and hundreds of Europainters per day. We flew him over to demonstrate the Europainter, because he was the best demonstrator, and sure enough, there was chemistry between us.

I hosted the show wearing a $43.00 sweater, and I kept looking at my watch thinking about how I was going to have to mortgage my house if the show didn't work.

Steve Moore directed the show. I produced and Bill Flohr was the floor director. It went on the air and did absolutely phenomenally. The Europainter was doing like 6 1/2 to 1 on the first three airings. I remember Nancy Langston calling me up and saying that there could have been an error at the answering service, but the initial response was that I wasn't going to have to pay for the show. I wasn't sure what she meant about the error, but it turns out we had blocked the answering service with the calls. People were not only responding to the product—they also loved the feel of the show, and the comedy and chemistry between Ian and me, and the fact that this was the first time they had seen a host who wasn't a celebrity.

*SD:* How long did it take to shoot the first show?

*ML:* About four hours. We shot two shows a day back then.

*SD:* How many people were in the audience?

*ML:* About 50. We couldn't afford to pay extras, so we figured out that we could hire a bus and go to Sun City, the retirement community. The retirees were more than happy to come out for the day if we would buy them lunch. So we trucked these people in. And this had a double purpose—they couldn't leave. It was 118 degrees outside. It was so hot in the studio, which was under-air-conditioned, that the paint on the floor stuck to my feet and we had to do retakes.

*SD:* What was the second show?

*ML:* I think it was HP 9000, the cleaner. And that was again a product that Ian had demonstrated. It was manufactured by a German company, and it was the weakest product in their line. When it became a hit, the company could not believe we were ordering 50,000 tubes at a time. Nancy arranged to have a 747 cargo plane go back and forth every Sunday loaded with HP 9000 to fill the orders. It became a real phenomenon.

The next really successful show was the Auri car polish, which my friends from Australia also brought to Positive Response. We took it to Media Arts. We used John Parkin, who is to car polish what Ian is to Europainters. John was selling various car polishes throughout Europe. And we found this car polish that had liquid Teflon in it, apparently one of the first times Teflon was suspended in a liquid that a consumer could use. It really took off, like wildfire on the hood of a Rolls Royce.

*SD:* How many of those have you sold?

*ML:* It would violate my contract with National Media to state that. Absolutely gazillions. We had to split the orders between two services to keep from blocking the answering services.

*SD:* How did you and Ian develop your back-and-forth banter, and the adding of product to the offer?

*ML:* During rehearsal, just screwing around. We were just goofing around trying to figure out what to put in the campaign and at one point Bill Flohr said, "We should have shot you right then." So we decided to make that part of the format. We agreed that if it didn't come off as sincere, we'd take it out. Ian and I had become hammy enough that I guess we were able to pull it off.

*SD:* How many *Amazing Discoveries* have you done now [as of September, 1992]?

*ML:* Forty.

*SD:* Of the forty, how many have been winners?

*ML:* I think about 28.

*SD:* That's almost three quarters. That's a very high average.

*ML:* Well, that's because we play it straight, we're very sincere, and we have fun doing it. The shows are structured to be at least 50% entertainment.

*SD:* Did you think your fire extinguisher show would work?

*ML:* I thought it was a very entertaining demonstration, but the fire extinguisher violates one of the rules of direct response, which is "Don't sell prevention."

*SD:* And why is that?

*ML:* Because the psychology of impulse is only motivated by a cure. Can you find a cure to something that people are suffering? And that sounds like I'm describing an illness, but you can cure a lot more than illness.

As I have said at every seminar I've been invited to speak at—and hopefully this will be my legacy when I go to the big dial tone in the sky—things that work in direct response are the things that fall into the categories of sex, vanity, religion or greed. Those may be bold words to be interpreted accordingly, and there are branches off these categories, but a prevention product does not fall into the realm of an impulse buying decision.

*SD:* Well, I'll take issue with you on that, because I think you could take any five categories and make something fit into it. For instance, BluBlocker sunglasses could be stretched into vanity, but I don't really think they belong there, and BluBlockers are one of the longest running products on television.

*ML:* People buy BluBlockers because they look cool.

*SD:* I think that even if they looked different, people would buy them because of the way the show is put together.

*ML:* Well, I can tell you that all of us producers would love to tell you that the show is everything.

But the product is very important.

In my opinion, the BluBlocker sunglasses are like a part of clothing that is related or identified with being part of your contemporary status. Dark sunglasses go back to 77 Sunset Strip with Kookie wearing the black glasses. And a lot of our audience members would like to image themselves after that. You can say the same thing about Auri car polish—a car is a status symbol. The old cliché, "You are what you drive."

*SD:* But in my mind that's not why people buy it. I don't think they buy it because it's a status symbol.

*ML:* Not a status symbol. It's almost a sexual thing. Sunglasses are sexual.

*SD:* I feel that in direct response you have to trigger something that makes people emotionally want to buy, and then you have to give them the intellectual reasons why they should.

*ML:* In direct response you also have to make the thought process complete within a few minutes, and then make viewers feel confident in reaching for the telephone and ordering. If you give them a message that is difficult to comprehend, where they have to go home and think about it and discuss it with their family, then the 800 number will never ring.

*SD:* Why do you think people bought the Europainter?

*ML:* You're addressing a chronic problem that they have. America hates to paint, but everyone has to paint. Women buy the product for their husbands to ease the burden. That's probably why 70% of our purchasers are women, even though you'd think it was a masculine oriented product. What you're saying is true if you look at it objectively, but the psychology of it is that you have to be able to cure a problem.

*SD:* Let's talk about how you research things at this stage in the game.

*ML:* I look for the problems, and then I try to find the cures. We don't try to find square things to fit into round holes—we try to find the holes first. I'm an avid reader via my three computer database systems. I probably read certain sections of about 400 publications a month now. I have the computer programmed to scan for certain sections. It gives me a window onto exactly the kind of stuff I want to look at.

*SD:* In using the databases, are there certain key words that you're always on the lookout for?

*ML:* I think if you would ever type in "phobia," you would spend thousands of dollars letting the computer run its course. That is an interesting search term to use when you're looking for products that cure problems. The thing that inspired us to pursue the Human Calculator was the American phobia about math. People are afraid of being put on the spot and having to figure something out with math.

**SD:** Was that a situation where you found the problem first and then found Scott Flansburg, or did Scott Flansburg come to your attention first?

**ML:** Scott Flansburg was introduced to Positive Response by Paul Simon, the real estate guy, who made one of the first infomercials ever, The Paul Simon Real Estate Show. Nancy Langston and Media Arts (before it was part of National Media) put it on the air, and it did $1.9 million over one weekend. Scott made an appearance on Gary Collins' *Home Show*, and was able to slip in an 800 number as a passing comment, and 22,000 calls came in the next two days.

So Scott came to us, and I then did a lot of research into this phobia about math. We put together the guidelines to create the Human Calculator home study course, which has sold, and continues to sell, hundreds of thousands. Scott is a remarkable person who has dedicated his life to helping children of all ages to learn to enjoy math and be productive at it. He flies around and gives seminars in schools and organizations, and he's made a big contribution to the educational system. It's a great feeling to be a part of that type of infomercial.

**SD:** Any plans to do a second show with him?

**ML:** I would like to. There was talk of doing a second show. I'm not sure what National Media plans on doing.

**SD:** So in that case you were introduced to them first. In other cases...

**ML:** In other cases we have made ourselves extremely sensitive to emerging needs of various types, through reading, advertising, listening to a lot of talk shows, etc. You have to be sensitive to what's going on around you, 24 hours a day, to be able to come up with decisions, products and creativity that sell.

**SD:** Do you do focus groups on an already completed show or on the product before the show?

**ML:** On the product before the show. I would never let a focus group write a show. The real problem is that if you use a focus group in California, you'll get a slanted outlook and you need to know how to skew for that.

**SD:** You've done 40 shows. The format has been copied tremendously. What do you think of the shows that have attempted to duplicate your success?

**ML:** The fan mail that we get tells me that the public is really insulted by copies. The public is asking the question, "Who are they trying to fool?" Sincerity is something you can't knock-off, and no matter how much someone spends to try to copy the *Amazing Discoveries* show, there's a certain magic that comes through that can't be manufactured. It can't be done with tricky editing, and it doesn't come through with the right words on the Teleprompter.

It comes through by having your heart in the right place. We have 28 people in our production group who do every single show with us. They all have a tremendous pride in this show. That comes through.

**SD:** You developed *Ask Mike* outside of the shows that you do with National Media.

**ML:** *Ask Mike* we developed mainly to generate a contemporary format different from *Amazing Discoveries* that would allow for this format to run simultaneously with *Amazing Discoveries* and not make it seem as if we were over-saturating the market. At any given time, a half dozen of these shows can run thousands of times a month. Another reason is that *Amazing Discoveries* is committed exclusively with National Media and we will do *Ask Mike* with other clients.

**SD:** Your wife Lisa has been producing your shows.

**ML:** Yes, she has been producing them for a long time. We have been producing the shows together. She comes from an acting background.

**SD:** How did you two meet?

**ML:** We met through some friends of ours who are also in the direct response business, direct mail. In fact, it was just after Europainter came out, and she looked at that tape and it almost ended the relationship. [Laughs]

**SD:** Really?

**ML:** She comically commented that, "You certainly are a nerd." She actually started out as a production assistant on some of the early *Amazing Discoveries* and began to really have a flair for making contributions.

As the shows progressed and the company grew, she took on the role of co-producer. She's essential because she brings the point of view of the female viewer, which is very important because of the skew that direct response naturally has towards females. Infomercials are even more skewed towards females.

There are times when Lisa comes up with little tidbits that, in my opinion, have brought in several percentage points of increased sales. Lisa put together all of the recipes for the Juice Tiger show and she devised the order of the demonstrations for the Juice Tiger. She also thought of the name Juice Tiger. So it's a family business! It would be very difficult for me to have the passion that I have for this business if I didn't have a wife who understood it and had the same passion.

*SD:* Before she met you, had she ever bought anything from television?

*ML:* Absolutely! She bought Anushka!

*SD:* Yeah! What changes have you seen in the industry during the last four years?

*ML:* The players who have remained in the industry are those who look at this as a full-time endeavor, a permanent endeavor, rather than those who are interested in the quick buck.

One of the predominant things I see in the nature of the product is that it is increasing in value. We used to focus our product selection on retail sales points of $29.95. Two things caused us to re-evaluate that—one being the increase in the cost of media, and along with that was the customer's desire for a more substantial product.

There are only so many substantial products that can stay within the $29.95 range. Car polishes and cleaners and some gadgetry, when purchased directly from the manufacturing plant without any middlemen, can fit within that price scheme. But when you talk about juicers and electrical items, you're not going to be able to stay within that retail price point and most of the time you're not going to be able to have the standard spread that we all have been looking for. The old rule of thumb of 6 to 1 or 5 to 1 cannot always be adhered to. You have to make up for it by having a high quality product and a high quality show.

*SD:* Have you had any shows within the past year that have had those kinds of ratios?

*ML:* Not exactly. The front-end did not fit within those ratios and the back-end made up for it. There's a lot more attention being spent now on the back-end. Continuity is becoming a way of life now. In the past, the utilizing of the list was not even a concern. Now, it's not uncommon for a direct marketing campaign to come out with a product and at the same time already have other products developed to work that list properly. The other products may be totally out of the original product category, but there have been crossovers that have been successful before. So it's not uncommon to say okay, as soon as we start generating 30,000 names a month, here's what we're gonna do with those names.

*SD:* Mike, who actually owns the *Amazing Discoveries* show and format?

*ML:* It's a loose relationship, and it's sort of in a dispute between National Media and Positive

Response. All I can say is that Positive Response produces *Amazing Discoveries* only for National Media.

**SD:** I'm kind of surprised that no one has jumped on the back-end bandwagon and come out with an *Amazing Discoveries* catalogue.

**ML:** Frankly, if I were the one who had to make that decision, I would have decided to put one together. This is one of the reasons we're putting together the *Ask Mike* format, because we'll have control of all the downstream and we'll be able to exploit all the different avenues of the name. But for whatever reason, National Media has decided not to develop the *Amazing Discoveries* catalogue. They had a catalogue about two years ago, but they had a complete turnover of staff and the catalogue project got dropped and was never picked up again.

**SD:** How do you see the future for infomercial formats and for the industry as a whole?

**ML:** In the future, the producers of infomercials have got to become aware of ratings. *Amazing Discoveries* generates good Nielsen ratings. And that allows broadcasters to look at our shows favorably with respect to their lead-in and lead-out value, the audience going in and the audience going out of the show. That often will dictate what they can charge for their spot advertising on the show that follows *Amazing Discoveries* or the one preceding it. As time is a finite entity. It's going to be important for people to pay attention to that.

I believe that producers have also got to be more sensitive to the entertainment value. We always give away something in the show in the way of entertainment or information that viewers can take away without having to buy the product. For example, on the Human Calculator show, Scott Flansburg taught the audience two techniques which they could try at home to prove to themselves that, hey, if they bought the course, they'd be fantastic. I believe that if I can give a message to someone and they go to the bar the next day after work and say to the person next to them, "Hey give me a number ending in 5 and I'll tell you the square root of it in three seconds," that person is going to be impressed and if they see that show again, they're going to buy. Very often the purchasing decision is not made on the first impact. The person watches the show several times and then they buy.

**SD:** Is there an average number of viewings before that happens, two or three times?

**ML:** The last time I measured that was three years ago. I'm not sure if this information is correct, but we came up with 2.3 times. I believe infomercials will become tools to create brands. Major companies will be able to spend money on research and development without having to maintain huge cash reserves to be able to go into a huge loss position to be able to generate a brand name.

For example, when Procter & Gamble comes up with a new product, they'll spend anywhere from three to eight million dollars to try to make the brand into a household name. That sort of expense can be self-funding with an infomercial. Now certainly not every product is appropriate for the infomercial format. But I think, as indicated by the number of Fortune 1000 companies that are calling us, we're going to see a lot of major corporations getting into infomercials. Hopefully they'll be smart enough to use the creative force that has proven successful in direct response. My hope is that they don't get turned off to the concept of direct response by trying things in-house and making mistakes.

*SD:* Well, I don't think there are very many advertising firms that understand direct response.

*ML:* Right. There are none.

*SD:* Based on the early experience of Volvo, whose show I don't consider successful, I think there's going to be a lot of that.

*ML:* Right.

*SD:* People who have the creative wherewithal to produce successful direct response shows, I think, are going to get more and more in-demand once the agencies find they can't do it in-house.

*ML:* Right.

*SD:* One of the biggest problems I see with the industry right now is that people see products advertised on television through an infomercial and then go to Costco or one of the discount warehouses and the product is there for up to half-price off.

*ML:* That's another example of greed killing the golden goose. Sometimes you have to hold yourself back from taking the big retail order so that your product name gets embedded in peoples' minds. National Media did a very good job on that. They held back on flooding the retail market with the Juice Tigers until the name "Juice Tiger" had been planted in as many American minds as possible. Then the flood went out. Now, that may or may not be a good example because the juicer has become a commodity, but it was a good way to do it, coming out right away.

*SD:* The Juice Tiger show is still running isn't it?

*ML:* Yes, but they can justify running it at a break-even or even a slight loss at times because of what the retail drive is providing.

*SD:* That is one of the products I saw advertised recently in a major department store's catalogues for $58 on sale.

*ML:* Well, we are in the process of re-editing the Juice Tiger show, and it'll be out at $99.

*SD:* Okay, but I think it's a major problem because all the viewer has to do is get stung once and then they won't order off television again. They'll just wait until the product comes to the store.

*ML:* That's one of the reasons we're going to start the *Ask Mike* format. Then we've got control of the situation.

*SD:* Do you ever see yourself doing an infomercial that is not a studio-based format?

*ML:* Yes, we are in the process now of doing that. We did one that was unsuccessful, *Amazing Discoveries On Location*, the dog show. It was a pet training course. But yes, we are going to begin doing some magazine-style *Amazing Discoveries* on location.

*SD:* That's great! We talked earlier about you doing them in shopping malls. For infomercials to really work, the products have to appeal to the largest common denominator, correct?

*ML:* Yes.

*SD:* You probably have more experience than anyone in the field with the sheer number of shows that you've done. How targeted can you get with products and still be successful?

*ML:* It depends on your overall goal for the campaign. If it's to have a profitable front-end and a profitable retail back-end, then you've really got to appeal to the masses. If you are willing to have a mediocre profit, or even no profit on the front-end because you see a potential for strong retail sales, then you can appeal to the niche—but your campaign will have to be very media sensitive. You'll have to pick and choose media based on location demographics and also viewing patterns of television.

One of the databases I use taps into viewing patterns. And if there is a niche, at Positive Response we will gather data that will let us look at products that might appeal to a more vertical market.

*SD:* I was interviewed today and the press source said, "These things only air from midnight till six o'clock in the morning. Who the hell are the customers? Blue collar workers who work swing-shifts?" How would you answer that?

*ML:* I think our customers come from all walks of life. But first of all, the shows don't just air from 12 o'clock to 6 a.m. National Media has some strong weekend time slots in Los Angeles. The media buying patterns are very heavy on the weekend during the day. And there are smaller stations that will air infomercials during the day on weekdays also.

But the only reason why the shows are usually on in the middle of the night is because the time is low-cost and it's available. But you'd be surprised who's up late, real surprised. There are just as many doctors and lawyers who are buying products as there are blue-collar workers. But they all go through very similar decision-making processes, and that's where the creativity comes in.

*SD:* There are a lot of products on the air that appeal to women. Have there been many products that appeal primarily to men?

*ML:* There are some that on the surface appear to appeal only to men, but the success of them is that a woman buys them for a man to get something done.

*SD:* Were women most of the buyers for the car polish?

*ML:* Yes.

*SD:* That startles me.

*ML:* It's difficult to determine the gender unless you're on the phone, because a lot of women use the man's credit card. So back in the days when I could get the customers names from Nancy, I would call the customers personally and do random surveys. You can't delegate that. I want to personally make contact with the customers. This business is so wonderful that you've got to have a passion for it.

*SD:* It's a 24-hour a day business.

*ML:* Yeah, and it's fun. I have several monitors in my office. One is tuned in to the Home Shopping Network, one has QVC, and one has CNN. And then I have picture-in-picture on one set, and I have Business Channel on it, which is interesting because you can see trends.

*SD:* Have you ever been on Home Shopping or QVC?

*ML:* No.

*SD:* Why not?

*ML:* Because I don't pitch products. You have never seen me pitch a product.

*SD:* That's true. You act as the Everyman host.

*ML:* There have been people who have tried to act like me, but they always come off as phony.

*SD:* Why do you think that is?

*ML:* Because they are phony. All they are concerned about is their override. Frankly, that's what Steve Weber's job is; that's why I never concern myself with the finances. We have a monthly meeting where we look at the financials, and then we go on to the next project.

I would much rather be in a studio 24 hours a day, seven days a week, than sit and thumb through my bank account. Certainly, anyone can determine that I've made a lot of money in this business, but not by the things that I own. Lisa and I are philanthropic.

*SD:* Aside from the media costing more, how have the financial realities of the infomercial business changed in the last couple of years?

*ML:* I think you have to be good at this now to do well, whereas before, the whole genre was so new that anyone who dabbled in it could make a living. Now it's sort of evened out. There was a peak, and then reality set in, which is good.

Now you can make accurate projections. Now you can run a real business, make two-year, three-year and five-year projections and business plans. Before, if you asked anybody in the get-rich-quick real estate campaign what their five-year business plan was, they'd say, "Well, I don't have one, but I'll come up with a home study course that will show you how to do one for $49.95."

I think flexibility is the key issue here. I think you have to be flexible, and cognizant of changes that are happening in the business. People have to realize that improvement doesn't just mean switching from video to film—improvement also includes the message, the psychology, the words that are said. Production quality covers a great many elements.

*SD:* You were the first person to try to get the audience, both in the studio and at home, really excited about what was coming next. You use lots of hooks before the breaks, and other elements. The viewer never knows what's going to come out of left field on one of your shows. The Tyee Productions shows are perhaps the opposite. They're shot on film with one camera, and are much more low-key and slower paced.

*ML:* Tyee stimulates your sense of aesthetics. We stimulate your diaphragm and make you laugh. Both approaches are extremely positive motivators, and both have merit. I think the combination of both can occur. I think to Tyee, a base audience is not important.

We're concerned about that viewer coming back again and again for another dose of *Amazing Discoveries*. When they hear our music or see my face, I'd rather they not be concerned with what the product is, just that they understand they're going to see a show and be entertained.

*SD:* So basically, in your case, you are the franchise.

*ML:* Correct. We're sort of like a Radio Shack.

*SD:* You are probably the one person in the industry who knows firsthand of the power and the clout of the producer versus the star.

*ML:* Yes. And it sure helps to be both, because the star never complains. He's cheap and he's always available. I know he's never going to say to me, "Where's my limo, and why is my dressing room not full of Dom Perignon?" Which is another reason I decided to create that franchise around me.

*SD:* You did it that early?

*ML:* Oh yes. I did a score of shows with celebrities, and I just cannot stand the prima donna attitude.

*SD:* Does being the star affect your clout when you get into deals with other companies?

*ML:* Yes. A lot of potential product suppliers come to me and the negotiation is good because they can also say, "Can we use your picture on the box?" I suppose there is a façade of talking to someone who is on television, although I really forget it until I've been out in public. Being out in public is a very strange experience for me. We were just out at a Japanese restaurant, and a guy came running out from behind the sushi bar and wanted me to sign his t-shirt while he was wearing it. But if I let that go to my head, then I wouldn't be good at this business. So I don't let it go to my head.

# PETER BIELER

*P*eter Bieler comes from a traditional background as a brand manager at Procter & Gamble in Canada. He entered the direct response business by forming Ovation, Inc. He was responsible for finding and developing the ThighMaster into an international sensation. Under one roof, he not only built up a direct response television business but his own retail and international sales. Peter subsequently was bought out of the company by his partners and went on to create a company that funds direct response television media roll-outs.

**Steve Dworman:** Peter, please tell us a little about your background.

**Peter Bieler:** My first real job was at Procter & Gamble up in Canada, where I was a brand manager. I left that to come down to USC Film School because I wanted to get into movies. After that I was in the industry for a good number of years, working at various studios—Quinn Martin, United Artists, and MGM. Then I was Associate Director at the American Film Institute. After that I had my own company making special interest home videos, primarily for Vestron. I then joined Alan Landsburg Productions as a production executive. And that's where I became aware for the first time what was happening in direct response.

Tony Hoffman had a show called *Everybody's Money Matters*. He was renting Landsburg's stage. That was a live show that was going with a new show everyday. When I first landed at Landsburg, I would park my car in the back and I'd walk by this studio, and I'd say, God, what is going on here? This is unbelievable. I wasn't seeing the show on television but I was seeing this activity. So I started investigating it and talking to people at Landsburg about it. And it was clear they had put together an ad hoc network. They were essentially their own network.

That's essentially what an infomercial does. Especially when you're doing a new show everyday. I mean, it's the same stations that are carrying it. I was really struck by that. I thought that was an amazing thing. And a couple of years later, when I felt that the video business wasn't where I wanted to be anymore, I looked at the direct response business. And a friend put me together with Pippa Scott, who is chairwoman of the board of Ovation, and Joe Grace, who is executive vice president. They were interested in being in the same business. And I put together a business plan and we started this company.

*SD:* Is Body Solutions a division of Ovation?

*PB:* Yes. There are two divisions of Ovation, Body Solutions and Home Solutions. Ovation is the corporate entity, Body Solutions obviously focuses on fitness products, and Home Solutions does household products, both expendables and small appliances.

*SD:* The first products that you started with at Ovation were infomercials, correct?

*PB:* Yes. What happened was when we started the company in the summer of 1990 I took about five months to tour all the state fairs, trade shows and home shows, looking really for a product and for a spokesperson.

I found a really terrific pitch guy in Miami. He was actually based in New York at the time, but doing a show in Miami. He just had the audience wrapped up in his hands. A lot of what the pitch artists do is very similar to what you have to do in an infomercial. You have to entertain, but at some point say, you have to say, I'm not going to entertain you anymore, I want you to buy.

It's interesting how the pitch artists do it, and I studied that. No matter how many jokes they tell, and no matter how fast they are with their hands demonstrating the product...at some point, just before they start to pitch—which is, you get this and you get that—they clap their hands, like that [claps his hands loudly]. And it's just to wake the people up from the kind of passive I-want-to-be-entertained mode, into, "Now it's time to pull out your wallet and buy the product mode."

And Tony Notaro, the pitch man I was watching, was really good at it. I felt this was the guy I wanted to work with, and we went looking for a product. He had a relationship with a company that was making janitorial products. They had a product they supplied in big bins to hospitals. What this product did was, you poured a little bit of it on a spill, and it turned the spill into a jelly like substance, making it much easier to clean up. I have to show it to you, this is really worth seeing. Okay, this is water, right? [Peter pulls out a plastic container that contains a powder, and a glass of water. He takes a teaspoon and puts it into the water, and stirs it up. It becomes what appears to be a hard gelatin that will not pour out of the glass.] Isn't that amazing stuff? I mean, it's a great demonstration too, right? My wife and I had used it around the house for a while. We found it a useful product. So I said, there has to be a home market for this. Instead of having paper towels, you could just sprinkle a little of this on the spill, and simply vacuum it up or sweep it up.

So we packaged the product, called it "Gone," and we made an infomercial. This was our first product out. It was a decent infomercial. Tony was demonstrating the product—how you could use it on kitchen tables, you could use it on kitchen floors, on carpets...all different kind of ways.

But I knew early we might have a problem. We were about three quarters of the way through the shoot, and the cameraman turns to me and he says, "You really think they're not going to want to use paper towels?" And I said, "No, no. First of all this product captures your attention, and secondly it's a lot handier..." and so on and so forth.

Well, he was right and I was wrong. We put the show on the air, and it simply didn't work.

I think probably I got a little carried away with just how gripping a demonstration it is. Ultimately America decided it was easier just to go grab a paper towel than it was to sprinkle this stuff on. So that was our first show, and it didn't work.

Our second show was ThighMaster, and we used the lessons we learned in the first show on the second show...

*SD:* ThighMaster was a spot, it was never an infomercial. What made you decide to do it as a spot rather than an infomercial?

*PB:* Well, we look at each product. And one calls for one, one calls for the other. You don't want to drag out a product into an infomercial form if it doesn't properly belong there. A $19.95 product, first of all, really doesn't support an infomercial. Secondly, one of the primary points you're making about *ThighMaster* is it's simple to use. So what's the point of trying to complicate the offer and complicate the explanation of the product with a half hour show?

*SD:* Did you ever contemplate bundling the video with it, making it an infomercial?

*PB:* Yes, we looked at that at the time. We looked at an infomercial, and what the offer would be. But the star of the thing was frankly the product. Everything else was really just support stuff that some people would find useful and some people wouldn't. And to force everybody to buy all that just to get the product just didn't make a lot of sense. As it turned out we were right. The thing worked enormously well as a spot. And maybe it would have worked as an infomercial too, but you know, we're not married to one form or the other. We don't see much difference in those two businesses. It's the same business as far as we're concerned. I think infomercials are a newer idea and so therefore get more attention. But we'll go either way.

*SD:* How did you find *ThighMaster*?

*PB:* The word was out that we were looking for products. This was during the same period that I was touring the shows looking for products.

*SD:* All of this was within the last two years. That's amazing.

*PB:* Oh yeah. Absolutely. A friend of mine had heard we were looking for product and he had a friend who had a friend who had this product which was at that time called the V Toner. The product's been around a long time, that's not necessarily of interest to everybody, but it's been around since the 1950s, in a slightly different configuration than the present configuration. It was first invented by a chiropractic doctor who put together a product that doesn't really look like ours, but has the same basic principles. And it was used up in The Ashram, which is a celebrity fitness spa, where real celebrities go... Oprah Winfrey, Shirley MacLaine, all kinds of people. And they were using this as part of their exercise program up there. And it came to the attention of a gentleman who had some real design smarts, and saw some value in making a change to the design.

What he came up with is very appealing. It's an infinity symbol. It's really nicely thought out in terms of its aesthetics. He said, "Listen, here's how we could change this basic product, which is not all that attractive, and turn it into something that has some resonance with people." And then he brought it to me. He had tried a couple of commercials on this product, and really hadn't been successful with it. He was emphasizing how many different kinds of exercises you could do with it, how many different parts of the body you could work on. Which is true. I mean, the product can be used for the biceps, the triceps, the stomach, a lot of different parts of your body. I felt that we should focus this thing. Let's just talk about one part of the body. People will be happy when they get it and find out they can do a lot of other things with it. But I think people really want specialized equipment. They want something that is really going to work. And that message is more cogently conveyed if you really focus on one part of the body. And those muscles inside the thighs are very hard to exercise. We had some tests done on *ThighMaster* at USC, and found it was an effective exercise for that part of the body.

I had dealt with Suzanne Somers when I was at Landsburg. I gave her manager/husband a call, and said I have this good product and we're going to launch this campaign...and wanted her to come on board as spokesperson. She tried it out for three weeks before she got back to me. She said, "I've been working on it. I like it." We got together and discussed whether it was going to be an infomercial or a commercial, and various marketing approaches to the product, and we came up with the approach and made the commercial.

*SD:* You had a previous relationship with her, but was it tough negotiating?

*PB:* Yes. There was a lot of excitement for the product right from the beginning, but these things are always a little difficult. One of the strengths the company's got is because of my relationships, and Joe's relationships, and Pippa's relationships in the industry. Which are substantial. We really do feel that we capture the ear of celebrities. And I would have to say it's more so now than it was then, because obviously people are aware of the huge success of *ThighMaster*, and it is generating a lot of revenue for Suzanne. So I think it's an easier sell than it was, but listen, the introductions are everything. Because it's not as though these celebrities are not being approached by everybody. I mean, I don't think there's a celebrity in town who's not getting a lot of offers. And we have to stand out from the crowd. And our personal connections help us I think.

*SD:* Did the negotiations encompass retail?

*PB:* Absolutely. We always knew that if it was successful we were going to go retail with the product. It doesn't make sense, from our point of view, not to. Advertising is advertising. And if you've got the public eye, you're leaving a lot on the table if you don't go retail.  But it's a wildly different business.

*SD:* Was it incredibly successful from the beginning?

*PB:* No, we went back and played with the commercial. It was always successful, but it was not as successful in the beginning as it was after we made some changes to it. We changed the offer at the ending. That was one thing I remember doing. We started offering the Suzanne Somers Center for Life plan, which was a free bonus. We made some other editing changes in the commercial. We re-shot a couple of scenes. I mean, that was our first two-minute commercial. And now it's simpler, because we've done it and we know what we're looking for, and we know what the formula is. But at that time we were still reaching for the formula.

*SD:* What is the formula?

*PB:* It's a three-part formula: There are three parameters to what I think you need to say to the consumer, to get their attention and to get them to reach for the phone. And frankly, that's a trade secret.

*SD:* Was that something you discovered by trial and error? Or was that something you got from watching the pitch man?

*PB:* If you look at direct response advertising, the greatest advantage direct response advertising's got over most image advertising is simply that you have real product differences. The guys who have it really tough are at Coca-Cola. I mean, how the hell they sell sugar water, essentially, which is very little different from every other product. I mean, it's a nightmare, from an advertising point of view. If you gave the average advertising agency on Madison Avenue the kind of product differences that we always approach the market with, they'd be in Heaven.

But at the same time, the difficulty is that you really have to create an ad that motivates someone to reach for the phone in the end. That's the hard part. The easy part is talking about the product. Because you're not going to go out there and talk about something that everybody else has got. But the hard part is how do you snap the viewer to action when essentially watching television is a very passive frame of mind?

Watching the pitch artists, making the ThighMaster commercial originally, then testing it to see where the weaknesses were, and coming out of Procter & Gamble and advertising in general, and understanding what the basic principles were...you know, all these things together helped a lot. It was trial and error, but there was also some pretty educated guessing going on. We figured out how to solve the problems just as everybody else does, in their own fashion, who has success in this business.

*SD:* Money wise, to test an infomercial is in the $10,000 to $25,000 range, depending on how extensive the test. Is it less money with spot?

*PB:* Well, to know if you've got something you should keep working at, costs you a lot less than that. You will know sooner than $10,000. We knew with "Gone." And that was an infomercial. We knew way before we hit $10,000 that it wasn't going to work. But once you get into testing time rotations, and testing areas of the country, and different kinds of premiums, and different scenes in the commercial...I mean, that's endless. When does a test stop and a roll-out begin? I mean, we're still changing scenes in the *ThighMaster* commercial.

*SD:* Really? After two years? You've got something to test against, though.

*PB:* Sure. It's partly to freshen the commercial, and partly to reflect the fact that the ThighMaster name has become as famous as it's become.

*SD:* Suzanne Somers did a phenomenal job promoting the product.

*PB:* Great job.

*SD:* Give me an average range of what you spend in a week to roll-out a spot nationally.

*PB:* That depends a lot. For one thing, it depends on what the mixture is between PI [per inquiry] and bought advertising. We buy an awful lot of time, but we also run on PI. Some of the major cable channels are more interested in PI than they are in selling you time.

But it's hundreds of thousands of dollars a week. For an infomercial, that's relatively substantial, but not unusual. Obviously, in terms of a spot, you're buying an awful lot of spots when you spend that kind of money. And you're getting an awful lot of penetration, and an awful lot of frequency. Because you have wider rotations, you're much more into day time, early frames, late frames, than you are with an infomercial.

*SD:* Were you able to target the spot?

*PB:* Sure. We knew what our target audience was. We bought some wide rotations, and some very narrow rotations. In fact we bought some shows. We found some shows where the cost per thousand for our target audience was very reasonable. So we focused on those shows. We ran them week after week after week. They were some well known syndicated shows that seemed to be very good buys for us. We also bought wider rotations. But we weren't afraid to step up to the plate. We had a program that was pulling a lot of leads, and it was clear to us it was catching a lot of attention.

*SD:* You had a slam bang product here. What's the advantage at that point with doing a PI rather than just buying the time?

*PB:* Well, I think that there are some cable networks that really prefer to deal with PI rather than sell time. In some cases, we bought and traded for PI on the same network. Broadcast is pretty much all bought. But with cable, some channels we were both buying and PIing, and some we were just PIing.

*SD:* Explain a little bit about how a PI deal works. Generally the station will take an agreed upon percentage of each sale. What is that range generally, on national cable?

*PB:* It's in the $5.00 range for a $20.00 product. And then on top of that you usually have a fee that's paid to the advertising agency that sets up the deal. The down side of PI is that you're paying per inquiry, not just per sale. So if you have a show which is pulling a lot of inquiry referral calls in relationship to the number of sales it's making, you can get hurt. But if you're closing a substantial number of your leads, it can be from a very good deal to an okay deal, depending on how well your CPO [cost per order] is on your bought time. But the reason to do PI is not simply to bring the rate down. It's that it's the only way to get some time. And when you have an offer that's really working, you're trying to buy as much time as you can, and get in as many channels as you can.

*SD:* What was the upsell when people called for the ThighMaster?

*PB:* We have an exercise video—actually we have two, we primarily offer one—which shows how the product can really be used for all different parts of your body. We focus just on thighs in the commercial. This videotape showed the exercise regimes that you could use for all the other parts of your body—your upper arms, your chest, your stomach, and so on and so forth. It's an exercise video, incorporating the ThighMaster. Then we had another one which incorporated the ThighMaster into an aerobics program. So we offered those two videos, and we did very well with them.

**SD:** In the spot business, does your product have to have a four or five time mark-up?

**PB:** Yes, it's the same kind of mark-up as in the infomercial industry.

**SD:** Why don't you talk about the process that you went through with retail, because you've ended up doing some very unique things.

**PB:** Well, it is our feeling that only about 20% of people will buy something off of television, even if they are attracted to the product. So there's really a large market that you can only reach through retail stores. If you have a product, and this is key, if you have a product that really stands up to that kind of scrutiny. And that's the only kind of product we'll do. It feels good. It looks substantial.

Going retail is a big financial investment. It takes a lot of bodies to go retail. A lot of the direct response business is done through vendors who handle small entrepreneurs, telecommunications and fulfillment services and so on. That infrastructure doesn't exist to the same degree in retail. So you really have to have it in-house. Theoretically, you could do a direct response offer with very few people. It takes a lot more bodies to go retail.

**SD:** There are a lot of companies that take products retail, but you decided to do it yourself. What was the thought process behind such a huge undertaking?

**PB:** It was a big commitment of money, and a gamble to some degree. The reason was that we intend to be around as a company for a good long time. We felt bringing products directly to the marketplace would be more effective. And we would control the quality of the service, and we would be able to coordinate the advertising and the distribution better if we were doing it ourselves. And ultimately if it was successful, the profits would be greater. I'm glad we did. There are people who will bring your product to retail quite effectively. We're talking ourselves about bringing other people's product to retail, who don't want to invest in the overhead necessary, and so on. And frankly, you need a substantial hit to break down the barriers. To get shelf space at Wal-Mart is not easy. I just picked that as an example, but it's true of all the other major retailers. I mean, that doesn't come easily. You have to have some staying power, and you have to have a product they really feel they can make some profits off of. We had all those things, and it worked for us. We developed a substantial rep force, and they have had a tremendous hit with ThighMaster. We hold the all-time sales records not only in fitness products but in any product, in some of the major retailers. I don't think there's a fitness department in the country that didn't owe a lot of its profits to ThighMaster last year [1991], and the first quarter of this year. Now going into the third and fourth quarter it is again doing very well. So it really paid the way. For the reps, and for ourselves. And it financed the development of all the necessary sub-structure.

**SD:** With the success of rolling it out in retail, you had knock-offs?

*PB:* Yes. You have to decide very quickly what you're going to do. We were knocked off really before we went retail. First by a local operator at the L.A. County Fair last year. We decided to be aggressive. We had a patent pending, but the patent had not been published at that time. Our first legal actions were based upon trade dress. And we bit the bullet, you know. It's very expensive. And it's very, very time consuming. The whole process, because there's so much at stake, and because the expenses are as high as they are, really takes a lot of the executive time. So you've really got to decide if it's worthwhile—consider the chances of success, and whether the product really warrants that kind of attention. We felt that was the case.

We won temporary injunctions very early on in the game. We won the right to seize product very early on in the game. We had federal marshals and a sizable force of investigators seizing product at a factory in the valley, and seizing product right out of the booths at the L.A. County Fair. We stopped that early infringer. We subsequently found out that this action was being fairly closely watched by other people in the industry who knew the success of the Thigh Master and were waiting to see how aggressive we were going to be legally.

So the local guys were not the end of it. They were just the tip of the iceberg. Our patent was published in January of 1992, and at that time we were able to, in court, defend it aggressively. It was very much a situation where the patent had to be defended. We learned that it was not an automatic thing. And I'm glad we did protect it. Because I think that a hot product that has patent protection, that is aggressively protected, is kind of an entrepreneurial dream.

*SD:* How did you get a patent if the product existed in other forms?

*PB:* Well, it's a design patent. The design is quite unique. This infinity shape design is really quite unique. It had been applied for by the people who designed it before it came to us. And it was their patent that came into effect that we had licensed.

*SD:* And then you came out with the ProMaster, which was a stronger spring, geared towards men.

*PB:* Yes. Forty percent stronger.

*SD:* Did you run any spots on that?

*PB:* Yes, we shot a spot. It's a good spot. [Steven Dworman and Peter Bieler view the spot.]

*SD:* We just watched the ProMaster Plus spot. Surprisingly, it's only 30 seconds long. Traditionally, everybody says that you can't sell something direct response on television with any less than 90 seconds. What made you decide to do 30? Did you think there was enough residual effect from the ThighMaster to carry over?

*PB:* Yes.

*SD:* Did you experiment with the longer?

*PB:* No. Just the 30.

*SD:* That's amazing. And it's working well?

*PB:* It's working. It's not a *ThighMaster*.

*SD:* Do you find now that you have to keep running the *ThighMaster* spots to support retail?

*PB:* Absolutely. In fact we made a new commercial recently which is going to start going into heavy rotation shortly. A whole new commercial which supports retail. The product is very, very widely available in retail. Our sales are primarily retail at this point.

*SD:* From the time you rolled it out in retail, were they automatically primarily retail?

*PB:* There's no question that retail substantially cuts into direct response. There's no question about it. Choosing the moment when you go retail is very important, so that you don't in fact kill the golden goose. Because the golden goose is the direct response commercial.

*SD:* What kind of rule of thumb do you have as far as when to roll it out?

*PB:* I can't tell you how I agonized over that decision. Exactly when the moment was, when we reached maximum penetration with our message, when we're timing it to retail season, when we felt that the direct response was starting to fall off, and so on. These are all factors. Plus there are others that we had to take into consideration. I think we timed it right. Exactly how we reached that decision we're going to keep to ourselves, because I believe it's part of our success. But I have to tell you that no decision I've made since I've been here have I agonized over as much as I did about that. And put as much thought into, and talked to as many people, and gathered as many opinions, and so on. I think as it turned out it worked pretty well for us.

*SD:* Would you never roll a product out in retail at the same time you were launching it direct response?

*PB:* I won't say never on anything like that. No, I wouldn't say that. I think some people have done that very successfully. And I think that there are other factors that come into these kinds of considerations, having to do with corporate life and so on, that you really can't make generalized rules.

*SD:* Being that you're taking the product retail yourself, how much more money do you make? Or is it a wash, when you deduct all of your retail expenses for rolling it out, in comparison with your immediate expenses and telephone and everything else. Are you making about the same amount of money off direct response as retail? Are you making more off direct response than retail?

*PB:* Your overhead goes up substantially when you go to retail. If you really want to penetrate the retail market, if you really want to go beyond 30 accounts, if you really want to get into all the stores out there, then it takes some energy, and some money. And you do still have to run the commercial to support the program, so you still have the advertising costs involved. But frankly, if you can absorb all that, the volume is substantial, and it makes it all worthwhile. We really are in a volume business. We're not interested in making a lot of money in a few sales. We're interested in making a little bit less money on a lot of sales. That's the only way to justify the kind of TV that we buy, that anybody in our business buys.

*SD:* The next subject I think is very important is the fact that I have never seen your product sell for less than $2.00 less in retail than it does on television. How do you maintain a similar price point on a retail level without getting into price fixing?

*PB:* Well, we have a pricing policy that we make widely known, and we've had very little problem. I mean, it's such a popular product that the incentive to discount it is not there, and that has made the job relatively easy. We're very open about our pricing policy, and people have paid attention.

I don't know what other people's experience has been. I've heard horror stories about people taking a product—particularly when the product is really tailing off and they're stuck with too much inventory—and really discounting heavily. I've heard those stories. That's not happened to us. I think that the impression that you're going to get killed, that people are going to drop the price so substantially that no one is going to want to carry it anymore, has not been a situation that we've had to meet.

*SD:* Going through the retail scenario, you don't really deal with distributors, you're your own distributor retail, right? So generally you sell it to a store at 50% off, approximately?

*PB:* No. Our margins are better than that. Because we advertise so much. We take on a responsibility when we go to these people. We say, listen, we're going to run some ads on this product. We're not just going to sell it to you and expect you to move it with your newspaper ads. We're going to run some ads here. We're going to do some substantial PR. Which we do, as you've seen. We're pretty active in that area. In return, if we're carrying that responsibility, which most manufacturers don't, we sell at a higher margin, or more margin to us.

*SD:* Well in that sense, that also helps to protect you on a retail level too, right? There's less margin for a retailer to discount.

*PB:* That's not our purpose, but I suppose that's true.

*SD:* So *ThighMaster* has now been running for about two years.

*PB:* It went on television in a substantial way in May 1991. And we went retail in a big way in December 1991.

*SD:* How many units have been sold?

*PB:* Millions and millions and millions.

*SD:* Over four?

*PB:* You know, there's a figure quoted a lot which doesn't come from us, which I think is four-and-a-half or something. I don't know where it came from, but not from us. We're a privately held company, so we're not obliged to say, so we say millions and millions. I think it is the fastest selling fitness product ever.

*SD:* With ThighMaster, you concentrated on setting up your retail, you rolled that out in retail, and all this time I would assume you've also kept your eye out on other products.

*PB:* Absolutely. ThighMaster was a crucial part of the profit picture for many major fitness vendors in the fourth quarter last year and the first quarter this year. And I think we're going to see some very substantial sales in the fourth quarter this year. The life of the product is quite amazing. Nevertheless everybody's looking for what's new. We think it's *BodySlide*.

*SD:* Your new product is *BodySlide*.

*PB:* Right. With Cheryl Ladd as our spokesperson.

*SD:* Where did this come from?

*PB:* Pippa Scott, who's our chairwoman of the board, developed the idea for doing this product. When she started to investigate this particular kind of exercise, she found out that there were other products on the market that were like this, but were much higher priced and were really more oriented toward the health club market. Our whole business is mass market, and putting an affordable product in as many homes as we can. So we found a way to make a quality product that could be affordable to the average person. Then we developed it. Just watching people skating, you knew that it had to be great exercise. In fact, speed skaters have been using lateral training devices for some time. So what we did was we designed our own product from scratch. And made it in a fashion that we could put it into the mass market. Add to this our kind of marketing and vision, and we'll see. So far it's doing well.

*SD:* You have a 120-second spot that's running now?

*PB:* Right. And a 60-second spot, which we're gradually moving into. And we're going to go retail very soon. You're going to start seeing them in the stores well before Christmas.

*SD:* That's great. Now, the price point on that is $49.95. For the people who haven't seen it, it's a specially coated plastic.

*PB:* It's not actually coated so much as it's a specially constituted plastic. There are special ingredients in the plastic that give it a special quality.

*SD:* You lay it out laterally in front of you, and you put these booties on over your shoes. And you slide from left to right, or right to left.

*PB:* Either way will work well. You push off from the bumpers and you slide back and forth. It's a very effective way of getting your respiration and heartbeat up in aerobic fashion.

*SD:* We tried it here, and my heartbeat got up very quickly.

*PB:* The thing of it is that it is an effective aerobic exercise that is also fun. That is basically the reason why we think people will want to buy it, and it is essentially the way we are pitching it.

*SD:* It is a lot of fun.

*PB:* It's like skating in place. It's the kind of thing you can quickly learn how to do, and then you can quickly start learning tricks. You can twist and turn and lift one leg and essentially dance on it, if you will. That adds variety to it. It makes it more fun. So it adapts itself to a lot of different levels of expertise. Therefore we think that people will stick with it.

*SD:* Is Cheryl Ladd doing the promotion for you?

*PB:* Yes. She did the ad and we're going to start a promotion tour. She's very gung ho. She loves the product. She tried it for quite a period of time before she decided to come on board. I think Cheryl had been approached by a lot of people when we came along. She had a lot of offers in front of her, and she chose to go with us partly because of who we are, but also because the product really stood out for her. There was nothing quite like it. So, yes, she's going to do promotions and she's very enthusiastic.

*SD:* Let's talk for a minute about the other side of your company, Home Solutions.

*PB:* We're currently testing a product, and we don't comment on products in test, so I don't know how useful this is going to be to anybody. But we're currently testing a product in two markets. It is a house-hold product, an expendable product. We're doing it as a key account campaign, which means it's essentially a direct response ad, but rather than have an 800-number at the end, it says, "Available only at so and so stores." That's what we call key account marketing.

The common denominator of our business is that it is television driven. But there's a lot of different ways in which you can distribute. There's direct response, normal retail, key account marketing, print, foreign export, credit card syndication. There are a lot of different ways in which you can capitalize on the television that you're doing.

So that product is not a direct response product. The economics don't allow for it. It's a $9.95 product, and it's hard to make $9.95 work in direct response. But we have a two city test running now and we'll be reading the results. It's longer reading the results, because you're reading store movement as opposed to phone calls.

*SD:* How long of a spot is that?

*PB:* It's a 60-second spot.

*SD:* Do you have to develop a whole new marketing strategy on a retail level, to get into home products?

*PB:* Yes. It's a very different approach for key account. You're really dealing with different buyers—promotion buyers as opposed to household buyers. Key account marketing has been around for a very long time. It's the original kind of direct response marketing. It comes out of Al Eicoff and those guys, in Chicago. That's how that whole thing got started. Before they had 800-numbers, that was really the only way to do direct response. But it's still valid, you still see quite a bit of it.

*SD:* Do you have an in-house graphic designer or do you use somebody else?

*PB:* We use outside people. We have a pretty large creative services department working under Carol Land. We do most of our own print copy in house, but most of the graphic design is done outside. For commercials we have a freelance production manager that works substantially for us at this point. And we hire freelance directors and writers and so on.

*SD:* You've grown from three people in the beginning to how many?

*PB:* Over 30 at this point.

*SD:* Within two years. That's amazing. How many people in your rep. organization?

*PB:* About 35. When I said over 30 people, that's just here, that doesn't include the salesmen, factories, warehousing, distribution, and all that. ThighMaster employs a lot of people.

*SD:* What do you contract out with the factories? You don't own your own factories.

*PB:* We don't own our own factories. Our primary factory is in Phoenix. They primarily make our products. But they do some other things as well.

*SD:* Did you have a problem, when you first rolled ThighMaster out and it was a big success, with keeping up with the demand?

*PB:* Oh! Keeping up with the demand in every possible way. It wasn't just keeping up with the demand for product, which was a big enough problem as it was. It was keeping the systems up. We knew we were going to sell some product, and we were prepared for it. But we weren't prepared for the kind of volume of paper work, and phone calls, and processing invoices, and collecting, and shipping product, and warehousing. It's a radically different business. And we were fortunate to have Joe Grace, who was very important in setting up the systems that make this company work.

And we're very edge of the envelope in terms of computers and systems. We're on EDI [Electric Data Interface] with many of our major accounts. So that all of the orders, for instance, from Kmart are all electronically communicated to us. We're able, if we choose, to read movement out of some of our major accounts at the level of the cash register. So we can really keep our finger on the pulse, in terms of the movement of our product. And that's all for a relatively small company, and certainly a very new company.

*SD:* With the EDI, do you actually track movement on a retail level through that, based on the amount of spots that you're running?

*PB:* Yes.

*SD:* So you can actually measure the next day?

*PB:* Yes. We keep track of CPO [cost per order] both on our direct response business and also on our retail business.

*SD:* How many major retailers are you up on the EDI?

*PB:* We're in the process of putting all our major retailers up. I think at this point it's two. But that's a very ongoing process. Talk to me next week and there will be one more.

*SD:* And how accurate are you reporting on that? Are you able to find out on an hourly basis how many units are moving per store?

*PB:* In some accounts we can do that.

*SD:* That's unbelievable.

*PB:* Yes. Well, it's crucial. I mean, one of the reasons that we kept retail in-house was that we wanted to be able to control the media. We make major commitments to media. And obviously we make bigger commitments where the product is moving well. Each broadcast of an infomercial is its own profit center. On short form it's not quite that, it's more like each station per week is its own profit center. But now add to this that you're reading movements through the stores. Obviously it's easy to track our own shipments to the warehouses, but that just reflects the enthusiasm of the buyers, who are very informed, mind you, and also know what's moving through our stores. But it's still a whole different thing when you're actually reading the movement through the stores yourself. You're able to react that much more quickly. And that's what we're capable of doing.

*SD:* That's fascinating. So you could actually air a barrage of spots at 2:00 in the afternoon, and then watch the rest of the afternoon to see if it has any results in retail.

*PB:* That's correct.

*SD:* Has it? Have you ever tracked that?

*PB:* It doesn't happen quite that quickly, because people don't usually hop right off the couch and go to the store. I mean, they might. But they're more likely to be aware of the product the next time they're at the store. Which may be the next week. It may not be the next hour or the next day. So the period you're tracking is a little bit longer than what you're suggesting. It's not hour to hour. Usually you're looking at movement on a weekly basis. We follow the movement at the store level on about twelve accounts. We track them every week. So we can and have pumped up the media in certain areas of the country where we've seen substantial movement. We've also cut back in some areas.

*SD:* Unless you can think of some other areas, let's wrap up with this: The fact that you are talking to other people about bringing their successful infomercial or spot products, and rolling them out retail. Because I know people are always looking for an alternative to that...an alternative source to do that.

*PB:* Well, we know how to sell direct response product in retail. I think the fact that we are the people who brought the ThighMaster to retail creates a certain kind of energy for our presentations. There's a certain level that you reach in terms of volume at which retailers start thinking of you as a partner. We think that we've reached that level.

# RICK CESARI

There was no hotter product in the early '90s than the Juiceman Juicer. Rick, with his brother Steve and spokesperson Jay Kordich, created this phenomenon. At the height of the infomercial campaign, juicers of every kind and brand name were flying off retail shelves so quickly that they couldn't be kept in stock. In this interview Rick spells out how it was done. After this interview was conducted, the brand name and product were sold off to Salton-Maxim, a major houseware company with products on high-end retail shelves across the country.

**Steve Dworman:** How did you and your brother Steve get into the infomercial business?

**Rick Cesari:** This might surprise you a little. I was a real estate broker in Florida back in the early '80s and I went to a seminar that Tom Vu put on. I know you know this guy, but before you say anything let me tell you this story.

**SD:** Okay.

**RC:** I went to the first seminar Tom ever put on. There were only eight people in the room, and he could barely speak English. Afterward, I went out and applied his technique. I bought a house and made about $12,000 in two weeks and said to myself, "Boy, this is great!"

Tom didn't know much about marketing—this was back in 1983. Basically it was just he and his brother. And then, over a period of time, I started working with him promoting his seminars. This was back when the real estate seminar business was going pretty well.

I did all the marketing, learning as I went. We built his seminar business up to the largest in the country, at that time. During the largest seminar, we saw about 13,000 people in one week in Los Angeles. I made the television shows for them and did all the media buying. Basically, I did all the stuff that preceded the infomercial business. This was in the early days, what I see as the beginning of the infomercial business. I think that the first guy on television was Paul Simon, doing an equity dissertation/participation thing. Basically, he did his 60-minute lecture and put it on cable and got tons of orders. Then Ed Beckley started up at the same time.

I worked with Vu for about two and a half years. I left because we didn't really see eye to eye on how people—both customers and our employees—should be treated. When I was with them we made a really first-class television show called *Secrets of Success*. A fellow named Mason Adams was the host. He had played the city editor on *The Lou Grant Show*. Ours was a really first-rate show. After I left...

**SD:** The girls came in...

**RC:** Yeah. That's when Vu started hiring the boats, the girls with the big boobs, and all the tacky stuff you see on television. Since I left, he has also been in a lot of trouble with different attorney generals in Florida and different agencies. So think I made the right decision back then. I learned a lot from them. All this leads up to how we were able to make the Juiceman so successful. I learned a lot about PR, media buying, and making television shows.

**SD:** Before we jump ahead, because it is such an interesting area that was so prominent for so long, why don't you talk a little bit about the lessons that you learned from the seminar business that you still utilize today?

**RC:** It was really interesting. Back in the early days with the real estate seminar business, we ran things a little bit differently than one does with an infomercial. Basically we would pre-empt a time slot on local television stations. We were after larger audiences, so we would buy a lot of prime access time. When a commercial would come on, we would invite people to come to a free seminar. In the free seminar we would tell them about an upcoming $295 two-day class and our speakers would then sign people up.

The most important skill I learned back then that still applies is the ability to create successful television shows. That was when I really learned how to work on the shows. We do most of our productions now in-house, and I'm largely responsible for that area. In the media buying arena, we basically went through the learning curve of what good television time is and what bad television time is. I had enough knowledge that we didn't need to go through an agency.

**SD:** What is good versus bad television time?

**RC:** You probably have heard this from other people, but we learned by trial and error. We would pre-empt shows like *Jeopardy* or *Wheel of Fortune* that had very large viewing audiences for their time period, but very little competition on other channels. So many viewers would tune in and stay tuned in because there was not much else to choose from.

To relate that to infomercials now, that's similar to the reason we like to buy Saturday and Sunday morning time slots, from 6:00 to 10:00 a.m.-because in a lot of instances, the viewing audiences are very good and there isn't much competition. That's one of the first things I learned back then. When you don't know anything about buying television time, you tend to think, "Geez, let's go out and buy prime time and buy a lot of viewers." But you'll find out that while you are buying a lot of viewers, you'll also run into lots of good competition for the audience.

The other thing we learned is the importance of lead-in programs where you could do specialty television buying and where you could follow sporting events so you would have huge lead-in audiences. That usually happens on Saturday and Sunday afternoons. You have to be careful during the sports seasons, especially football season. You don't buy time opposite the local team's football game or you'll get blown out. Just little lessons like that. People might know them today, but back then we still had to learn. And when stations would not sell us time, we taught them creative ways of selling it to us. Instead of running a two-hour movie, for instance, we would tell them to run a 90-minute movie and put us in the last half-hour. There was this one fellow whom now I am using as a television buyer-Raul Vasquez, he's just a one-man shop. Again, this was in the early days of infomercials and we weren't able to crack the big markets like New York and Los Angeles. Raul wrote a letter to the owner of Metromedia, one of the richest guys in the country today. Raul got an appointment to see him and told him that he wanted to spend $1 million a week on television time. I think that got his attention. Raul flew to New York, met with this man and, as far as I know, was the first person to open up television time on the Metromedia stations in New York and Los Angeles. That helped make the real estate seminars at that time such a success. We were the first ones to get in on those stations. I still use Raul today to buy media because he is very aggressive and creative at coming up with ways of using the media to make money, or using television buying as an art to making additional money.

*SD:* What is the name of Raul's company?

*RC:* It's Multi-Media Marketing Group, located in Tampa, Florida.

*SD:* After you parted ways with Tom Vu, what did you do?

*RC:* I was looking for something to do, so I went to the bookstore. This was in 1986 and the stock market was the hottest thing around with all the takeovers. Bookstores have sections on how to make money, so I went there and found a book entitled *How to Make a Million in the Stock Market.* I bought it and read it. The author had created a mathematical system for investing in the stock market. I called him up and talked him into doing a television show on the hunch that it might be something that would be attractive to people.

We put together a home study course that explained his program and we made a television show named after his book, *How to Make a Million in the Stock Market.* The show was a moderate success, from the standpoint that not everybody in the country is going to be interested in how to make money in the stock market. But we ran it for a couple of years on most of the cable stations and especially FNN. It did very well.

That was around 1986 or 1987. After that, I made a television show on a weight-loss product called NewDay. It did about $20 million in sales and that was during 1987-1988. I was just kind of going along—I don't know how to describe it—maybe, as a one-man shop. I would just get an idea, make the television show, have a small staff buy the media time, and go from show to show.

*SD:* Let me just stop you for just a second. Wasn't NewDay a protein powder?

*RC:* Yes. It was called a protein-bearing modified fast which is a fancy name for a protein-based drink. But this one was tailored after the products they sold through the hospitals like Optifast that Oprah Winfrey used. The product had extra calories in it so it was safer than the medically supervised ones.

*SD:* Was that an existing product that you happened upon?

*RC:* Yes, that was an existing product.

*SD:* So then you made a deal with the manufacturer to do a television show.

*RC:* Right.

*SD:* How do you work a deal like that, Rick? How do you go to the manufacturers of an existing product and tell them you could probably expand their market considerably? How do you structure the deal for yourself?

*RC:* Every deal in which we have been involved has been put together in a very similar way. Basically, it is a royalty arrangement where we go to the person we want to make a deal with and say that we will do everything—take care of all the costs of production, the media buying, the fulfillment, etc. Their only participation will be input in assembling the show, for instance, in defining the important aspects of the product.

In the case of NewDay, the manufacturer created the product and the weight-loss system that went with it. It was a pretty simple and straightforward deal. We took care of all the expenses, all of the marketing, and everything involved in the product. Then we paid the manufacturer a royalty on the gross sales, a simple and straightforward method. We just had to determine what the fair royalty amount was. We have done royalties anywhere from 3% up to 10% on gross sales. It depends a lot on the product's margin and also how big a role the person or the company will play on an ongoing basis.

*SD:* If you had a royalty deal with the BreadMan for example, would he be paid on the bread mixes on the back-end as well?

*RC:* Probably yes, depending on what the back-end product was. But we usually don't do a flat royalty arrangement. For example, with the Juiceman, we paid one royalty rate with seminars, another royalty rate for direct response, and a different royalty when we put the product into retail. A lot of it has to do with the available margins. We've always used a straight royalty arrangement on gross sales, but adjusted that depending on the avenue of distribution.

So to get back to NewDay, I guess that product did about $20 million in sales.

*SD:* Was there a large back-end on that?

*RC:* Yes, it was very large in continuity sales. You see a lot of people doing this today, having a lower front-end price to get the customer into the system. With the NewDay product, the only vehicle or distribution channel to the market was the infomercial. This was the vehicle that created new names in the system.

But every infomercial has a life span. Back then we had tunnel vision about marketing. We believed that once the infomercial stopped working, the whole program would end and we would just go on to the next television show. We didn't look at the other options available, such as bringing the product out into the retail marketplace.

*SD:* So in essence, every year or two you had to look for a new business.

*RC:* Absolutely. That was exactly what we did—start a new business. Those were the kind of things we learned along the way. Our knowledge about exactly what an infomercial could do and couldn't do went into the development of our long-term strategy for the Juiceman. It gets frustrating when you build up a business and then the show stops working. With an infomercial, you can go from zero to $20 million in the course of a year and you build up a support staff to manage that level of business. In a lot of cases, companies had to go out of business. So from day one with the Juiceman, we asked, "How can we create a long-term business with this product?"

*SD:* You must have had to watch your media dollars very carefully for the day when, all of a sudden, your show would stop working.

*RC:* Infomercials tend to work in a bell-shaped curve. You have your support structure that is totally supported by the infomercial when it is working, but then when the show stops working, you have to find another vehicle. But the media spending is just part of the difficulty. You go from the place where just about every media buy works, to a point where you have to be very, very selective about how and where you are spending. You can go from spending $1 million a month down to, in the final stages, annual spending of only $50,000 dollars.

*SD:* After NewDay, what did you do?

*RC:* After NewDay I looked for a new business to get into.

*SD:* Did you keep your support staff in between businesses?

*RC:* In the case of NewDay, when the infomercial stopped working, we sold our customer database back to the manufacturer. I think we had approximately 400,000 customers. And we also sold back the remaining assets of the business. I left and began looking for a new business.

I went to a kitchen show at the Seattle Coliseum. The Juiceman was there demonstrating product. He had about a dozen people around him and was doing his pitch like I had seen him do on television. He was very captivating, but that was just one of the things that caught my attention. Personally, I was interested from a health and nutrition standpoint. Even before meeting Jay, I was juicing as part of a healthy lifestyle. So I really understood the health benefits of juicing.

This is back in 1988 and Jay was running his own business with the help of his wife. It was kind of a mom and pop operation where they would go from kitchen shows to state fairs and show the product in a booth. We talked at that time about getting involved together, but for one reason or another, we never did anything about it. Then, after the NewDay job, I thought about Jay again and decided that it would be a good time to pursue that. This was in the spring of 1989.

*SD:* So you called him up...

*RC:* So I called him up. He had just moved from Seattle to San Diego. It turned out that he was coming back up to Seattle. Jay had a business advisor and friend named Jack Lee, whom he had hired to help him find someone to do an infomercial with. It turned out that he had negotiated a contract with Dave Del Dotto's group and was very close to signing.

I called Jay and he said that his and Jack Lee's business advisors were coming up to Seattle and that they'd like to talk to us. From a business standpoint, I wasn't really prepared. I didn't have an organization at that time. I was by myself again. Dave Del Dotto was on television, had a big telemarketing set-up and a big support system. What I had to offer from a business perspective probably wasn't a match for that. But I think Jay and I hit it off because we were in tune philosophically, from the health perspective. We didn't want to do this just to make money. We wanted to help improve people's lives and make them healthier. I think that is one of the things that convinced Jay and his business advisor to sign a deal with us.

*SD:* Was that a straight royalty deal?

*RC:* We started out in the very early days as a partnership deal with the provision that it could change over to a pre-arranged royalty within the first six months. That was, indeed, what we ended up doing— probably in the second or third month. It was just much easier to keep the roles clearly defined. It also made it easier for Jay to determine how much money he could make.

When we started out with the Juiceman, I used a lot of the things I had learned over the years in all the different shows I had made and the different marketing I had done. In the early days, we would go to a city and get Jay on radio and television talk shows. We started out using a public relations firm in New York called Planned Television Arts. That's the public relations firm for Chuck Gibbons. Chuck does the real estate and financial planning thing. He gets great public relations. He's been on every show possible. We used this firm for six months and then switched over to a company called Jericho Communications in New York, which we still use today. Public relations has been an integral part of our marketing plan from day one. At the end of all the local radio talk shows and morning television shows he did, Jay would announce that he was going to do a free lecture at, say, the Marriott Hotel. People would show up, we would have juice machines in the back of the room, etc. We did that for about a year, just doing seminars that way. They were moderately successful.

The problem was that because it was public relations, you couldn't really control your destiny. In other words, we might go to a city and find that the talk show had been canceled, or we might have been promised a 10-minute segment and then been given 30 seconds. Meanwhile, we'd have already booked a hotel and incurred the expenses. We did okay, but we were just getting by. Then I started to use the same skills I had learned in putting on real estate seminars to make a television show, and that's when things really started to change for us.

Let me go back a second, because I forgot something that is really important. Jay had been on a local talk show in Minneapolis. The producer of that show got hired by WOR in New York, which had a show called "People Are Talking," hosted by Richard Bey. Jay had been such a phenomenal guest for that talk show from the standpoint of response. When he went on the air, the phone lines would jam with calls from people asking for more information. So when this producer was looking for someone to fill in at the last minute, she looked for Jay. She called me up. I was taking the business calls at the time. I think it was June 28th and I think they said they needed Jay to be on the air June 30th to fill in for some guest who had canceled. So we flew Jay out to New York. We agreed to do the show if they would put up our office address at the end of the segment so viewers could send for more information.

Jay flew out and did a 20-minute segment on the talk show and they put up our address for about 30 seconds at the end of the segment.

Over the following weekend, my wife and I were at our cabin in the mountains. When we came back from the cabin on July 3rd, there were three huge postal sacks that the postman had dropped off—this was the response from that one appearance. Overall we got 15,000 letters from just that one appearance. That was the very first thing that kicked off the business. From that point on, we knew that because Jay has such a strong appeal, if we marketed him right, the business would easily become very successful.

We later used public relations appearances to create a big segment of our business. Jay would sit at home and do radio interviews all over the country with different shows booked by our public relations firm. At the end of the radio segment, we would give out an 800 phone number so people could call for more information. We would mail them information on the juicer and created a huge business through our office phones that way.

*SD:* Would the 800 number go into your office or through a service?

*RC:* It depended on the size of the show. If it was a smaller show that Jay did during office hours, we would put the calls through to the office because we could convert the calls to sales more efficiently. If they were large shows—for example the WOR show—calls would go into a service bureau because we could get thousands of calls in a five-minute time span.

When you think about it, the public relations fees for booking this kind of appearance are very small when compared to the results you get. It is almost like doing infomercials on radio and television without the advertising cost. So that was always a very important segment of our business. Plus, a public relations appearance has greater credibility compared to the infomercial. In the early days of the business that's all we would do—send Jay around from city to city and out to do seminars. People would show up and we would sell them the product. We did lots of public relations and generated sales through the office.

*SD:* Just a practical question, when you walked in that day and found those sacks of mail, and were basically running the operation yourself, how did you answer all the letters?

*RC:* That was funny. My wife, my sister, and I spent all of July 3rd and 4th opening up letters. On Monday, we ran down to a quick printer. This was before we even really started the Juiceman business per se. We ran off an information sheet on the juicer with our address and office phone number. We would simply mail that sheet back out to people. You talk about hands-on!

After reading through 15,000 letters, we felt we really understood what aspects had excited people about the juicing business and about Jay. This of course helped in all the subsequent marketing. But to answer your question, just the three of us sat there and opened up 15,000 letters over two days.

*SD:* Did you hand address the envelopes?

*RC:* We had to hand address the envelopes. It was fun. Because what a way to start off a business, what a way to start money rolling in! While it was tedious and boring on one hand, it was very exciting on the other. From an entrepreneurial standpoint, who wouldn't love to have 15,000 potential customers on practically the first day you open your door? And again, reading all those letters gave me a lot of insight into the product's appeal, which helped in all our subsequent marketing.

*SD:* Any idea how many juicers you ended up selling as a result of sending that information sheet out?

*RC:* No, we weren't even set up to measure the response and apply it directly to those letters. But we realized that the information sheet could be a very good marketing vehicle to use on an ongoing basis; in fact, we did just that.

*SD:* At that point, did Jay have the juicers manufactured for him?

*RC:* Jay already had a relationship developed with a Swiss company called Rotel, which made the juicer for Jay. He had sat down with the engineers and told them what he wanted from a juicer. They developed a juicer that, while crude compared to the juicers we have today, was really head and shoulders above anything else on the market at that time. The Swiss company's manufacturing plant was in Poland. Very early in the business, I had to fly over to Poland. I had to go over our marketing plans with the factory, tell them about our manufacturing requirements. It was quite an experience to be going into Poland at that time. The factory was about 80 miles from the Russian border.

In the early days of the Juiceman, our marketing was always ahead of our manufacturing. We were never really able to turn things loose because we were always playing catch-up with the manufacturing process. Skipping ahead, we eventually ended up hiring an engineering firm in the United States to create our own juice machine—that was the Juiceman II. To find the best manufacturing relationship, we had to go shopping all over the world, including in the United States. We ended up settling on a Korean company that had done a lot of private label manufacturing for Samsung.

*SD:* I remember that there was a big glut of juicers.

*RC:* Last year I heard that eight to nine million juicers were manufactured and shipped to the United States. They sold between two and three million. So you talk about a glut of juicers—for the cheaper, lower-end models without an established brand name, you can't give them away. I know a lot of people have taken a bath, probably the manufacturers and maybe some other people. You think about more than six million unsold juicers—that's a lot of juicers. That is why you see some juicers on sale through discount stores for $19. You figure they're not really getting their money back for even the cost of manufacturing.

*SD:* So back to Poland...

*RC:* I'm in Poland getting my manufacturing straightened out; giving the factory the projections; finding out how many we could get in so that when we got back to the United States, we could do our marketing. One reason we got involved with the Juiceman is because very early on it was evident that Jay had a fantastic television presence—he was a draw.

I had all the knowledge necessary to go out and make an infomercial right away. But we didn't make an infomercial for almost two years because we wanted to be in a position with our manufacturing to keep up with demand when we broke the infomercials. With the manufacturing capabilities in Poland at that time, we wouldn't have been able to keep up. That was one of the reasons we waited two years before we started selling with an 800 number on television.

The other reason was because of my familiarity with the infomercial business. I knew that as soon as we used the 800 numbers on television, the competitors would come out of the woodwork. Then our product's life cycle on television would become very short. So we were planning from the very beginning to build up a base. Then when we were ready to launch the infomercial, we planned to do it on a big scale and be ready to move out into retail. This is kind of how it worked out, although there were some bumps and turns along the way.

*SD:* Let's go back to when you shot your first infomercial. That was to promote the seminars?

*RC:* Yes, that was to promote the seminars. It was kind of a no-brainer, where you figured Jay was on television with Richard Bey and he got 15,000 letters from one 20-minutes appearance. So I thought, "Geez, why don't we just call up Richard Bey and see if he'll fly to Seattle? We'll get a studio audience and let those guys interact, just like it was a talk show." We gave Richard Bey an outline incorporating all the feedback from the letters and everything else we wanted him to talk to Jay about. We shot them live. There were three half-hour shows. Then we went back and edited the best pieces together and came up with the talk show. It's funny, you hear about big budgets for television shows but I think we did the entire show, including Richard Bey's compensation, for between $35,000 and $40,000.

*SD:* Wow.

*RC:* And that was the first Juiceman show. Again, it's easy when you have a personality like a Jay Kordich. Obviously when you do a studio shoot, it is a lot less expensive than when you do a documentary-type show.

*SD:* I remember that show airing in Los Angeles. I went down on a Friday night to the Miramar Hotel in Santa Monica. I got there a half an hour late and was stunned to find that there were 1,000 people inside with 500 people waiting to get in. They had to have security guards to make sure people went in one at a time.

*RC:* Yeah, that was a little bit later on. Let me tell you what happened in the first place we tested the show. Jay had always been very popular in Salt Lake City. People there tend to be very health conscious. So I figured the first market we'd test in would be Salt Lake City. We patterned these seminars according to the lessons I had learned in the real estate seminar business, where we used to run the show. You buy it differently than you buy infomercial time. You buy a whole bunch of time grouped together over the weekend. For instance, you'll buy Saturday afternoon, or prime access, although you will probably buy Saturday through Tuesday. You might spend anywhere, depending on the size of the city, from $15,000 up to, in a place like Los Angeles, $100,000 for your seminar.

But in Salt Lake City, I think we spent about $15,000 or $18,000. Then you pick different hotel locations. For me, I think the most exciting part of the infomercial business is when, whether it's a seminar show like we made or an infomercial, you have finished the show and you get to put it out to test. You sit there with your fingers crossed, holding your breath, and waiting for the result. In this case, the seminars we promoted through public relations drew 100 to 400 people total for the entire city. When we ran this first show in Salt Lake City, I think more than 600 people showed up at the first hotel location and we still had two more days—which right away told us it was going to be a phenomenal success. During the next year, we hired speakers in addition to Jay, mostly health professionals, to go out and give the health lecture that Jay had been giving.

Our seminars helped to promote the business in several different ways. We would send speakers, including Jay, into the city, and while they were there doing the seminar we would book local public relations appearances on radio and television talk shows. At the same time, we were running the infomercials. We were killing two birds with one stone. We were getting all this public relations plus the seminar business. The seminar business can be very profitable when it is done correctly. We did the seminars for about one year before we made the first infomercial. At that time, I was waiting until we could get our manufacturing into a position to support the growing business with the Juiceman. We decided to make a direct response television show because there was such a good response, like what you saw at the lecture in Santa Monica.

All of a sudden, the Juiceman wasn't a small business anymore. People were starting to write about it, hear about it, and I knew it wouldn't be long before somebody else would try to do a show on television. I wanted to grab the lead by being the first one to do an infomercial. We made the infomercial in the spring of 1991. We used the same television show and made a different commercial with an 800 number in it.

The television show was working great for the seminars. Like you said, we would go to a city like Los Angeles and we would do lectures over the course of a week in five different locations. We were in Santa Monica, at the Pasadena Hilton, we were at the Anaheim Hilton, which holds something on the order of 3,000 people. Altogether, I think we sold 10,000 people over the course of one week. We did two lectures a day, one in the afternoon and one at night. They were very successful for us. We also started to read in the trade papers that all the juicers in the retail stores had started to sell like hot cakes. I think we were making a ton of money for other people like Braun and Krups. Their juicers were flying off the shelves. At first, they didn't know why.

*SD:* Here in Los Angeles, for example, there is a chain of discount department stores called Adray's. When your first seminar show hit, they had maybe one juicer on their shelf. Within six months, they were carrying nine different juicers and they couldn't keep any of them in stock.

*RC:* Right, that is what happened. And the reason for that phenomenon was that nobody had the manufacturing capacity for juicers. When we started doing this in 1989, the total number of juicers sold at retail was just under 300,000. Nobody had them in stock, nobody had the manufacturing capacity, and this trend hit so big and so quickly that it created a huge demand. Then everybody rushed out and created manufacturing capability. Nobody really knew where the top of the market was. First 389,000 were sold, then about a million in 1990, in 1991 maybe 1.5 million, and I think last year about 2.5 million. At this point, it looks like the peak of the market was somewhere between 2 and 3 million units sold. Meanwhile no one knew that and everyone was rushing out to fill the huge demand. That's what caused the big glut of juicers on the market.

*SD:* I imagine that when you actually started selling the juicers on the air, your sales skyrocketed.

*RC:* Let's talk about the infomercial first, because around August of 1991 we released that product on television with the 800 number. Meanwhile, we were also doing the seminars. They were working great and the direct response television was working great.

It's funny because in the infomercial business these days you hear about different companies using infomercials to stimulate retail sales, and it is a very hard relationship to do correctly because the operations are definitely at different ends of the spectrum. When you have a successful direct response campaign, and then you try to switch it to retail, the retail will kill your direct response show. So in a way, you are killing the goose that laid the golden egg. It is very hard to have both avenues of distribution survive. That is the challenge and the struggle. You have to devise a strategy to use the infomercial to stimulate retail sales, but then prevent retail sales from killing your direct response business. That is a big challenge. Our idea was to do it through two different units.

*SD:* Which is a great idea.

*RC:* In the beginning, the Juiceman II could be bought only through television or our seminars. For retail, we introduced the Juiceman Jr., a lower-priced model that was more competitive with other products at the retail level. At first, the only place you could buy that one was through department stores and health food stores. Then we released the Juiceman II into the health food market, which is what that machine is better adapted to.

That didn't really have an affect on our television show because the price it sold for at a health food store was the same as on television. But as you go forward in the process, the competition at retail forces the product to lower and lower and lower price levels. In the long term, it kills your direct response business.

One thing I want to comment on—which is a mistake that we made going into retail, and it is something I read about when you interviewed the people that did ThighMaster—is how they went directly to the retailers. We went through a distributor and I think, looking back, that is something we would not do again. We would rather establish direct relationships with the retailer. If you haven't had any retail experience, you might think this would be an overwhelming task. But if you're looking at it from a long-term strategy point of view, it only makes sense. For us, going through a distributor was a mistake. If we had to do it over, I would go direct to the retailers, starting on a small basis. That is, I'd contact a couple of retailers, make deals with them, go through a learning curve to figure out how the retail business works, and then slowly spread out over all appropriate retailers.

We did kind of a shotgun approach with our distributor. We went totally national within the first few months. We went from zero retail, meaning zero percent of our business came from retail, to as high as 80% of our business in less than a year. That was with very few employees in our organization and without much knowledge about retail, so we went through a tremendous learning curve under a lot of pressure.

*SD:* Rick, what problems did you encounter utilizing a distributor?

*RC:* Because there was such a huge demand for the Juiceman, we had a tendency to be a little less conservative and to say, "How can we get this out into all the stores?" We sat there reading, just like you were telling me, how stores all over the country were selling out of other manufacturers' juicers. So we were in a hurry to get into retail. We used a national distributor, a company called PHD, Professional Housewares Distributors, which is the largest distributor of small appliances in the country. They do rival products, such as Black & Decker, Oster, and many others. PHD gave us the opportunity to get out nationwide very quickly, compared to what we could have done by ourselves. But by going that route, we lost the opportunity for direct feedback from the retailers so we could know the pulse of the business.

With a distributor, you don't hear directly from the retailers what the sell-through is: how many units are actually being sold at retail. We went with a distributor just because we had the manufacturing capability at that time and it was the fastest way to get out into all the stores from Macy's and Bloomingdale's on the east coast to the stores in Florida to the May Co. out on the west coast, to Dayton Hudson. It was like, "bang," a shotgun—we were out there all at once in all these stores because the distributor had the relationships set up already.

Looking back I think it might be good advice for other people to deal directly with the retailers and build their retail business more slowly. Now with that said, we are still in a good position in retail because of the strength of the brand name. I think that the Juiceman owns over 50% of the market share in department stores. So as we work our way through this glut of juicers, many brands will fall by the wayside while we're going to come out the other side in a very, very strong position.

*SD:* In utilizing the distributor, do the department stores still have return privileges to you?

*RC:* Yes, because our inventory, the distributor's inventory, and the store's inventory are basically all one inventory. If stores are not selling the product, they will return it to the distributor, who in turn won't buy more units until their inventory is depleted. So the arrangement has the same affect as the store being able to return unsold items directly to us.

*SD:* So having the in-store feedback is extremely important.

*RC:* Oh, yes. It is extremely important from a manufacturing perspective. We went out into retail in the spring of 1992 when juicing was hot. The topic was in all the media. And because there were no juicers in the pipeline, many stores put in huge orders for juicers, for which we had to gear up manufacturing operations six months in advance. Through the distributor, we geared up to manufacture a huge number of juicers—and then it turned out that if we had been dealing directly with the department stores, we would have been able to have the department stores put up letters of credit for their orders. With the distributors we didn't do that. Then the department stores turned around and said, "Oops! You remember that order we put in for 20,000 juicers? Well, we're only going to need 3,000."

And that is really the biggest problem of not dealing directly with the retailers. We would have gotten information faster. We would have realized that there were problems before they arose.

*SD:* In retail you lose pricing control, as well.

*RC:* You lose pricing control and you lose control over your product. During our first year in retail, only the Juiceman Jr. was available in retail. We were able to maintain some semblance of pricing control. But if you go out with the same unit that you have on television, the first thing the retailers will do is sell it for less than you are selling it for on television in order to get the customer to come into their store and buy the product.

The first thing you will see is a full-page advertisement in *The Los Angeles Times* or *The New York Times* advertising the Juiceman for $20 less than the price advertised on television. It is just a cutthroat market. So while retail dramatically increases your dollar volume of business, your margins take a big hit. Whenever you read that you can sell five or ten times as much product at retail as on TV, you have to know that your margins will take a tremendous hit and that you will need the added volume to just make up on a margin basis what you were making on direct response.

But still, you need to go to retail. Like when we started out—first we did the seminars, then we started selling directly through an infomercial and people didn't have to go to the seminars anymore. Retail was the next avenue of distribution.

It's funny, the department stores sell the product at a less expensive price and insist that they put the lower price in their advertising, which kills the infomercial. Then you have to take the infomercial off the air because it is not working and the retailers moan and groan about not having a vehicle to drive the product off their shelves. It is a vicious cycle.

*SD:* Did releasing a less expensive model at retail contribute to the demise of the Juiceman II show?

*RC:* A little bit. We became a victim of the pricing. We had to price the Juiceman II at around $299 in order for it to work on television. The Jr. cost about half that much and was the best unit in its price range, although the Jr. was not as powerful as the Juiceman II. People will naturally gravitate towards a less expensive model. The less expensive retail model did contribute to the TV show's downfall, but at that point I think the show was reaching the end of its natural life cycle, anyway.

*SD:* Which was about how long?

*RC:* A year, I would say. We are still running it in some isolated places, but on very low media dollars.

*SD:* The next step for the next Juiceman show might be to get even more involved scientifically, to go to some of the research clinics and show the specific results and benefits of the nutrients received from juicing.

*RC:* That is exactly the direction we are going. We used Jay Kordich as a spokesperson up to a point, but Jay is not a scientist. Jay can get people excited about juicing, but I think that the product's longevity will depend on the addition of a scientific perspective. We also have some really exciting things coming up on the sports nutrition front that incorporates juicing. I can't go into details, but we are working with several professional sport teams that are using juicing and a combination of supplements and they are having remarkable results. Probably in the next few months you will see some items in the press about it.

That, combined with credible scientific information on the benefits of the nutrients in juices, will sustain the business as a credible product over the long-term. It is not going to be a fad. Actually, marketers that jumped on the bandwagon for the short term are now going through a bloody process and they are all falling by the wayside. When we come out on the other side, we will have a good, stable long-term business with juicing.

**SD:** Let us go back for a minute, Rick, and talk about the fact that you decided to produce the show to sell the juicers direct over the air. Were you surprised by the results when the show first came out?

**RC:** I shouldn't say surprised, I should say happy. Our results were just phenomenal. We were getting returns of five and six and seven to one—that is, for every dollar spent, we would take in five or six or seven dollars.

**SD:** Wow. This was in 1991?

**RC:** Yes, they were just amazing results. It was definitely a very successful show. I wasn't surprised because of all the people who had shown up at the seminars, as you experienced first hand. Something about the message was very attractive to people. I knew the product would be successful on an infomercial basis. I just didn't know how successful.

**SD:** Essentially, you were able to do a couple years worth of market testing, find out what buttons worked, why people went to the seminars and then incorporate that information into the infomercial.

**RC:** Oh, absolutely. I make sure that I personally read all of the testimonial letters from people who use our product. We have files full of letters that say, "I've started juicing and it has done this for me," "I've started juicing and I lost weight," "I've started juicing and my cholesterol came down," and "I was so tired I could never get out of bed and I started juicing and it did this."

I know that from a scientific basis, but this is anecdotal evidence. I literally have thousands and thousands of letters. Hundreds of professional athletes have taken up juicing. So have entire baseball teams, the Texas Rangers, a lot of the Los Angeles Dodgers, the Milwaukee Brewers. Nolan Ryan called the office one day and ordered a juicer. Carl Lewis is a big juicer and credits juicing with helping him to maintain such a high level of performance. This evidence tells us that the business and the product itself have long-term viability.

**SD:** You are one of the few companies in the infomercial field that have managed to build a brand name.

**RC:** I don't look at our company as being an infomercial company anymore. We are a health and nutrition company and we use infomercials as one of our marketing tools, or as part of our marketing mix.

Obviously, public relations plays a big role and books play a big role. We've had two books published: *The Juiceman's Power of Juicing* and *The Breadman's Healthy Bread Book*. The Juiceman book was #11 on *The New York Times'* list for all of 1992 and the Breadman book was 29th on *The New York Times'* Bestseller List.

A book does a lot of things for you. With a book as successful as the Juiceman's, you can make close to $1 million. But what the book really brings you is credibility. It opens up the door in public relations. You can get a lot more talk shows than you would have gotten without the book. You can get a lot more media coverage, especially if your book hits *The New York Times'* Bestseller List. Then everybody comes knocking on your door, which gives you much more exposure.

There's a cycle. You mention the book in your infomercial and you do millions of dollars worth of advertising every month, and that pushes the book out of the bookstore. Meanwhile, the public relations appearances help give credibility to your television show. All these things together create brand awareness that helps push your products out of the retail market. Dollarwise, books don't look that big compared to retail sales or infomercials, yet they are a really important piece of the puzzle.

*SD:* Do you think that the Breadman book didn't go as high on the bestseller list because it lacked television exposure?

*RC:* Absolutely. The Juiceman had two years of grass roots marketing where we did seminars and Jay was on radio and television all over the country. By comparison, the Breadman came out and we took everything that we learned from the Juiceman and compressed it into a couple of months. We released the television show, we went into retail, we did the book—everything hit at the same time, so it didn't have a chance to build like the Juiceman did. But the book has legs of its own. It didn't come out with a big bang, but it is constantly selling and the numbers are doing very well.

That is partly attributable to the fact that the bread machine segment of the market is selling really well. Both the Juiceman and the Breadman books were put out in all the department stores. In the back of the books, we have our 800 number so customers can order the product from us directly. The books are also in all the bookstores, the Price Clubs and Costco's. It just helps to get further brand awareness for the two products, not to mention for the spokesperson on the cover of each book.

*SD:* For the Juiceman, you have also been publishing a monthly four-color newsletter. In the early issues the newsletter seemed much more like a sales-oriented tool, but recently it seems to include a lot more editorial copy.

*RC:* We started the newsletter as a sales tool to move product, but we are finding that it is succeeding as a newsletter unto itself. We were moving towards a magazine format because we are getting a tremendous response, a lot of subscriptions. The newsletter goes way beyond the Juiceman now, and has become the mouthpiece of our company as a health and nutrition company. We market this newsletter as focusing on the most current topics in health and nutrition. We use it to communicate with the subscribers. For moving product to our database customers and our subscribers, we found we did much better with a direct mail piece than through an advertisement in the magazine. So we are moving back towards more of an editorial newsletter format and when we want to market a product to the subscribers in the database, we do that through the direct mail.

*SD:* Interesting. At some time you might even consider turning the newsletter into a magazine and bringing that out to the newsstand.

*RC:* We were thinking about that earlier, but I guess that was a business I didn't want to get into, so we are going to keep it just as a newsletter.

*SD:* Do you believe that the newsletter will be self-sufficient, supported by subscription revenue?

*RC:* It has been so far.

*SD:* That's great. And that, I am sure, further helps build the brand name.

*RC:* Yes, exactly. Again, we are trying to create an awareness of our company that goes beyond the juicer and the Juiceman. Early on, we did a mail survey with our Breadman database and found out that people were interested in bread machines, but maybe didn't know a lot about them or didn't know which one to buy. When we announced that we were coming out with the Breadman and we went out to film testimonials for the Breadman show, almost every single person mentioned the quality of the product. The reason they decided to buy a Breadman from us was that they liked the quality of the Juiceman machine. They felt they could depend on us for quality and reliability.

Customer relations is another important aspect of our strategy to become a long-term health and nutrition company. That's one of our highest priorities. If you have a short-term perspective and say that you are just going to sell juice machines and you don't care what happens to the customer, you just want to make a lot of money, that mindset will hurt you as soon as you try to come out with another product. With the Breadman, we believe that we have reaped the benefits of the way we treated people before. Customers have faith in our company. They know we offer quality products and they know we will stand behind them.

*SD:* Let's talk about the Breadman for a minute, Rick. From a marketing point of view, the Breadman almost goes counter to what you did with the Juiceman, in the sense that there were a lot of breadmakers at the retail level, they are very expensive machines to produce, and I would think you couldn't get the kind of margins that are generally considered necessary in infomercials.

*RC:* Correct.

*SD:* So you probably count primarily on retail distribution to make your profit.

*RC:* Right.

*SD:* Why don't you talk a little bit about the different experience in the marketing of the Breadman?

*RC:* We decided to do the Breadman not because it would make a good infomercial product, but because we looked at the product from the point of view that as a health and nutrition company, our main message is to try to get people to eat better. You know, to eat more fruits and vegetables, more grains and legumes, and more whole grains. A juicer can help people eat more fruits and vegetables, and the next logical product is a bread machine that can help people get more whole grains into their diet. We approached the bread machine from the standpoint that it was a great product for our company.

If we'd evaluated the bread machine as an economically viable infomercial product, we probably wouldn't have done an infomercial because with the Breadman, the margins aren't there. But we looked at the Breadman from the standpoint of our company's mission and the fact that we were trying to establish in the retail marketplace a concept of products that make it easy for people to eat healthy. Also, we already had the Juiceman out there and we knew the Breadman could ride on its coattails into retail because consumers were familiar with the company and the quality of our products. From that point, the decision to do the Breadman made sense, even though we knew that at best we would have an average-earning infomercial.

Again, if we'd been just an infomercial company looking at a bread machine, we wouldn't have done the Breadman. That is probably why you haven't seen too many such products on television. But we wanted to go out and do all of the things we had incorporated in the Juiceman. We had a spokesperson named George Bernett who with his family has owned a natural foods bakery for the last 20 years in Montana. George was also one of our speakers for the Juiceman seminars, so we knew he could speak in front of a crowd and sell a product.

George was a good choice for the Breadman. Rather than taking a known personality like Tony Robbins or a Juiceman, we decided to create a Breadman personality, which was kind of an interesting concept to try. We did everything that we did with the Juiceman, except that we compressed the process into a shorter time frame. The idea was that we were going to put the product out into retail, we were going to run the infomercial, we'd have a book come out the same day that the infomercial hit the air, and then we'd have a 35-city public relations tour at the same time. All this stuff happened in a three-month time frame. We planned it that way to take advantage of the retail sales from the minute the television show hit the air. The book worked well, and the retail sales worked well, but the infomercial didn't work as well as we had hoped. So we went back and made some changes to it and now it is working better for us.

*SD:* You re-shot the whole show, didn't you?

*RC:* Yes, basically.

*SD:* It's a much better show.

*RC:* I have always been able to make successful infomercials when dealing with a person or product that was already successful in the marketplace. It doesn't matter on what level. If somebody is out there doing seminars on a small scale or if they are selling their product somehow, the infomercial acts like a giant magnifying glass. It takes a successful product out to the public.

We did the Breadman show without having any of the feedback from people who were using our bread machine, without the benefit of all those testimonial letters we'd had for the Juiceman show. We had George Burnett who had never sold machines in his life, but knew a lot about baking whole-grain breads (that is what his entire book is about), and he adapted recipes to use in the bread machine. Only after the show's big launch did we gather all the information necessary to create a more effective show.

*SD:* That brings up a very interesting point. In the case of Jay Kordich or Tony Robbins, you have a personality that has had the time and the seasoning to refine their pitch.

*RC:* Yes, that's exactly what they have done. And that is the same thing we are finding with this McDougall program. It has proven to be a very successful show for us. There are people out in the marketplace who are already successful on a smaller scale and all the infomercial will do is take that success and magnify it.

One person I have been reading a lot about lately is Susan Powter. She is a perfect example. She has the same type of magnetism as Jay Kordich or Tony Robbins. To make a successful infomercial with a person like that is a no-brainer because they already have this magnetism, this passion that comes through. While Jay has a passion for juicers, she has a passion for diet, and Tony Robbins has a passion for the things he teaches. That comes across on screen. You find that with the McDougall program, the guy has a passion for his diet and health program and that credibility comes across on the screen. When you start with a personality like Richard Simmons, doing a successful infomercial is easy.

*SD:* Would you say then, that finding the personality is more important than finding the product?

*RC:* This is just my opinion. I gear my marketing around a personality. So I do look for personality when I'm looking for a project to get involved in. I know that there have been a ton of successful infomercials that are done just on a product. But I look for someone with a good personality because if a successful personality isn't already selling a product, you can usually create a product around that person.

McDougall is a good example. He is a successful personality, has his own radio show, and he has his Santa Rosa Health Clinic, similar to the Pritikin Clinic, at St. Helena's Hospital. So we created the product around that. The books and tapes are basically a home study version of what you get at the live-in clinic. If you have that powerful a personality, you can create the product around it.

I prefer to do this because it gives me a lot more marketing options. I can do the public relations and the books and create a lot more excitement other than with just the infomercial. There are a lot of people out there who just take a product, gym equipment or whatever, without using an exceptional personality, and the product itself is selling and works very well. I just prefer to do it differently.

*SD:* A lot of people have done that. Tony Robbins didn't have his Personal Power Collection until the association with Guthy-Renker, and Susan Powter created her weight-loss cassette series after the infomercial came into being. It's a very good point. Now that I'm thinking back on it, it's very hard—with a few exceptions like BluBlocker Sunglasses—there haven't been many dynamic infomercials that have pulled for a long period of time.

*RC:* The other benefit that you get from attaching a product to a personality is that it becomes harder to do knock-offs. In the case of a juice machine, yeah, it's easy. You can sell other juice machines. But in the case of Tony Robbins, why do you think he has been able to stay on television for several years? Because you can't duplicate Tony Robbins. Richard Simmons sells diet products, and many other diet products come and go, but he stays because of his personality.

With the McDougall program, we expect to be around for several years because of McDougall and his personality. And you just can't duplicate that. Look at Dave Del Dotto and real estate. Look at how many real estate programs have come and gone and he has stayed. If you attach the product to a personality, you are looking at a much longer run. And when I say a personality, I don't mean a Hollywood star who's pitching a product, because that is different.

*SD:* Your shows don't use any celebrities?

*RC:* No, we don't. I'm not against it. It's just that I feel you can be just as successful without one, so why pay for one? I'm sure the time will come when we feel that there would be a benefit to using a celebrity. I'm not for it or against it. It's just that if you can do it without one and the show works just as well, why pay for one unless it's just for your ego?

*SD:* Let me back up here for a minute. When you rolled Juiceman II out into retail, did you ever get letters from people who had bought off television and were upset when they found the product cheaper at retail?

*RC:* I read all the mail that comes in and that has never happened. The reason we eventually rolled the Juiceman II out into retail is not because we received complaints, but because at that point the television show had run its course. We weren't getting much mileage out of it and so it was time to move the Juiceman II into retail at a lower price point. It was just a natural progression.

We chose to put the product out in the upscale department stores first. But that really is not a good place to sell high priced items like ours because they have all the less expensive juicers already. We ended up putting it in Costco. That really was a place where, from a margin standpoint, we could make as much or more money as by putting it into the department store, and at the same time the stores are able to sell it at a lower price. And because the product was in a Costco, people expected the product to be priced lower.

*SD:* How were you able to make as much money selling to a Costco, when Costco might be selling it at 40% off the retail?

*RC:* This is what you get from dealing directly with the retailers. You learn that if Costco—and I'm sure all the price clubs and warehouse places work the same—is selling your juicer for $199, they work on only a 10 or 11 point margin, so they are paying $175 or $185 for the product. When you sell to a department store, and the retailer wants to sell the product at $199, or even $249, they will pay you to get the margins that they need to operate on, which is actually less than what Costco will pay you. If both the department stores and Costco were selling the product for $199, you could sell it to Costco for $180, but you'd have to sell it to the department store for $140.

*SD:* That is very interesting.

*RC:* But again, you have to make a choice. If you put your product into Costco and you are already in the department store, you will kill the department store business. There are so many different avenues of distribution, and they have to stay unique. The best way, and what a lot of larger manufacturers already do, is to create different products for the different distribution systems. This is what we are doing with the juice machines now. Some products are unique to the department stores, with unique features and unique price points, and then other products are unique to the price clubs.

*SD:* How else can you differentiate?

*RC:* Some of them just do it with different colors. You take Kitchen Aide, which is an upscale mixer. I think they just put different colored products out there. I don't know if you want to quote me on this, but that's the thought process.

*SD:* How are you going to incorporate that into your future product plans?

*RC:* Well, the Juiceman Jr. will be going out to the department stores and the II is already at the price clubs. I think we are going to come out with two new models: an improved version of the Juiceman II which will be at the upper end and that will go to the department stores; and an improved version of the Jr. that will also be at the department stores. Then we will take the current Jr. and move it out to the price clubs so we will have two units in each area of distribution.

*SD:* I think that it becomes very apparent to the consumers that you are not in this business just to make a quick buck. The things you seem to be getting involved with have a lot of integrity behind them.

*RC:* I guess it is just a thought process from a business perspective. I have had what many people consider to be an infomercial company where—and there's nothing wrong with this—you just go from product to product to product. Sometimes it doesn't make as much sense to devote so much time, money, and effort to long-term customer relations and quality of product because basically you are on the air, off the air, and then off to your next product. People don't usually buy from an infomercial because they recognize the name of the infomercial company that is doing it; they buy it because it is a powerful show, and it works. That is the short-term infomercial mentality, which is fine.

I just chose, because I was tired of going from business to business, to become involved in something that lasted, that put the customer first, and would be in the area of health and nutrition. What that enabled us as a company to do is generate a lot of money from our database because of people who are happy with what they bought from us the first time. They know that if they have a problem, it will be taken care of. That opens up the door to any product. If we introduce a good product, we can get a lot of sales from our database.

*SD:* How large is your in-house staff at this point?

*RC:* Right now we're right around 100 people.

*SD:* You're that big, huh?

*RC:* Yes.

*SD:* Do you do everything now pretty much in-house?

*RC:* We do most everything, customer service, phone sales. But we use an incoming service bureau for the television shows. We do some out-bound telemarketing in-house on a test basis, to get a feel for what programs are going to work. Then we throw it out on a large-scale basis, and take it to an outbound telemarketing company. Customer service is very important to us, so it's in-house. Customer service is the segment of the company that has the most people in it. Then we have the retail staff, the direct marketing staff, the accounting, and the other normal business things.

**SD:** Now, you have the Juiceman, you have the new version of the Breadman show you are about to roll out, and you have got the McDougall Plan—is that it, those three shows at this point?

**RC:** Yes, that is what is happening on the infomercial front. We have some other businesses that aren't infomercial related that are doing quite well for us. Early on in the juicing business we went out and purchased a company called Nutri-Faster which created the best commercial juicer in the country. We did this with the thought that as we made juicing popular, the demand for juicers out in the public would increase. And that is, in fact, what we are seeing happen. Actually, that is a business that is getting ready to explode. We have been in contact with TCBY Yogurt about putting commercial juicers in all of their stores. We have also been in touch with Burger King, and people contact us on a weekly basis about opening up juice franchises.

We are exploring all the possibilities, but just from the standpoint of manufacturing and selling commercial juicers, it is a very profitable business for us. Again, it is just something that has sprung up as an offspring from the success of the infomercial and the brand awareness that it created. Then we have our sports nutrition, which came about because of athletes buying a juice machine and feeling the benefits of juicing. We hired a man named Robert Hackman, who has a Ph.D. in nutritional biochemistry and teaches at the University of Oregon, in their College of Human Performance. He put together our sports performance program that incorporates juicing and supplements. We are rolling this out on a professional level right now, with great success. As I said, in the next few months you will start hearing about it, reading about it, reading about which teams we're working with and so on. As you become successful on the professional level, you roll it out to the colleges, which we will be doing. You know, up until recently, athletes have always been very concerned about their workouts and exercise, but you would be shocked at how little professional athletes know about nutrition. So that is what the sports nutrition program is remedying. It is very successful and is going to be a successful business on its own. It might have the capability of being a potential infomercial in the future.

**SD:** So are you going to be selling vitamins?

**RC:** It is a whole supplement package that is designed specifically to enhance endurance and increase muscle mass. It is really scientific. The co-developer of this system is a man named Alexander Volkoff who was a nutritional biochemist in the Soviet Union and was the chief man in charge of all nutritional training for the Soviet athletes. They were and still are light years ahead of our athletes in their nutritional training. It is just amazing the system that they have. I can't talk about it too much, but down the road you are going to be hearing a lot about it. So there are a lot of little businesses that have sprung up from our infomercial, that are doing very well for us but are totally outside of the infomercial business.

*SD:* Where do you see the infomercial business going in the next couple of years?

*RC:* Where do I see it going? That's an interesting question. I always look at the infomercial business and compare it to Hollywood. I think there are a lot of similarities between the infomercial and movie businesses. The fact that there is a constant production of movies, and the same thing is true with infomercials. Very few of them are home runs, but when you get a home run it pays for all the ones that aren't successful. I just see it as several larger companies dominating the business, like in the movie industry, but there is always room for an independent. The thing that generates everything is the production of a successful show with the packaging of a product and a personality. That is what creates the success. So whoever has the ability to go out and make a successful show—and nobody has a lock on that—can go out and do it. There is always, in my opinion, room for the small guy.

When you talk about the big Fortune 500 companies coming in, the problem is that not every product that they market is going to be right for infomercials. They might look at this as long-term advertising, and if they are going to spend money on advertising, they might get more bang for their buck doing an infomercial. But unless it is the right product that generates good returns and large sums of cash, there is always going to be room for products that are right and can do that. I guess the biggest question is what is going to happen to the availability of television time, as that gets more and more competitive. Television time has already been getting scarce as far as good time spots. They are getting locked up and more expensive. The ability to get television time is really, I feel, the key to the business, just like making a successful movie.

I don't know how the influx of Fortune 500 people is going to affect media buying. But I think that having the right product and access to television time are the keys to moving forward. And I still say, for the right product, it is a business that someone can be very successful in without being a Fortune 500 company, without being a big Wall Street company—if they know what they are doing.

*SD:* You still think there's room?

*RC:* Oh, yeah, definitely. Because you could take Joe Blow off the street and if he creates a show that comes in at 3 to 1 or 4 to 1 or 5 to 1, there is always going to be a place to put that show because it has the potential to make 10, 20, or 30 million dollars. The reason independent producers can survive in Hollywood is that they can create a movie—even though they are getting more expensive—that can generate big bucks. While the Fortune 500 foray onto infomercials is an interesting trend, that is great for business from their perspective—and it's great if you are in the infomercial service business, like the telemarketing companies, and the production companies. But there is still room, as we've been saying throughout this interview, for people to use infomercials as part of their marketing mix.

*SD:* Most of the Fortune 500 companies coming in are looking at infomercials to drive sales at a retail level. One potential danger with that is that they are not going to really care what the media dollars are.

*RC:* Right, because they are going to spend them anyway. So if you try to predict the future, that, theoretically, is going to drive up television time, and that is going to make it harder to make infomercials that work. But I don't know, I haven't seen it and I don't think it has happened yet.

*SD:* No, it hasn't happened yet.

*RC:* Well, if that starts happening, that is what will drive up the media cost. Everybody else, even a very successful one like the Braun Oral B—when I say it's successful, I mean that when I saw it I thought it was such a great infomercial that I did a little checking and a lot of the retail stores are sold out of Braun Oral B electric toothbrushes—found success because their infomercial works. If the infomercial hadn't worked, would Braun still make the decision to spend the media dollars all over the country, several million dollars a week? If an infomercial doesn't work that means it doesn't work as an advertisement. That is very important. Does that make sense to you?

*SD:* Yes.

*RC:* In other words, the beauty about direct response advertising is that you can measure the results. So, if you produce an infomercial and you get dismal results, that means that it is not generating an impulse for people to buy. So why keep running it? Again it goes back to creating infomercials that really work. You know there are exceptions, you read about them, like GM with the Saturn infomercial, or Volvo. They are doing them for different reasons, for lead generation, for image. But still you don't see any of those much. You only hear about those infomercials because they aren't plastered all over television like Tony Robbins or Cher, or the infomercials that are really working.

*SD:* No, but what I think will happen is that you will see some of these large retailers put an 800 number in the show to either send the caller to the retailer or to get some sort of discount coupon or whatever to purchase a product at retail.

*RC:* Oh, absolutely. And I think that is being creative. I think that's great. We looked at things like that and actually are still looking at ways to interact with retailers. But what it boils down to is creating a program that makes people take action, whether it is to call an 800 number to get a coupon, or to run out to the store and buy the product.

On the other hand, you hear about all of the cable stations opening up, and I don't know when that is going to happen. Probably one thing that could happen with the infomercials is that it could become much more segmented. Like there is a fishing channel, so that is where you would have fishing infomercials, and then there is another channel that has to do with healthy cooking and that is where you would see healthy cooking shows. I don't know if that is a possibility and I don't know how far down the road it might happen, given that the current number of cable stations is going to be expanding to 300 or something like that. But things are getting much more segmented and targeted. When that happens, it opens up the television time because in the free market, if there is this huge demand for television time, that is going to open the door for more places where you can spend your money. Then rates will come down again.

*SD:* That's true.

*RC:* I don't know, it is hard to predict what effect the Fortune 500 thing is going to have until we actually see some results from somebody. But you have to give credit to people like Braun who saw what happened with juicers and then went out and did this infomercial with the Oral B toothbrush. I know that there are some other people out there doing similar infomercials. They are really on the cutting edge of it.

*SD:* Is there anything else you can think of that you want to add?

*RC:* No, I'm getting hoarse from talking so much. Did I ruin my reputation by admitting I was involved with Vu in the early years?

*SD:* No, I think people will be fascinated with that. You got out before the boobs came in.

*RC:* Oh, yeah, when I was there we did a really classy show.

# JAY KORDICH

❧

*J*ay Kordich is truly a sales pioneer. As a young man he was struck with cancer. Believing that drinking the fresh juice of vegetables and fruits saved his life, he traveled across the country for 40 years proclaiming the value of juicing. He sold his own juicer everywhere, from retail store demonstrations to county fairs. He did this often sleeping out his car as he traveled from venue to venue. When his Juiceman infomercial hit in the early '90s it created a national juicing sensation. After 40 years, it was only when Jay was in his '70s that he experienced fame and financial success. This is a fascinating story told by a mesmerizing storyteller.

**Steve Dworman:**  Why don't you begin by describing where and how you got started in juicing.

**Jay Kordich:**  I trained to be a teacher and a coach in my college days and then when I developed a tumor in my bladder, I got in with some people who said that I should try natural treatment. When I went to see Dr. Max Gerson in New York, he put me on a juice program. It worked so well for me that I went ahead and joined the juicing team. I went door to door, one on one. I felt that more people had to know about juicing, but I could never reach more than a couple of hundred people a year that way.

**SD:**  Let me back up for one second. What kind of juicing team did you join?

**JK:**  There's a company, Norwalk Press, which sells a very expensive juicer. It runs about eleven hundred dollars, but back in the '40s it ran about $395 to $450. That was big money in those days. It's a quality machine, but it had two steps and this made it very difficult and time consuming to operate. I used to go out on leads for that company. People would call or write and say, "I'm so and so and I live in Pasadena, Sierra Madre, or Westwood and I'm bed-ridden, or I have lymphoma, or I'm incapacitated." I would have a little ice chest, with a little bit of produce, and a couple of pamphlets. I would go into their home, talk to people and show them different juicing combinations. Because of the price level, people often could not afford to buy the juicer and this was hard because I was working on commission. But I was an eager beaver and sometimes down the line, somebody that you met in April would buy the juicer in September. Then you'd get your commission and that was nice to get two or three sales in a week like that.

*SD:* How did you go from having your treatment in New York to selling juicers in California?

*JK:* I decided that was my life's work, but also, I'm from California. I went to the University of Southern California. I played football for them in the Rose Bowl after the Second World War. Then in 1948 I signed a contract with the Green Bay Packers. But when I developed the bladder problem, I slowed down five steps. I went to Dr. Max Gerson, though I didn't have any money to pay him. He taught me about juicing and he didn't charge me. He was just a good Samaritan. I even had to take raw liver juice at that time, but I couldn't hold it down. Then I found out that there was a great juicer company, called the Norwalk Press. Dr. Walker taught me a lot in 1948, 1949, and 1950. I didn't know anything about juicing when I first started. I had never had a glass of juice in my life. I went out into the field for over a year, until I found another little juicer company, the Hollywood Juicer. I went to J.J. Newberry's and I demonstrated for them. Then I met a couple of old pitchmen who used to come in and watch me. They said that if I wanted to meet people, I had to go to the fairs. That was my first exposure and I loved it. I loved talking to people and showing them juicers and watching their reaction. A lot of times, Steve, it would be trial and error. Maybe I'd be putting carrots in the juicer, but I'd be talking about cranberries and oranges. It didn't really make any difference what you were showing because the people would have their eyes on the machine. I don't know if they listened to me and heard me or were just transfixed by the juices coming out of the machine. I found out that you can talk about anything when you're juicing because people are watching your hands as they operate the machine and they never put two and two together.

*SD:* It's amazing.

*JK:* A lot of times, you'd sell a juicer, and then maybe another. Then all of a sudden there would be a line and you'd sell maybe 14 juicers. I'd ask, what did I say to sell those 15 juicers? I talked about the ileum, I talked about the fiber going right through you and not entering the blood stream. Then I coined the term, "It's the juice of the fiber that feeds you." That's what I mean by trial and error, it wasn't a sudden scenario, it wasn't something that happened overnight. You had to try this and try that and mix this word with that word. Let's get down to fundamentals, you have to create in people a burning desire to have your product. You have to make people want it so much that even if they don't have the money, they're going to go out and raise the money to get it.

*SD:* How do you do that Jay?

*JK:* You've got to look the people in the eye. You've got to romance what you have. An old pitchman from Redbank, New Jersey said to me that I did something very special, I was unforgettable. People never forgot what I said. They always remembered, whether they bought a juicer or not. He said that I was subjectively creating the cancer. "You put the seed in their brain and they can't shake it. You're enveloping their brain with the cancer, making them want your product." First of all you have to have a product that you really believe in. If you don't have something you believe in, you can be the greatest actor in the world, but people will pick up on your true feelings. A lot of people don't believe in the things they sell. They're doing it for money. You have to believe in your product, that's number one. You have to use that product and be involved in that product. That's the basics for selling. You have to be sincere and level with people and you have to romance what you sell.

*SD:* Are there any stories that you can tell to illustrate how you changed things in a pitch or did something differently, and it had a profound impact?

*JK:* The most important thing that I have learned is that one good television show reaches more people than you could possibly reach in ten life times, one on one. I'm not talking about door knocking, like I used to do when I first started, I'm talking about standing there at the booth, at the Pomona Fair, or the Minnesota State Fair in St. Paul, where you have no less than two to five hundred people around you at every moment. One television show will supercede that, maybe tenfold. It's incredible. That's what I found out personally. You can become a star. Were you there at NIMA [an infomercial conference], when I gave that little talk on being a pitchman?

*SD:* I had to have been.

*JK:* I talked about how I didn't like to be called a pitchman because I had gone to college and I thought I really should be a teacher or an educator. Then I met a guy in Toronto, at the Canadian Exhibition, who told me that I should never be ashamed of being called a pitchman. He said, "Hold your head up high and be proud because you're doing something phenomenal. You're showing the people something they would never have known about. You're demonstrating a product, whether it's a frying pan or a pair of fins, and showing them the ins and outs of that particular product." He said everything in this world is a pitch. I used a little analogy of President Nixon and John F. Kennedy vying for the Presidential nomination. They were both on nationwide television selling their wares in the greatest pitch of all time. He knew I was insulted when somebody called me a pitchman because to me it inferred that I was a carnival worker. So I was always insulted by the word pitchman. When I analyzed my feelings, I realized that he was right. Being a pitchman is a pretty darn good thing to be. I told people that they were lucky that they didn't have to go to fairs the way I did. In the last few years, we have seen superstars in infomercials, and they have become a household name. You mean everything to people and they are believing in you. People who get a chance to do an infomercial are very fortunate. I feel very fortunate.

*SD:* Don't you think that the background that you had in the county fairs, dealing with people one on one, is one of the main reasons that contributes to you being as effective as you are on television?

*JK:* Absolutely. I was speaking from the heart, it wasn't canned.

*SD:* In the new informercial, you're basically doing a show for vitamins. If this was your money, if you were actually putting the money up to do an infomercial on vitamins, would you go out on the road before doing the show?

*JK:* If I was going to take these vitamins, I would definitely put the Vitapower, that's our trademark now, in the hands of all kinds of people. I would monitor them. I would give it to people that I know needed it and see what the results were. Antioxidants are on the cutting edge of nutrition today. We used to call them free radical scavengers, but they have refined the terminology a little bit and they are now called antioxidants. They neutralize the free radicals. That's what Vitamin C and Beta Carotene do all the time. You can't get enough of these substances unless you take them in supplemental form. You can't get enough from your food because the soil is depleted by 85%. Anything you grow today is going to be depleted. The wave of the future is going to be organic produce. Produce grown in soil that is enriched. If people drank two quarts of juice a day, which very few people ever do, they might have a chance of getting the nutrients that they need, and they wouldn't have to take supplements.

*SD:* Right after the Vitapower show came out, there was an article in *USA Today* where doctors basically said that you are much better off getting your vitamins and minerals from fresh fruits and vegetables because there are elements in them that have not been put in the vitamin pills, at this point.

*JK:* Exactly. I've said that all along. You can take the most supplemental one-a-day multi-vitamin mineral type of thing and those are only bits and pieces of it, they're not the whole picture. There are a lot of unidentified elements that haven't been pinpointed, as to their value. They don't even really know what they are. That's what you get out of juices, plus, you get the enzymes. Vitamins don't have enzymes, they're catalysts, they can help you in many ways, but you can't get enough of them by just eating them. This was my thrust when I sold juicers. It was a proven fact that cellulous fiber, which plant life is structured of, is relatively indigestible to humans. The purpose of juicing is to release the juices from the fiber, which the body tries to do anyway. The body is literally a juice machine. It tries to break everything down to liquid. Dr. Kershner and Dr. Henry Sherman, probably the greatest authority of all time on the human body's requirements, from Columbia University, wrote the book *The Chemistry of Food Nutrition*. They said, back in the '40s, that when nutritional knowledge is sufficient and widespread we will all be asked to eat at least 15 pounds of raw plant life a day. That's impossible, so that's where the juicer had its impact.

You know what I'm really doing when I'm pitching or doing a demo? I'm really painting a picture.

*SD:* I was noticing that. A lot of the things that you are saying paint internal images in the mind.

*JK:* Exactly. Something that's indelible. You've got to paint this picture. It's like my kids' puzzles. They lay all the pieces down and start looking at them and pretty soon they put together a beautiful country scene or an army marching or something. The pieces all start to fall into place. This is what you're supposed to do when you do an infomercial. You're supposed to paint a picture that becomes imbued in a person's mind, that he can't shake.

*SD:* When people buy the juicers and they start juicing using the produce that they get in the stores, could they potentially be doing themselves harm, if they juice a lot, with all those pesticides put on those fruits and vegetables?

*JK:* That could very well be if they don't clean the pesticides off. They're putting a concentrate of juices together. Usually you chew on one carrot, but for juicing you use 20. My kids can eat one or two apples before they're filled, but you're juicing 7 to 10 apples. If you don't address the fact that they might have external pesticides, you could have a pesticide build up in your liver. You have to be careful. That's why I recommend organics. Plant your own garden. My dad's 100 years old, down in San Pedro and he still gardens.

*SD:* How would you summarize the steps one should take for optimum health?

*JK:* Number one is juicing. Number two is Vitapower. You can't get enough quantities of Vitamin E, Selenium and Vitamin C, unless you take supplements. Next is antioxidants which is on the cutting edge of health today. That's the big topic on the *Today Show*, the *Good Morning* show, and in magazine articles. Nothing works without minerals, those are the key to the body's building structure. You've also got to have food enzymes, to keep the thymus gland from having to produce enzymes. The thymus gland should produce T-cells to fight thyroid conditions, particularly HIV virus. This is all proven. So what I've done is to integrate four pieces of the puzzles of life. I've put it all together and made it very cohesive. I've only taught the first one and I'm doing the second one now. When I put the other two into perspective, it doesn't really make much difference what else you put into your body.

*SD:* Do you eat cooked foods?

*JK:* Just certain foods like rice, beans, or maybe an ear of corn once in awhile. But I'll go out with Linda and I won't even eat a vegetarian sandwich when the vegetables are cooked. I won't do that. Cooked food is dead, it takes 48 hours and longer for the body to digest that food and evacuate the waste and residue. I'll eat raw food and if I do eat anything cooked, what I'll do is take the enzymes. That's what I stress. Digestively speaking, you're not supposed to have any liquids during a meal. It dilutes the gastric juices. But if you eat anything cooked, that food is going to tax your immune system, your internal organs, so you don't want to eat cooked food unless, and here's where it comes in handy,  you have food enzymes, or you can sip on a glass of vegetable juice. That puts the enzymes in there and keeps the brain from asking the pancreas to do extra work. The pancreas has two primary jobs to do. The first job is to produce insulin and the second job, and the most important job, is to repair, restructure, and to cleanse.

Dead food cannot rebuild the body. If you eat late at night and then go to bed, you have no enzymes to break down the food. Enzymes are delicate entities, they are catalysts and are destroyed in a very low heat, 102 to 126 degrees. At 126 degrees, you and I wash our face with a face cloth. Raw food digests itself, it has its own enzymes. It's a well known fact that raw food is digested and evacuated as waste matter within 17 hours—31 hours less than cooked food. It's incredible, isn't it?

*SD:* It is incredible.

*JK:* People don't understand this. Here you are with a big blob of cooked food. The brain says, wait a minute, how are we going to compensate? How are we going to get that food out of our stomach? Late at night, it calls upon the pancreas. If you want to eat cooked food, have it for breakfast, have it for lunch, but not in the evening. Don't eat cooked food at night. If you're hungry, eat a slice of watermelon, eat a raw salad. Don't put anything cooked in there. Here the brain calls upon the pancreas to produce enzymes, to help digest cooked food, when it shouldn't have to. It puts a burden on the pancreas. The pancreas now is overworked, doing a job above and beyond its calling. The typical pancreas, which is about 85 grams in weight, blows up like a big bloated sponge, maybe three and a half to five times its normal size. It's like starting to lift weights. You're lifting weights and lifting weights and your arms go from 14" to 16" biceps, maybe they'll get to 23", but they'll puff up from work. That's what you've done to the pancreas when you're 10, 15, 20, 30. All your life you've had cooked food. You've had hot dogs, you've had macaroni and cheese, you've had this, you've had that, you've had whatever. Even though it's big, it falters, and loses the ability to produce enzymes. The pancreas is overburdened. It starts to falter. That's the organ that protects you from any viral condition, by producing the T-cell. People with AIDS are unable to build up their immune system to fight off the viral condition they have when they eat cooked food. They need to be juicing. Don't burden the body. Put the things in that can give benefit and rebuild. I look at this fax, this book, this magazine—these things can't rebuild themselves. They deteriorate and in 100 years from now, if I just left everything here and closed up the house, everything would be rotten. But you and I have the propensity to rebuild. Everyone of our cells is like a body unto itself and it can rebuild. Everything is determinable by what you put in your mouth, good or bad. That's what you're going to be made of and that's been my story.

*SD:* It's amazing to me that basically, your success story has taken place in about the last five or six years. Tell me how that came about.

*JK:* Now Steve, I was always successful. I didn't have any money, but I was always successful. I turned a lot of people on to juicing. I've helped thousands and thousands of people with their health. Through juicing, I've helped them with ulcers, heart attacks, liver trouble, skin problems. It's the same thing I feel about antioxidants, minerals and food enzymes. Once I finish this story it's going to be terrific. By the way, Linda's book is going to follow that. I'm going to co-author it, though it's mostly her recipes on how we eat here and how we feed the kids and how we juice. It's called, *Married to the Juiceman*. Do you like that?

*SD:* I love it, Jay. You made a comment that when you met Linda, you were penniless pretty much.

*JK:* Yes, for many years.

*SD:* And here's a woman who fell in love with you and there's around a 40 year age difference?

*JK:* Thirty-three. She was just turning 25 and I was 58.

*SD:* How did that happen?

*JK:* It was love at first sight. It was just one of those fantastic things. I knew her mom and dad. Her mom bought a juicer from me and loved juicing. She was a vegetarian. I found out later, after I met Linda, that Linda had been a vegetarian since she was 9 years old. I'm talking hardcore vegetarian. I knew her mom and dad real well. Her dad and I used to talk a lot about juicing and he used to say, get your own juicer, you're making these companies millions while you're starving to death. So finally, I had a chance to get a little machine from Switzerland and I called him up and I said, let's meet, I got a little juicer that just came over from Europe and I could import it. I used to go to the consulate in Germany and France and they used to help me find different products. He calls me up, we're going to have lunch in a Mexican restaurant, rice and beans. He says, do you mind if my daughter shows up? I said no, that's okay with me. We're sitting there and Linda walks in. She worked at that time in an escrow office as title representative for a big real estate company. She came in to hit her dad for some money. I looked at her, she was attractive, businesslike. She had a nice business suit on. We talked. She was happy, with a big smile. I was involved with other ladies, I didn't bother. A few months later her dad called me saying it was his daughter's birthday. He said, here's her phone number, when you get a used juicer, something in real good shape. So I said Bob, I just happen to have a great juicer, so he said, give her a call. It was Christmas. I called her up and we decided to meet. We were both in San Diego and I was still working at Green Tree Grocers and Hadley Farms. Her dad was going to buy the juicer from me for 50 bucks, a $200 juicer. That's what I took as a trade in. The minute we met, that was the end, we never left each other's side. Then her mother found out about it. Her mother said to Linda, if you marry that dirty old man, we're never going to talk to you again. They literally disowned her. Isn't that something. Linda didn't care, she follows her dreams. My book, which was a best seller in the *New York Times*, told the truth. There were a lot of times when she was pregnant with Johnnie, that she said, "Jay we can't sleep in a hotel. We can't afford it. Let's sleep in the car, in the pickup truck." When I married her I said that I was going to take her to the best places, to the best hotels in the world. She didn't know that I meant sleeping in a pickup truck behind the hotel. She thought we were going to go to the Sheraton and the Hyatt and all that. But we always found a good hotel, with good parking and security, and we'd sleep in the parking lot. Whatever city we were in, we always found a good hotel that had a restaurant, that was 24 hours so we could use their restroom in the middle of the night. But it was convenient. She loved me for me. She didn't care. That's why she deserves the financial rewards that have come upon us now. It's great, I just love it. Money never made any difference to me. I went out and did my thing and that's what comes through in me.

*SD:* It does.

*JK:* People know that. It's a nice afterthought, it's a nice benefit, a nice bonus for all your hard work. I told somebody just today at the health show that somebody up there must have looked down from the heavens and said that old guy down there needs a break. He worked his heart out.

The Clintons better thank their lucky stars that I taught the people in this country and the medical doctors all about these juices and foods. I've pioneered this thing.

*SD:* Yes, you have.

*JK:* Steve, I don't want to be recognized as a champion of the people or anything like that. I'm not on an ego trip. I just love what I do.

# JERRY WILSON

❧

*J*erry Wilson, is a true entrepreneur in every sense of the word. He invented both the Soloflex machine and the innovative method of marketing them through infomercials before anyone else ever conceived of such a thing. This is the first time he ever consented to do an interview on the subject of his business and marketing methods. This interview stirred up much controversy amongst competitors in the fitness industry the moment it was published. Jerry's marketing methods are still being copied today by companies such as BowFlex.

**Steve Dworman:**  You are truly one of the innovators in this industry, and I admire a lot of the work that you've done.

**Jerry Wilson:**  Thank you. We've toyed with the idea of picking up other clients. We have people submit things to us all the time, but we made a commitment early on that we were going to master what it takes to learn to advertise and market our own product, and that's kind of where we stayed. Although if I'd been selling refrigerators on infomercials, I'd probably have made a lot more money. If I'd been selling Cadillacs, I'd have made even more money. And I've always wondered why others haven't seen that opening with infomercials. You can make a presentation that you just can't do in 30 seconds, or in a magazine. You can only make a claim in those things, you can't demonstrate the truth of that claim. But with an infomercial you can come pretty close to telling the whole truth—to showing what your product can actually do.

**SD:**  Let's go back to the beginning of Soloflex, before the infomercials.

**JW:**  We were just advertising in magazines, after trying several things including newspapers and direct mail. The only thing that really worked for us was the national magazines. There was also a tremendous social acceptability in *Time* magazine and *Sports Illustrated*. We were hitting a money-making audience. There were a lot of reasons that magazines were a good place to introduce the product. What we were trying to do more than anything else was to develop a social acceptance to weightlifting. This type of product had always been sold from the back of Spiderman comic books, or some other relatively low rent media, all positioned to people who didn't have much sense, and certainly didn't have any money. Even though there was a real strong demand, there was a real strong peer pressure to stifle that kind of activity. And even the coaches had a prejudice, but they got over that in the 1960s. The professional sports teams and athletes know that the more they pump iron the better they play, so they couldn't deny the proof there, and the old adage that "if you're muscle bound it slows you down" was getting disproven by everyone that pumped up. But still you had that major class bias out there. I had witnessed the motorcycle companies from Japan repositioning their product with American advertising and giving social permission to the American male to own a hundred-mile-an-hour racehorse. And they did it with Norman Rockwell type scenes that made it a socially acceptable part of the media they put it in. Harley ended up with, I think, 3% of the American motorcycle market, and were selling more motorcycles than ever. It was the social permission that was critical to reaching a mass market. That was the same problem we had to overcome. So a full page ad in *Time* magazine seemed like an appropriate place to do that, and it was. It was received with open arms—there was a huge demand. At first people bought it despite how we chose to market it, and how we manufactured it. But over time, with enough trial and error, and a commitment to really try to do everything as well as we possibly could, we finally got to where we could turn out a good ad, and we made a really good product.

*SD:* What year did you start with magazine ads?

*JW:* 1978.

*SD:* That was very early. Was it mostly copy or photo?

*JW:* Actually, the ad didn't even have a complete picture of the machine because I couldn't decide whether I wanted to leave the base plate on or not. It was all makeshift. I went down to a little art house and had the pictures taken and pasted up what I thought explained the machine. I bought a regional section of a national magazine and made sure that I had an 800 number. It didn't matter what I put in the ad; there was such a pent-up demand for a home weightlifting machine that people would have bought anything that faintly resembled one. The product was good enough that people bought them in spite of our efforts. We had a commitment to not only manufacture the equipment itself, but to also manufacture the sales. And I think that was the most critical decision we made, to do our own marketing.

*SD:* What was your background before that?

*JW:* I was a professional pilot.

*SD:* That's a long way to come.

*JW:* Well, I'm still the captain of a machine of sorts—the critical thinking, the overall perspective, the detail. Most people don't stay with any one thing all their lives. Once you've mastered one thing, it kind of gives you the system on how to master anything else.

*SD:* What got you interested in weightlifting?

*JW:* As a kid, I always thought people who pumped up their muscles looked great. All kids flex their muscles in front of the mirror, but not all of them know how to make them bigger. I took a weightlifting course in military college, which was a full semester of circuit weight training with free weights. Everything they were teaching then in 1965 is exactly the dogma that is still accepted and still proving itself today. So I was well versed on state-of-the-art weightlifting, most of which has been adopted and picked up by body builders and by coaches. But trying to stay in shape out in normal life is another thing altogether. I always had a set of weights that I was clanking my foot on or my wife was tripping over, and I'd sell them every time we moved. For five years I just wanted a weightlifting machine. The first time I got under a Universal [machine] I thought, "Boy would I like to have one of these in my house." I'm sure that's what occurred to everyone who ever got under one, but who had an extra $10,000 or $20,000 when you consider you have to build an extra room onto your house? And I sure wouldn't want to transport it when I moved. I could see the geometry of the machine, and I realized you could probably capture all those exercises if you wanted to re-configure it into something smaller, because the basic range of motion is either a press or a pull through a relatively short range of motion. It took me a year to find that perfect geometry, with no extra parts, and so that everything works the way it's supposed to. It was by trial and error. A lot of talking to body builders, strength coaches, a lot of research. And there was no time limit, so I just kept working on it.

*SD:* It's the first time to my knowledge that the bands were used as resistance.

*JW:* That came from airplanes. I came into this thinking like an aviation person and not a body builder. You can only invent with what you know. I was looking for something to replace the actual plate itself, because that's what gets dropped on your foot, and what pinches your fingers. That's also what's so expensive and hard to ship. I talked to people and asked them what was wrong with free weights. The body builders complained about muscle tics—where a little piece of ligament pops away from the bone, because you get so strong as a body builder that sometimes you're too strong for your own good. It hurts like fire, and it's the bane of body builders. When Arnold Schwarzenegger endorsed the machine back in 1980, he had just gotten another tic in his shoulder. What was needed in there between the unstoppable force and the immovable object was some dampening—like you have in your car. Without shocks and air brakes and rubber tires, your car would crack and fall apart in no time at all. Rubber is a most unique property. It can actually turn gravity in any direction you want it to. It's a perfect dampening type of resistance. We've sold a half a million machines, and probably several million people have pushed on those things for quite a bit of time. And we have yet to hear of any body suffering a muscle tic. We've managed to duplicate all the free weight exercises and do it in a way that people don't get hurt. I've seen all the other products out there, I discounted them in my search for what I considered to be the ultimate in functional simplicity. If you can get that, you can get some elegance along with it. You can't even think about selling these things until you can get people to bring them in the house. So that was a real important feature.

*SD:* Infomercials didn't really begin broadcasting until government deregulation in 1984, so you must have learned a lot through print advertising.

*JW:* We learned how to present the product through print advertising, which is basically the story boards you'll need for any kind of moving action. I had been on the phone for years at that point trying to tell people what I had invented, and I got pretty good at it. So that helped to write the copy. I was just looking for a more cost-effective selling technique, and to try to get a demonstration. It occurred to me that magazines were going to fade for us, and I would have to look for other media. I was well aware that VCRs were becoming more popular, and that tapes were not that expensive, although they now cost about 20% of what it used to cost to produce and dub a tape to mail. So we went out and risked $90,000 to produce a demonstration tape of what the thing really was, and that was our first infomercial. Although we did not broadcast it—we never anticipated that we could broadcast it—we just mailed it out to people when they asked to see it, from the magazine leads. In about 1984, we started mixing in network television spots. We ran during the Super Bowl twice. It wasn't possible to capture all the names that came in during the spot, but the first night, we got about 12,000 calls, from one Super Bowl spot. All of the magazine sales picked up after that too, so we learned to mix regular commercial television, which was more expensive per inquiry at that time, but we learned to boost magazines and gain credibility with it. It took about five years to deplete the magazine audience, and during that time our selling costs were getting higher and higher because the price of a page doubled, and the circulation had dropped. We're like farmers. We had depleted the soil. We needed to move on to something else. The videos were helping, but the magazine inquiries were still so expensive. We were actually losing money.

*SD:* The magazine ads had an 800 number to call in for information...

*JW:* Yes, a two step thing. We were trying to sell the brochure.

*SD:* Did you use any telemarketing to follow up on the leads?

*JW:* No, we felt that was too rude to even contemplate. The best time in the world to make a sales pitch to someone is when they're actively engaged and looking for something. A magazine is ideal, no matter what page you're on, because a person is looking for something to engage their mind. You're not going to interrupt them—they'll be just as engaged with an advertisement, if it is something they have an interest in, as they will with an article. It's a very socially acceptable way to make a presentation. The worst way is when you start knocking on doors, because your cost per sale is going to go way up, and the customer is paying for that high cost.

The second worst way is an unsolicited phone call. While it may work in some industries for some products, people generally despise it. Unsolicited mail is also a disruption of sorts. While people may be looking through their mail for something that interests them, it's not really given much credibility. All three of those types of selling have exceptionally high selling costs. You may need 10 times your manufacturing costs to get it to pay. And then you have television. You may be interrupting people with a 30 second commercial, but it is socially acceptable. It does give you some credibility. And that's where everybody is, and you have to be where everybody is. But still you're interrupting people, so television commercials are not necessarily the best vehicle. We thought and proved—to ourselves at least—that magazines were really where it was at for our product, and that was our only option. We finally realized when we started to broadcast our 30-minute videotape on cable television that it wasn't traditional television that those people were watching; it was a video brochure that they were flipping through. It took me four years of flipping to realize this, but finally I noticed, there's the Super Bowl spot at $600,000 for 30 seconds, and my next flip on the dial is an ironing board for sale, and then maybe a black channel that the cable operator isn't getting a dime for. So our first test was to go in and buy an entire week of an LO—local origin—channel on our local cable system, and we just looped our 30-minute film nonstop for an entire week. That was very cost-effective for us. We just went on from there. There were about 8,000 cable systems in the United States and we actually went in and built an infrastructure to the top 4,000 of them; we could come in with the promise of a hundred hours of time that they weren't going to get anything for otherwise. None of these 4,000 cable operators had anybody to take our money—we had to actually teach them that they had something up there that they could get quite a bit of money for. I could play my 30-minute commercial 200 times in a guy's house for less than I could mail him a post card. And he could flip through it over and over again.

*SD:* What year was this?

*JW:* 1986. It didn't take very long to go from there to making the buy of an entire system, which was about 1.6 million households, 35 different channels. But it was kind of like going to ABC and saying, "I'd like to buy a spot on your network," and ABC saying, "Well, you have to go out and negotiate with each individual affiliate," because they didn't even have a pricing structure set up. I couldn't understand this, because the value of cable systems was skyrocketing at this time. But none of the operators had anybody to take your money.

*SD:* So you had the foresight to approach the cable operating systems rather than go to the individual stations.

*JW:* Yes, we did end up going to the networks and negotiating really good deals. Our cost per inquiry went from nearly $20 per call, which it had risen to with the magazines towards the end, to less than 80¢ per call, with much more qualified calls. So our margin went through the roof. It was phenomenal. We rode it as far and as long as we could. We knew it would also deplete over time as more and more people came in to buy this cable time. So of course the cost of this cable time has risen dramatically. We got there first.

**SD:** What did you learn from the print advertising that you brought over into television?

**JW:** Art direction, media selection. Media buying is really where it's all at, and where the advertising industry seems to be the weakest. They are really creative and entertaining, but not many of them seem to understand marketing.

**SD:** In what sense?

**JW:** I've never met an advertising agency person who didn't spout the cliché, "Well, half your advertising money is lost." When we place ads, we know the cost efficiency of every nickel. Each ad on television has a different phone number, so we know who's overcharging, and who's delivering. It has nothing to do with Nielson ratings or what the rate cards tell you. But those are easy things for the agency to present to the customer.

**SD:** It has come up over and over again at our conferences that ratings have nothing to do with viewer response.

**JW:** And the same is true of magazine readership. It's just an arbitrary datum line to charge people on. It is a fact that all advertising agencies charge the customers whatever they can to get their 20% profit. I even went to a seminar once where that was stated. Because you can't grow a company on anything less than that. The actual negotiating to make the good buys and find out what really is working and what isn't is something that none of the agencies were qualified to do, because not one of them does it. We just couldn't tolerate that kind of inefficiency. It was our own dollar that we were spending, and we knew we could negotiate these things better, and that we'd spend more time with it. When we had an agency for a short period of time, we couldn't get them to pay any attention to the media.

**SD:** You started right at the beginning, buying your own time in-house on the cable systems.

**JW:** Yes, no agency would do it or could do it.

**SD:** You aired the video as a lead generator, and that was effective. What went into your first official infomercial?

**JW:** I wrote the show with a really good copywriter, and my philosophy has always been that if you're not teaching, you're not selling—and that teaching and selling are similar words. If you can just teach a person what you have and how they can use it, it's really their business if they want to buy it or not. So I always soft-sell and try to be polite. And if you're going to be out there you might as well try to be entertaining as well. We don't try to be funny or anything, but we want nice film work and good art. We want to take the same care with the advertising as we do with the manufacturing, because that's all they see at first, and that reflects on the product.

*SD:* Was there a theme to the first show?

*JW:* There was a cute little kid flexing his muscles in front of the mirror, trying to do push ups, flashing over into showing the guy giving the actual demonstration of the machine. It was real nice film, we spent a lot of money on it. It was a big risk, and we didn't realize what we had until we started broadcasting, but once we did that, we really knew. We were down at that point; the company had equity of about $4 million, and we lost a million dollars in equity with the selling costs going way beyond budget. We were just groping. Luckily it took off. During our peak year, sales were around $100 million. We were making 8,000 to 10,000 machines a month here at the factory. That was fun. We had no idea how high it would go, how long it would go.

*SD:* The first show aired for a year?

*JW:* It took us about a year before we decided we needed additional programming. We've never stopped making new shows, new brochures. Sometimes we do better, sometimes we do worse. It's a habit more than anything else. You need fresh stuff.

*SD:* What was the second show?

*JW:* We filmed more of an at-home set, and accentuated the woman more than in the first one, made it more life-stylish. It worked well, but none of the shows worked as well as the first one until this current one.

*SD:* At what point did you start working with Tyee?

*JW:* We went to them to do the first one we were going to try on our own. Our director on the first one had moved to Chicago, and we sat down and wrote it ourselves. We weren't sure what we were going for, so we ended up spending a lot of time in editing. We ended up with a pretty good show. We shot that one on video, because we weren't exactly sure what we wanted to shoot. And then we came back in and did it again. Both Tyee and our people were still learning at this point about how to be more communicative in these things. We've never stuck with one production company too long. I don't remember if we did two or three with Tyee, but they all worked out really well. The last one that they did was really first rate.

*SD:* Was that the Soloflex Heroes?

*JW:* Yes. Some of the shows really get you, and some aren't so great.

*SD:* Tyee talks about the way they structure shows with pods, figuring that every seven or so minutes the viewer will switch channels, so they try to build a whole story within seven minutes.

*JW:* Yes, the whole concept is that people will flip through this—they're not going to see the whole show.

*SD:* Do you measure the rate of responses at different times during a show, so you know at what point most of the calls come in?

*JW:* The calls start coming in almost immediately and go on for 30 minutes or so after the show.

*SD:* You were doing things no one had done way before other people started doing them, and you've gone through the whole experience much earlier than others in the industry.

*JW:* We're from Oregon, we're supposed to be pioneers. I don't want to go down the beaten path, there's no opportunity there. Getting away from the crowd allows you to see better. I identify with the scouts on the wagon train. My wife is a better wagon master than I am. I prefer to get out there in unknown territory, explore for opportunity and unknown obstacles, try to see what's out there and then find the path back to the wagon train.

*SD:* For awhile you had your own retail stores. The infomercial industry has just discovered in the past two years that infomercials can tremendously boost retail sales.

*JW:* Well, we never could prove that we were selling more Soloflex machines in the areas where we had those retail locations, and there was a tremendous overhead. Over the years we found some really good managers that we've been able to pull back into the company, so from that sense we profited. But as far as the whole retail experience goes, it was a bust. Plus there was the extra expense of collecting sales tax. Once we had a location in San Francisco, we had to collect sales tax from all sales made in California, which had never occurred to us.

*SD:* So even though say 95% of all sales in California were through direct response, you still had to collect sales tax on all those sales?

*JW:* Exactly. That's something that everyone should seriously consider before opening a retail location. Oregon doesn't have a sales tax, although they're always trying to change that.

*SD:* Hasn't there been a lull between your last 30-minute show and the new one?

*JW:* Yes. It was just getting harder to buy those 30-minute spots, and they weren't working as well. The cost has gone up tremendously, it's four or five, sometimes 10 times more expensive than when we started. Our selling budget is fixed, and once it goes over budget, we just can't afford it. But we're not giving up. We've tried to make a better commercial, and better videos. The whole economy suffered after the Gulf War, and it never really recovered. So we've been unprofitable the whole year, and we've never been unprofitable before. But our sales are back up, and our closing rates are even a lot better now. I don't know if it's because we just got back to basics, or if it's the economy. I don't really understand business at all.

*SD:* Now you have competition breathing down your back from NordicTrack, Fingerhut and numerous other machines.

*JW:* Those things have been coming out ever since our first magazine ad. People who were capable of manufacturing something like that were painting them gold or orange and stepping on our patents and trademarks. We filed one action early on. Not because we thought there was anything to gain by doing that, but because our lawyers told us that if we didn't file against someone that we knew was infringing on our patent, then we could lose the patent. So it's a catch 22. We went into that litigation and found out the guy was totally broke, and was sitting on a big inventory that he couldn't sell. But all we wanted was for him to stop, so he agreed to stop. This NordicFlex thing is a very strange situation, why they would target us and mimic us the way they have. I don't really understand their ulterior motive, and how they thought they could get away with making the false claims that they have.

*SD:* Why did it take so long to file the suit against them?

*JW:* Well, you have a bias against suing in the first place. A lot of people took charge at us, saying that our machine didn't have a leg extension. Well, it has five basic, and most important, leg exercises, which were more than most people were doing anyway. No one really needed the leg extension. I've always given the customer what they needed, instead of what they wanted. But all those who took charge at us faded pretty quickly. So we'd seen false claims and hyped up stuff before, and my bias is not to sue. There's an old quote that says, "The buyer needs 1,000 eyes, the seller not one." Our system kind of runs on that. There are regulators in the government on fair trade and all that, but they only deal with those things that can harm people physically, like medicine. Trademarks are so easy and fast to rip off. When it gets into political campaigns or consumer products, there are no regulators. It's up to the competitors to file a complaint when somebody breaks the law. And there are rules and laws out there, but they're designed to be forced into court by competitors. And that's the only protection you get. When my patent and trademark attorneys come out and they'd seen the NordicFlex thing for awhile, and they pointed out all the places that they had broken the law, I'd had enough experience to realize that the sales they were taking away from us were the people who didn't know anything about weightlifting, not the 50% who do. I concluded that filing against them was my only choice of weapon if I was going to get them to stop, because it didn't appear they were going to stop on their own accord. They had damaged us severely. It's a machine that only pushes in one direction. They were stating that it was a iso-kinetic exercise, and it is not genuinely iso-kinetic. They said that by doing less than half of the exercises, because the negative is the part you get the growth on, you could have 70% faster muscle gain, which is a blatant lie. It was like standing up and saying the world was flat, with absolutely no evidence. The only proof they did offer was a study that had been discredited in trade magazines by the professor that was supervising it. But that didn't stop them from including it in the brochures. They intentionally went to try to knock us out of the field and try to be the name in home fitness. I don't know what they could have possibly gained from taking the approach they chose. They tried to use our production people, our models. They wanted everything to look exactly like Soloflex. And then they turn around and say, "Soloflex is no good, this one is much better." They lied about everything. The cost, they said their machine was one third cheaper, and it wasn't. It cost about the same, if not more. The charts and graphs were dummied up.

*SD:* When do you expect that to come to trial?

*JW:* We filed in Oregon, where all cases have to come to trial within a year. Instead of answering the suit, they filed a totally separate suit in the same federal court, in Minneapolis. They're doing whatever they can to confuse and jack the price up. They're basically not very ethical people. I think most people recognize that from what they see on TV.

*SD:* In all this time, it doesn't appear that you've made any changes to the Soloflex machine.

*JW:* There have been minor changes, the quality of the materials has been beefed up here and there as we get more experience over the years. We try to make the machine last forever, which is almost un-American. To make a product that doesn't wear out goes against the mindset of almost everybody in manufacturing in the United States. America makes Chevrolets, not Mercedes. They make things that you throw away when you're through with them, and you don't put more into them than you absolutely need. When we were going around to vendors and sub-contractors in the early days, the first question that would come up was, "How can we make this thing so it will break down?" Of course they didn't get the job. We're dealing with one of the most hazardous activities a human being can do here, kind of like airplanes. There were something like 66,000 people badly injured last year just trying to lift weights. We're trying to make something safe, and operating with very high pressures and very heavy loads, so let's over-build it, and maybe we'll get a good reputation and people will continue to buy it.

*SD:* Do you get as much resistance on the negative as on the positive with the rubber bands?

*JW:* Sure. You move slowly, and it stores the energy you put into it and brings it right back down on top of you. All the control group studies we've done, or that others have done, show that you get identical gains pushing on a Soloflex as you would pushing on a Universal or free weights. We've never been able to find any difference. And it's much easier and safer to use. I don't know how many injuries have been prevented, but it's a lot.

*SD:* The new show is absolutely gorgeous, and it's your first show in three or four years.

*JW:* Thanks. My wife did this one, start to finish. She wanted to produce it and she knew what she wanted to produce. She pulled together all the Soloflex people, and outside cameramen and gaffers and everything else. We have our own off-line Avid system for editing. So we could really take our time in building the story. The last show has over 500 cuts, and it really moves around nicely. She just took everything that we had learned, all the mistakes she had watched me make. She's really produced this whole company, actually. She's the brains behind it all.

*SD:* What did the show end up costing?

*JW:* About $300,000. When you get in and do it yourself, become the contractor, you can really keep your costs down. And you know who to blame if it doesn't work out.

*SD:* How long did it take to produce the show from start to finish?

*JW:* About three months.

*SD:* Including scripting?

*JW:* Yes. It's primarily storyboarded, with pictures, and then the copy is massaged for a great deal of time.

*SD:* Is this the first time you've actually asked for the direct sale on the show?

*JW:* I believe so.

*SD:* It's a multi-pay offer?

*JW:* You can buy one outright, but we talk about the payment options. Being able to finance the machine allows us to sell twice as many as we would otherwise. We've had over 10 million calls from all media. That means that one out of every seven households in the United States has called for our brochure. That's a deep penetration. But actually only about 5% of the households in the United States can afford one of these machines. And we've sold them.

*SD:* Have you ever developed an additional product line to sell to customers?

*JW:* Well, I'm an inventor by hobby, and I like to find better ways to do things. We've come out with a new squat machine that we're going to sell to health clubs, and possibly into homes.

*SD:* I read that you had developed a swimming-type machine.

*JW:* Yes. I was trying to come up with something I could get older people to use, and this is an iso-kinetic device that won't make you sore, won't make your muscles any bigger, but will tone and strengthen. My mother, aunts and uncles all had a bias against weightlifting, and thought that swimming was the best exercise. I'd never tried to develop a product for someone else before, I'd always tried to design for myself. So I thought if I came up with a wide range of swimming movements, with the resistance, it would work. The people that bought them absolutely love them, but it's so difficult to get older people to get up and exercise, and I really don't know how to communicate to them. The machines are selling well in Japan. But I'm not personally enthused about the product.

*SD:* So you've never done anything with books or tapes or supplements to go back and market to your buyers?

*JW:* No, but every week I get from two to ten proposals for products to sell to my Soloflex buyers. I've yet to see one that I felt was worth the effort.

*SD:* The most amount of money you'll ever spend is getting the customer in the door the first time.

*JW:* When we decided to go ahead and manufacture the leg extension we mailed it back to the Soloflex buyers and they ate it up. There was a six month backlog of orders. So if I could find the right thing, I suppose I'd do that again. The Soloflex really does every exercise you'll ever need. The reason we made the squat rack was because people were skipping that exercise, and it's a very important exercise. So we felt it was important to make that more comfortable, and easier to get in and out of. You can lie down while you do the exercises—it locks you into perfect form for all squats. It's the only machine I know of that allows you to do a free weight barbell squat with perfect form, safely locked in.

*SD:* It uses band resistance?

*JW:* Bands and plates. The Soloflex was initially designed to be used with plates. When you put the plates and the weight straps together, it gives you the nicest feel of any press or pull you've ever experienced. I've always used plates with my machines in addition to the weight straps.

*SD:* Do you sell the plates also?

*JW:* No, anybody can get them locally very cheap, if they don't already have them. When I designed this machine, there were seven friends I used to hang around and play basketball with, and six out of the seven had a set of plates resting in their garage. I always knew there was a demand for a home weightlifting machine. I waited five years for Universal to build one and they didn't do it, so I did. I was flying around with a lot wealthy people, flying Learjets on charters, and picking their brains. And they also told me that if I wanted to sit in the back of that Learjet with them, I'd have to design something, and control the manufacturing. The manufacturing is where it starts, and that's where it all ends. And I believed them. I looked for something that was a mass market item. You're much better off trying to design something that will satisfy you, knowing that you are more like everybody else than different. So if you're solving a problem for yourself, you're probably solving a problem for other people.

**SD:** Is the magazine that is enclosed with your literature subscription-based or just a sales tool?

**JW:** It's basically a re-mailer. We try to give people something that they'll sit around and read.

**SD:** Have you ever met anybody who worked out exclusively on the Soloflex who amazed you with what they were able to do?

**JW:** Sure, we get letters all the time. It's just weightlifting. If you do any kind of weightlifting properly you'll get the gains out of it. We're not surprised to see people who use the machine and make phenomenal gains. But it's hard to stay motivated, I've had my share of those problems. If I hadn't, I never would have invented that machine, to make it more convenient, hoping that would keep me sticking to it.

**SD:** What do you have to say about the infomercial industry at this point?

**JW:** It's taking the path that I anticipated, that people would see that this was a cost-effective way of reaching people. The advertisers and marketers were all looking for better ways to sell their products. It took about the same amount of time for us to deplete the infomercial market as it did the magazines. It's not totally depleted of course, but our margins are a lot smaller than they used to be.

**SD:** What do you see people in the infomercial industry doing wrong?

**JW:** Selling garbage. I don't know why more legitimate companies don't do it, although I shouldn't say that because I have a hard enough time competing for the media time as it is. I suppose it's because all the big companies turn their marketing over to advertising agencies, who only do half the job.

**SD:** There are some major companies that are starting to come in.

**JW:** Why didn't they do it six years ago? There were many times that I wanted to throw everybody in the jet and go back and make General Motors a presentation. But I don't make cars, I don't want to sell somebody else's product. And how big do I want to get? Do I want to be an advertising agency? I don't think so.

*SD:* You said at the height you were grossing about $100 million a year, and what has it dipped down to?

*JW:* We'll probably do $30 million this year. And that's still a lot of money, if your costs are in line. We intend to be profitable from this month on. We've got such a good company. About four out of five of the people that have worked here don't work here now. I don't know how to build a Super Bowl team except to cut the draft and let the best players play. We've made those hard decisions. Even if it means taking some of those profits that we made early on and subsidizing the company and keeping everybody here so that we would be able to turn it around. My bias was to ease off and scale it down, but we chose to keep the company together, which cost us about $8 million.

*SD:* How many employees do you have?

*JW:* About 130. For the sales we were doing six months ago, we should have been at one quarter of that number. The extra profit that we made during the Republican administration has now been used up. It's subsidizing labor to keep the company afloat. If the opportunity does come back around for heavy production and heavy sales, I'll have to have these people around to capitalize on it. So that was all part of a bigger gamble that looks like it's going to pay off.

*SD:* Due to the new show?

*JW:* And a new brochure we've worked on. There have been so many false claims made about our products that we have to answer. When you're number one in the marketplace, you don't compare yourself to anyone, you sell the benefits of whatever it is you sell. So we never wanted to be pulled into that trap.

*SD:* How many of the 130 are in your manufacturing division?

*JW:* About 40%. The rest are in marketing, research and development, tooling, customer service, shipping, and accounting.

*SD:* You do your own fulfillment?

*JW:* Fulfillment, customer service, financing—everything. If you're going to make a commitment to be a manufacturer, you've got to manufacture everything. Sometimes when you scale up, it becomes more cost-effective to subcontract it out, sometimes it's more cost effective to pull it in-house. But you can't run away from the work. The money goes to whomever does the work.

# STAN BRUCKHEIM

❧

The Russ Reid Company is one of the pioneers in developing long-form advertising for non-profit groups. Their use of statistical analysis in measuring long-term results is light years beyond anything that is currently tracked in the commercial infomercial world. They have systems in place for tracking the long term worth of a customer. They have proven that a customer ordering at one time of day can be worth more money over the long term than someone pledging money at another time of the day. I'm pleased to say that this interview presents in-depth information never before revealed. It should absolutely open your eyes as to what is possible and doable in the statistical realm of television response rates and what it teaches us about sales behavior.

**Steve Dworman:** Who and what is Russ Reid? They aren't generally known in the infomercial business.

**Stan Bruckheim:** Right. We will be celebrating our 30th year next March, and yet we are not known in the commercial marketing arena because we've been specializing in non-profits and cause-related markets for the past 30 years. We're the largest agency in the country that specializes in cause-related marketing and fund raising. We're the 12th largest direct response agency in the country. And nobody knows it.

**SD:** The Russ Reid Company has entered into direct response television and the infomercial realm. What are some of the infomercials your company has been responsible for?

**SB:** We've been the agency for World Vision for over 25 years. If you're not familiar with the name, their shows are usually hosted by Alex Trebek or Sarah Purcell, as well as a number of other hosts, and the cause is world hunger and relief. We've also worked with St. Jude's Children's Research Hospital, and in the areas of child abuse and substance abuse on television.

*SD:* Did you do the series with Sally Struthers?

*SB:* No, that show is often confused with World Vision. That show is for the Christian Children's Fund. We do a similar genre, but I think if you line the two shows up against one another, there's a very significant difference.

*SD:* What was the first infomercial that you did?

*SB:* Our first program-length advertisement was done in 1970. That shocks those people who look at infomercials as coming out of deregulation in the 1980s. In the early 1970s, there wasn't regulation against it. It just wasn't done. The only people doing any kind of program-length direct response were ministers and non-profits. Our first was "America's Best Loved Hymns" featuring Bud Collier. When the advertising industry was regulated as to how many minutes of commercial programming could air, that did not affect cause-related advertising. So we could continue to produce what are now called infomercials.

*SD:* So you had a 15-year jump on what we consider to be the pioneers of the infomercial industry. Did you at that time have to buy the media?

*SB:* Yes. We've been buying the media since 1970.

*SD:* What were the rates like in the 1970s?

*SB:* The stations didn't know how to price their time. They weren't used to selling blocks of time. When our predecessors went into a station in the early 1970s to ask to buy time, it was something that had never been asked for. Stations didn't know how to compare that to selling spots. There was the ease of selling an entire hour of time, but there was also the inconvenience to the station's programming department of scheduling that hour, and questioning whether that programming would yield a significant audience, especially in sweeps period. They didn't know how to price the time, and we didn't know how to gauge it. Over time they learned how to price time, and we learned how to gauge response.

*SD:* At that time there was no national cable. What sort of rates were you paying for, say, a Los Angeles O & O [Owned & Operated] or a major independent?

*SB:* It was certainly a fraction of what it is now. Possibly 10% to 15% of what it is now. We wouldn't mind going into late or late-late night if the price was right. We had a pledge-to-cost ratio, what we call a "PC," and if we paid $1,000 for a period of time, we needed a 4:1 response, or $4,000. If we got it, fine, we'd go back and buy it again. And if we didn't, we'd go back and re-negotiate the price for next time down. And at that time, all avails that began to come through, came to the Russ Reid Company. Station representatives like Bob Steres and Jim Miller who have been around for a long time, when they got an hour avail (and they were generally hours back in the early '80s) it went to the Russ Reid Company. There was nobody else who would take them. We either agreed to them or the station broke them back into programming and spots.

*SD:* For non-profit, what do you find is the best time of day?

*SB:* There is no particular day-part that is across the country better than others for non-profits. You have to look at it for each market and each station individually, and if you make the mistake of accumulating all of the day-parts across the country and come to the conclusion that primetime works better than late night, that does not apply to each and every individual market without looking specifically at that market and that station. The cost and the front-end return is certainly better in late fringe and late night, and for years that is why we all relied on late night avails, because that is were our margins were greatest. But when you factor in long-term customer value, and for us long-term donor value, then we begin to see that other day-parts are as good or better over the long haul as late night.

*SD:* Does Russ Reid do the production on the shows?

*SB:* We are a full service advertising and marketing agency. We do the strategic planning, the positioning within the marketplace. We do the entire production from writing the treatment, to talent, production and post production, and then planning, buying and analyzing the media. And the very important continuity series, following the acquisition of a new donor, and building the relationship. We're about 40% direct mail, 40% media—television, radio, newspaper, magazine, outbound and inbound telemarketing—and 20% other services like public relations and development.

*SD:* Do you do your own telemarketing?

*SB:* No, we hire centers. Over the years, we've used several, and think that we've found what works best for us.

*SD:* Who do you use?

*SB:* For outbound, our primary center is Infocision, which is the largest center for non-profits. We generally use two centers for each of our programs to test both the center and the cause.

*SD:* What about inbound?

*SB:* Some of our clients, World Vision for example, have great in-house centers. In addition, we've used many centers for one day events, such as telethons. For the on-going airings we have, we use two centers right now, MATRIXX for volume, because they can handle it, and a group called CDA here in Los Angeles for smaller print accounts, with a little more personalized approach.

*SD:* So you are working with non-profits, but you are utilizing direct response mail, television, and telemarketing. You're controlling the whole campaign from your company. You are very experienced in taking a campaign and making it work from a multitude of media, and I see a parallel here to the major consumer marketers who are now recognizing these opportunities. What is the range of your cost to produce a half-hour show?

*SB:* Our shows range from $150,000 to $750,000. The high end is for a World Vision show that would include going overseas for a survey trip, and then a filming trip, and a crew and talent to go over there as well.

*SD:* Do you script these in-house?

*SB:* Yes, all of our scripts are written in-house, in association with the client. And it's very scripted.

*SD:* And do you have an in-house producer and director?

*SB:* We have an in-house production team, but not in-house production facilities. We use existing facilities we have relationships with.

*SD:* What is the time frame from when your client says, "Hey, we're ready to do an infomercial," to actually airing it?

*SB:* I'd say an average of six to nine months. However, there are some shows where we will follow the progress of a particular child over time, so that time factor needs to be considered.

*SD:* Do you ask for a set figure for donations?

*SB:* Yes, and we often give an option of set donations. But all fundraisers have found that asking for a particular donation, or offer, will always get you more than leaving it open for the person to make a decision of how much to spend.

*SD:* Have you found that there is a range of amounts to ask for that is more successful?

*SB:* Yes. There's a range for each particular client. For some, such as World Vision, it's an ongoing need to help an orphan overseas, so we ask for a monthly pledge of $20. And that by definition becomes a continuity plan; it continues over time. We've gone as high as testing $27 per month. Most of our clients are in the $15 to $22 per month range, and average one-time gifts range from $30 to $50.

*SD:* These are the campaigns where you sponsor a child and pay for their clothing, their shelter, etc.?

*SB:* Exactly. You sponsor one child. Life and death is what people respond to initially. But sheltering, clothing and medical care and then long-term development are also important to our donors.

*SD:* Have you been greatly effected by the recent escalation of media rates?

*SB:* In television, yes, significantly. Ten years ago we were getting all of the avails, and now there are so many infomercials out there competing for air time that rates are rising significantly. There are increases in printing and postage and other areas that affect us, but nothing at the rate that infomercial air time is rising. The competition has grown exponentially over the past two years.

*SD:* Is it still profitable for you to produce infomercials?

*SB:* It is, but we're having to find new ways in terms of content and buying. On the production side, we have to find ways of building a better show, a more compelling show. On the media side, we've got to be more savvy in buying the media, for example trying new cable networks, or buying blocks of time.

*SD:* How do you actually test one of your infomercials from a media point of view? Are there differences between your shows and consumer product infomercials in the way that they're tested?

*SB:* It's probably similar. First of all, a lot of our shows have been one hour. Now we're moving to half-hours because we have to. When the infomercial industry started, most of the avails were hours and then the infomercials broke them down into half-hours. We would set up a test using several different offers: we may ask for $15, we may ask for $17 and $20, and each of those would be a panel. A test panel would give us a representative mix of day-parts, regions of the country, days of the week, market size, urban versus rural, affiliates and independents, local cable, and national cable. So a test would give us a representative mix of all those media factors. A typical test of a one hour show might be 25 to 40 airings, an average of $1,500 apiece, a $40,000 to $50,000 test.

*SD:* How do you test different price points?

*SB:* It's actually very simple and this is attributable to commercial marketing. When you buy, you buy two of everything. You buy the next two Tuesdays on KCAL at the same time, and every airing you buy, you buy two in subsequent weeks. And then you give one panel the first airing and the other panel the second airing. Then you reverse it so that you have half of your first airings in one panel and half of your first airings in the other panel. Then we have what we call matched panels. And you literally have the same markets, same stations, same costs, same times, just a different date, separated by a week, and you match up the first and seconds.

*SD:* If the results you're getting are not satisfactory what's the first thing you consider changing?

*SB:* When we debut a show, we always do a minute-by-minute report which gives us the response from the phone center by when they called. We analyze what parts of the show are strong and compelling and what parts are not. So we'll look at, from a production standpoint, what can be done to the show to make it stronger. Then from the media standpoint, we'll look at the media factors that I listed and see if there is a media factor that is conclusively hurting us. Is there a certain day-part that we shouldn't be in? Or is there a certain market we should not be in, or type of station? That's often hard to test to be conclusive in an initial test. For example, you might do 30% better in most day-parts but not so well in prime, but that might be because of four or five airings and you certainly shouldn't rule out prime time for your rollout on that basis.

*SD:* The 40 airings you talked about, do they include the price testing as well?

*SB:* That would be per panel. Twenty-five airings is plenty if your broadcast traffic people are real efficient at getting the right tapes out to the right stations and your stations are real efficient at airing your right tapes, no mistakes. We can usually get away with 25 airings.

*SD:* You normally test two or three prices?

*SB:* It depends where we are in the relationship with the client. You can only test one thing at a time from a production/content standpoint to be conclusive about what's working. If you test more than one factor, you're not keeping the control constant. If price is the most critical, then that will be. For some clients we've been doing TV for so long that every couple of years we test price, but that's not the primary criteria for a new show coming up. We've produced probably 150 shows over 20 years and I'm sure there's 750 versions of those shows and price is only one approach. It could be different talent.

*SD:* You would do the exact same show with just different talent?

*SB:* We may have different use of talent. We may have three hosts and try it with just two of them at certain points. Or we may use talent in a phone center or without the phone center scene. We may do a long-term development focus for several segments and pull that out if we don't feel that's a risk. And, yes, for our newest show, we've filmed four different versions, with four different sets of talent.

*SD:* What is the first element you do check on a show? Is it the price?

*SB:* Probably the stories. For non-profits the stories are critical; that's the piece that's compelling you to go to your phone. The mix of stories is important too. Price would probably be secondary.

*SD:* In testing the story, what would show A have compared to show B?

**SB:** I mentioned long-term development. We may need eight stories for an hour show, but we'll film twelve. We may feel that we know which are the best and most compelling stories; but there might be two of the extras that are in long-term development and we substitute them in for two of the other stories. We usually have extra stories in the can that can be substituted in for the weaker stories or for an important test. For our newest show, story mix is an important criteria we are testing.

**SD:** Is that something that you do after you test it? Test the initial show and look at it minute by minute?

**SB:** It depends on what the original strategy is for testing the show. Originally, if you know what you'd like to test, then you go in and A-B it.

**SD:** What is it that you want to test in a new show?

**SB:** We don't always test two versions. When we do, I would say the order is: 1) story  2) price point and maybe 3) continuity.

**SD:** Tell me some incident from your own experience where you had to change stories and how that altered the response, taking you from where to where?

**SB:** Something that we'd like to show more but that doesn't often work is long-term development, World Vision for example. As a potential donor to World Vision, you would like to see positive strides in long-term help that your money is making. And that is a natural thing for all of us to want our money to go toward. So our natural instinct is to add long-term development and see how that works. I think most of the times we've tested that against a child that needs to be fed today, or needs severe medical, life or death care, then long-term is much harder to make work. And that could have a 20% affect on response, and 20% lower pledge-to-cost might be the difference between success and failure.

**SD:** If it's harder to make work, do you try and make it work because it's ultimately more effective? Why do you take the trouble to do it if the other is easier to make work?

**SB:** We will test it as long as it is viable to do as well. If we're trying to elicit a TV response which is spontaneous, then we may go back to the immediate need, the hunger and the shelter.

**SD:** Give me an example.

**SB:** Here's one we can all relate to. We work with the Los Angeles Mission and about 40 rescue missions around the country. And most of us have a rescue mission within our market. We've tested ads about long-term rehabilitation, we've tested ads about bringing families back together, and use different longer term approaches, but what we always come back to—and is always most successful—is feeding the person today because that is the immediate need. And that is the most compelling fundraising approach. And if you look at the ads in today's *Los Angeles Times*, you'll find that most of them will go back to the immediate need of feeding the hungry. It doesn't rule out long-term, it's just harder to make work.

**SD:** How can you apply that to the selling of consumer products through infomercials?

**SB:** Take fitness products, for instance. I think what people want is short-term benefit more than long-term health. And those products will probably give you both. But if you tested a show that was really designed to increase your health over the coming years versus a version that promised weight-reduction and great looks in the short term, that latter version will significantly out-pull the long-term benefit approach.

**SD:** Let me refine that even more. If you were taking an exercise device, for example, would it be more effective pointing out how it will solve the problems you have with lungs, cardiovascular, and so on ,or would it be better to stress the long-term health benefits, or would you do both?

**SB:** My gut would say that a positive approach would sell more than a negative approach.

**SD:** But don't you have to set up a negative and then offer a positive solution?

**SB:** Right, but I'd devote more time to the positive future rather than the negative past. And remember, specificity is important. Clarity is important, and simplicity. And don't forget endorsements. A significant part of our shows feature endorsement by talent, either political or entertainment figures, both local and national figures. But most important are probably the testimonials by either the donors or users of the product—the customers.

**SD:** That's a really interesting point. I think on the commercial side there's been an overuse of celebrities. They might not have as much credibility as everybody gives them credit for. The actual donors, as you've said, are much more real.

**SB:** It's very important for the viewer to see someone like themselves, and sincere, giving, as an endorsement of the cause.

**SD:** Okay, how do you use that endorsement in a TV show?

**SB:** You'd call it a testimonial. We would probably film the person in their living room in a comfortable and relaxing, casual, sincere setting. Keep it short but have them explain what benefits they've received from the product. How their life has been enriched.

*SD:* Are you still doing hours or half-hours?

*SB:* It's interesting. We're doing both, and only because we have to. Over the years, hours have worked significantly better than half-hours. But we've had to produce half-hours because 90% of the avails out there now are half-hours, and that's a figure that's growing and you have to change with the times.

*SD:* It's interesting that the hours have performed better. Why?

*SB:* We're still researching why. Our shows have always been built on 15-minute pods, and then we go back to another similar pod and do that four times an hour. Well, if you take the best two pods and make a half-hour, you'd expect to have a more powerful show than the best two plus two more as an hour. But that's not the case for us.

*SD:* When you run your minute-by-minute reports from your telemarketing center, in an hour show where is your response coming from?

*SB:* The first time we put the 800 number up is usually anywhere from four, six or eight minutes into the show. We don't put the number up immediately. Response comes in as soon as eight seconds after that number comes up. It doesn't end until the show is over and then there are drag calls and cleanup calls after the show is over. We find that we get the most response after stories from the field, when we're back in the studio with the host pitching hard. The best response is when the host is in the field pitching. The stories are always of one child per pod, per story.

*SD:* Do you get an equal amount of calls after each pod, or, as in the commercial infomercial business, do the calls stack up as the show plays on?

*SB:* There are more calls in the last quarter of the show, as in the commercial infomercial business. But also, viewers tend to tune in and out for 15 minutes or less. We tell the whole story in 10 or 15 minutes so the viewer doesn't have to finish the infomercial to get the whole feel in order to respond. For some things, like the Philips CDi infomercial, I imagine most of the viewer response comes after the viewer has been able to digest the whole thing. More viewers don't get the whole feel for the product until the half hour is over. For us, those are 12 to15 minute segments.

*SD:* Have you ever experimented with doing longer segments, where maybe one segment would be a half hour instead of 15 minutes?

*SB:* No. The length of the segments came about as the result of a lot of testing in the 1970s. We haven't changed that thinking. What we've done is change the pacing within the segments. We've made the pacing faster, more documentary style—a longer story, different paces of editing.

*SD:* I'm fascinated in how sophisticated your analysis is of your shows and response. Can you comment on that?

*SB:* We plan our media, and we'll negotiate very hard, because that's our nature with non-profit clients. Then results come in the same way as a commercial, from phone centers. We will look at both short-term response from that airing and then we will build a relationship with those donors over the course of months and years, and then look at the long-term value of those donors. So it becomes database marketing. The donor begins to get a constant stream of personalized communication, everything from personalized mail and phone calls, updates, newsletters, and information. With database marketing, you realize the individuality of your donors, or customers. You build a database that summarizes how each of your customers is different based on key marketing criteria.

*SD:* Can you give me an example?

*SB:* Club Med, for example, has a membership program whereby once you go to Club Med, you are a member. Certain people who go there are singles, some are families, some are couples. So that is one field to segment them by. What sports do they enjoy? And this is all data you get from them. Are they volleyball players, or do they like to play bridge and bingo? When do they make their travel decisions? So then you segment your database based on those criteria and market to the people based on their interests and their needs, and their buying habits. It's extended psycho-graphics, and you market based on that. Rather than selling what you want to sell to them, you sell them what they want. So the customer could conceivably get a letter from Club Med three months after his trip (which is when he's making his vacation decisions, because Club Med knows that, based on information you've given them) which says, "Dear Steve, we have a new village we want to tell you about, and as a volleyball player, you'll be interested to know that there's a great volleyball court at this new village. And because you are a member of Club Med, we're going to invite you to a special viewing of this new village in Los Angeles." So there are several variable inserts that are taken advantage of in this mailing, including your personalized name, special interests, and location. The key to database marketing is realizing the individuality of your customers. Consumers are becoming too sophisticated to be treated as a mass market. And advertisers are recognizing that, and the technology is there so that you can do the segmentation based on your key marketing criteria, on a cost-effective basis. So you are doing vertical marketing to each of your vertical niches.

*SD:* And how do you actually apply that?

*SB:* Once someone gives to one of our clients at the organization, we will send them an immediate follow up letter thanking them for their gift, with an envelope to begin the pledging. Then we will send them a newsletter several times a year. We might send them an invitation to an open house, if they are in the area of the mission, or if it's a special event. If they are high-end donors, we might send them a videotape appeal. We would call them first to verify that they have a VCR, and tell them that we'd like to send them an 8-minute video about a new program that we are launching. And you have to be very attentive to what they say. If they say "take me off the list" or "don't send me any more of these kind of mailings" or if they say "send me more of these mailings" you have to have the ability within the database to do that. So you build a relationship and make them feel that they are a special friend of the organization, because they are.

*SD:* Do you use an outside mailing house for that?

*SB:* We do all of the strategic planning, the creative. We rent the lists, we do the print production work. We do everything except the actual production and mailing of the letter itself. Now, going back to the long-term value of donors, I can give a good example of that. Of our 40 mission clients, the average donation from a space ad in the *Los Angeles Times* is around $30. Yet over the relationship of the cause with the donor, our average is over $150. And that says that only $30 of the $150 you will receive from this relationship actually comes in when you first market to this person. The value is in the long-term stream of communication through database marketing. So those who are ignoring the benefits of long-term relationships through database marketing are left with the $30. So when you look at the initial call-to-order as just the first in a series of steps to building a relationship, that's when you maximize your profits. And your costs will never be higher than in getting that $30 than initially.

*SD:* What's the drop-off rate on a program like that?

*SB:* We have people that are asked for a monthly donation. We have people who give for years and don't drop off. We have people that give for a few months and drop off. And we have people that never start (unlike commercial advertisers, we don't get a credit card number up front.) We usually send a letter with an envelope because normally people prefer to use their check than their credit card. So the credit card rate is much lower for non-profit than it is for commercial applications.

*SD:* How many people actually do send the checks in?

*SB:* A typical fulfillment rate on a one-time offer, we get 80% to 90%. It can actually go higher, over 100%, because people who say they may give actually do give. When you add that to the people who actually said yes to begin with it sends the rate up to, say, 105%. One time donors are, typically, 80%. Monthly donors can range from 40% to 60% of an annualized gift.

*SD:* I want to back up for a minute because that's an astonishing number to anybody in the consumer product infomercial industry, where a 20% to 25% response is typical. Is there anything specific that you do? Or is it that donors are making a verbal commitment over the phone to pledge something that sways them over? What, in your mind, is the deciding factor?

*SB:* That's an interesting question because in a commercial application they're getting something in return that is very tangible. They're getting a product and they're willing to pay for it. For us, what they're getting by calling is the satisfaction of knowing they're helping an important cause. So you'd think the fulfillment would be greater on a commercial product, but with us I believe it's a matter of the follow up that is so important.

*SD:* Tell me how much response can alter from something as silly as whether a stamp is on it or it says "no postage required" on the outside envelope.

*SB:* That's very particular to what the cause or the product is. Certainly there is a greater cost but a greater potential benefit if someone sees a stamp there—that you took the trouble to use a live stamp. They may feel more beholden to send in their payment than if it's a typical "no postage necessary" BRE (business reply envelope). That's something I'd test if I were a commercial marketer. You could also test when you send the package out, the affect of sending it out faster. We get ours out within 24 hours. Nothing could increase response better than having that product there within less than 5 days. There's an old axiom in fund-raising that every day you lose getting the mail to your pledger, you lose 10% of your response.

*SD:* What is an effective package to get the consumer to get them to send their check in?

*SB:* Consumer application is very different from not-for-profit. For non-profit, it's a very warm thank you letter that also shows need, that follows the theme of the show. It should first say thank you, then restate the need as presented in the show and the direct effect their gift is having. It also includes a response device of some sort, either a tear-off at the bottom of that page or a separate response device that can be personalized or simply be pre-printed. Again that's a test that you do. It also includes the business reply envelope or the live stamp envelope. It might include a kind of lift note, for example, some newspaper headlines splattered across a sheet that give your product some validation. Or a lift-note from the host of the show that says thanks again, etc. It could be a lift note from someone not in the show but affiliated with the product or organization.

*SD:* Define a lift note.

*SB:* It could be anything from a pre-printed "post-it" to something on a monarch-sized letterhead that says, "From the desk of Mayor Riordan," saying, "Thanks again, etc." Again, the great thing about direct marketing is that you can test all this and come to conclusive results and base your future on the tests that have given you the direction you want to go into. And it's imperative that you continue to test and you don't rest on what you learned last year to be applicable to next year because the economy and our customers change constantly.

*SD:* Tell me what the difference is in the way you follow up on the people who have sent in their check as opposed to the people who pledged do so but still have not come through?

*SB:* If they send their check in, they must get a thank you letter. If they don't send their check in, then they must get a reminder letter about 14 to 21 days later that says, "Thank you again for giving. We apologize if our letters have crossed in the mail but in case you have not given yet, we hope you do so" and re-state the "need" factor. And there may be a third letter—a delinquency letter. And then there's the people who did give, and it's different for every client. If it's a monthly giving program, then they get an envelope every month for monthly gift and a reason to give that gift. They get a newsletter three to 12 times a year depending on the client. They may get a special appeal, if something happens like a major earthquake. If they fall into inactivity for some time, we would usually send about three reminders and then not count on them anymore. We do mail to our inactive donors, but we take a different approach—possibly a less personalized, less expensive mail piece because the return will probably be smaller. And then you mix in, possibly, telemarketing. You could use the telephone to make special appeals when necessary. We haven't found delinquency calling to be extremely successful, but that can be an approach. Telemarketing, in a commercial approach, is probably more appropriate.

*SD:* Talk about long-term donor value and which media has been responsible for attracting them and keeping them.

*SB:* That's a very important question. Basically, you take the donors or customers that were acquired as far back as you can go with reliable data and track their response over time and decide how much money they have generated for your cause. It's critical to track the donor response as to which media they were acquired by.

What's the donor value for those media? That's critical because if someone was first acquired through TV and they're worth $150, but someone you acquired through direct mail is worth $170, then you can back up and say, "I can afford a lower response on the front-end for mail donors. So understanding your long-term donor value by media is very important.

*SD:* And there's no way of tracking that unless you keep their histories.

*SB:* Right. But history could be one year. Compare your TV response to your mail response. Who are your repeat customers? The extension to that is to track within the media, break a single medium's usefulness and effectiveness down into smaller parts. For instance, in TV, how are the primetime donors in the long-term responding to all of our continuity compared to late night generated donors? What you might find is that you have different qualities of customers. You could look at it by language. We found that Hispanic donor response is generally equal to general market donors. Yet, on the front end they are 20 to 40 percent more responsive on a pledge-to-cost basis.

*SD:* What have you found about "day of the week" and it's effect on donor response?

*SB:* We found that day of the week is not a big determinant. We separate the days of the week by "weekend" and "weekday." Day-part is very important. And for certain products, of course, region of the country is going to be very important. Or urban versus rural market for certain products is going to be very important.

*SD:* Looking at your tracking reports, the detail is incredible.

*SB:* Thanks, Steve. When someone calls, we track how they were acquired, which media they were acquired by and within that media, which airing generated their interest. The date of the airing, type of airing, the station that aired the program, the type of station, be it cable network or otherwise, and any number of other factors we want to track in long-term fulfillment. All that becomes part of the individual donor's record on how they began their relationship with the organization. Then down the road, we'll take a look at all the donors that were acquired in particular categories. If we know that a typical donor is worth $150 over the long-term, we can break out that worth by day part in which they were acquired.

*SD:* You're not only tracking the numbers of calls, but you're tracking the individual people that call because you're capturing what they're pledging and then you're capturing whether they send the money in or not. So you can look back and see what individual donors pledged to send and what they actually sent.

*SB:* Most importantly we can determine the quality of the donors over not just months, but years. The fact that a prime-time donor is 40% more reliable means that you can go back and pay more for prime and get a lesser immediate return cost per order and still you should be in prime. So looking at strictly the cost per order is no longer anything more than a short-term indication on how you should do your buying. But your overall marketing strategy should include an understanding of these media factors and how they vary for your particular product. So then, you've got your short-term revenue, you've got your long-term revenue, you've broken it out by all of the media determinants, and you've gone back and given yourself short term goals by day part, region, day of the week, etc.

*SD:* To give the reader an example, I'm looking at one of your show charts and, boy, you can see right here the difference in responses between 1988 and 1990.

*SB:* Right, because the initial pledge-to-cost ratio is actually higher in 1990. But since this report was pulled in December of '90, some of these people have only had three months to fulfill, whereas others have had two years. Very short-term fulfillment data is really not reliable.

*SD:* How do these figures compare to the current figures, the ones from '93?

*SB:* Because of the rising infomercial rates, it becomes harder to yield the same figures. Our results are 25% down from what they were three years ago.

*SD:* To my knowledge, nobody is doing this kind of tracking in the infomercial product business. Tell me how this works. You have your inbound telemarketing people capture your information, but then how is this data stored and checked to see that pledges are sending their checks in and so forth? How is that mechanically handled?

*SB:* Generally that's handled by the clients or a database management firm. We only coordinate the processing of the data.

*SD:* So that the database manager has downloaded the names from the outbound telemarketing company?

*SB:* Yes, it's often done that way. World Vision works that way. But some clients are not that sophisticated.

*SD:* The non-profit organization, it seems to me, has to be well-funded to operate in this arena.

*SB:* Yes, for a non-profit to get into TV for example, they have to be significant in size and they have to be able to generate mass audience appeal.

*SD:* What kind of money does a non-profit need to bring to it?

*SB:* Well, there's a huge range. We have a Los Angeles client that's limited to the local market. We have a national account client that spends up to a million dollars a month.

*SD:* A million dollars a month for an hour show?

*SB:* Yes. We raise about $450 million a year for charities. That's significant. One hundred fifty thousand hours of TV programming over the course of 24 years. It's quite a history. We're a marketing firm that has a media buying division and that's one of our significant assets.

*SD:* For a charity, what is an acceptable cost of advertising?

*SB:* Charities report their net profit to watchdog organizations and to federal entities and to donors. And you want to know if you're a donor that only a certain amount is going to overhead. For our clients, generally, their overhead is no more than around 20%, which is acceptable to the watchdog organizations.

*SD:* So $90 million of that $450 is going toward media and production costs? A net profit, then, of $350 million?

*SB:* We don't call it profit because those are funds that help them serve their community.

*SD:* How does your agency take their piece?

*SB:* We are an advertising agency in structure so we get a standard 15% agency commission. It is not dependent on how successful the campaign is. On the production side we mark up costs, standard agency markups. And we bill hourly fees for departments like PR and development.

*SD:* I'm flabbergasted by the fact that your overhead cost is only 20% of the money you're bringing in.

*SB:* Most of that revenue comes over the long haul and is not the initial buy, the initial gift. We break even on direct mail in the short term, and then we do much better over the long haul.

*SD:* Most infomercial companies don't approach it that way.

*SB:* Right, they're looking at quantity, not quality, of customers. They're looking at units sold, not customers. But customers are your life's blood, not how many units did you sell last quarter.

*SD:* Talk a little about the upselling and the cross selling in your business.

*SB:* We certainly don't call it upselling and cross selling. We don't use those sales terms in fundraising but it's similar to what we do when we make a special appeal after an earthquake or natural disaster. That is a form of a cross sell. Cross marketing, yes, we do a lot of that.

*SD:* With your background and your sophisticated approach to the monitoring of this, let's say you decided to start your own infomercial company. Where do you see the industry going?

*SB:* We are taking a look at applying what we've learned in the non-profit world to commercial applications that are consistent with who we are. That is, we'd select our clients very carefully. We feel our experience in the non-profit field would significantly help us with our commercial clients, and vice versa.

*SD:* If you were advising infomercial producers on what to do in these economic times, with what's going on in media, what would you say?

*SB:* We would take an overall marketing strategy to what they're doing. They're an infomercial product. If they wanted strictly the media buying service, fine, we'd do that. But if they wanted to talk about the range of media we could help them with then we'd probably want to talk with them about their overall marketing strategy—TV, radio, direct mail and so on. There are two kinds of clients, those that want to use us as a buying service because we have a wonderful buying team and database, and there are those interested in TV production or getting into the Hispanic area. Or direct mail. We're one of the largest in that on the west coast.

*SD:* How would you advise an infomercial producer who wants to penetrate the Hispanic market?

*SB:* What we would suggest is that you create a show that is completely Hispanic, that is not designed as a translation, certainly not a dubbing of an English show. You produce a whole new show. And the back-end, the product fulfillment has to be in Spanish. That commitment can be rewarded in significant revenue. There's a huge market there for beauty products, for example. It's a huge and growing marketplace. We're the largest buyers of Hispanic infomercial time in the country. We've recognized the importance of that market.

*SD:* Any other advice for commercial infomercial producers maximizing their results?

*SB:* Take a look at what you're doing with your customers once they become customers. You have a show and let's say you're satisfied with the show. That's not the problem. Then take a look at what you're doing to get repeat business from these customers. The cross sell. And that's probably where the greatest opportunity is, taking your existing customers and moving them to a relationship and selling more to them. Repeat business is key, and that's the whole database marketing issue. And the first step there is understanding who your customers are and coming up with a marketing plan that addresses their individuality, their needs, and their buying habits.

*SD:* Stan, I'd like to thank you for taking the time to discuss Russ Reid.

*SB:* Thank you for the opportunity to share this with you and your readership.

# MARVIN TRAUB

Marvin S. Traub is the president of his own marketing and consulting firm, Marvin Traub Associates, Inc. (MTA). Prior to creating MTA, he was Chairman and CEO of Bloomingdale's for 14 years, as well as Vice Chairman and Director of Campeau Corporation, and Director of Federated Department Stores. At MTA, Mr. Traub specializes in working with major corporations in manufacturing, marketing and retailing. His clients include Jeanne Lanvin in Paris, Jones NY, American Express, Federated Department Stores, and Saks Fifth Avenue. From the moment Marvin Traub first spoke at our 1992 New York Conference, major corporations started to take the use of infomercials seriously. At that conference he stood up on stage and announced that he'd never seen anything move product in such tremendous volume at retail as a successful infomercial.

**Steve Dworman:** Why don't you give a brief synopsis of your background.

**Marvin Traub:** I live in New York. My mother and father were involved in the retail business. I was interested in retailing from my teens on. Stanley Marcus sent my letter of recommendation when I started out in Bloomingdale's right after graduating Harvard Business School. Bloomingdale's was a store with no particular distinction and it went through major changes. Bloomingdale's saw a somewhat different role for itself than other stores, in the sense of not simply being a middleman between the manufacturers and the consumer but rather developing products that we thought would be appropriate for our customers. That was the major difference at Bloomingdale's. We built a reputation of having a unique store. We worked with a new generation of designers worldwide, people like Ralph Lauren, Calvin Klein, Halston, and later Donna Karan here, and Lagerfeld, Missoni, Ungaro in Europe. We helped to popularize the designers to celebrity status, almost like rock stars.

We also created our unique effort of marketing ourselves through things like advertising shopping bags or the various special events such as tying in with China, India, the Philippines. We also invited the Queen of England to come and she did. We could say it was like no other store in the world and mean it. We think we had a lot to do with retail changing in the '60s '70s and '80s.

**SD:** Let's talk about defining the store as having merchandise specifically for its customers. I'd like to get a little more specific with that. How did you know who your customers were? Did you do surveys? And when you did know, did you go out and find the merchandise or have it manufactured specifically for you?

**MT:** Well no, retailers can depend almost too much on surveys. We started by defining who we wanted as our customer. We exclusively defined them as a sophisticated person who lived on the upper east side who had some travel, some taste, and some sophistication. We defined Bloomingdale's by that particular customer. We then created a synergy in all of the price points and the look, style and taste of the merchandise that would work. The customer who comes to the store to shop for her apparel should find similar things—taste, price point—in home furnishings or the children's section.

**SD:** How did you really know after defining who the customer was whether they would buy specific kinds of merchandise?

**MT:** Oh, you didn't. You'd find that out only at the cash register. Sometimes you're right and sometimes that's what a markdown is for. But retailing is also very much about risk, Steve. If the retailer is not willing to go out and say, "I believe that whether it's the maxi coat at one point or the mini skirts or country French, then they're not serving the function that we think retailers should. So when you say you believe in something then you have to back it up really with the merchandise to demonstrate it. Similarly, trying new projects such as building a catalogue or creating airport shops, it's all about trying to be a little bit ahead.

**SD:** It was also interesting to me that you were the first to really promote designer relationships.

**MT:** When we started to try and change the image of Bloomingdale's, the Fifth Avenue stores were doing line-for-line, copies of the couture. And we said we wanted to be different so we saw this new young group of designers going forth. Calvin Klein was then selling coats that he designed and we started with Calvin in the coat area. The designers who were developing and learning about their own business sought a store they thought they could be comfortable working with and I tried to build relationships. Rather than starting with a collection, I tried building them up in the stores as personalities so they could benefit enormously from the exposure.

**SD:** Essentially building brand name.

**MT:** Yes, the designer is absolutely, Steve, a brand name. You say to the customer that that shirt is from

Ralph Lauren and the customer immediately has an image, as opposed to saying that's a good shirt.

*SD:* Did you have any exclusives on the designers?

*MT:* Oh yes.

*SD:* You could absolutely benefit then from the building of their name.

*MT:* We did a couple of things with some of them. We were the first store to launch Ralph Lauren's women's line. We were the first store to have Ralph Lauren home furnishings, or Ralph Lauren's cosmetic fragrance. Over time, if you have ties to the designers, you help launch many of their things. The store is constantly looking to find ways to work with the designers to get products done especially for us. Perry Ellis did a collection for us, as a promotion, called South China Seas. You constantly try for ways of trying to make your store different. That's one of them and that's still going on.

*SD:* In essence though, that's changed a little bit, hasn't it? Some designers have now come out with a high end as well as a lower end?

*MT:* Well what you're talking about is the development of the bridge business. Designer prices got more and more expensive, so the designers developed a business called bridge. Instead of "Donna Karan," it's "DKNY." Instead of "Ralph Lauren," it's "Ralph." Instead of "Calvin Klein," it's "CK." They joined an existing group of other designer's companies, like Ellen Tracy and Anne Klein, who had already been in the bridge business. For many stores, the area just below designer is a much faster growing portion of the business. The bridge business gives you the advantage of the designer name while giving you a lower priced collection.

*SD:* Would Armani starting his own lower-end stores be included in this trend?

*MT:* Armani is really three different price points. I should have included him as one of the designers we were closely involved with. We saw him grow and develop. I say in the book that Armani was the single largest volume European designer at Bloomingdale's. Armani is really three different collections, at the very least. There's the Armani couture, Armani black label, which is in very few stores across the country. There's Armani which is called "The Collection," which is more widely distributed and that would be somewhere between bridge and designer. Then you have "Armani Exchange" which is both more popular price points and more aimed at casual wear built around denim.

*SD:* There's been a tremendous amount of consolidation of department stores recently. Most department stores reside in malls, but the malls themselves for all practical purposes are like a department store within itself. For example, Victoria's Secret takes the place of the lingerie department, etc.

**MT:** Well, let me put it two different ways. The first one is periodically someone says the department store is a dinosaur, the department store is going to disappear—that is the wave of the future. Customers look for more than just price when they are shopping, although value is clearly an important component. The department store meets a valid convenience of going to one place and buying an entire outfit. It's the convenience a woman cannot get from going to ten different stores in a mall. It is a convenience to be able to shop in one store and it meets the need of the consumers. So they will survive based on that. On the other hand, you have to learn to be a low-cost operator, and I think that's driving the consolidations and driving some changes in the structure of the stores where they're not only combining so as to create bigger stores, but they are lowering costs by combining buyer organizations. On another hand, the malls really depend on the department stores for drawing traffic, and these specialty stores feed off the traffic generated by the department stores.

The change that's happening is stores such as The Limited have become a more complex company. You have a Limited Express, a Victoria's Secret for lingerie, Structure for menswear, and a Lane Bryant for special sizes. Those have been a series of separate stores. The Limited is putting these six to eight stores together, taking 70 to 75,000 sq. ft. in some of the new malls, with all of the stores together. They've almost made The Limited into a junior department store.

**SD:** On the other hand, you have the discount retailers—the Costcos, the Wal-Marts—coming in. People will make an afternoon out of going to the Costco.

**MT:** People talk about retailing, Steve, as if it's one form of shopping and one consumer. We're a country of 240 million people. Everyone has their own ways of shopping and their own ways of what they like to buy. Now just because the Costcos are aimed at a different market than the department stores doesn't mean there isn't some overlap. But the Costcos really are the ultimate in the value appeal of the late '80s and '90s. They've really proliferated enormously. Now they're flattening out or even having comp store drops because Costcos draw from a fairly substantial distance. When they began moving into each other's turf, they flattened out the comp store growth a lot. Because they work on very narrow margins, 11% to 12 %, inevitably there is some failure. You've seen what's happened to Pace. You've seen some of the combinations coming out of that because they need large volume and you have a shake out in the large volume/lower price club industry where the number of players is dwindling. It is another form of retailing, but it doesn't have unlimited growth potential.

**SD:** Do you think that the success of the Wal-Marts and the Costcos will change the department stores? For example, department stores don't carry the electronics like they used to.

**MT:** I think that's happening anyway. I think the major competitors in electronics are the Circuit City's and the specialists in electronics. The department store can offer product differentiation in apparel a lot easier than it can offer product differentiation in electronics. There's very little reason, other than price, to shop for a camcorder.

*SD:* Let's shift now into the electronic retailing infomercial world. You said at our conference last year that if anyone had told you a year before that you'd be speaking at an infomercial conference, you would've thought they were crazy. Why don't you talk about how you first discovered in Bloomingdale's the effects of infomercials?

*MT:* I think I commented then I was surprised in the sudden pick up in demand for juicers from Mr. Juiceman and the steamers from the steamer infomercial. It was apparent to me that people who watched infomercials would also look to the department stores for some of the products, rather than simply buying them through television. I felt then, and I feel now, even more strongly, that the direction of the future was really the combination of the infomercial with an ability to sell the product in stores as well.

*SD:* You were involved with QVC at a relatively early level.

*MT:* I was involved really with Diane Von Furstenberg. I brought her down to QVC.

*SD:* So you're the one who took Diane down there, and then she took Barry Diller.

*MT:* That's right. The *New Yorker* article about Barry comments on that. We were all struck by QVC's enormous potential. We helped put together Diane's first apparel presentation for QVC.

*SD:* One thing that's never been sold successfully on infomercials is clothing. I've always maintained that clothing would be a nightmare to sell on television because you have different colors, you have different sizes, and people have a hard enough time finding something that fits just right in a store. Returns could be potentially terrible. But you have the inside...

*MT:* Steve, I can answer that quickly. In terms of infomercials, first. The value of an infomercial is the ability to repeat it. The only kind of clothing that would work on an infomercial is something nonseasonal with a very long life. The most basic thought is: turtlenecks, athletic apparel, etc. It's not a natural venue for selling apparel. I think the experience of some of the home shopping channels is to sell a lot but then get a lot back because the woman gets the dress home and it doesn't fit right, regardless of the price.

*SD:* What else can you tell us about what you've learned about apparel on QVC for example? What works, what doesn't work, what doesn't have return problems, what does?

*MT:* Diane Von Furstenberg has clearly been very successful where you had a combination of a designer name and attractive prices on silk merchandise. I was also responsible for bringing Saks Fifth Avenue to QVC. That has worked, in terms of good sales response, in bringing in a very satisfactory result. This is how a retailer can make money supplying QVC. There has been much discussion, and appropriately, that you can't have two sets of markups and give the right price to the consumer. Someone's going to have to figure out an accommodation in the pricing structure that can work for both.

*SD:* Would the retailers have to have their own labels?

*MT:* There's no sense for a retailer to sell a Liz Claiborne, or an Estee Lauder to QVC. The only thing that would ever work for retailers would be private label products specially made for that retailer. We also did home furnishings with Diane which did not work, partly because they had some problems sizing and getting the goods in on time. Not everything works. We made an infomercial that didn't work.

*SD:* Somebody develops a successful infomercial and creates a winning product. There's been a tremendous amount of controversy about what you do with it on a retail level. Some people have said that if you get it into the discount stores, the Costcos, the Wal-Marts, etc., you are going to move a lot more volume with the television ads driving the sales. On the other hand, you don't really create a brand name by doing that. What would be the best way to market infomercial products at retail with the show driving sales?

*MT:* I don't think, Steve, the answers are the same for every kind of product, nor is it the same for any point in time. If you're building a brand of spa cosmetics, for example, I think you'd be much better distributing it with the service that is tied in with a department store. Some types of appliances might work better with a mass store distribution. Or you may have a product that you introduce on an infomercial that goes through the classic cycles and then after a year or two at department stores, as the product begins to run down, you move to the second stage, into more mass marketing. So there are different ways that can work. I think that both the infomercial world and the electronic shopping world prices had to be lower than the department stores. I think it is just now being realized that in some cases it can be the same. On the other hand, if they were to take a product they were promoting and offer it to the Costcos, I doubt if the Costcos would be very happy to have the same products at the same price as in the infomercial.

*SD:* If you take something like the Jet Stream Oven, its price is not substantially that different at the discount store as it is on TV. With Jet Stream you're looking at $299 on television including some extra accessories, and with a few less accessories you can find it at the Costco for around $229. The other thing that I've heard is that by going to the mass merchants, you're not at the bid of the department stores telling you what price they'll buy your product for.

*MT:* In some cases, you have a real advantage. The other thing that I find people are doing is, as in the case of the Juiceman, one model is sold electronically and then a smaller model is released at retail to take advantage of the exposure you get on the air. This may be an area worth exploring, as you have a separate product line, yet you're still building the name and the reputation with the electronic media.

*SD:* What other type of products launched through infomercials would be advised to start retail distribution in retail?

*MT:* Skin care. Most haven't worked and I suspect at some point some will. I also think that some sort of specialty appliances, whether it's a juicer or an iron, or certainly the vacuum cleaner. I think an infomercial is successful particularly when you can have a host demonstrate the benefit of the product. It's hard for a consumer going through a store to see quite all the great features of a vacuum cleaner. If you make that kind of fun, and yet have the chance to seriously tell the customer all it can do, that's where the electronic media works well.

*SD:* A tremendous amount of the cosmetic companies buy their display space in department stores. Tell me a little how that works and how somebody from the outside gets into the department store.

*MT:* The major brands in the cosmetic industry essentially have long standing relationships with the stores. They supply the product. And though the manufacturer supplies the sales staff, it is jointly paid for by the stores and the supplier. So the stores have minimum risk and the major brands are supplied the real estate and the prestige of the store. It works well because the actual cost of the product leads them to spend considerable dollars on marketing the product. It would not be easy for someone to get a product in a department store because, you're right, they'd have to get the space. It would be easier for a Revlon, or someone else, who already has the space, to make an infomercial work through retail, although we have said publicly, we are working on a new cosmetic line.

*SD:* Through an infomercial?

*MT:* Yes.

*SD:* Before we talk about your new venture, why, after woks had been one of the big successes in the early infomercial industry, did you decide to come out with a Thai wok infomercial?

*MT:* We needed something, we felt, to make the infomercial work to build up the retail sale, which may or may not have been good logic. What turned out was that the Thai food sold and the Wok sold separately. But not on the infomercial.

Steve, if I were to ask you, what percent of infomercials are successful, meaning they make money off the infomercial itself, what would you say?

*SD:* Less and less at this point. I would venture to say probably 1 out of 15.

*MT:* I'm fascinated because I always figured it was 1 out of 5. I'm sure you're more right than I am. So the infomercial has to really generate retail sales, but it also has to generate enough of a response to justify the exposure on the air. Whether conceptually it could be argued that woks were overexposed, or the approach which was taken, which was essentially soft-sell, didn't work, I suspect I would not do that again. I would try to have more urgency, more sell, more endorsement.

We are absolutely not discouraged. As we speak, we are exploring who to work with on making an infomercial sometime next year. The product is there, the distribution is there, and will tie in an infomercial with retail. Our own projections regard the infomercial as the plus and a selling tool, but not as the basis for putting a company together.

**SD:** I think you're right on the money with that plan. Media rates keep going up and unless you have the retail in place, as you're qualified to do, it's going to be tough to make the front-end work.

**MT:** What do you think is going to happen with the proliferation of the electronic shopping, HSN and QVC?

**SD:** My opinion has always been that the talk of the 500 channel universe is overblown quite a bit.

**MT:** I think the whole area of electronic shopping is overblown.

**SD:** When people talk to me, or I read in the press about a 500 channel universe, my first reaction is that 400 of those channels are going to be pay-per-view events and it's going to create the demise of the video store, more than anything else.

**MT:** I think people's imaginations are taken with this idea of electronic shopping, and I think that it's going to grow. I've been going around the country saying that if you view the whole world last year of home shopping channels, and all the infomercials, that was less than a $3 billion business. I'm sure you have the same numbers I do on that. All of electronic shopping is roughly 20% of JC Penney's sales, or less than half a percent of total retail in the United States. It puts things in proper proportion. If home shopping grows dramatically, and it can, it's still not a major enough form of retailing to justify all the media attention it gets. On the other hand it will grow. It will change.

It's never been clarified whether this is 500 channels across the country, or do you mean in New York City you will have a choice of 500 channels, which is impossible. Nobody can choose from 500 channels. So, yes there will be more choice, there will be more channels aimed at specific viewer types. But I think this is much overblown. I think even in the case of interactive television, while it interests me, it has been tried a number of times, unsuccessfully. There is a long way to go between where we are today, and this information highway with a black box in everyone's home. First of all, who's going to pay for the black boxes? So I'm interested. I'm going to keep on top of it. I think it's going to grow, but I think this enormous enthusiasm may be a little premature.

*SD:* In my mind, the scenario I see in maybe 10 or 15 years down the line, might be an interactive system where somebody is interested in a lawnmower and they can look up on their system and find out how different lawn mowers are rated by Consumer Reports. They could then view maybe a 15-minute video clip on the benefits of each one, and then automatically scan retailers or cataloguers all over the country to find the best price, receiving it by Fed-Ex within two days.

*MT:* I think the Time-Warner interactive experiment tested out very much that practice. What's interesting for me is to have some of our key managers from Bloomingdale's move into this field of electronic marketing, with a little of my encouragement. Gordon Cook who did our mail order is heading the Time Warner effort. Jim Held is Sr. Vice President of QVC, working on the Fashion Channel and QVC. There are going to be big opportunities and some Bloomingdale's trained executives will be there to take part in it.

*SD:* I've heard rumors of QVC developing their own product lines. The products would launch on QVC and if successful an infomercial would be created around it. I assume after the infomercial they'd launch at retail.

*MT:* I think QVC very much is going to be in that.

*SD:* The one fascinating thing that I think I wrote about years ago about QVC is that because you get instantaneous reaction when pitching a product and actually see what buttons are causing the consumers to pick up the phone and dial, it can serve as a very effective blueprint for knowing what hooks need to be in an infomercial.

*MT:* QVC has an enormous advantage in the sense of their having an opportunity without an enormous expense of testing product. One of the things that I discovered QVC had not been particularly successful in was selling books. I happened to bring Robert Taylor Blackford down and introduce the format where the author appeared, talked about the book and signed copies. It was very successful. It demonstrated you could do that. Some other authors who have written books were not quite of the same sales appeal. I'm going to sell my book out of QVC. It's fun. We'll see how that works.

*SD:* Let's talk just a little bit about the kind of margins that the various types of retailers work off of.

*MT:* Well, you have to differentiate between markup and margin, the margin being the number after you take the mark down. Department stores typically look to have a margin. They don't always succeed. But if you bring a product into a store, they are going to be looking for a margin between 40 and 50 percent.

*SD:* What about returns?

*MT:* Returns are all reduction from the margin. If you have to mark it down when you take it back, you're an extra expense. If you are selling jewelry you're going to get less returns than if you're selling dresses.

*SD:* How do the returns work for the manufacturer? Does the store have the right to send back all unsold merchandise?

*MT:* No. The manufacturer, when he sells the product to the store, expects the store to sell it or to mark it down. If the manufacturer has a very large business with the store, he may try to develop a joint strategy for solving stock problems or mark down problems. But it's done not as a matter of course.

*SD:* What's your timeframe on your beauty line?

*MT:* We hope to be out in spring sometime. The product is done. The packaging is done. We think we are very far along on the retail distribution.

*SD:* Is it your intention to have it in retail as the infomercial hits?

*MT:* Yes.

*SD:* Will they also be able to order the product directly on the infomercial?

*MT:* Yes, I think it should work. I think it's all part of a marketing matter. You sound surprised. Do you think it should be another way? Do you think the infomercial should hit first?

*SD:* It depends on what you're ultimately trying to do. It's been demonstrated over and over again that as soon as you let your product into retail, it kills your direct response sales. If you're prepared for that and you're looking to drive the retail sales and not make a profit off TV than it's fine.

*MT:* What makes you think the product has to be the same? The infomercial can be a kit, a package of everything together. The cosmetic business, the retail sales is sort of one-on-one.

*SD:* You're saying put a starter kit together on the front-end. I think that makes a lot of sense. That's never been done before.

*MT:* It should have been.

*SD:* It should have been, but it hasn't. Generally they'll sell the same product, with the exception of the Juiceman, to my knowledge, they'll sell the same product off television as they do on the back end. Changing the subject, does Barry Diller have a vision of where electronic retailing is going, or is he along for the ride with everyone else?

**MT:** I believe he knows where he would like it to be. I can't tell you I'm privy, except I think he sees it.

**SD:** Thank you very much.

# A.J. KHUBANI

At the time of this interview, Telebrands was grossing over $100 million per year. Beginning from his kitchen table in 1987, creating direct response print ads, A.J. Khubani added direct response television spots and retail distribution—within a short time building up a real marketing machine. He is known as getting products on the air and into retail distribution faster than anyone else. Although on the surface his manner is very gentle, he is a fierce competitor who has employed some of the country's leading patent attorneys.

*Steve Dworman:* Why don't you give me a little background of where you came from and how you started?

*A.J. Khubani:* My father started an importing business in 1961. When I graduated college in 1982, I joined his importing company. I was always curious about mail order. I'd think that these guys are working on incredible margins. They're buying things for a dollar in the Far East and selling them for $10 to $20 in print. That seems like a great business. So I figured I'd give it a try. I made fantastic connections in the Far East. I could buy practically anything. So in 1983, just one year out of college, at the age of 23, I ran my first print ad. It broke even. But it was very exciting to see this mail coming in.

*SD:* What was the product?

*AJK:* The product was an AM/FM headphone stereo, like a Walkman. Walkmans were very hot back then. And I sold them for $9.95. I was buying them in the Far East for $4. I ran the first ad in the *National Enquirer*. I bought a junior page for $7,000. I had $20,000 to play with, that I had earned playing the stock market in college. I was living at home. I said I'm going to take this $20,000 and try something. The AM/FM radios I bought from my father's importing company on credit. I worked out of his office in New York. He didn't charge me rent and I did everything myself. I didn't hire any people. I opened the mail, typed the shipping labels and went in on the weekend and shipped everything out. I'd write the ads myself and run out and have them typeset. The first year, 1983, I did $60,000 of business.

*SD:* With the same item?

*AJK:* Yeah. I tried a few different versions of the ad. Nothing really made money. In 1984, I tried a few other items and again, really didn't do much, a couple hundred thousand dollars in sales and didn't do any money. I kept on turning this $20,000 over and over again, just didn't make any money. I was determined to do something. In 1985 I came up with an ad for massage slippers. I sold it in print for $9.95. I bought them in the Far East for $1.50. That ad made money. By the middle of the year, around July, I made about a hundred thousand dollars in profit. I thought, this is a great business. I was 25 years old and made a hundred thousand dollars on just wasting a few print ads.

*SD:* Using an 800 number or mail?

*AJK:* Just mail with a coupon.

*SD:* You were doing the fulfilling yourself?

*AJK:* I was shipping everything myself. I hired my grandfather to work for me and a couple other people. I kept it real low cost. Then, towards the end of the year, 1985, I ran an ad on a 35mm camera for $10 and I was buying them in Taiwan for $4 and that ad did fantastic! The year 1985 ended with one and half million dollars in sales. Ended up making a profit of about a quarter millions dollars. Seemed like easy business. In 1986, I kind of got the hang of this, finding items and running them, writing the print ad. I always wrote all the ads myself. In 1986, I did $11,000,000 in business in print. And made a net profit of $3,000,000.

*SD:* A lot different than the infomercial business.

*AJK:* I said this is great. I ran out, bought a nice house, bought a nice car, did everything. In 1987, I decided this print business seemed pretty easy. How can I expand the business? What else can I tackle? I remember seeing all these ads on TV. I said maybe I should try some TV. I started out by partnering up with Mike Sander, who is now a partner in TV Products. Started a joint venture with him in 1987, called Value Connection. I owned 80 percent. Mike Sander owned 20 percent. And I gave Mike three items to make commercials on right away. One was a product called Easy Cycle, another was called Flea Zapper, and the third one was a product called Amber Vision. I gave him those three commercials to do and he did the three commercials, did a great job. Actually Collette Liantonio produced all three commercials. All three commercials hit. I said this is easier than the print business. The

Flea Zapper I had patent problems. I ran it for about a month and I had to stop. I wasn't that knowledgeable about patents back then. Amber Vision was phenomenal in 1987 and 1988 on TV. This was two years before [Joe] Sugarman started running his BluBlockers on TV.

*SD:* And you were running a spot?

*AJK:* I was running a spot, ended up selling just through mail order almost two million pieces. It was fantastic. That was the first item I ever ran. Everybody knew the brand Amber Vision. I said, this is a brand name and I bet if we put this into retail stores it would sell. So that's when I got interested into going into wholesale. I took it around myself and started calling some accounts. I spoke to Bob Schnabel over at Fitness Quest. Bob said, "The formula's working for us. We're selling this Easy Glider into retail and the formula really works. You advertise it on TV, bring it into retail. Make a lot of money." The stories he was telling me about how much money he was making in retail really inspired me to look into this retail business further. He told me about a rep group I should use, Leisure Marketing, who took some of their products into retail. Leisure Marketing put us into Herman's Sporting Goods, the first account we were able to break in. Amber Vision was really tough to get into retail.

*SD:* Why is that?

*AJK:* First of all, the stores were really not to into this "Seen on TV" business. To them, this was a company bringing in one pair of sunglasses, one color and one style. They'd say, "This is ridiculous. I got a whole rack of sunglasses. I've got a reliable sunglass manufacturer. He gives me a hundred different styles. He sends his guys in on a weekly basis to refurbish the rack. He pays for the rack. Why do I have to buy one pair of sunglasses?" Nobody wanted to buy it. We were pounding doors all across the country. Finally, Leisure Marketing asked me to come down personally. I went down to the meeting with the buyer. And I was giving the guy the best sales pitch I could possibly give and the guy wouldn't listen to me. By luck, the president walked into the office and said, "Amber Vision sunglasses. I've seen that on TV a hundred times. Put it into the stores." So I said fine, we've got an order now. I didn't have a package. What am I going to do? I had mail order boxes and I had to put it into stores. I've got an order from Herman's Sporting Goods so what am I going to do? I had to do something quickly. People are going to want to try on glasses. They're going to want to look at themselves in the mirror. I can't do all that, it's too expensive. So finally I came to the conclusion, let me just slap a label on the brown box and we'll put them into a floor display and send them out that way. We put it into the stores and they sold out immediately. The one SKO sunglasses outsold five times the entire rack of sunglasses that they had in there. It was unbelievable. Just by a lot of hard work and pounding on doors, and telling the story of what happened at Herman's we were able to get more and more distribution. And we found the formula: get it on TV, bring it out to retail. It works tremendously and we've been following that formula ever since.

**SD:** What were some of the surprises you learned about retail being a novice back in that time?

**AJK:** The surprises were the amount of chargebacks and returns you get from retailers. It's just incredible. I always felt that you buy a product for $3, you sell it to an account for $6, you make $3. You don't make $3. The net profit, the profitability was a big misconception.

**SD:** What is the average return and chargebacks from stores?

**AJK:** The average varies from industry to industry. Within our industry, we're running 10 to 15 percent.

**SD:** That's pretty close to what you get on TV isn't it?

**AJK:** Yeah, we get a little bit less on TV. We're getting 10 to 15 percent chargebacks and we just figure that into the numbers. There are various reasons for it. First of all, these items are fairly short-lived. They have very short life cycles, most of them do, because competition comes in and undercuts your price. So the first type of disillusion comes from marking down your product. We'll come out with a product for $19.95 on TV, wholesale it for $12.50. We'll get that for a period of three months and finally, because of such cheap competition being out there, we need to reduce our price to $9. When you mark down your product, you need to give a markdown to all the product on the shelf. Say I have a hundred thousand pieces out there, I have a $3.50 price reduction. I've got to pass that on to the people who have it on the shelf. Now I've given them $350,000 of mark-down money. That happens constantly. Of course, you have your returns that come in. People return things very easily at retail. The return rate at retail is always higher than it is at mail order. Just because of the ease of returning it. The mail order customer has to wrap it up, call UPS or go to the post office. It's a headache.

**SD:** How long did you continue with Leisure Marketing?

**AJK:** It was pretty short. They weren't really that successful with Amber Vision. We kind of went out on our own, hired our own internal sales people and actually did a better job than they were doing. They wanted Amber Vision nationally and they weren't capable of doing it. Leisure Marketing has a very good rep for the sporting goods industry. They were very instrumental in taking ThighMaster to retail. Actually, we just hired them again to take AbFlex into the sporting goods accounts. We're not that strong with the sporting goods accounts, but they are.

**SD:** At that point, when you got it into the first store, you let Leisure Marketing go and then you did it yourself?

**AJK:** We kept Leisure Marketing on for Herman's Sporting Goods. We figured out that they weren't strong in the mass merchandising, so we said we would handle the mass merchandising, you stick with the sporting goods category. We really didn't let them go. We just isolated what they were good at. I brought on my brother Andy, and Keith Mirchandani, and these guys went out and pounded the pavement and started getting in more and more accounts.

**SD:** Calling on the accounts yourself, the major retailers, tell me about your reaction to that. What kind of terms they were looking for, return privileges, guaranteed sales. That can be pretty scary to somebody without huge amounts of capital.

**AJK:** First of all, all the terms were net 30. What I did initially, because I saw the sales results at Herman's, and nobody wanted to listen, I told our sales people at the time, any first order into the account is a guaranteed sale. I knew once they got a taste of the sales of it, they would continue to buy. The first order would blow through and re-orders were not guaranteed sales.

**SD:** That was smart.

**AJK:** How much of a risk was there? I knew the thing was going to sell.

**SD:** And they went along with that when they saw how great the results were?

**AJK:** Once they saw the results, they were buying it like crazy. To date, we have sold over 15,000,000 pairs of Amber Vision.

**SD:** What was the wholesale and retail on it?

**AJK:** The retail was $10 on TV. The wholesale was $6.50 initially. This will be our last year with Amber Vision, basically closing it out for $2 apiece.

**SD:** In retail you sold it for the $10 also?

**AJK:** Initially $10. It came down. A lot of competition came in. I stuck to the box concept, which nobody had ever done before with mass merchandising. They were always on a rack. Nobody ever bought sunglasses in a box. But we kept it that way and it continued to work. Then, later when BluBlockers came to retail, they did the same thing. They put it in a box.

**SD:** Why do you think that works?

**AJK:** First of all, you make it different. It's not just another pair of sunglasses. This is something special. It comes packaged in a box, plus you've educated people from TV. They've seen it, they know what it is. It's not just a fashion aspect. They're buying it for the utility.

**SD:** When you were gearing up in those kinds of quantities, what did you do monetarily? Did you have to get financing at that point?

**AJK:** Luckily, we were profitable enough to finance everything ourselves. I funded everything to our profits. I kept all the money in the business. I never took out much for myself, except for that first year when I went a little bit crazy. But after that, kept it in the business. If we were going to be getting into retail, I needed to keep this money in the business. I took just the bare minimum amount out of the company for myself.

**SD:** I would assume you were still running your direct response spots for Amber Vision?

**AJK:** No, actually, we were so slow, moving it from TV into retail. The TV campaign died down completely in 1988. I only had one solid account in 1988, that was Herman's Sporting Goods. It just died a natural death on TV. But it continued to sell in retail, 1989, 1990 and so on. Amber Vision was very profitable for us. I had a cost of the thing in the package of a dollar and was selling it for $6.50. That's a nice profit margin. Because of those profit margins, we were able to finance our retail growth. In June of 1994, I finally got outside financing. We just couldn't keep up anymore. Now I have a $25 million bank line. It's very difficult to convince a bank to give this kind of business financing, because they don't understand it. That was a big challenge. I had been looking for financing since 1990. I could show them great statements, great profitability. But the banks couldn't understand the business. They couldn't comprehend it. They said, "You don't have a line. You're not selling a line of toys or shavers or garments. We don't understand this business. One minute you're selling sunglasses, the next minute you're selling car wax, the next you're selling a cooking gadget. This is not a line. This business seems too risky to us. You may have been profitable, but you have to come up with new items all the time. How do we know you're going to continue to come up with new items?" So it was extremely difficult.

**SD:** How do you answer that?

**AJK:** The answer is, here's our track record. Every year we come up with new items. Every year we have something to sell. We've never had a unprofitable year. We've always made money. We've always found items. And I think we can continue to do this.

**SD:** So what happened after Amber Vision?

**AJK:** In 1990, we started to really progress. In 1988 and 1989 we were very slow in retail. Just a few million dollars. In 1990, we got up to $6 million in retail distribution. The next big item at retail was the cat and mouse watch in 1990, which was a huge direct response success.

**SD:** Describe what that is for the people who didn't see it.

*AJK:* The cat and mouse watch is a watch with an illustration of a cat on it and the second hand was a mouse that went around. And the cat was in a position where it looked like it was trying to catch the mouse. It sounds ridiculous. Where I found this item is a story within itself. Believe me, if someone had walked in here with that item and said, "A.J. You should do a TV commercial on this," I would have kicked them out. What happened on this was a guy named Harold Schwartz, who was a former president of Hanover Direct, he was recently hired as president of Joan Cook. The guy that runs my fulfillment was very good, close friends with Harold Schwartz. Harold, after going to Joan Cook, said he would like to meet me. I went down to meet him. He said, "A.J., I have a great idea. I have this catalog. I can only make so much money off this catalog, but I have information in this catalog which I think can be very valuable to you. I can tell you what my hottest items are. I can show you my numbers. And I can tell you if something is really blowing out that's novel, that you could take into print or maybe onto TV and maybe into retail. I'm going to show you my first item." And that was the cat and mouse watch. I said this is never going to sell. He said, "A.J., look at my numbers. Not only is it the best item in the catalog, it's the best item we've had in the past five years. We're selling it for $44. I know you could make this thing in the Far East for $3.50." And we did. I gave it a shot. We put it on TV. We were selling 60,000 pieces a week off of spot.

*SD:* At what price point?

*AJK:* At $19.95. It was so hot. And we took it out to retail. I had very limited retail distribution at that time. I was selling it at $10 wholesale. I wasn't smart enough to sell it at $12.50. We could have sold it at $12.50. We ended up selling, just through retail distribution about a half million pieces. Today, if I had that item, we would have sold at least five to ten million easy, with our retail distribution.

*SD:* Bring it back.

*AJK:* That was 1990, it's 1995 now. It might be time to bring it back. That one really helped us out. Then, we went out aggressively, constantly looking for the next TV item, which started to become more difficult for us to do. It wasn't like in 1987 where the first three were winners. It was increasingly more difficult to come up with TV winners. And we started seeing these infomercials popping up all over the place. And I said no one is doing these infomercial products in two minutes, nobody's taking them out to retail, why don't we just attack these items? Anything that looked good in an infomercial that we thought we could buy cheap enough and sell in spot and bring it out to retail we did. And that formula was terrific. Because you had a very high likelihood of hitting with a spot success if it was a success at infomercial. Worked like a charm and really helped us build the business further. We continued to come up with winners. We continued to supply the retailers with winner after winner after winner. And we continued to build our relationships. And the retailers love us. We bring them hot items consistently.

*SD:* Were there any television items that you tried in spot from an infomercial that didn't work?

*AJK:* The three-step tooth whitening system worked well. There was Natural White on TV, we came up with Dazzle. That did tremendous. The ColorSmart was terrific. The Color Coat was on TV from National Media, and we came up with ColorSmart and put it on spot and brought it out to retail. The Jack LaLanne Mini-Stepper in 1992 off of the Super Step. National Media had the Super Step with Bruce Jenner. We came up with the Mini-Stepper and that did terrific. Even stuff that didn't work for us in spot, like the juicer didn't work for us that well in spot, we put it in retail and blew it out.

*SD:* Do you think it was too high of a price point for spot?

*AJK:* Yeah. The food dehydrator did not work for us in spot. But we sold probably a million pieces at retail. What we did was, anything that was on an infomercial, we just came up with our own version of it and sold it to retailers. The infomercials were making the category hot.

*SD:* At that time, there were probably a lot of infomercial companies that weren't very happy because you beat them to the punch.

*AJK:* They weren't taking them to retail.

*SD:* That's true, at that time they weren't.

*AJK:* There was an opportunity there. Now, things are getting much more competitive at retail. Since last year we've taken the strategy that we want to get the original infomercial product. It really gives you a competitive edge. Last year, with the SmartMop, there are so many knock-offs of the SmartMop out there, even Guthy-Renker did one with Victor Grillo called DynaMop, which Greg calls the DynaFlop. But what was even more interesting, the two largest mop companies in the country knocked it off. Suburbanite and Quickie, they both knocked off the SmartMop. Even with that happening, we were able to get in, using the original SmartMop and presenting it to retailers as the original SmartMop, talking about all this media behind it and get a higher price point. Everybody was out there with a $6 price point. We went out at $8.50. And we sold, last year, three and a half or four million mops. To date we've sold over five million mops. With all this competition out there. That really convinced us that the original is the way to go. We can get more money for it, we have to pay a royalty, but the sell-through is better and the life of the product is usually longer. These knock-offs come in and they go out. We're still selling them like crazy. It's still one of Wal-Mart's top items. Then all of a sudden, it was like an influx. Every infomercial company all of a sudden in 1994 started coming to us. It really expanded our business. We got the Miracle Thaw from TV Products. I had a big litigation with them in 1989 regarding some other product. We've been arch enemies since that time. With the TopsyTail, that was when it really came to a head. They came out with the TopsyTail, which is a patented item. Because of this on-going battle, I said anything they come out with I'm going to try and hurt their business. So I came out with the PonyFlip, which got around the TopsyTail patent. But they sued me anyway under the Doctrine of Equivalence. So they came in very strongly, they spent almost two million dollars in legal fees. I spent over one million dollars in legal fees and I ended up winning. Next winter, in December of 1994, they came knocking at my door, "A.J., how would you like to take our product to retail." I was very happy to talk to them.

*SD:* That's quite a compliment to you.

*AJK:* I think what convinced them, was, first of all, we knocked them out of a ton of accounts. They had the original TopsyTail, they had a five month jump on us. We came in and got the Wal-Marts and the KMarts and all the major distribution on it with our PonyFlips. I think that's one thing that convinced them. And I think another reason they probably came to us was if they were dealing with Telebrands, Telebrands wouldn't be competing with them. I think that made sense too. We worked out a deal they were very happy with, I was very happy with. We'll end up selling almost five million Miracle Thaws this year.

*SD:* From not knowing anything about retail, to in such a short time having such a powerhouse retail distribution system, how did you accomplish that?

*AJK:* It hasn't been without its growing pains. First of all, we ran out of space very quickly. I originally had a 30,000 square foot distribution center in Roanoke, Virginia that we used for our mail order. I was running out and renting any available space we could find. We ended up with five warehouses for a total of over a hundred thousand square feet spread all over the place and had trucks running back and forth. Last year we bought a new distribution center in Salem, Virginia. Two hundred thousand square feet. Then, staffing up, getting the right people, the right systems in place, setting up with EDI, getting a national sales manager. Getting our regional sales managers in place, starting to have our national sales meetings and regional sales meetings. All kinds of stuff. It's a whole business.

*SD:* You're one of the few people in this business I think that has successfully gone from being totally an entrepreneur, doing everything yourself to all of a sudden running an organization. That's tough.

*AJK:* It is tough, and it is extremely challenging and that's one of the things I love about it. It's not the same old thing I was doing ten years ago. I'm not just sitting here writing print ads and putting them out there and opening the mail. Now I'm running an organization.

*SD:* Have you found people that can do the print ads as well as you were able to?

*AJK:* No I haven't. And quite frankly, our print business has suffered quite a bit. We don't have much of a print business. Last year, we ran the Whisper XL in print, which did about $10 million in print. But I wrote that ad personally. It was a huge success for us.

*SD:* So that's where one of your major talents is.

*AJK:* I never get a chance to utilize it. I very seldomly do. I just started getting back into that a little bit. I want to see that pick up. The print business is a great source for driving the rest of the business. If something works in print, it will work on TV. It works on TV, it will work at retail.

*SD:* Give me a quick lesson on what you've learned about print, as far as do you buy the ads at remnant rates? What seems to work better?

*AJK:* You buy at the mail order rate or the remnant rate. Certain magazines and publications have regular mail order rates. And some of them have remnant rates. The FSIs have remnant rates. It's really supply and demand. Everybody bids for the remnant rates and whoever pays the highest price gets it. *Parade* magazine is terrific. There's a huge circulation. You can make a lot of money if you can make it work. I'll give you an example. I had an ad in there in July of 1989, my best ad ever. At that time, I paid for a full page, full run about $210,000, which was still a lot of money for me back then. I had an ad for the Magic Hangers. I went out there in print. Just to give you an idea of how well the print did, that single print ad from *Parade* brought in a net profit of $1.7 million.

*SD:* That's after the ad was paid for?

*AJK:* After the ad, after the merchandise, I'm talking net, pre-tax $1.7 million off of one ad. People don't realize the amount of money you can make in print. I look at the magazines and papers today. There's nobody who's really doing a good job in print. Because nobody really realizes how much potential there is in print.

*SD:* Were there any other secrets or tricks you learned in print?

*AJK:* I think it's all trial and error. Just to find out which publications pull the best and sort of coming up with a system of testing and rolling out. We can today go out with a $10,000 print test. And if it looks right, we can proceed to a $3 million roll-out. Again, I learned this all myself. Nobody taught it to me. One thing really important in print, you need to know in a short period of time what your results are. On TV, you know instantaneously, because everyone calls the number. You have your results in one day. How do you know in print? You start getting a few pieces of mail today, a few pieces tomorrow, maybe a bundle the next day. How do you know how well a print ad is going to do unless you wait for two months and wait for all the response to come in?

*SD:* And?

*AJK:* We set up response curves based on history for every single publication we've ever run in. And we have those response curves. So I know that a week from the Monday after an FSI runs that I'll have 40% of my response in. So if I have a thousand orders in, I multiply it by .4 and I know what I'm going to get in. And that helps us roll out. If we're testing, within a week of the time that the test breaks, we know what it's going to do and we decide to roll out on it, based on our projections. And those response curves hold up. It's miraculous that people respond in the same way over and over again.

**SD:** When you were playing around with the ads, were there any elements that you tested more than others as far as headline, price or whatever?

**AJK:** It really depended on the item. Sometimes the price would be the big thing. Like when I first sold the 35mm camera, I sold it for ten bucks. That was a big thing in 1985. Nobody had ever heard of a 35mm camera for ten dollars, so I really played that up. Sometimes it's just the key benefit. Just like a spot, you need an attention grabber. The headline and the layout have got to do one thing...stop the reader. Think of when you read a magazine. You're flipping through it. You don't stop and read these ads unless you see something really catchy that stops you. On the 35mm camera, "35mm Camera $10.00." That will stop people.

**SD:** I remember that ad.

**AJK:** You do?

**SD:** Your impression when you read it was, how could they do this?

**AJK:** That's right. Then you tell them how. You come up with some reason why you're doing this. "National publicity campaign" was a good idea. "National publicity campaign" to promote this camera, that's why we're giving it away for ten dollars. You're giving them a reason that's logical. Not that I was able to buy them in the Far East for four dollars. Or just a headline. When I sold Amber Vision, I didn't play up the price in print. The headline was, "These are not sunglasses." And it showed a picture of sunglasses there and it made them read the ad. They're going to stop, number one. Number two, they're going to start reading the ad. And then you've got to entice them initially. And then you've got to close them. They've got to act now. They've got to order this now. They shouldn't do anything else because once they turn the page, or once they put down the magazine, you've lost the order. You've got to act right now. So deadline dates are very good, even collectibles use them all the time. You must order before this date, otherwise this offer will not be around anymore. I used it in spots a lot too. I said you must call within the next five minutes to get this extra bonus. Act now. Because if they don't act now, they may never act.

**SD:** All the elements are there in print, which translate to television. But of course, there are very few people, even now, that I think still understand that in this business. There aren't a lot of direct marketing people in this business.

**AJK:** No, there's not. It really amazed me. There's nobody really that strong in the print advertising business. I look around, there's nothing creative. People are just taking items, throwing prices and coupons and hoping that they make money. That's not the way to do it. So, I've taken a real interest in the print advertising business again. I think if we get some creativity back into print, that we could do a big job with it. I think there's a hundred million dollar business just in print. I really do.

*SD:* I think you're right.

*AJK:* Especially considering the fact that nobody's doing it. Everyone's complaining about the media rates. The biggest media in print is the FSIs.

*SD:* What does FSI mean?

*AJK:* Free Standing Inserts. Those are the coupons in your Sunday paper. That's got 53 million circulation weekly. Accounts for about 50% of all your print business. The FSIs have not gone up in price, not anywhere near where everything else has gone up. The FSIs, back in 1985 when I first started running them, I was paying $2.10 a thousand. I just booked a full run in September at $2.35 a thousand. That's nothing. It's unbelievable. We just tested a very successful print ad.

*SD:* For which product?

*AJK:* A product called Silver Lightning.

*SD:* What does it do? It's a good title.

*AJK:* Silver Lightning is an item that's been around direct response on and off. And nobody's ever done a big job with it. It's this tray that you put in the bottom of the sink. You add some baking soda, put in your silverware and it cleans it within seconds.

*SD:* I think I've seen that somewhere. Did they try and do something on TV?

*AJK:* Yeah, there's something on TV called Quick Silver. It was kind of on and off. Earlier this year, Brockway did a commercial for Silver Star. They actually took the commercial that was running in Spain and Americanized it and brought it over here. They weren't doing a big job with it. I looked at it. I said, nobody's doing a big job with it, this seems like a good item. We actually re-did a spot. We did our own spot with Robin Leech. The commercial is doing great. We've ordered a million pieces. We've already started to distribute. We sent out samples to retail. We're taking orders already. We'll start shipping in September, but we're going to do a big job with it.

*SD:* What is it that you do that enables you to get things into the stores faster than anyone?

*AJK:* Don't forget, since 1990 we've been coming up with hot items. And the retail business is really relationships. We've managed to build a good sales force. We've got over a hundred sales people on the road. And that's really it. We've come up with a new promotion. We just came up with Silver Lightning. We've got our samples ready, we got our marketing strategy ready. We sent out a memo and samples to all the salespeople. My national sales manager and Andy will go on the road. Everytime we get an item my sales managers go on the road, visit the accounts, visit the reps, walk into the accounts with them and really do a road show. And just get it in. Get the positioning, get the endcaps, whatever we have to do. We just have a very aggressive team that doesn't let it go. We know that this item is going to last for a very short period of time. We've got to milk it while it's hot. We've got a window of opportunity. We've got to hit it. If we don't hit it, we're not going to make it up four months from now. The item may be dead four months from now.

**SD:** To maintain those relationships, you've got to make good on the inventory the stores are left with in some way don't you?

**AJK:** Absolutely.

**SD:** How do you do that?

**AJK:** Nothing we sell is on a guaranteed sale anymore. Not even the first orders in. We've gotten completely away from that. We work with the accounts. Items slow down, the first thing we do is mark it down. We mark it down, try lower price point. If it still doesn't sell we mark it down and mark it down again. We continue to mark it down. 99% of the time the markdowns wipe out the inventory. Very seldomly do we have to take the goods back.

**SD:** You're giving them credit all this time when you mark down?

**AJK:** Right.

**SD:** You presented at a conference two years ago a very interesting example of, I think it was, three different versions of your tooth whitener spot. Talk a little bit about the differences between them and the surprises at what worked and what didn't work. Two of them had Morgan Fairchild. One of them was a real glossy version and the other was more of a direct response with her. The third one was without Morgan, but real direct response. If I remember, the one that was a combination of Morgan and direct response far out-performed the other two.

**AJK:** What happened was Guthy-Renker came out with their Perfect Smile, and it was a hit and we heard right away that it was doing big numbers. We started looking into it right away. We wanted to market a similar product. So we got the product and we saw the patent and couldn't figure out a way to get around the patent. My lawyers were doing a patent search, going crazy trying to find something. And they found another patent. This guy, Dr. George, in Atlanta, Georgia. I called up Dr. George and he tells me this story about how Vanna White is ripping him off. He's got this patent on this item. Vanna White and Guthy-Renker are infringing on his patent and he called up Guthy-Renker and tried to do something with them, asked them for a royalty, sent them a copy of the patent and got blown off. I think about that and I said, boy these guys are really stupid. This is like a loose end that is perfect for me to take advantage of. So I go down and meet with the guy. It turns out, both the patents issued very close to one another. And what it had come down to in the lawsuit was who conceived the idea first, which is almost impossible to get proof of. They put into use at the same time according to the papers they submitted. They both got the patent in the same year. The patent office screwed up is what happened. They shouldn't have issued both patents. They both cover the same invention. So after giving it some thought and discussing it with my attorneys, I said let me license this patent from Dr. George and let me sue Guthy-Renker for patent infringement. If I sued Guthy-Renker for patent infringement, the most likely scenario is that we would settle and end up cross-licensing one another. And that's exactly how the scenario played out. It was all pre-planned right from the beginning that we would end up settling and cross-licensing one another.

*SD:* Did anyone end up paying anyone else money?

*AJK:* I'm not allowed to disclose that. Guthy-Renker really screwed up, they should have paid this guy, 10¢ a unit, 20¢ a unit. He would have gone away and they would have had the whole item to themselves. The second thing that happened, when I met Guthy-Renker at ERA [Electronic Retailing Association] that year, I said you know guys, between us, we own the patent on this item. Let's work together and really control the market here. Their response was, you have to go talk to Victor Grillo. And that was the end of it. I explained this to Victor. Victor said, "A.J., you turn the whole thing over to me, I'll give you a quarter a piece and that's the end of it." He was sitting on a high horse. He was the king and I was like a peon to him at the time. And not only that, but he, for some odd reason, he thought he could beat me at this lawsuit. At that time, the TopsyTail lawsuit was going on. He said, "We're going to put you out of business anyway because we're going to win this TopsyTail lawsuit and you're going to be liable for $15 million in damages." At the time he didn't even want to think about working with Telebrands. So that didn't go anywhere. It's unfortunate, because we ended up doing a much bigger job with it than they did. Getting back to the creative, Dr. George has a very heavy southern accent. But I thought there was a certain benefit to having the true inventor in the commercial. And I had read recently about certain hometown commercials with these guys that can't speak well, but end up doing a good job because they're credible. Like Carvel Ice Cream. This guy used to do the commercial, the owner, he was terrible. The commercials were very effective because he was credible. I thought Dr. George could end up being credible, even though he didn't speak well, and he had this heavy southern accent. The commercial worked okay. It came in a little bit over break even. I said we have something here. Let's get a celebrity and do a commercial. After two months of searching and negotiating, we finally ended up with Morgan Fairchild. We did the commercial. I went out and hired more upscale producers, these guys from DRTV. They did the commercial and the commercial didn't perform any better CPO wise as compared to the original one, even with Morgan Fairchild. It was upscale, it was slow, it wasn't hard hitting, the way I would have done it.

**SD:** That's another case where you kind of drop back and let others do it because you're busy with the business.

**AJK:** They did it, and I ended up with a better credit card percentage, about 10% better. But still, the commercial wasn't making money. And I said this commercial sucks. We have to make a more direct response commercial. So I was viewing the two commercials over and over again to figure out what to do. I said, that first spot we had was really a good spot. The only thing wrong with it is Dr. George. And this Morgan Fairchild spot, in the beginning is very good and Morgan at the end is very good. What we're going to do is take the beginning and the end of the second commercial and wrap it around the first commercial. That's all we did and the thing took off.

**SD:** Price and everything else was the same?

**AJK:** Everything else was the same. I sat at the edit myself for two days. We picked up the pace a little bit. We did a new voiceover. I personally picked the music, really lively music and put it together. And at the same time was prepared to roll out at retail with this thing. I figured, even based on what the infomercial is doing, it should sell. I said, we've already booked a half million pieces for retail distribution, let's just roll out with the commercial and see what happens. If it doesn't look that good we'll pull it back, we'll fix it up, we'll cancel some markets, whatever needs to be done. But let's just take a shot and roll out with the Dental White commercial. And that's what we did. We rolled out at two hundred thousand dollars a week without testing the last spot and the most exciting part is that it paid out.

**SD:** And drove the retail. At that point, I think Guthy-Renker had a strategy of coming out with the high-end Vanna White product and doing a low-end product also.

**AJK:** What they did to combat us, they came out with a low-end product called Smile. They were out there hustling it for $4 I think. And actually, Victor Grillo, at the meeting said, "You know what, A.J., I'm going to kill you at retail. I've got this item, I'm going to wholesale it for $3 or $4, whatever it takes to get you off the shelf." He went out there with this product, the package was lousy. It didn't look like anything. It wasn't well thought through, because his strategy was just to kill me. It didn't kill me. It didn't do anything to me. We ended up getting all the distribution. We had Morgan Fairchild, the retailers were seeing it all over TV and wanted ours. Our product sold like crazy and the Smile product didn't sell.

**SD:** Well so much for that.

**AJK:** And Victor's great strategy was that once he got me out of the market, he was going to take over the whole market with the Vanna White product, which he's trying to do now and it's too little too late. He's not doing anything with the mass merchandising.

*SD:* Let's talk for a minute about hair. What happened with hair at retail?

*AJK:* A couple of things happened. First of all, our deliveries were late. We were supposed to start shipping retailers in January and at the same time, Positive Response's deliveries were also late. And we were joint venture partners on the whole deal. We said it's more important to fill the mail order, so let's put all the combined production into filling the mail order orders. And then we'll go out to retail. Our first orders started going out in March, got on the shelf, looked very good. So we continued to bring in more hair, and put it on the retail shelf. And by the time we reached the end of April, the beginning of May, the item just dropped dead. I don't know how it happened. We've come up with theories, ideas, whatever. But the item is completely dead at retail.

*SD:* There was less being run on TV at that point wasn't there?

*AJK:* There was nothing being run on TV at that point. That could be one reason. Still, it shouldn't have died that fast. I've seen items that have been off the air a year and the products still sells at retail. We had a ton of media that was run on hair. Forget about just Perfect Hair. What about Guthy-Renker's and American Telecast. And all three combined, you probably had as much media exposure on this category as you did on the juicer. And this item should not have died this fast. But it did. Now, I've talked to people in the wig industry, they've said yeah, wigs don't sell in the summer. People don't like to stick stuff in their hair when it's hot out. They say the item will pick up again in the fall. I don't know. I will soon find out. I'm currently sitting on like a hundred eighty thousand sets of hair. And we've got the merchandise placed for the fall at a substantially reduced cost. Still at a profitable price, we're not selling it below cost, we're still making a profit on it. I've got it placed in most mass merchandisers and we'll see what happens. And we're re-selling at $29.95, which I think is a very strong price point. And it could go. It may not go. But I gave it the best possible shot.

*SD:* What do you see out there with the other two companies at retail?

*AJK:* Guthy-Renker, I don't see them any place at all. And American Telecast was making a big push into salons and quite frankly I don't know what they're doing. What's amazing though, is that the item is still selling in catalog. The catalogs I have it in, they're very happy, the item is continuing to sell. So I don't know.

*SD:* That is amazing. Do you have any estimate on how many hair units across the board it ended up selling within the period of time it was being blanketed on TV?

*AJK:* I really have no idea. I think I ended taking in a total of 350,0000 pieces. Now, of 350,000, I have 180,000 left. So just under half sold. I sold in April and May when the item was dead. The other thing was, I was wholesaling the item at $40. Now, I'm wholesaling it for roughly $20. And the price point is now $29.95 versus $69.95. I think it's going to sell. It's not going to end up being a big problem. Sure, if everything went right, I would have sold a million. Based on our previous experience with other TV items and TV exposure and the initial reads we were getting in March, I should have sold a million. But there's an unknown factor and the item dropped dead. It was something out of our control.

*SD:* Does that happen often?

*AJK:* Not this badly. I have never seen anything drop dead like this before. We'll get out of it, we'll be okay. The overall campaign we might end up breaking even on it or making a few bucks. The thing that really killed Positive Response was that they had these projections with their shareholders and they got upset when they didn't come through. They don't want to hear about how or why we misprojected. They don't want to hear any excuses. We're supposed to be God. A public company is supposed to know exactly what they're doing. And nothing should go wrong.

*SD:* When you're dealing in those kinds of volumes though, with something like the hair that required processing and everything else, it's got to be so difficult to try to keep your hands into everything, from the manufacturing overseas to making sure the shipments get out on a timely manner. It's a big job.

*AJK:* What's really difficult about this business is everytime you roll out with something, you're making something completely different. What did we know about hair getting into this? We didn't know anything about hair. We've never dealt with any suppliers, we don't know which suppliers to go to, which suppliers are reliable. The only thing we can go by is looking at the track record of the supplier, how long they've been in business, and just do your homework with the supplier and hope that what he's telling you is true. We had no experience with this guy. And obviously everything he was telling us was a crock of s---. And not only our supplier, but Positive Response's supplier. We found two suppliers that were full of s---. And these are two of the biggest suppliers in China.

*SD:* With that kind of problem, have you ever looked at or attempted to concentrate on one thing and build a company around that?

*AJK:* Around that one product line, develop a line?

*SD:* Yeah.

*AJK:* When Fitness Quest told me, in the late '80s, that they were only going to do fitness items and build a line of fitness through direct response. I thought to myself, it's difficult enough to come up with a winner, without limiting yourself to a single category. I don't want any limits. I want to be able to get into any category. These days, manufacturing most products is not all that difficult. And if you do your homework and you find the right supplier and you do it quickly, it can be done. And we've done it over and over again.

*SD:* It's tough though as you pointed out, when you're dealing with the volumes of having a successful television product. It's very easy to find out that you didn't have the right supplier too late.

*AJK:* It is. You've got to be very careful in selecting a supplier. And you've got to have a team of qualified people who are following up with the suppliers, who are constantly staying on top of it. And we've built that up here.

*SD:* Being the entrepreneur, I bet there are many days when you say, I should have done that myself.

*AJK:* Absolutely. The problem is, you can't do everything yourself. I look back and see the things I don't do anymore. I don't open the mail, I don't type up the shipping labels, I don't come in on the weekends and stuff the product into jiffy bags and ship it out. I've given up a lot over the years.

*SD:* You still do all your own fulfillment for the direct response side of the business?

*AJK:* Yeah.

*SD:* Developed your own custom software and everything to handle it?

*AJK:* Yeah. We started that fulfillment center in 1987 and I was very lucky to get a very qualified person to run it.

*SD:* Do you do much back-end marketing to your customer base?

*AJK:* Not much. We have a catalog called the "Uncle Bernie" catalog that's really not that big. The guy that was president of Joan Cook, he's running the "Uncle Bernie" catalog for me now. He comes in twice a week. He's semi-retired. He's trying to get it off the ground. We'll see what happens.

*SD:* What can you tell me about the chopper?

*AJK:* The chopper story. I was going to do a two minute spot on a chopper last fall. And it turned out that Jon Nokes walked into my office and saw this sample sitting on my desk. He said, "A.J., what are you doing with that chopper?" I said, well, I'm going to do a two minute spot. Jon said, "A.J., do me a favor. I'm just in the middle of doing an infomercial. Don't do it. If mine works, I'll give it to you for retail." It turned out that he tested it and it was very successful. Now, why was I interested in the chopper to begin with? This item was a very big success in short form throughout Europe. We're tapped in all over the world, so we hear what's hot all over the world. This item was never really done properly in the states. It was attempted earlier, by somebody that tried to position it as a salsa maker. I always thought it was the wrong position. It should have been positioned exactly the way it was in Europe. Pretty much lift the European version and Americanize it and run it the same way and then you have a chance of making it work. Nobody ever did that. Jon Nokes did. He took the key selling points from the trade shows in Europe, that's where it started, and made it work in half hour. So he started running it. Then we got the retail distribution. We started shipping it recently. We went through all this and my patent attorney calls me about a month ago and says, "A.J., we never did a patent search on the chopper." I said, you're crazy, it's selling in Europe, it's been out in the states and it's been here in the pitch market, everybody's been selling this thing. He says, "A.J., let's be thorough. Let's make sure nobody has a patent and nobody will come after us five years from now and say you violated their patent." It's just good business. So I said alright. Two days later, he calls up. Bad news, there's a patent that's right on. You're violating a patent. You're infringing this guy's patent and so is everybody else that's selling this thing. What am I going to do? I've got a half million of this thing on order. This guy could all of a sudden wake up one day, or maybe he knows what's going on and he's planning to come in and get all of his damages in some future date. This is a major problem. Now, I've found the patent, now it's willful infringement if I continue. What am I going to do? Where is this patent holder? Maybe I can buy the patent or license the thing. He does a search. The guy lives in Taipei, Taiwan, owns a U.S. Patent. We got a private investigator to find out where the guy lives and works. Within 48 hours, I'm on a plane to Taipei to visit this guy to see what I can possibly do. Very risky, because I could have gone and met the guy and he could have said, "You're Telebrands, you're infringing my patent and you owe me a lot of money. And I'm coming after you right away." Or it could have turned out the way it did. I ended up buying the patent from the guy.

*SD:* Did he know what he had?

*AJK:* No.

*SD:* You were lucky.

*AJK:* I was very lucky. The guy didn't even know that the item was popular in the states. He invented this item back in 1991 sometime, and his attorneys went ahead and filed the patent for him in the states. And he was really on to some other phase in his life. He had started a direct selling company in Taiwan, similar to AmWay. And was very successful, it was taking off like crazy and really couldn't care less about the U.S. market anymore. He said, "You want the patent, take it." We came to an amount and I bought the patent from him. It puts me in a nice position now. I protected myself. I'm not infringing and I can go after everybody that is infringing. So, we're planning to do that starting next week.

*SD:* That worked out well for you.

*AJK:* It worked out very well. So anyway, there are a bunch of guys that are infringing. We'll go after them and lock them up. What's nice about it is they're all my competitors. I get all my competitors in one shot. Keith has got one, Mishan's got one, Sonny Howard's got one, K-Tel's got one, you name it, they have it.

*SD:* That's going to be fun.

*AJK:* It will be a little distracting, but it will be fun too.

*SD:* Where do you see the industry going?

*AJK:* It seems like it's really difficult to come up with winning infomercials. But don't you see that people are still coming up with infomercials? And these Fortune 500 companies really haven't come in the way that everyone thought that they would come in. The majority of the infomercials on the air are not Fortune 500 companies the way everyone thought a few years ago. The majority of the infomercials on the air are entrepreneurs who have come up with something and get it on the air. I've always thought when media rates go up and things become more difficult, what it does is, it makes the people who are better at what they do, it gives them more opportunity. It gets the people who are not that good out of the way. What's out there? Are media rates going down?

*SD:* No.

*AJK:* Why aren't media rates going down? Because there's so much demand for the time. Why is there demand for the time? Because people are paying out. There's only so much airtime. All the airtime that can possibly be bought is being bought. All that happened is you had a maturing of the industry. In the mid-'80s, any idiot could have put anything on the air and sold it, the media rates were so cheap. And that phase is gone and that's never going to be here again. But it's like every other business. The best people will survive. The best people will continue to come up with winners.

*SD:* You need a lot more cash now though.

*AJK:* You need a lot more cash. Survival of the fittest. The people who are smart enough to really leverage their winning infomercials into retail and international distribution and print and syndication and everything else that goes along with it, those are the people that are really going to survive. Because they're milking every last penny they can out of that infomercial. And I really think that the infomercial companies that either do retail themselves or align themselves with a solid retail partner like Telebrands will have a much better chance for survival. There are companies that don't have any retail distribution or don't have the right retail distribution partners, like Guthy-Renker. I don't know who their retail distribution partner is right now. It's either Victor Grillo or Keith [Mirchandani] and neither one has ever done a good job for them. Look at Smart Inventions. Nobody ever thought these guys would survive. Guthy-Renker thought these guys were idiots, that they'd go out of business, they'd be gone. And these guys probably made more money last year than they did. I'm sure they did. And Guthy-Renker's been spending a fortune on shows. These guys produced one show and made millions of dollars off of it. Their second show made millions of dollars. They're not going crazy producing shows. They've produced two shows and both were winners and they did them both low budget. They spent $60,000 for their mop show. And these guys came up and they made a lot of money. And one reason they made a lot of money is they hooked up with us right in the beginning, as stupid as these people were conceived to be, they managed to buy their media time, they managed to fulfill their product, they managed to manufacture product. They hooked up with Telebrands. They got total distribution. They sold five million mops at retail and made a lot of money. So, as stupid as they were thought to be, they turned out very smart.

*SD:* They've done that. And Positive Response has done that with you as well.

*AJK:* We haven't been as fortunate with Positive Response, but we're looking forward to a very good relationship. We're going forward. We're working on the Eagle Eyes with them. And we're working on the Cyber-Edged Knives with them. They see it. They're smart enough to realize that there's big money in retail. Actually, Smart Inventions made much more money off of their relationship with us than they could ever think of making off the infomercial.

*SD:* How are deals with you structured?

*AJK:* I'm very flexible. Whatever makes the most sense. And also, what the other party feels comfortable with. What I feel the most comfortable with, let me take over the production of the product. Let me finance everything for the retail side and let me pay you a royalty. That's what I feel the most comfortable with. That's how my Super Slicer deal with Positive Response was. We tried something different with the hair, it didn't turn out. They don't like being a joint venture partner because they don't like sharing in my risk. I've got a huge amount of risk out there. They want to go back to the royalty situation. With Jon and Thomas at Smart Inventions, they feel more comfortable having some control. They like the idea of manufacturing the product and selling it to me and using my money to do it. So that's what they're doing. They have the product manufactured in Los Angeles, they sell it to me on a C.O.D. basis and I buy in huge quantities from them and they have their profit built right into that.

*SD:* What are your parameters as far as making deals on product? What kind of products do you look for? How do you know whether something's going to work or not?

*AJK:* I look for stuff with a history. Stuff with a history has the highest likelihood of working. You look at a catalog company. A catalog company will test in every issue of their catalog a hundred new items. And maybe half of those will make money and half of those will lose money. Out of the thousand items that they test in a year, they'll come up with one or two super hits. They've done all the testing for me. I've just got to know what those super hits are. I've learned from the cat and mouse watch. Find out what the super hits are and you have a much better shot at making something work in direct response. Why should I test a thousand items? I can't afford to test a thousand items. Find something that's working in some other vehicle, whether it be Home Shopping Network, catalog and retail stores. Stores take chances on entrepreneurs all the time. Try the item in the retail store and all of a sudden it's a big hit. So be tapped into what's going on and what's coming up.

**SD:** Have you done any other arrangements after the success with the cat and mouse watch with catalog companies?

**AJK:** I have several arrangements, those are confidential.

**SD:** It would seem like a very smart relationship to have.

**AJK:** It's a great relationship. Especially now, catalogs are really hurting for business. They're hurting for profits, I should say. Paper and postage has really killed them.

**SD:** Do you have a problem with that though in that most catalog items, the catalog companies don't have retail?

**AJK:** It really doesn't matter. They're basically selling me their information, which they have every right to do. Here are my numbers. What I do with those numbers is my business. Whether I go and find the original supplier and make a deal with him, or come up with my own version of the product as long as it's not infringing the guy's rights, they don't care.

**SD:** Talk a little bit more about retail. Your strength is really in the mass merchants. Is there anyone else in the industry that you see is doing a decent job in retail?

**AJK:** Right now, there's nobody close to what we're doing. And I really have to give the credit to my brother Andy. He's an extremely aggressive, extremely bright guy. He's gone out there and done a hell of a job. Andy is just a towerhouse. We need a minimum of five to ten new items to retailers every single year. They don't like suppliers that come in one year and then have nothing the next year. They forget about you. You have to be constantly in their face. Your sales reps, you have to constantly feed them. The more business they have from Telebrands, the more loyal they're going to be to Telebrands and the more they're going to think about only doing Telebrands stuff.

# STEVE SCOTT

✦

$\mathcal{S}$teve Scott is the creative partner of American Telecast Corporation. He, along with producer Frank Kovacs, has created some of the biggest successes in infomercial history. Their shows include: The Total Gym; Lori Davis Hair, featuring Cher; Jane Fonda's Treadmill; Victoria Jackson Cosmetics; Where There's a Will, There's an "A," and many others. The Total Gym alone has generated over $750 million in sales. This is the first interview Steve ever consented to do. It gives a real sense of how a true marketing mind generates ideas and concepts that compel consumers to buy.

**Steve Dworman:** Why, after years of silence, did you decide to write *"A Millionaire's Notebook"*?

**Steve Scott:** Basically, it started as a fluke. My kids have all grown up seeing dad as successful. They never knew how it happened. They all knew my partners, they all knew American Telecast, but they didn't know what my role in American Telecast had been. They didn't know about all the failures that I had been through. I started thinking, if I don't teach my kids the difference between failing and succeeding, nobody else is ever going to teach them that. I actually started writing the book to show them that dad had lots of failures in his life, and that it was learning to deal with those failures that ended up becoming the difference between succeeding and failing. I had written about five or six chapters and Stephen Covey's agent was in my office and saw the manuscript laying on the corner of my desk. She asked what it was, and I said it was a book I was writing for my kids. She asked to read it and took it on the plane back to Dallas. She called me from the airport and said, "I can sell this. This is terrific." I said, well, I'd have to re-write it and make it a little less personal toward my kids. And she said that was all I had to do. I did and she sold it to Simon & Schuster.

**SD:** On the book jacket itself, you list your first nine jobs and how you either quit or were fired from all of them.

*SS:* I really had nine jobs in the first six years after college. It was during those nine jobs that I had a lot of failure and learned what didn't work. On my ninth job, I actually had a boss who gave me my first chance to come up to the plate and take a swing at the ball. I did and I hit a grand slam home run with the help of a tremendous batting coach named Bob Marsh, who owned a little media company called the National Media Group. He and I put together a program that doubled Ambassador sales from $30 million to $60 million. That was the beginning of my current career. I worked for banks, I worked for research departments of banks, marketing departments of banks, just lots of different jobs and I couldn't seem to succeed in any of them.

*SD:* You made a statement earlier that was very interesting. That was that you learned from each of these failures. I see a lot of people in day-to-day life, and they'll get angry, but they don't take the time or have the insight to really learn.

*SS:* Failure is something that hurts so much that you want to run away from it. I was fired from a job at a mail order insurance company where I was humiliated. I was fired in front of the department. I was told to go clean out my desk. I was told that I was the biggest disappointment in this particular person's career and that I would never succeed in marketing. I was about 23 years old and I was crying as I was emptying out my desk. Everybody had been told that I was going to be fired and they were watching me. It was a terrible, hurtful experience. But it was probably one of the best things that could have ever happened to me. When the dust settled and when the pain stopped, I went back and I said what went wrong? Why would that man say that I was such a failure and that I would never succeed? What did I do wrong? I found some insights from that and from that point on, every single time I struck out, whether it was on a project or on a job, once the pain stopped, I would go, get a pad and paper and I'd start writing down why. Why did this project fail? What did I miss? Here I thought I was going to hit a home run and I struck out. What happened? So I learned to analyze my failures. The more failures I had, the more I learned what didn't work. Edison failed over 500 times in creating the lightbulb. He tested over 500 filaments before he found a carbon filament that worked. With each failure he knew what wouldn't work. We were fortunate at American Telecast, in that most of our learning days were in our first 12 years, when we were in the 2-minute business. Learning was a lot cheaper. Failure was a lot cheaper than what failure is today in a 30-minute commercial. When you fail with a 30-minute commercial you can lose a half a million or a million or a million and a half dollars. When we failed with a 2-minute commercial back then, we were failing with $15 or $20 thousand.

*SD:* Back then, when this was going on, did you have a picture in your mind or a goal in your mind of what you wanted to achieve?

*SS:* I always have goals on individual products or projects. I'd never had a corporate goal. We never had a goal where we said we want to achieve $50 million or $100 or $200 million in sales—how do we do it? Rather, I would get a vision for a project. One of the concepts that a *Millionaire's Notebook* teaches is a process called dream "conversion." Everything has to start with a dream. Then you have to convert that dream to a set of goals. You convert those goals into a set of tasks. You convert those tasks into very specific steps, then you take the first step. Most people never go through that process.

*SD:* Give me an example of that process.

*SS:* One of my goals is to be the best husband I can be. So that becomes my vision or my dream. My wife is such a wonderful person, she really deserves the best. Now, I break that goal into some tasks. One task would be to gain a mentor, someone who is really a great husband and learn from that person how they are such a great husband. So I decided I wanted a mentor named Gary Smalley, who's one of the best husbands I've ever seen. So I went to Gary and asked what can I do that would really make me a better husband. So that was one task. The step was going to him. Another task was I went to Shannon and I asked, "What are some things that I could do that would really make you feel fulfilled and happy?" She gave me some things that I could do, and I wrote them down and started doing them. Those became the tasks and the steps.

*SD:* Pretty simple just to ask the questions.

*SS:* Questions are how we learn. I do the same thing in a business. I get a vision for a project and I break it down into some goals. And then the goals into the very specific tasks. The book gives several examples. Throughout the book, any concept that I teach, I usually give an example from both the personal side of life so a person can apply them to their daily lives in non-business areas. Then I usually give examples from the business side.

*SD:* When you were in college, did you want a career in marketing?

*SS:* By the end of college I did.

*SD:* How did that come about?

*SS:* I started out in political science and found out I wasn't going to make it with my political views. I changed to marketing and two professors in particular were very motivational and inspirational. One was teaching for a dollar a year, had been an executive vice president with Foote, Cone & Belding, had created the campaigns that launched Dial Soap and Clairol—"Does she or doesn't she, only her hairdresser knows for sure." They made it seem so fun that I really wanted to get into it.

*SD:* What about it seemed fun?

*SS:* That you had a chance to really persuade and influence people. I had always enjoyed speaking and writing and anything persuasive. I'd always been a persuader, even back in high school I used to persuade the people around me to do the things that I wanted to do. Persuasion always came easy to me.

Marketing was simply focusing the persuasion on getting people to buy the things you wanted them to buy. So there was a real natural fit for me. I was only good at two things in high school. One was typing and one was persuading. I enjoyed both very much. So that's what I've spent my life doing.

*SD:* [Laughs] Maybe this is a good time to throw in the Spielberg story.

*SS:* Okay. One of the things that was another motivation for me writing the book was the realization that most people that I meet are stuck. They're stuck at their current level of success. They're stuck at their job, their careers, in their relationships. I have never felt stuck. Just the opposite. I felt stuck for the first six years after college, but after that, once we broke through and started American Telecast, I've never felt stuck. I've always felt like there was no limit in what we could achieve or do. Yet most people I meet are very stuck and frustrated by the fact that they're not able to achieve the things they want to achieve. I began asking myself the question, Why are people like that? I traced it back to high school. In high school, we're all judged based on three things: grades, popularity, and athletics. If a person isn't a homecoming king, a star quarterback, or a straight A student, they graduate from high school thinking of themselves as average or ordinary. That's what happened to me. In fact, I was kind of below average in high school. I never had a single date, I was in a military organization that was frowned upon in the '60s. I went to every football game, not playing on the field or even in the band, but I went in a military uniform as part of a color guard raising the flag. I was a mediocre student, not popular, excelled in absolutely nothing significant. Every football game, I sat next to a guy in the band who was in the same situation. He was below average as a student, excelled in nothing significant, and was not popular in any way. That was Steven Spielberg. So looking back, what did Steven excel in? Why did he become Steven Spielberg? When did he become a genius? Well, the reality is, even in high school, even though he excelled in nothing significant, he did excel in two things. He was a great clarinetist and he made terrific home movies. I excelled in nothing significant, but I learned how to type and I learned how to persuade. One of the things the book teaches is that we, as teachers and parents, have done a big disservice by accepting as a standard of significance the standards that are put upon us in high school. In reality, what really is significant isn't grades, or athletics or popularity. What is significant to any individual are the areas that they have a passion for. Steven had a passion for making home movies. I had a passion for persuading and writing. It took six years before I was able to get into a field that utilized my passions. It took Steven a couple of years after high school, three or four years. Then we both did the exact same things, oddly enough. He found a mentor, I found a mentor. His mentor was Sid Sheinberg at Universal, my mentor was Bob Marsh. He found partners, guys that he could dream with, visualize with and create with. I found partners that I could visualize with and create with. There were really three keys to both of our success. Number one, we were mentored. Number two, we built our lives around our passions. Number three, we were able to recruit external resources, in my case wonderful partners, that enabled us to turn our passions into reality. What the book really focuses on isn't infomercials and it's not about making money, but rather it's taking six critical elements that have meant the difference between no success and phenomenal success. Every superachiever I've ever met in my life, and I've met some who have made millions and some who have made hundreds of millions, they've all had those same things in common. They've all done the same things. These same techniques and strategies can be applied to any area of one's life, personal or business. They're critical to achieving extraordinary success.

*SD:* What are those elements?

*SS:* There's really six areas that make an incredible difference in success. They all start with a "P" oddly enough. The first is passion. A person has to be able to have fun in what they do. Steven Spielberg and George Lucas were creating the first Indiana Jones movie. Right after they filmed Indiana being dragged by the truck, Spielberg looked at Lucas and said, "Can you believe we get paid to do this?" That's how I've felt about my job for 20 years and it's always been fun. If a person is not in a fun job, they have to learn how to bring fun into their job. As they have more fun in the job, their success rate will go up and that becomes the key to getting an even more fun job. The second area is partnership. Nobody can achieve extraordinary success in any area of their life by themselves, they need the help of others. The book really focuses on how to recruit the right kinds of partners, mentors, advisors, counselors, financial advisors and so on. The next critical area is productivity. Super-achievers are incredibly productive. They achieve more in an hour than most people do in a year. There's about four or five keys to becoming a lot more productive. The book shows you how to make the most of your time, of your money, of the limited talents and abilities that you have. The next element is persuasive communication. This is the area where most people fall down. Most people are very poor communicators. Communication isn't simply saying or writing something. Rather, it's enabling the person you're communicating with to understand what you're saying, feel what you're feeling, and be motivated to do what you want them to do. That's persuasion. So the book dedicates two chapters on how to be far more persuasive in your communication. The next area is power. How do you increase your power? Success, like batting in baseball, is a function of three things: how often you come up to the plate, how consistently you hit the ball and how hard you hit the ball. That area of how hard you hit the ball is the area of power. The book teaches you how to play to your strengths, how to strengthen your weaknesses, how to convert strike-outs into hits and hits to home runs. The final area that is critical to extraordinary success, all the super-achievers I have ever met have learned how to use this area, and that's persistence. Persistence isn't coming up to a brick wall and hitting it one hundred times until it finally breaks down. You hit the brick wall and now you're going to come at it again, but from a completely different angle. You're not going to keep hitting it, but you're going to keep coming back to figure out how to get around it or over it or under it until you get through it. I teach a concept called "creative alternatives"—how to develop creative alternatives when you encounter road blocks. For example, what to do with criticism. There's good criticism and bad criticism. Criticism is either our best friend or our worst enemy depending on its source, its accuracy and how we respond to it. Everybody's life is filled with criticism and we need to know the right way to deal with it.

*SD:* Now, all those are very powerful processes. I can't imagine anyone not wanting to pick up the book to discover the intricacies of how to make them work for themselves. One thing I've noticed in getting to know you is you have an incredible ability to focus on what you're doing at the moment, at the expense of blocking everything else around you out. I would imagine somebody could put you in the middle of a construction zone, in the middle of writing a script, and you wouldn't even notice that there was chaos going on around you.

**SS:** It depends on what stage of the script I'm in. If I'm starting the script, I couldn't start it with chaos around me. I have to run away. I run up to the home I have in the mountains when I write until I do get everything out. But once I'm in the middle of it, you could drop anything around me and I wouldn't notice it. I do focus, when I'm on one project, I put everything else aside and focus 100% onto it until I know the direction I'm going. Once I know the basic direction and what I want to communicate, then I can leave it and come back to it as often as I want.

**SD:** Were you always like that or did you do anything specific to develop your concentration skills?

**SS:** No, I've always been like that. Once I have a vision for something, I am relentless in pursuing it. Let me give you one of the reasons I've flunked out of so many jobs and one of the reasons that I've succeeded with American Telecast. My attention factor is pretty short. I'm usually good at focusing on a project for two or three months. Every corporation I worked for wanted me to do the same things over and over and over again, day in, day out. I couldn't do that. What would happen is I would start thinking about other areas to improve the business and my bosses would always tell me, "That's not your concern, just do your job." When Bob Marsh decided to bring me in as a partner he knew that I could not be happy on one project a year. The worst thing he could ever do is say, "Steve, this is your project, make this work and then go on to the next one." That's not how I am. I'll get something working, and in the process, think of three or four more different things on different projects and so on, and I'll jump off my project, go on one of those, come back and so on. Bob never tried to make me be a person who simply fills a job description, who's assigned to one thing, or one part of a project or one project. Rather, he let me be an entrepreneur, while working for our company. Consequently, this is the first company that I've really had tremendous success with. It's lasted for 20 years. It was Bob's genius and his love for me that enabled me to be that way. So any time I'm working on one project, long before I finish it, I'll have started two or three other ones.

**SD:** Bob Marsh is Dave and John Marsh's father.

**SS:** He is the founder of American Telecast.

**SD:** And the two of you really started the company together?

**SS:** What happened was he owned a media company that he had purchased and started running in September of 1975. I was working at a mail order catalog company in 1976. Bob came in and we convinced that company to let us create a TV campaign for a product. We launched that campaign. As soon as we launched it, we saw that it was going to be a big home run. That it was literally going to double their sales in a year. With that in mind, the first week that we were testing this program, Bob said to me, "If you could ever find a product that you and I could market, we could start our own marketing company. There's a lot more money to be made in marketing than there is in buying TV time." And with that, I started looking for a product. Two weeks later I found the product, I quit my job at Ambassador, moved 3,000 miles across the country to Philadelphia, and we started a little marketing company.

*SD:* So you started by selling your products with 2-minute spots?

*SS:* Exactly.

*SD:* In another conversation, you had brought up the importance of constructive criticism. That's something that isn't talked about very much.

*SS:* No, people usually just criticize. Very rarely is criticism constructive. For criticism to be constructive, it has to be offered in the right spirit, it has to be offered with the right goals in mind, and it has to be received with the right spirit. There are some people I would never criticize, even if I could give them constructive criticism, only because they don't know how to receive criticism. In Proverbs it says, "Never scorn a scoffer." The worst thing you can do is criticize someone who can't deal with criticism. When a person is willing to receive criticism in the right way, they can become far wiser. So a wise person welcomes constructive criticism. Now constructive criticism is criticism offered in the right spirit, meaning I have the other person's interest in mind as well as my own interest. I want to help them, I don't want to hurt them. I don't want to say I told you so, or why didn't you do this or why didn't you do that. I want to help them to achieve their goals. Part of the book focuses on helping others around you and beneath you to achieve their goals. Once I have the right spirit, I have to offer criticism in the right way. I teach a process called "sandwiching." Sandwiching is simply never offering criticism by itself. It's like a piece of bologna. You put it between two pieces of bread, which are encouragement and praise. So if I'm going to criticize somebody, the first thing I do is I encourage them and praise something that's worth praising. I point out something I like about the person, something I like about what they've just done. Then I get around to the criticism. It isn't offered with a pointing finger. Usually it's asking questions. What do you think went wrong? What do you think could have been done to make it better? Did you think about this? Would this have helped? Then it's leaving the person with the attitude of let's work together on it. How can I help you? Then criticism is constructive. Even when people have criticized me with the wrong motives, where they've been mean and cruel, if I go ahead and just accept the tangible aspects of the criticism, not the emotional ones but the logical ones, then I can usually get smarter from the criticism, so I welcome it. There's a wonderful verse in the Bible that I love that says, "The wounds of a friend are better than the kisses of an enemy." There's another verse that says, "When all kinds of trials and tribulations enter into your lives, don't resent them as intruders, but welcome them as friends. Realize they come to test your patience and produce in you the quality of endurance." When I would fail at something, Bob would call me into his office, not right away, and he would say, "Are you ready to take a look at this?" I'd say okay, I'm ready now, and we'd sit down to discuss it. It was always so enlightening. It was the nicest thing Bob could have been doing for me. The worst thing he could have done is said, "Hey Steve, you gave it your best shot." I don't need to hear that. I need to hear how I could have done better. And if there's anything we can constructively think of that would have made it better, I'll use that the next time I create something. Bob is really brilliant in so many areas. He has so many strengths.

*SD:* How much time would he let go by?

*SS:* He would wait until I was ready and with me that's usually a couple of days. It's not weeks. I swing, miss, fall hard on the ground, get all dusty and cut and bruised. I get real upset for probably a day or two. I have the best partners in the world. They have always gathered around me and they have always picked me up off the ground and accepted me and my failures. Then, when I felt ready for it, after a couple of days, then we would sit down and analyze what went wrong.

*SD:* Let's talk about the unique partnership relationship you have. The company is set up in a different way than most companies. Talk a bit about that.

*SS:* Sure. Most partnerships fail. They fail because the partners are either the wrong partners or they don't understand what a partnership should be. American Telecast exists today, not because of Steve Scott, not because of John or Dave Marsh, or Ed Shipley or Jim Shaughnessy, or Ben Weaver or Jeff Heft. If you picked seven strands of thread, each one of them is so weak. But when you intertwine seven pieces of thread and try to break that, it'll rip a hole in your fingers. Our partnership was based upon the example set by Bob Marsh. Bob Marsh established the partnership around love. He had a tremendous love for each one of the partners and wanted to see us succeed. Rather than motivating us with threats, he motivated us with love. We all wanted to succeed because of him. That's how we started. Within a year, each of us really grew to love one another. It became important to me that not only I succeed, but that Ed Shipley would succeed, that John and Dave Marsh would succeed. It became important to each of them that I succeeded. Everybody became desirous of helping one another succeed in their own personal areas of the business. The other thing that was so wonderful about the partnership was Bob Marsh. Rather than holding all the ownership and giving us little tiny pieces, he did just the opposite. He gave away the vast majority of ownership to each of the partners and kept a little piece for himself. We knew if we hit home runs, we were all going to go around the bases together. And if we struck out, we were all going down together. It's a partnership that has, at its center, the love that Bob Marsh helped create. We had time to learn together. The book teaches a person how to recruit the right kinds of partners. Now that I know what right kinds of partners are, the book shows you how to determine your own need for partners.

*SD:* Also in the book you make a statement: "If you follow the following rules, you can double your batting average in thirty days." It sounds like an infomercial.

**SS:** You can double. I think that's being conservative. There's probably about two dozen different techniques and strategies that are revealed in the book. If a person were to apply any four or five to any particular area of importance to them, whether it's business or personal, they will see a radical improvement in their success rate.

**SD:** Talk a little bit about what you call your "laws of achieving success."

**SS:** The book gives insights for success and laws for success. Basically, these resulted from me looking back over the last 20 years and saying what worked 100% everytime it was used. If it worked 100% of the time, it became a law for success. If, on the other hand, it worked a lot, it usually resulted in success, then it was an insight.

**SD:** Have you gotten any reactions yet from people who have started applying them already?

**SS:** I've gotten a lot of good responses and some really nice endorsements from people that I really respect. A person from one company that received an advanced copy called me and said, "I read your book and I want to now make some of my key employees partners." They now are using the basis from the book to move some of their key employees into a partnership position. So that was gratifying. They've also used the book to take some of their key employees and discover what those employee's dreams were. The chapter on dream conversion is really important. They discovered the dreams of some of their key employees, and now they're focused on not only achieving their corporate goals, but helping those employees achieve their personal goals. That makes a huge difference in a person's fun factor on the job. Fun isn't something we need to bring into a job for the benefit of having fun. We bring it into the job in order to have higher degrees of success. When a job is fun, people always do it better, because they end up giving more hours to it, they get more creative and so on.

**SD:** Most of the book deals with a person achieving success wherever they apply it, but a lot of what is in this book can be applied very specifically toward infomercials. Weren't you afraid of your competitors reading this and discovering some of your trade secrets?

**SS:** Some of our competitors already use some of these things. I think they probably use more than they don't use. I wasn't really afraid of giving too many secrets that they don't already know. What goes along with the knowledge is the willingness and the ability to apply it. I can communicate the techniques. I can communicate the strategies and the formulas. But a person has to be willing to apply those and that's where our competitors may fall a little bit short. For example, some of our competitors love to do creative, beautiful productions that are very artistic and gorgeous. One of the things that the book teaches is that artistic swells and logic sells. That person that tends to be really artistic will have a difficult time putting their artistic desires aside to just get logical and to sell. Even though they learned that from me that artistic beauty has never been a key part of selling as much as logic, they may say I'm still going to make it the way I want to make it. One of our keys is that we are willing to spend whatever it takes to do something right. A lot of people aren't willing to take that kind of risk, because the risk could be a million or two million or three million dollars to do something right. Our company is a little bit different in that we don't have to get a lot of people to sign off on a concept or a script or a celebrity. Most companies deal with ad agencies, or different people within the marketing group and there's a lot of egos involved. To get all of those egos to sign off on something because it's the best thing to do versus something that gratifies their ego, that's somewhat difficult. Anybody in the ad agency business would know what I'm talking about. Bringing all of these things into sync to apply my formulas and techniques is not going to be the easiest thing in the world. We are in an ever-evolving business. We still have lots of failures, we still have lots of successes. We're forever gaining new insights. The book, in essence, captures a freeze-frame of what's been helpful to us so far. It's not necessarily what's going to get us through the next stage of success.

*SD:* What about a product will make you step up to the plate in comparison with another product?

*SS:* If it appeals to our target market. We know who our market is, we know who we can reach on television most efficiently. Five criteria in the book that I use for product selection separate probably 990 products out of a thousand that are presented to us and disqualify them. Product selection is very difficult. A lot of people have an attitude of throwing a lot of products against the wall and hoping one sticks. That's never been our approach. We spend a lot of money on each infomercial that we do and on each project that we test. We don't want to test a project that has a high possibility of failing. Instead, we like to test the ones that have a high probability of succeeding. One criteria is, does it fit our marketplace? Another, is the math there? You can have a great product that will appeal to the marketplace, but won't have the math necessary for infomercial marketing. That can disqualify one as quickly as anything else. Can I see the logic, the reason for the consumer to want that product more than anything else they can buy in the store? If I can't separate it from what's out there already, why take a chance on it? There's quite a number of criteria that we give.

*SD:* One of the things that I was really interested in, in the book, was the fact of the thought and the logic process that you go through with a particular product before you actually sit down and start scripting. You answer objections, you come up with all the benefits, you come up with any doubt that would be in the mind and try to assess how best to answer objections. And you always have the highest respect for the consumers' intelligence while you're doing it.

*SS:* That goes back to something that happened in college. When I was in college, this professor who really motivated me, had, as a speaker, Fairfax Cone, who was one of the founders of Foote, Cone and Belding. He spoke for 45 minutes and I don't remember a thing that he said except one statement. He said, "The woman in the supermarket isn't an idiot. She's your wife. And she's the smartest shopper in the world. Twenty-five thousand products on the supermarket shelves and when one goes up a nickel, she knows it. So treat her with the respect she deserves." When I heard that, from that point on, I thought he's right. I have always taken an approach that treats my market with respect. I know a lot of people disagree with that. They say you've got to make the impression, you've got to make them remember. And if it means having people pilot canoes in toilets, whatever it takes, that's what you've got to use. I disagree with that. I would never use that even if it could make me successful. I respect women and women tend to be my marketplace. That becomes a foundation for what I do. It is honoring and respecting my target market. Then, building a logical reason for that person to choose my product over anything else that is available.

*SD:* How much research do you do on competitive products in the marketplace before you sit down to write?

*SS:* Very little. Usually, it's a few phones calls and seeing what else is out there. I'll call somebody who's real smart in an area and they'll say yes or no and I'll ask how successful is it. I do a little bit, not a lot.

*SD:* The other thing I've always been amazed at, is that with the amount of success that you have, you have a very lean company. There's between 50 to 60 people working there. Are there any words of wisdom of how you get so much achieved from your people?

*SS:* Yes, you treat everybody with respect and you honor the people that are there. Once again, that started at the top with Bob Marsh treating everybody like they were highly valued in the early days when we only had 15 employees. Then it was up to John and myself and the other partners, as we grew into our positions, to treat those around us with respect. You treat people like they're family. We've always felt real fortunate that we've had the employees that we have and how hard they work and how productive they are.

*SD:* You've been in the business almost since the inception. Can you talk a little philosophically about where you see the business going?

*SS:* I would think that five years from now, there probably won't be a direct response infomercial business. Television time continues to skyrocket. The companies that don't have to measure the effectiveness of their advertising can afford to pay whatever rates they want to pay once or twice. Pretty soon, they're going to want to measure the impact of an infomercial. I think there's a lot of smoke and mirrors in our business. I think there's a lot of people that think they are getting a lot more bang for the buck than what they are. Infomercial prices are not related to sizes of the audience, unlike 30-second spots. I feel that the actual reach of an infomercial isn't near as great as what other people think it is. Because the rates are going up and will continue to go up as long as people are willing to pay such exorbitant prices, I think we'll see a lot of direct response marketers fall out of the business in the next few years, leaving the business primarily to the people who aren't mail order. The same thing happened in the free fall insert business. We helped build a life insurance company years ago around 6-page free fall inserts. The pulling power of those inserts was unbelievable. Then, one of the printers we hired created an insert for consumer goods companies, like Proctor & Gamble. Today, your Sunday paper is filled with lots and lots of non mail order inserts and very few mail order ones. It used to be just the opposite. I think that could happen with infomercials.

*SD:* Where does that leave American Telecast?

*SS:* Well, American Telecast works really hard at creating businesses that will be non-TV dependent or non-infomercial dependent. We'll keep going in that direction. I could be wrong. Everything is a function of supply and demand. If, all of a sudden, the demand for infomercial time falls into the waste basket, then rates will come down. If they come down, people will succeed and we'll be right back where we were three or four years ago. We could see a big falling out, we could see rate adjustments, of course you don't know what the stock market is going to do or anything else. There are so many different influences that are out of our control.

*SD:* A lot of people have been talking lately about the potential infomercial or direct response television market overseas. Is that something you're exploring as well?

*SS:* Yes we are. We have several people in our company that are well focused on that. I don't know if that will ever become anything big or not. Once again, you're dependent on so many different factors. Oftentimes TV broadcasting in foreign countries is strictly regulated by the government and one single stroke of a pen can wipe out an opportunity much more easily than it can in the United States.

*SD:* Can you make some comments on the types of infomercials you're seeing right now?

*SS:* I'm disgusted by some of the ones that I'm hearing about. I've heard that O.J. Simpson is doing an infomercial. There are infomercials that make me embarrassed to be in the business. I know ERA was founded originally to try and bring some self-regulation, and I think they've been successful with a lot of the companies. But I see some of these things and I think where is the FTC? There are some abuses that are going on in our business that really have me discouraged. I have tremendous respect for some of the players in our industry who really create quality products, quality presentations of those products and respect the viewer and I applaud them. There are others who really don't care what they sell so long as they can get a buck out of it. Some of them have been highly successful. They bring the scorn of the community, of broadcasters, of news organizations upon our industry. I feel bad about that.

*SD:* What's on your plate?

*SS:* We're always looking for new products and we're always looking for new businesses that we can create around those products.

# MIKE LASKY WARREN

❧

*M*ike Lasky, known in his earlier newsletter days as Mike Warren, is a one-of-a-kind individual. A complex man, with many sides to him, Lasky created and executed the Psychic Friends Network in 1991. As you will read, getting the concept up and running involved having AT&T do things that hadn't been done before. His direct response background before entering this business gave him the tools and know-how he needed to build the largest cash generating machine in the history of the industry. At the height of the business, Mike woke up every morning to learn he had generated over $1 million while he slept. He is a very driven man. This interview with him was conducted at 1:00 a.m.

**Steve Dworman:** So why don't you start out giving some background on yourself. Where you came from and how you got here.

**Mike Lasky Warren:** I was involved in sports information. Primarily a direct mail, telemarketing company that supplied information to the sports public on events that one could have a financial interest in, and one that would have a strong television interest in, I suppose. Something you'd like to watch—some sport like a football game, a basketball game, a horse race. And I had a newsletter, *The Warren Report*, and it is quite successful. When I was doing it full time, it was much more successful than it is now. Actually, I launched an industry. Before that time there really were no professional handicappers selling their service to the general public.

**SD:** Like a Jim Feist?

**MLW:** Yeah, Jim Feist and I were always the competition in the business. As a matter of fact, Jim Feist and I spoke recently, and we were thinking of going back on TV, on a show we've been wanting to do for a long time, because we were competition and friendly adversaries and have like a Siskel and Ebert thing in football.

*SD:* That'd be fun.

*MLW:* It would be. Professional ones like Jim and myself who have an opinion really bring a different angle to the handicapping than the people that you see out there now. Most of the people that are handicappers, they talk about the big stars and this and that. They really don't get behind the game, behind the line, what the numbers really mean, what the spread is and the odds are. And sometimes you see how uncannily accurate the line is, the Vegas line is, it's so accurate. And to pick with it or against that number, it becomes a very difficult thing.

*SD:* So you were writing the newsletter yourself, and the copy, to sell it?

*MLW:* Yes. We had a newsletter and we had a telephone service. Always had a telephone service.

*SD:* Okay.

*MLW:* Because that's the latest breaking information you can get.

*SD:* And in sports it's essential to be right on top.

*MLW:* Oh absolutely, because you have to deal in real time, real time situations. I used to tell them to please call for updates, or weather changes, or injury changes, personality changes, line changes. You know, positions come in that people take on an event, the whole line changes. So, if you have an interest as a fan or the betting public, the information you need is very important.

*SD:* So this was the start of the 900-business for you?

*MLW:* Well, actually I did it the old-fashioned way, through 800-numbers. They would pay for the service, you see. And then after that, the 900-numbers came open and we went into the 900 business. So they could pay for it when they liked it, and they could get the information that way.

*SD:* This was around the mid-'80s?

*MLW:* That's about right.

*SD:* So you built that business up and that was successful. Did you sell that business off?

*MLW:* No, the business was being run by my brother for a long time, who handled it quite well. But I don't have time to do anything with it anymore, and he handles it quite well.

*SD:* So where did the psychic idea come from?

*MLW:* Well, I was looking for other things to do, you know after a while you just need other challenges, and with a background in direct mail and telemarketing, we saw a real need, about five or six years ago. People were interested in the horoscope reports and the astrology reports and psychic information, and we did a direct mail program. But it was old already. It was six, seven days old when you got it, or two weeks old or three weeks old. It really wasn't styled for the individual call. It was sort of like a broadbased report. So what I decided to do was astrology readings or psychic readings live. I started to do a mail campaign, and it was successful. The problem was that I couldn't see it getting bigger. It was almost impossible because the mechanism was a live psychic, or a live astrologist if you will, talking to a live subscriber or customer. And I reasoned, in order to get big, you need thousands of people calling, and thousands of psychics responding. In those days, when I started, what was happening is you would do it out of a central station. We would look for psychics all over the city or town or place, and try to get them in to work, and it took us 24 hours a day, seven days a week. It's at the customer's convenience, not yours. So it was difficult to fill a room with enough psychics to warrant the advertising investment. If you didn't have enough psychics, it wasn't worth it. That was the problem. The real genius of what we did was the Mohammed-on-the-mountain routine. We used the computers, not to bring the psychic into a room, but leave the psychic wherever he or she is, in the home, on the road, wherever they work, and we could make the call come to them. That was the key. Once we were able to do that, once we figured that out, then we were able to broadbase our market. What I should have done is patented that discovery, and I wouldn't have had any competition probably into the next century. Hindsight is always 20/20. But it gave us enough time to get away from the entire field and to establish a name, the Psychic Friends Network.

*SD:* It's a great name.

*MLW:* Yes, and that was done for different reasons. The name now has been trademarked because it's been around and it is such a wonderful name.

*SD:* It's warm, and friendly.

*MLW:* Yes, but the trademark is the key. No one else is trademarked. So it's become part of Americana. In the *New York Times* last week, they had the crossword puzzle, and it said, "The ------- Friends Network." And of course, the answer was the Psychic Friends Network. So we're even in the *New York Times* crossword puzzle as a part of Americana, which is great!

*SD:* How long did it actually take you from start to finish to set the network up?

*MLW:* Once we got on it, it really wasn't that long. Four months, perhaps.

*SD:* What was the criteria you were able to use for the psychics themselves?

*MLW:* What we believed in and what we did with AT&T was help write all the laws. We absolutely wanted to give people not their money's worth, because that sounds hard, or cruel, but giving them what they wanted. And giving them the help they need. A lot of people out there need help. And these psychics are phenomenal. They really get behind a person and really help them on a friendship basis. You'd be amazed to take a reading and see what comes of it. You'd absolutely flip out. I know I did when I first started to do that. So what we looked for was the best psychics. We'd take them through tests, we'd take them through readings, and we'd take the ones that we'd think are good. We check them all the time. We're constantly rating our psychics. So we get the criteria of master psychics. And it's proven because our psychics have been with us for a long time and our customers have been with us for a long time. Any time they stray off and go somewhere else, they always tell us the poor experience they've had, and they come back.

*SD:* The ingenious thing about this whole system is that in the relationship they build up with the psychic, you've got the ultimate continuity program.

*MLW:* Yes, that's right. We monitor a whole network by calling in, by checking the lines, by seeing that the customer is getting the value in what they're supposed to get all the time. There's a lot of work and it doesn't just happen. We have people up all night doing this.

*SD:* Do you ever call in?

*MLW:* Oh yeah.

*SD:* Anyone ever know it's you?

*MLW:* No, I never tell them. I'm good at voices and changing position. They're pretty good. They're pretty accurate. They have a sense of things. You have to call and try it. It really is wild.

*SD:* How long does the average reading take?

*MLW:* Well, we found that a good average reading, if you really are a good psychic, you really have something to say and the client wants to hear it. So it should take at least 10 minutes for a fine reading.

*SD:* So it's an average $40 call.

*MLW:* I would say so.

*SD:* That's not bad.

*MLW:* If you're going to get our television prices down for advertising, it could really be a good business.

*SD:* Tell me a little bit about how your direct marketing background really came into play in putting this together.

*MLW:* A lot of people I meet in the infomercial business are quite knowledgeable in movies or television commercials, and that's important. But they don't think of the continuity program. Direct mail is based on continuity, as I said before. The back-end of our business is the recall. It's not getting the call the first time, it's the call the second, the third, the fifth, the tenth time. And that's done by giving value, by giving service, by constantly monitoring and checking your machinery to see if it's right, if it's working. When you're selling a product, like other people in the infomercial business that sell a product, they may sell two or three of it, but that's about it. So they sell a product and that's it. The product we have is a service. And we re-sell that service over and over again. So it has to be of value. It has to be good. It has to be accurate. If they keep calling back, and calling back, and we've been successful over a five and a half to six year period, there has to be something good in it. We've had over 10 million calls. And that in itself says something.

*SD:* Would you say 50% of the people call back a second or third time?

*MLW:* Well, I think without the competition it was higher. Of course there's more competition now. They're two different things. The customer suffers because he used to get the warm and fuzzy feeling from the old. Most of the others at least, they're not really concentrating on the reading, they're concentrating on the sale. It tends to denigrate the entire market. But I think over the long haul, if you stick to your deeds and your creeds, it comes back again. I don't see the astrology/psychic business fading away into the sunset. It's the oldest profession in the world, older than the other profession you would think of.

*SD:* I didn't know that.

*MLW:* It's out of the Bible. It's the first profession. And it's a worldwide phenomenon. There are psychics all over the world. People believe in it.

*SD:* Have you been able to expand overseas?

*MLW:* We're working on it right now, as we speak.

*SD:* With the limitations with phone systems?

*MLW:* Yes, but they're catching up quickly. They have different ways of billing and charging. If I could, I'd bring the 900 system with me and install it for them. I could put the system in for the entire country. Of course I don't want to lay lines, the phone lines, and do that, but if they have a system that is good, I can overlay it with a 900 system. Which costs millions of dollars, and I would do that, and work a deal with the government. So that's one of our programs we're working on.

*SD:* You were the first person that I'm aware of that did a global campaign around the infomercial. You ran print ads, you did spots, I don't know if you did radio or not.

*MLW:* We tried to do radio, it just wasn't accepted at the time. But we're doing radio now. You have to hit all the bases. And in the old days, no one did that. But everybody is catching on fast. The thing I can't figure out is retail. I'm really not sure what's the best way to go with that. They take these products and they advertise them very heavily for two or three months and it goes to retail and the product becomes a retail product, but certainly after they put it in retail you really can't sell it on television anymore.

*SD:* It's the same thing as doing a product infomercial. You're in, and then you die.

*MLW:* Yes, but I'm not sure if that's the best way to go. Perhaps it should be sold only on television, as opposed to giving it away in retail, because there's so many things that apply in a retail deal. I'm not sure if it isn't counterproductive.

*SD:* I'm gonna ask you a tough question now. What happened with Linda Georgian, that you can talk about?

*MLW:* From beginning to end, when we got involved with Linda, she was a psychic and we loved her dearly and she loved us dearly. I think she's quite talented, and she's a nice person, and we tried many things with her. A lot of it worked, a lot of it didn't work. We had a great time together, but the contract expired, actually unbeknownst to me. It wasn't renewed, unbeknownst to me, and someone made a faux pas, and she felt the need to go on with her life. She thought she could make a lot more money dealing with other people. We weren't going to give in to her demand for more, and her manager/agent decided that they could get more someplace else. I guess that's what she's doing. Linda Georgian is not the Psychic Friends Network. The Psychic Friends Network is made up of thousands of great people who are in fact psychic readers. We wish Linda great success and great luck.

*SD:* So have you filmed the new show?

*MLW:* With Linda?

*SD:* No, she's not in the new show, is she?

*MLW:* We've filmed the new show, yes. It should be going on shortly. As a matter of fact we have a new show without Linda that's on right now. We have another show that we shot that will be going on in a couple of weeks, also without Linda, which is quite a good show.

*SD:* Did you get anyone to basically fill her position in the show?

*MLW:* Yes. He's very, very good. And we have someone new for our newer show, and we had a meeting today with a psychic who is unbelievable, maybe the best I've ever heard or seen. A real leader. People all over the world come to him, to learn psychic wisdom. A very wild guy. Very, very good. We have no problem getting psychics. We're negotiating with some very big names, which we're working on, and hopefully it'll come to fruition in a couple of weeks. And life goes on. No one is bigger than the game, so to speak. There's no baseball player bigger than the game of baseball. And there's no psychic that's bigger than the psychic phenomenon that's sweeping the world.

*SD:* Talk a little bit about how, out of the gate, you produced your own shows? You'd never done that before. How did you pull that off so successfully?

*MLW:* That was really not that difficult. We've been involved in direct mail and marketing for a long, long time and I had to write copy and talk to the public and sell to the public and get across our point. What we needed was for the person to take the copy into the screen, into television. I hired Rob Hoffman to help me do that. And we did it. We did some other shows, and different things, and we've been successful with it. As you get bigger, you tend to do less of that, and do more of business, and it gets you out of your game. So now I became a big businessman and I do less copy and production, and I should probably stick to that, which I like better anyway.

*SD:* I was going to ask you about that, because my talent, if I have one, seems to be with the writing, but the day-to-day stuff just takes me so far away from it.

*MLW:* It does. And then you have to utilize other people to do the craft that you do better than they do. Then you have to coach them on the side, so what you're doing is two jobs now. And that's the problem. So it's very important to have good people working with you. And even if they don't stay with you, they want to pursue their own individual career, you have to let them go. You have to become a teacher so you can expand your business. It works, because if you teach them, they have the ability to go on by themselves. So you're constantly teaching. You have to teach to be good. To get bigger, you have to teach people.

*SD:* How much has the competition within the last two years really hurt your bottom line?

*MLW:* Interestingly, it really hasn't because of the foothold that we have in being the Psychic Friends Network. We've had so many calls for so long a period of time that people have known we're the standard and have come to depend on us. I would imagine [people] do try them, but I think they come back to us. Our numbers have not diminished, and we have not done what the other companies have done. We don't market the way they do. We don't do some of their programs which at best, are questionable. If anybody would do an investigative report on it, I think it would be somewhat shocking.

**SD:** Are you talking about how some of the other companies attempt to get the people locked into continuity programs where they're charged automatically every month?

**MLW:** Yeah, it seems to me it's not just bait and switch, it's just clear deceptive advertising. I myself called for it and I asked information and I got a bill at the end of the month from the telephone company, and it was called voice mail or something. I had no idea what I was getting, I didn't ask for it, I didn't agree to it, and if that happened to me, a sophisticated person in business, it's happened to thousands of people. And perhaps even more.

**SD:** And the problem is if there's a crackdown, you're going to get fallout from the publicity.

**MLW:** Perhaps as a business, but we're so careful, and we're not tainted. I think certainly the people we deal with like AT&T know what we're doing all the time. I don't think it would affect us at all. I hope it wouldn't affect the psychics because it took me a long time to grow the psychics into a part of Americana. When we first started, people didn't know what psychics were. They were heretics or devil worshippers or lunatics. It took us a long time to work on the persona and the personality. To have some people work it over and try to wrongly defame it just for the sake of a dollar is absolutely preposterous. But these are the same people that were in the adult business. When they cracked down on the way they were advertising and marketing, some of them just automatically started over to the psychic business, just thinking it was so successful. When everyone hears how successful something is, they want to try it.

**SD:** With Barbara De Angelis, her two shows, *Making Love Work*, have been very successful. I think the first show was more successful than the second one. Originally, wasn't the plan to do a whole 900 call-in thing with her?

**MLW:** Yes, actually we had a lot of plans to do a lot of things with her when we first started. I felt that Barbara could be and should be a real mentor, a real leader. It's 1996, it's the age of the woman, and people are looking at women not just from the neck down but from the neck up. And she's extremely bright and talented and she can help people in need. She really can help people, she has the gift. And she can produce, she can write, she can do anything. Barbara is a phenomenon unto herself. The reason you said the first one was more successful than the second, because the second was really very similar to the first, and only Barbara could have made it work. Because it's so honest, it's so good, if you see the infomercial, and read her reports and books, she's just so good. We haven't gone where we wanted to go with Barbara, and that's what we're working on now. We're sort of up and running again. Using the Web as an example, I could see using her on the Web to do huge audiences. I could see her in big seminars, in shopping malls being broadcast back to regular TV. I could see her doing so much good from perhaps her own clinics where she helps people. I don't think we've seen all of Barbara yet. I think the best is yet to come with Barbara.

*SD:* So you're doing a new show with her?

*MLW:* Oh yeah, we're working on a new show and new concepts, and not just the same kind of show, but different stuff. She should be hosting her own television show and I don't mean a game show. She very well should have millions and millions of people following her. She could be a great help to a lot of people who need it. And who doesn't?

*SD:* I'm looking forward to seeing those. We didn't talk at all about charge-backs on the psychic lines, but one rumor or misconception that's floating around, is that you have to keep the Psychic Friends going indefinitely or else the chargebacks would catch up to you.

*MLW:* If that's the rumor that's out there, it would probably keep everybody out of the business. It's probably disinformation. It's probably some spin that someone had on it. I don't think Visa or Mastercard would keep you if you got a lot of chargebacks.

*SD:* Can you give me some idea of what the average range is for chargebacks on 900 psychics?

*MLW:* I think their chargebacks could be as high as they were when these people were in the adult business. And I think that ranges anywhere between 35 to 70 percent. And you really can't make a living on that. The chargebacks come in months later. The telephone company has to hold out so much money, to make sure that there's a bankable amount that they can pay off to irate people. Once the telephone companies get wind of it, they tend to try to take these people off the air. But of course, everybody has the right to be up. You just can't make a person guilty without their being guilty. So it's a process, you know.

*SD:* All right, now I'm gonna ask you a question that I think a lot people have kinda scratched their head over. There's this image of you as a street smart kid, that you don't want to screw around with.

*MLW:* I hope so. That's the image I want out there. I am a street smart kid. I don't particularly knock anybody off, I don't particularly copy anybody's style or copy. I'm very fast to give a compliment to something I think is good. I don't like to be tread on, I don't like to be played with. I consider myself to have honor, and I treat people that way, and I expect them to treat me that way.

*SD:* Talk to me a little bit about the other worlds you want to conquer? You were getting into the motion picture business.

*MLW:* I'm doing that with my son, because he wants to go into that. It isn't a thing that I would pursue. I believe in commerce. I like selling. I like inventing. I like consumer products. I'm not into art for art's sake. A lot of film is subjective. Also the games they play, let's say I was talking to an actor about doing a net deal. As soon as you say "net deal" with them, they get sick. I didn't understand why, until I saw what they did to them in the movie industry. It's net after they're paying everybody from here to China! There's nothing left. For me, a net deal in the infomercial business is only, there's such a margin left, we're talking about two different things. So, it's different. The infomercial business is a great place to be, if you have the product, and you can wait for the right product, and you can show it correctly, you can have big winners!

*SD:* You have to have deep pockets nowadays, though.

*MLW:* Not really. I don't really think so. You know a bird in the hand is worth two in the bush. You have a product, you can speak to other people about helping you get it to market. You don't have to go up and spend hundreds of thousands of dollars on an infomercial right out of the bag, and the infomercial companies don't have to do that to get a guy who's coming to them with that. I spoke with someone the other day and these people said they're gonna get 8% and this deal and that deal. And I said, what are we talking about? You want 8% of what? Is that more than my percent of what I'm gonna make? It's all nonsense! You want to talk real dollars, talk real dollars. Everybody talks percent, they want this percent, that percent. Well, you deal with certain people in the industry, you'll get that percent.

*SD:* What about the huge increase in the media cost?

*MLW:* There's a saying where I come from that "cats look down at you and dogs look up at you, and pigs look you right in the eye." The pigs out there will look you right in the eye, and take your money. You have to be strong enough to say no. A lot of times they say, "But someone else is going to take it, they're going to take it." The truth of the matter is, after a while, they're not going to take it. And there's wholesale time out there available. If I see a number that they're putting out, I know what I have to sell to make it work. And I know that if I can't sell it to make it work, then no one can make it work. They could say, "Well, they're making it on the back-end, or a continuity program." Or this or that, and okay, I have to see those numbers too, because to me, they are their own market. It would be better to say no and keep the money in your pocket than giving it away. It becomes a situation where if you don't do it, they all talk about back-end marketing. Well they mean that if they don't do back-end marketing, they can't make any money. So they've shot their whole business.

*SD:* I would imagine that you saw much more significant profit on the front end in '91 with what media rates were, than you do now, but you know that you're getting it on the back end too.

*MLW:* Well, we haven't established that, but yes, it was a different time, it was a different horizon, it was new and there were people who have come in and taken it over. But you know, there's gonna be another thrust up, there's more space that's coming on. Another good story—when I was younger and my children were younger, I was going to an affair with my wife. I had a tuxedo on. I had this full-length mirror and I put my bow tie on and I thought I looked like the cat's meow—young and handsome and tan, feeling good, looking good, working out, and I looked in this mirror and I put my bow tie on and I said to my daughter, "Do I look great or what?" And she said, "Compared to what, Daddy?" And that was the greatest line in the world. So everything to me is compared to what? There's things I want to do, there's things that have to be done. As compared to what? The competition? Who's the competition? They're here today and they're gone tomorrow. And you see that, it happens all the time now. You see big companies going out.

**SD:** There's even been talk about either you merging or being acquired by somebody like National Media.

**MLW:** That could happen. There could even be funnier things. It could be a combination of, who knows, maybe I would merge or Guthy-Renker would merge with me. There's a shortening of the market. By doing that, you can bring your overhead down because you don't need duplicity, you don't need four offices, you don't need 10 advertising buyers, there's a lot of things you don't need. If everybody does the same thing, there'd really be no point in doing it. But if you bring different things to the table, then there is a point. I think that an entrepreneur like myself is not necessarily a great leader of a company. Because I have an entrepreneurial spirit. I don't like custodial work. Running a company is custodial work. That, to me, is extremely difficult, extremely unrewarding. But that's what any business is. Being a baseball player you have to do the same thing over and over and over again. I don't like that. I like the creating, I like the pizazz of it. But then again, you need an entrepreneurial guy to create the business. So, if I was with a company, or maybe my own, if I put a good CFO up, or even a president, and I can go out and find other things to market that's what I like. So that's the reason you hear these reports about me doing something else, or a lot of people think that I'm so good. Every time I make a lot of money, I'm great. Every time I don't make a lot of money, I'm not great.

**SD:** Did you ever dream you'd have this kind of money?

**MLW:** I've been asked that so many times. The truth is, I think yes. I'm not in awe of it. I think it's funny that I was chosen. I was always a little different, and thinking a little differently. So yeah, I think I kind of expected it. To tell you the truth, I expect a lot more. I could come out very egotistical. I don't mean it to be. I certainly do pay the price for it. The truth of the matter is, you go to work at 8 and you leave every night at 9. You put the time in. I feel fortunate that I can put the time in and make a lot of money, because I had a father and a brother who put a lot of time in and didn't make any money. There are many people who work hard just for a salary every day of their lives, and they're not any dumber than me, or any less swift, or kicky or street smart. So luck is very important in there.

*SD:* For somebody who wants to achieve a high level of success, is there any secret?

*MLW:* The secret is, what are you willing to give up? Think about what you have to give up. Not what you might give up, or could give up, but what you will give up for this craziness that people like me do. I want to tell you something—you'd pick me on your team if there was a gas strike or if there was a food strike. You'd want me to be with you. You ever see the movie *A Few Good Men*? When Jack Nicholson said to the lawyer, "You need me." At certain times, people want me for my drive and my tenacity. They like that. And I have it. This isn't something I asked for. I didn't go to school and learn. I have it and it's there. It drives me, it constantly drives me. When I get into something, I want to complete it, and I want to finish it. I don't like to play cards against friends because playing cards is not just a game of skill or chance, it's a game of ----ing the person you're with. So I don't like that. I don't like to do anything against my friends. I don't take a position against friends. But business is business. By doing that you have to give up a lot of friends. I can't, personally, socialize and be friends with people I'm doing business against. How can you really root for a guy not to succeed and be a friend? I root for my friends to always succeed, and in fact I root for my friends to succeed greater than I do. Because if they're my friends and if they're greater than I am, and I have a problem, they'll help me! I always look at it that way. So it's difficult. You give up a lot. By working from 8 in the morning till 8 or 9 at nighttime, you're not with your family that much. Your whole family suffers. You may give them the fruits of your labor, but the whole family suffers.

*SD:* Was your goal to earn a lot of money or was your goal to see an idea and run with it and find out where it ended up? Or both?

*MLW:* I would think both. I was poor growing up as a young person. And yes, I wanted to make a lot of money and live the American Dream. But it's also pride in winning and being successful. I always used to say that I don't worry about money. You just be successful, and you'll make the money. You shouldn't work for money. I remember *The Godfather*. When they were in Cuba, one of the guys was telling Michael that there's a little insurrection going on right now, but they'll put it down, the government is very strong. And they were looking down the street, and there was a shooting. The guy, the rebel, shot somebody important and they shot him and Michael said, "I think I got a problem here. These people are willing to die for what they believe in." True believers, you don't beat. Anybody can hire a mercenary. But a mercenary will run, or someone'll pay them more money. But a true believer, what do you do with that person? So I get into a friend and I'm a true believer, and how do you beat me? To beat me, you'd have to kill me. Or beat me square up, and then I'll love you. But if you don't beat me square up, then we have a problem, 'cause I'm there. I'm not leaving town, I'm in your face.

*SD:* You didn't make a success when you were real young. Are you grateful for that?

*MLW:* When I was 28, I was getting pretty wealthy already.

*SD:* Interesting. The last subject I wanted to touch on was that Don had spoken to me and kind of alluded to, and he was very general when he said it, but let me give an example that you take a fitness product, and you get somebody like Nike to sponsor it, and if the infomercial works, Nike's name is all over it and they'll put up money that goes toward the media buying.

*MLW:* That's something that could be. I'm not actively pursuing that end of it, but that's something that's done in movies all the time. They have different spots, and they show a car or Nike shoes, and they pay to get in with that. It's a retail commercial. I would love to do an infomercial to sell a car, something big like that. Because that's really the way to sell a car. The scariest thing in the world is going into a showroom and talking to a car salesman. Everybody's afraid of a car salesman. And I can sell a car right over the phone. And I can do it in direct mail with the real pointed commercial that shows the sales. A real direct marketing program in there. Whereas now, they run a commercial, and they spend X amount of dollars, they take in Y, and they deduct one from the other, and say well, we're successful. But I can do a commercial and I can do it for cities and towns. You tell them to go into Bob's Chevrolet tomorrow and there's a lot of ways of doing it that would be better. I can really explain the car in half an hour, what it does and what it doesn't do. There's a lot of big benefits. The infomercial business, the education end of the infomercial business is certainly the way to go.

*SD:* Any final words?

*MLW:* No, I really don't know. I've read some of the other interviews you've had. I hope this is as good as the others. I try to be as honest as I can. I really am a very private guy. I don't like to give away too much information. If it isn't informative...

*SD:* Oh I think it's a great interview.

*MLW:* My natural tendency is not to give anything away, like the American Telecast people. I'm not looking to hog the airwaves. I constantly see National Media in and I constantly see Guthy-Renker in, and they have a whole PR organization that keeps everything going. There's reasons why they want that to be. It isn't our program to do that at all.

# DAN DANIELSON

&

# JOHN CABRINHA

an Danielson and John Cabrinha are two of the humblest men in this industry. Beginning in the early days of the '80s when the business was just beginning, they joined up as partners and have driven their company, Mercury Media, to be the leading media buyer in the direct response television industry. Mercury books over $140 million in media business annually. Their computer system contains data of every media buy on every television and cable network they've made, making it easy for them to test new products in similar categories to what they've already run. They have solid data with which to measure a test against. In a business in which competition is tough, everyone in the industry has nothing but wonderful things to say about these men and their company.

**Steve Dworman:** How did the two of you get together and what were you both doing before Mercury Media?

**John Cabrinha:** Around 1982, I started as an operator for a company called Telephone Auction. At the time, I didn't even know what home shopping was. I was asked to come down and help out my sister, who was answering the phones for this auction at the San Jose flea market. I started answering the phones and we were handwriting orders. After we would write the orders, we would call the credit card companies and get the approval numbers. We'd send it over to shipping the next day. That took off in 1982. The company lasted until about 1987. At that point, I moved over to a company called Sybervision. This is where Dan and I met.

*SD:* I remember the Telephone Auction. It was on Saturday or Sunday morning?

*JC:* It was on at various times. We bought broadcast for it. It was an hour show and we'd run about 60 products in an hour.

*SD:* Why did the company go out of business?

*JC:* A number of reasons. They were having to purchase a lot of their own inventory and warehouse it, so they had huge cash outlays. If they weren't selling all of their inventory, it was very hard for them to liquidate it. A lot of their cash was tied up in the inventory and they couldn't purchase the necessary media. Once they got behind in their media, they had a vendor that went under. I think they lost around five to six hundred thousand dollars in that one hit. They started getting canceled out on their media. And they were running terms too. Once the media started drying up, they went into a tailspin. They were doing everything themselves. They were trying to telemarket, trying to ship and fulfill, and they were purchasing their own product and warehousing it. Nothing was on consignment.

*SD:* It sounds familiar. Those problems haven't left us.

*Dan Danielson:* No, it's pretty much a repeat. I graduated from college and started working at a company called Sybervision, back in 1986, in their marketing department. They came up with the bright idea of doing a one-hour commercial. We had about 15 products being sold in one hour. We realized that about 80% of the sales were coming off of one product, Neuro-Psychology of Weight Control. They decided to do a half-hour show on that one product and sales went through the roof. We started calling up stations all across the country and tried to secure half-hour time periods from them. That was when we hired John. We had three media buyers. And in the course of three years, with five shows on the same product, we did about $100 million in gross sales. We purchased about $40 million in media to do that.

*SD:* So John started as a media buyer and you were working in marketing?

*DD:* I was in marketing and was asked to start doing media buying. John was still working at Telephone Auction and we hired him away to do media buying for us.

*JC:* I had started as a telephone operator [at Telephone Auction] and worked my way through the company in various stages and ended up as a media buyer.

*SD:* So, John, you've been in this business for 15 years.

*JC:* Yeah, you can look at it that way. I try not to date myself by telling people that.

*DD:* He's done everything. He started as a telephone operator, he was an on-air demonstrator of products, he processed credit cards, he trafficked tapes, he tracked orders, he bought media. He did all that at Telephone Auction.

*JC:* Which I won't do anymore.

*SD:* Unless the offer is superb. John, with you having background in every sector of this industry, haven't you ever had the desire to do it yourself?

*JC:* Yes and no. Yes, it would be great, and for all the same reasons that you did a show. But I don't think I would do it, mainly because of our position as an agency. We hold very true to the philosophy and belief that Mercury Media is an agency and not a marketer. We want to keep that line as solid and distinct as possible.

*DD:* It would become a very strong conflict of interest for us if we were to ever get into the marketing business. Our clients would then have to compete with us.

*SD:* And what happened with SyberVision?

*DD:* SyberVision was essentially a similar premise to what happened with the Telephone Auction. We've seen it happen with a lot of companies in the industry. When John and I started there, they had about 30 employees in about 7,000 square feet. At its peak, we had 150 employees in 36,000 square feet. They tried to do everything themselves. They did their own fulfillment, their own telemarketing, their own media buying, their own production. Once they had built up the big infrastructure, they had to feed the beast. When they stopped feeding the beast, everything crashed around them. They only had one product on the air that was driving the whole system.

*JC:* They became so operations intensive that they forgot to really look at developing the product for the infomercial. Infomercials were definitely the driving force there. But we all know how volatile infomercials can be and you are really relying on your last hit. The product was always the same, Neuro-Psychology of Weight Control. They did five versions of the same infomercial. The other products they put on the air and tried to do infomercials with didn't have the same impact as the weight control product did. They could have, but there wasn't enough time to focus on those other products.

*DD:* They got detracted. There were a lot of problems. They eventually put themselves up for sale. They were sold and the last we heard was that SyberVision had about four employees in a 600 square foot office.

*SD:* I guess it's hard. The Neuro-Psychology of Weight Control is a subject that appeals to a great common denominator, but then using the same formulation, everything almost becomes a sub-set of that.

*DD:* We tried a few shows, but they were all niche in comparison. We did a foreign language show, a self-discipline show...

*JC:* A staying young show...

*DD:* And a golf show. They were there, and were actually ahead of their time. The products were just a little off the mark. Had [SyberVision] said they were going to be an infomercial company, I think they could have been so much more successful than what they were. They had a good product base. They had a memory product, but they never got out with it. They had a skin care/cosmetics show, but they never got out with it.

*JC:* They had a relationship show.

*DD:* All those things we've seen work in infomercials, they had product of, but never pushed.

*SD:* How long were you there?

*DD:* I was there for four years. John was there for three.

*SD:* And you both left at the same time?

*JC:* Basically, and this was one of the trickiest parts of Dan's and my partnership there.

*DD:* The company was up for sale and we knew it was going to be sold.

*JC:* Once it was sold, Dan left. I remained there as the sole media buyer. But it was pretty hard because I was there as a media buyer, but couldn't buy any media. The new company wanted to over analyze everything.

*DD:* It was analysis paralysis.

*JC:* I was stuck there, just trying to hold the schedules as long as possible. The only solution I could see was if Dan and I could start up an agency and I could become independent and run other shows and buy volumes so that I could keep the shows alive for SyberVision. I had to resign from SyberVision and convince them to come on board with us as our first clients.

*DD:* When it was up for sale, we had decided to start a company. We started one as soon as I left and called it Direct Ventures Marketing in San Ramon. John convinced SyberVision to become our first client. One of our other big clients that we were selling time to was Mercury Media. Marilyn Carr, the founder and owner of Mercury Media, was in need of airtime because she had two hot shows on her hands, the SnackMaster and Tony Robbins' Personal Power. So we helped her acquire airtime to meet her needs in a high-demand market.

*SD:* With SyberVision having financial problems, were you ever worried about not getting paid?

*JC:* No, they were still pretty solid.

*DD:* At that time, they had just been sold.

*JC:* We didn't have that concern. Once we started our business, we had two clients right off the bat. We were working out of a little office. Dan and I were sharing the office. It was like the two guys with their desks facing each other.

*DD:* We ran that company for a year and a half and were doing pretty well in Northern California. And one day, Marilyn Carr called us and asked if we would consider moving to Southern California.

*JC:* She called us on more than one occasion asking us that. At the time the response was always no. One day she called and told us she wanted to retire, she wanted to merge our company with hers and wanted us to move down and buy them out. Marilyn was in partnership with Richard Dubois, the other owner of Mercury Media. So we came to a deal and the next thing you know, we were living in Los Angeles, running Mercury Media.

*DD:* That was in September of 1991. That year, we had nine employees and about a $15 million year.

*SD:* Where are you at now?

*DD:* In 1996, we closed out the books at $75 million in media placement and in 1997, we'll end somewhere in the $80 to $85 million range.

*SD:* So that really makes you the largest domestic buyer of infomercial media time.

*DD:* We just know that we're one of the biggest ones. We'd like to remain that way and do the best job that we can.

*SD:* It doesn't seem as though you toot your horn very much. You basically keep it very close to the vest and very quiet.

*JC:* For us, it's very difficult. It's our clients that we're representing, and it's hard for us to go around tooting our horns when our clients are the stars. There's not a whole lot that we can say, nor should we say, because it's our clients that are responsible for that.

*DD:* We could brag, but we don't. We try to do a good job. The amount of billing we're doing and the campaigns we run have been indicative of that.

*SD:* At one point, Guthy-Renker was the majority of your business. That has changed drastically hasn't it?

*JC:* Yes, that was our biggest challenge when we first came down. The scariest thing for us when we came down six years ago was that Guthy-Renker was around 80 to 90% of the business. And we were buying into a company that was solely dependent on one client. Our immediate objective was to diversify the client base. We thought that by diversifying, we could become a better service to our clients in this game. Since media airtime, infomercial airtime, is almost a commodity base, the more you have the better your clients are because they have a better base to run within. Now...

*DD:* Guthy-Renker constitutes about 30% of the business.

*SD:* They're doing a lot more in-house?

*DD:* They do the cable buying in-house.

*JC:* Mercury Media was never responsible for their cable buying. Their cable buying was always done either through [Doug] Bornstein, [Nancy] Langston, or in-house.

*SD:* Let's go back. In the early 90s, how different were the success ratios?

*DD:* The success ratios were much higher in the late '80s and the early '90s. I think there are a couple of reasons for that. Media rates have escalated. We've charted it for 11 years now and seen how it has risen over that course of time.

*JC:* Are you talking about success rates of new infomercials that are coming on or individual airplays of previously tested shows?

*SD:* Well, for example, I was really blown away when Bill Guthy told me that in 1989-1990, the first Personal Power show was only doing a 2 to 1. At the price point they were charging and the cost of goods, it was a phenomenal success. But everybody has heard for so long that in that time period people were doing 4 or 5 to 1.

*JC:* That's kind of a myth, too. Yes, you may do 4 or 5 to 1 in your initial test, but everybody loves to blow up their numbers and say how well they are doing.

*DD:* When all is said and done, it's interesting to look at SyberVision, who was one of the first major players in the business between 1986 and 1990. We did $40 million in media and about $100 million in sales. It's just over a 2 to 1 mark. It wasn't a 4 to 1, or a 5 to 1.

*SD:* What was their price point?

*DD:* It was $69 and $89 with the upsell.

*SD:* Was it a one-pay?

*DD:* No, it was a three-pay. They were one of the first to do that.

*SD:* It might not have been as golden as everybody thought. The big difference was that the media rates were lower and there were also more eyeballs-per-station.

*JC:* I can't quantify the whole eyeballs per station thing. The media rates we can quantify. They aren't that far off from four to five years ago.

*DD:* From 11 years ago, it's dramatic.

*SD:* Give me some examples from 11 years ago.

*JC:* I was buying some network affiliates 11 years ago for around $2,000 for an hour.

*SD:* And today?

*DD:* Stations back then were roughly about 20% of what we pay now.

*JC:* We had an affiliate in L.A., during the SyberVision days, that had a half hour on Saturday mornings for about $8,000. And we're not talking about six in the morning.

*SD:* And today?

*DD:* It's in the 20's.

*JC:* Those are phenomenal changes. Obviously because they stick in my mind. For the most part, you can't milk that much blood out of a turnip from a station that's probably charging $400 or $500. It's not going up to $1,500. In a lot of cases, the only reason the prices have gone up on a lot of stations is merely because they work that much better or they work that well for clients or marketers. The prices go up because we pay them.

*DD:* The marketers have gotten smarter. Back in our SyberVision days, we just took the money off the front-end. TV was it. That was where you made your cash. We didn't work the back-end like we do now. We did a little, but not like now with retail, print, credit card inserts, international, etc.

*JC:* I would say that most of the campaigns we are doing right now are doing as well or better than they were in terms of overall ratios.

*SD:* It's hard to believe because so many more shows fail.

*DD:* My theory on why so many more shows fail nowadays is because there is so much more out there. You're throwing a lot more stuff up against the wall. How many new shows came out last month? If you go back to 1987, you're lucky to have 20 shows come out—and that is a random guess. But there were probably 80 or 90 shows last month.

*JC:* Tony Robbins' fifth version, overall, did much better than his first. Quick'n Brite, their ratio has probably doubled with the most recent version over the first and second ones.

*DD:* Not that the ratios doubled, but that the ability to spend on the show has doubled. The ratios stayed the same, but the life of the show and the return on investments has increased. And that's because the marketers are becoming better at producing these infomercials. These two that John just mentioned are able to hit the hot buttons much better than when they initially came out. They know how to market their products better than they did four or five or six years ago.

*SD:* They need more capital, too.

*DD:* Correct.

*SD:* With the early examples you gave, you've seen the same scenario happen to National Media, Regal, and Synchronal. Who's next?

*JC:* I don't know who's next, but I do know that there are lessons that we learned from SyberVision and Telephone Auction. I was pretty young at the time, but I do remember hearing management and administration saying, "Gosh, we could run this company with 14 people if we could source things out."

*DD:* That was CyberVision's ending story: "We could have run this company with 20 people." That's the stance that John and I have taken in running our business. We run a lean, mean ship. We were able to stay that way because we haven't gone in and built a big infrastructure that requires you to keep feeding the beast.

*SD:* How many people do you have working there now?

*DD:* Fifty-six.

*SD:* That's pretty lean with the amount of media you're buying.

*DD:* Correct. We have 12 media buyers in long form and three in short form.

*SD:* How have the media rates been affected, if at all, by the Fortune companies entering this industry?

*JC:* There wasn't any *Fortune 500* company that came in and blew rates out of proportion or was around long enough to do it. Microsoft came in and did the Windows 95, but it was a whole separate buy, away from traditional infomercial time. It was for two days. That didn't even have a huge impact. The industry does about $8 million a week in airtime. It would take a lot for any one *Fortune 500* company to come in and have a huge impact on us. The other thing is that we hyped the *Fortune 500* companies up a lot, but they didn't stick around.

*DD:* They come in and spend their million dollars and then they're gone.

*JC:* The ones that do stick around are playing the direct marketers game. They're buying the time based upon their results. And that's very important about keeping the *Fortune 500* companies co-habitating with the entrepreneurs.

*SD:* Have you run any *Fortune 500* campaigns?

*DD:* We have tested several and run James Bond, PeeWee Herman, Elvis Presley. We worked with Revlon, Redken, Merle Norman. Those were tests.

*JC:* Origins, Estee Lauder, Sony.

*SD:* Is there a lot more time involved in those campaigns?

*JC:* You'll kill yourself trying to answer every little question that they have fears and paralysis over. But at the same time, when you do get the one company that starts to think like direct marketers, they have a greater chance for success.

*SD:* And do most of them, going in, have any idea of what their goal is?

*DD:* They all do. Every single one of them that we have talked to has had an objective to hit. Unfortunately, most of them haven't hit their objective, so they're quickly out of the game. Some of them come up with an objective and they hit over it, doing better than they aimed to. So they change their objective to be even more direct marketer oriented.

*JC:* One of the biggest mistakes that we see with the *Fortune 500* companies is that they have too many objectives with the infomercial. They try to do too much within that half hour. They think that they can do the awareness, drive the retail, without upsetting the retailers they try to offer a product. Most of the time, what you're trying to do with an infomercial is get someone to pick up the phone and make a call. And they forget a lot about making the phone ring while trying to do the other items.

*SD:* They fall in love with their product, too?

*DD:* Every client does.

*JC:* You have to.

*DD:* As media buyers, we have to fall in love with them. That's one of the reasons why we make things work. We love the products we sell. We believe in the stuff we sell.

*SD:* Mercury is very well known for being able to test for a low amount of money. What is your philosophy about testing a show?

*DD:* Basically, for the low amount of money we test, one of three things is going to happen. You're going to know if you've got a dog on your hands. You put the show out there and the shows don't ring. We're putting you on such proven time periods, such proven stations. We're not testing the stations or the time periods, we're testing your show. If they don't work on these A+ stations, they aren't going to work anywhere.

*JC:* Typically what happens is that people walk into a test and assume they're going to be able to test everything all at once: your markets, your day parts, your time periods. You really can't do that. Your test early on is just the show. We're just testing whether you're going to be able to make the phones ring or not. That's going to be your big deciding factor, before you go into testing everything else.

*DD:* If on that first weekend, you come in and you die, we don't recommend that you spend any more money. We recommend that you revisit your campaign. Look at the product, look at the presentation. Something is dramatically wrong here. If you come in that first weekend and break even, we say, "Hey, people did pick up the phones and they did call. Now what can you do either in our strategy of buying, in your price point, upsell, or telemarketing script to get more people to convert to the sale?"

*JC:* Typically, in situations where they are a break even, enough phone calls were made to the telemarketing centers to actually make a profitable test. The problem that occurs is that not all the phone calls are actually ordering. So you've got to figure out what the hindrances are. Why are people calling, but not ordering?

*DD:* The third scenario, being the best, is that you've doubled to quadrupled your money. At that point you've got a hit on your hands and we still recommend further testing to make sure we're pricing it at the best level.

*JC:* Your first stage is to simply find out if the infomercial works. Second stage is to find out markets and day parts. You'll see off your first test the different nuances in your test are in your markets. And the third stage is there to set your budgets up. At that point we make the recommendations to what degree can we roll this show out. How much can we spend for the client to reach the peak profitability. We're usually pretty right on in our marks.

*SD:* For a successful show, how much should you be spending a week?

*DD:* It depends on the show. We've had shows on the air that we consider successful that have spent $25,000 a week, and they did that for two years. Their objective was a 2 to 1, and at $25,000 a week that was all they could do. It was a small company and they made nice money, but it was a niche product. On the other hand, someone else's show might go up to $600,000 a week. Their objective could also be 2 to 1, but because it's a broader show with a broader audience and appeal, we could roll it out much further.

*SD:* Talk to me a little bit about when you're buying multiple shows and you've got commitments for certain airtime. How do you juggle who gets what airtime?

*DD:* Basically, the way we do it is to buy airtime for specific shows. People have this feeling that there is a finite amount of media. We've always been able to buy more media for clients for their show specifically.

*JC:* Let's say you're looking for a 2 to 1. We have a $10,000 buy that's pretty hot and guarantees a 2 to 1. What would be the problem with coming up with ten $1,000 buys on a 2 to 1? We're doing only $80 million out of $400 million. There is time to be bought there. It is just a matter of making sure everybody has the right mix in their portfolio. We get clients who want to air during the "hot" time periods. They think these large time periods are the hot time periods to have. In actuality, they really aren't. It's very hard to put clients into those time periods because they can be large risks. If you're running shows at $40,000 to $50,000 a week and you're putting in two time periods that equal $20,000, that's half of your budget. Frankly, that's too much weight to put into two time periods.

*DD:* Mercury Media's average media buy last year was $700. That means that where we're making money for our clients is in that $600 to $1,500 media price range. That's where the bulk of our buying occurs.

*JC:* You do the large time periods for a specific reason because you know it is going to work, but it is not the name of the game.

*SD:* Talk a little bit about the variances when you're running a show. City versus rural, morning versus late night.

*DD:* Our database has over $350 million worth of media buys in it. I can access data going to back to 1988 right now. If you're looking for a show that appeals to women that are 35 to 54, we go into our database, find those shows, and we buy media in accordance with that.

*JC:* From there you have to go into your ongoing testing for the campaign. You may have a celebrity that has a big appeal in one region, but none in another. You do market comparisons, knowing that one market acts similar to another market. This is more of the art form than anything else. We know this from experience. We know the different characteristics of each market, then we have to compare as we're rolling out.

*SD:* How often do you analyze this?

*DD:* Every single day. That's where we make our money, by analyzing every buy to see what's working and what's not and making sure the shows you're placing now are hitting a similar demographic to what you've done in the past.

*SD:* Do you see any trends as far as what kinds of shows are working?

*JC:* I think right now, what you see a lot of is what's working.

*DD:* People are always wondering what's working. If you flip on the TV on a Saturday or Sunday morning, between 7 and 10 here in Los Angeles, what you'll see is a lot of paper and tape, a lot of self-improvement. It's much more than we've seen in the recent past.

*JC:* There may be room now for demonstratables again.

*DD:* Kitchen items are coming back. There are two or three strong kitchen items. One thing we've learned in all the years in this business is that it is a very cyclical business. We started off with weight control in 1986. Around 1991, weight control was back in. We've seen weight control have a resurgence this year, 1996 to 1997. We're seeing it with kitchen items. We've seen them come and go two or three times. Real estate, home business opportunities, too.

*SD:* Who's making the most money?

*DD:* The guys that retired a few years ago and are out of the business.

*JC:* Dan is.

*SD:* And who's second?

*JC:* Marilyn.

*SD:* And Richard is probably third, so who's fourth, John?

*JC:* My girlfriend.

*SD:* Now really, who's making the most money?

*JC:* In the industry?

*SD:* Not necessarily in the industry. But of people you know, who is actually pocketing the most profit? It doesn't have to be your clients, but who do you think, with the way they're set up, is seeing the most profit, not necessarily the largest grosses?

*JC:* I would say the marketers are the ones who make the most money. The product owners who market their own products make the most money in this business.

*DD:* No one prints their bottom line. We thought we made a lot of money with SyberVision, but when all was said and done, they didn't walk away with a whole lot of cash.

*SD:* The average infomercial company that has successful shows on the air, when everything is said and done, their net profit might be between 10% and 12%. And then taxes take almost half of that. It's one of the few business where you can spend hundreds of millions of dollars and be left with gum money.

*JC:* It would be interesting to compare the percentages between a large infomercial company compared to smaller to mid-range companies. If you put Guthy-Renker and National Media on the high end and then somebody out there with one or two products on the low end, see what the percentages are then.

*SD:* Is there anything else that you would like the readers to know that we haven't covered?

*JC:* Dan, where do you see the industry going?

*DD:* I always see it doing what it is doing right now. It is very entrepreneurial in nature. The media vendors will continue to sell media. Infomercials will continue to work. New productions need to come up that have new tweaks, new angles, new twists to get the audience to pick up the phone and call.

**SD:** When you get right down to it, is it all a numbers game? Do you just throw everything against the wall and hope something sticks?

**DD:** No, in fact, I think if you look at the history of the industry, a lot of companies got into trouble when they started throwing stuff against the wall and it didn't stick.

**JC:** I think the times we've seen the greatest failure rates of companies are right after they start throwing everything up against the wall. They don't take the time to see what the elements are that make a particular product work within an infomercial.

**DD:** And they usually only do that out of desperation.

**JC:** It's either desperate or greedy when they start doing that. They assume they can get anything to work and they start throwing things up.

**SD:** That's also the problem of feeding the pipeline when you're doing everything yourself.

**DD:** When you've got that beast to feed, you're very tempted to throw a lot of stuff up and hope and pray that something sticks.

**JC:** Another good question is what are the challenges for our industry? I would say our number one challenge is keeping the media vendors happy, making sure they continue to supply us with airtime. The over-purchasing of airtime for specific product categories and then turning that airtime back in left a bad taste in their mouths. Not that we did anything wrong, we just over-committed. Therefore, they felt like they had most of their time sold and it came down towards the end of the year and we turned it back in. That kind of stuff doesn't sit too well with television stations. Media vendors would like nothing more than to not run infomercials or run infomercials in their current state. What they would rather do is to run programming that either creates a better feeling towards their audience, or actually garners a better audience. Now if we can do both within an infomercial, that's great. But it's not common. For the most part, these media vendors are looking for ways out of the infomercial. It just so happens that the money is intoxicating for them.

**SD:** On that point, are the broadcast stations more flexible with their rates than cable?

**DD:** That's a case-by-case situation. Some stations, in both instances, are more flexible and some are more rigid. I wouldn't throw them into a box saying one is one way and one is the opposite. You'll find broadcast stations that are more strict and more stringent than cable.

**JC:** If you're looking at some broadcast stations that are $400, the broadcaster can take you down to maybe $350 or $300. Anything below that, somebody else is going to gobble the time up.

*SD:* Have either one of you seen any breakout shows for fourth or first quarters yet?

*JC:* We hear that a few have tested that are doing very well. We haven't seen them roll out yet. I'm not at liberty to name them.

*SD:* There doesn't seem to be a lot though, does there?

*DD:* No.

*JC:* I'm not hearing of any forest fires out there. I just got a note here that says, "Stock market crashing. Deal with it now." With that in mind, it will be interesting to see what happens with the rest of the fourth quarter. I think this may have a big impact on us in the fourth quarter.

# BURL HECHTMAN

❦

*W*ith a background as an agent at the William Morris Agency, Burl Hechtman creatively put a lot of music projects together in his career. He was hired personally by Michael King to head a new division of King World called King World Direct. In a few short years, Burl built the business up to be an extremely profitable division selling video series such as *Wild America* through direct response televisions spots. He left King World to start a spot division for industry leader Guthy-Renker. After heading that company up for a number of years, Burl left and is now consulting for a number of companies within the industry. When Burl began in this industry he literally knew very little about direct response. He is one of the best students I've ever run into and could now easily teach—as he does in this interview.

**Steve Dworman:** This is one of the strangest stories I've ever heard in my life. The industry will be talking about this one for weeks to come. Why don't you tell me how you first met Mark Simon?

**Burl Hechtman:** Well, it was in a bathroom. I was at the left-hand urinal, he was at the right-hand urinal.

**SD:** Uh huh.

**BH:** And I was looking straight ahead—as you're supposed to do. I felt a tension in the air, so I turn over to the right and I see Mark there. And he says, "Could I come and work for you, I'd like to get into direct marketing?" And I said, "Why are you approaching me in a bathroom like this?" He said, "Because I've been trying to get in and meet you and I couldn't get an appointment and I want to get into direct marketing." I said, "Well, of course, if you're this persistent and aggressive, um, tell me about your background?" He told me about his background—by now we were washing our hands. He was a

USC film school graduate who really wanted to get into direct marketing because he felt there was a big business there. I said, "I didn't have any openings for him but if you want to start as a trainee, even though you have a college degree, I'll give you a shot." He said, "Yeah, I want to do it, and I'll prove myself." And, that's how we met.

*SD:* Did he wash his hands?

*BH:* Let me go back. Did he wash his hands? Yes, he did. That was after the urinal. I don't remember if he dried them though.

*SD:* Okay, and what position does he have now?

*BH:* He is the Vice President of Production.

*SD:* But you are still paying him minimum wage?

*BH:* Well, now I'm not paying him anything. Now he's just doing it for the title.

*SD:* Uh huh, that's how this business works.

*BH:* Yeah, titles are very important.

*SD:* Well that's fascinating. Did he ever tell you how long he had been waiting around the bathroom?

*BH:* He had been there for somewhere between two and three weeks. He knew eventually I would come in there, and he was right. I did.

*SD:* How did he know what you looked like?

*BH:* You know that's a good question. I'll have to ask him that. I guess, maybe, he just asked everybody who came in there. "Are you Burl Hechtman?" Eventually, somebody—me—said, "Yes."

*SD:* Really?

*BH:* What's funny is, in that same building was Fred Silverman. You know, he could've been in television if he had asked him. Mainstream television. But I think that Fred Silverman's office was on the 8th Floor. And I was on the 12th. Different bathrooms.

*SD:* He must have been told that you are a large man?

*BH:* I guess he wanted to confirm it for himself.

*SD:* Why not?

*BH:* That's one of the things I teach. You know, never trust anything and always go and do your due diligence. Check everything out for yourself. Yeah, I guess that's what he was doing, that's very good. I guess everybody knows now.

*SD:* I always found that a fascinating story.

*BH:* It's really the basis for my success, that story.

*SD:* Why is that the basis for your success?

*BH:* Because Mark is really great at what he does.

*SD:* What does he do?

*BH:* He goes to the bathroom a lot. In his spare time, he oversees all the productions that we do, and he also finds a lot of great products.

*SD:* You start getting worried and insecure every time he goes to the bathroom now, right? You think he's looking for another job?

*BH:* Not really, because I go with him. I won't let him go alone anymore. Especially when he goes to the bathroom wearing a tie. Then I'm really very concerned.

*SD:* Yeah, that's bad. Now let's talk about your background.

*BH:* Okay, I started in a bathroom. Okay…my background is that, ah, my background in the direct marketing business or my overall background? I'll give you my overall background.

*SD:* Give me your overall background.

*BH:* Graduated college from Roosevelt University in Chicago with a degree in marketing and decided I wanted to live in California because the cold weather of Chicago had gotten me as much as it could. Graduated college on a Saturday and the next day, on Sunday, got married to my wife Betty. And we are still married all these years later. Drove out to California and went through a series of around six jobs in two years trying to look for the right thing to do.

I thought I wanted to become a CPA because I had done well in accounting courses and business courses, I was all set to take a job at Southland Corporation, which is 7-Eleven, to be an accounting clerk while I was going for my CPA degree or whatever. And basically I called up one place that had an opening—another accounting clerk opening—before I took the job at 7-Eleven. It was the William Morris Agency. On the phone, I gave them my qualifications and the personnel person said I was overqualified—you have too much education for our accounting job but you sound great for our agent training program. I said to them at the time, "What's an agent?" Because I didn't know what a theatrical agent was, you know being from Chicago and being in the Midwest and just generally my degree in marketing, and she told me about it and I said, "Wow, that sounds great!" She said, "Why don't you come in for an interview?"

I went in for an interview, and said, "Wow." This had sounded great, $90 a week, had to have a college degree, and all that kind of stuff, then when I left there, I found out that the only way to really get into that program was that you had to have connections, you had to be a relative of someone there or have a very strong friend, you know, your parents have a very strong friend or something like that and that made me want to have the job that much more. I was getting a little tired of the accounting courses anyway because once everything balanced out, there was nothing else to do in accounting. So what I did was, I wanted to get that agent training job.

I was driving my wife to work one night—she was working at the phone company to help us get by— and I saw a Western Union office there. This is in North Hollywood, on Magnolia, and something hit my mind saying, what I learned in business school, whatever, you know, let's do a telegram—different ways to get to people to get what you want, stand out, be special, that type of thing. So, I sent a telegram to William Morris, a sales telegram, wanting the job, and this is after about three months of waiting and calling every week waiting to see if there was an opening in the program. Well, it so happens— this is before fax machines and e-mail and all that stuff—when I sent the telegram, it got on a thing called a telex at William Morris Agency which went to all of their offices around the world, where they transmitted offers. And the telex was seen by the top executives, president and top vice presidents of the company. It must have impressed them because when I made my weekly call to personnel they said, "Well, Mr. Hechtman you've certainly made an imprint here with your telegram, and we'd like you to come in and start in our training program." So then I went in, got the job and that's how it started. I started in the mail room there.

Eventually, I signed a couple year contract with King World. Michael King said, "We're doing a promotion for *Wheel of Fortune*. Could you put it together?" I said, "Sure." He said, "Put it together. We're planning on spending a couple of million dollars. See what you can do." Well, to make a long, long story short, I put together a deal with Toys For Tots and Pizza Hut and *Wheel of Fortune* for a big promotion with a 900-number where people call in. Basically, they got a $5 coupon at any Pizza Hut and they also had a chance to win major prizes and it cost them nothing other than the 900-call.

Well, I had never done 900-calls before, so I made a deal with a company called Call Interactive. We had no idea how many calls we were going to get. It turned out that it was a huge success. It was one spot within *Wheel of Fortune* for three weeks, 15 shows, during November sweeps. We ended up averaging 360,000 calls a night. The interesting thing was that we got about 100,000 of those calls from about an hour after the show until the next day's show. So, I started learning about drag, calls coming in, whatever. And that's where I started learning about fulfillment because we had to fulfill the coupons.

We ended up fulfilling something like 4.5 to 5 million coupons in three weeks. It took one year of customer service after that to deal with the 10,000 people out of the 5 million who didn't get their coupons. The reason they didn't get their coupons was with Call Interactive. I learned all this after the fact. Only about 80% of the calls are transcribed properly. About 20%, the operators can't understand the people's address, phone number, etc., and they didn't get the coupons. And 10,000 people actually cared. So we had to go and fulfill these 10,000 people for one year after.

But it was a huge success. Ronald Reagan gave a $1 million check to Toys For Tots. Ended up giving around $3 million to Toys For Tots. So a promotion that was supposed to cost King World $2.5 million ended up making $3.5 million, of which, all the money was given to Toys For Tots. They set up a foundation, which to this day I believe is still going—every Christmas, they give toys to kids. So that was a really good feeling, very successful thing.

Michael wanted me to be in promotion now. I told him I didn't want to do that. I can do it, but you have a whole department with 15 people doing that. So, he said, "You've got to do a promotion for *Candid Camera*. We're launching it with Dom DeLuise and we want to get a good tune-in." Since I had a contract, I was there, I did it. Again, I brought in Pizza Hut, who I had a relationship with. We did a watch-and-win contest again. I brought in movie theaters to do trailers before the films of maybe 5,000 to 6,000 movie screens. We did a whole big promotion. It worked in the sense that *Candid Camera* came out with a 6.5-7 rating the first two weeks, so it got the tune-in. The show ended up not going past the year, but I did my job to get the tune-in to get the people to watch the show.

While that was going on, I was looking to create something for myself. I told Michael I wanted to form a direct marketing company. He said, "That's interesting, but we have no budget for you." I said, "Well, I want to do it." He asked, "Why?" And I said, "Because I think there's a big opening there and there's a lot of available time in direct marketing." I was starting to be intrigued by spots that I would see in the middle of the night. One spot in particular was this Time/Life spot called *The Camelot Years*, where they sold a John F. Kennedy tape. I'll never forget writing that number down at 2:30 in the morning and seeing that spot. It was a very moving spot. Three days later, I called the number and ordered the product. The interesting story that I tell people, which is true to this day, I've never opened that tape. But I was moved by that commercial enough…

*SD:* I thought you were going to say you never got the product.

*BH:* [Laughter] Yeah, I never got the product and I'm still trying to get it. It's taking me ten years! That's funny. And that's what intrigued me about this business. That you can send somebody your money and never get the product and still keep doing it.

*SD:* And it took you three days to call.

*BH:* Three days to call! But I liked it! I said this is something I can do. So I got the product...

*SD:* Wait a minute. Do you ever breathe? You just talked for 15 minutes without taking a breath.

*BH:* No, I don't breathe. I don't have time to breathe. I breathe on the weekends, sometimes. So, basically, I was intrigued by that, the Time/Life thing. I said to Michael, I want to do something. He said, "You have no budget. If you're not going to do the promotions, what are you going to do?" I said, "Direct marketing." At that time you—Steve, had introduced me—because I had found you somehow, through your *Infomercial Marketing Report*—you had introduced me to Joe Sugarman. And, Joe as you remember, this is around '92, was very hot with his infomercial for BluBlockers. I got a call from Roger King who said, "We're going to launch *Inside Edition* on the weekends." It was a Monday-Friday show. This was July. He said, "Look, we need 70% of the country to get national advertisers. Right now we're only going to have about 35 to 40% of the country, so we can't get any national advertisers, but we're holding three 30-second spots in the show. And, we can only go to one station per market. Can you do anything in direct marketing with this?" Because he had known that I was interested and my main contact there was Michael on the west coast, because Roger worked out of New York. So I said to him, "If I can put the three 30s together and make a 90-second spot, I think I can sell that and make some money." He said, "Go see what you can do." So you had introduced me to Joe Sugarman. I was talking to Joe and learning and studying. I want to thank you, Steve, this is on or off the record, I don't care, for all the introductions of people—from Gail Eberline to Jeff Glickman to fulfillment houses...

*SD:* You're welcome.

*BH:* So, in the year '92, I was traveling all over the country meeting different media companies. Eicoff in Chicago, Corinthian, talking to Wunderman, to fulfillment houses, telemarketing companies, the whole thing...doing my due diligence, because Michael wanted me to prove to him there was a business. At the same time I was talking to Joe Sugarman and Roger called me about the show and Joe said he could put together a 90-second spot of BluBlockers. So, I swung a deal with Joe where for 52 weeks we would be in the Saturday-Sunday edition of *Inside Edition* and it was a flat fee against a percentage. It was basically a 50/50 deal. Put the spot in there and I was amazed. Because I had never—I had the 900 experience of *Wheel of Fortune*—but I was amazed how this one spot running in 35 to 40% of the country generated so many orders. And orders throughout the entire week. The shows aired Saturday and Sunday, but we got as many orders Monday through Friday combined as we did just on the Saturday to Sunday. That drag factor. Also, the upsells and the whole thing and I learned a lot in that year from Joe and watching how it worked.

I made enough money where I had around $250,000 profit from that. At that time, still they were thinking, that's interesting, but all you've got is that $250,000 to play with Burl. Even though King World has hundreds of millions in the bank, they were a very conservative company and didn't want to get into a new business they didn't feel they had expertise in.

So a friend of mine, Paul Gilbert, who was working at King World in the syndication department, transferred a call to me from Marty Stouffer. Marty had a PBS series called *Wild America* and Marty wanted King World to syndicate the show. Well, King World wasn't going to do weekly shows. So, Paul, knowing that I was looking to do direct marketing, thought maybe this was something I would be interested in.

I got Marty on the phone and told him about the Time/Life success, and I met with him and made a deal for the entire library, because they were having trouble syndicating the show. As a matter of fact, they just recently syndicated it for the first time to Rysher. Because of the success, I believe, of what we did in direct marketing and they even got a movie with it. Anyway, I made a deal with him and thought all the Time/Life stuff that was out there was very violent and it was doing fantastic, you know, *Predators of the Wild* and *Trials of Life*. So, I said to him, "Let me have your library and let me reformat it into concept shows." They gave me the library and I reformatted them. And rather than having animals chase animals and get eaten up, I figured, let's root for the underdog. Let's do one where the animals chase the animals. They catch them, but they escape.

So I created a concept called *Great Escapes*, a $19.95 offer. I felt the perceived value of video was about $10 to $12 a video, looking at retail and prices going down. So, I couldn't sell one video for $19.99, we had to have two. So I made a premium of *Wild America: The First Ten Years*. An existing half-hour show of one of their 195. Gave that as a premium. Now you have two videos for the price of one, the second one was free, the reason to motivate people. Came up with the formula and it was a big success. This was in September of '93.

**SD:** Now you had to be dealing with pennies there, giving two tapes away with all your overhead costs.

**BH:** Yeah, I was dealing with pennies, but what I had learned—remember that year in '92—that to make a business work in direct marketing you have to have a back-end business. You don't want to have a one-shot business, because if you do, it's only one shot. I had learned in business 101 in school, and throughout my whole business life, you want to build businesses there needs to be a back-end. I was looking to build a *Wild America* business, with foreign, with as many of the back-end things as possible. Outbound telemarketing, with Jeff Glickman being very successful and helping me a great deal in that. It worked in foreign and outbound telemarketing and it worked on television. We made money on it because we sold huge numbers of it. It didn't work in other areas, such as print and direct mail, but not everything works in every area.

To make that business work, you had to do volume. You had to hit a nerve. I kept it out of retail by design, because I looked at the retail marketplace for animal tapes and they didn't do well. From Time/Life to National Geographic to Discovery Network tapes, they didn't do well, so I kept it out of there and made it "Not Sold In Stores." Plus the things that I had learned, the things that motivate people to buy, are things such as, free, where you give the second tape free, the premium. Also, "Not Sold In Stores," a reason for urgency—you've got to buy it now. And, the perceived value of two tapes. We were able to move tapes. The good thing about videotapes is you don't have inventory risks because you really manufacture to order.

Since I only had $250,000 to play with from the money I made on the BluBlockers, I couldn't get into a business that was infomercials, which were hot at the time, because I couldn't afford to do one infomercial. So, I was positioned back into doing short-form, and short-form that didn't have inventory risk. So, I was positioned to doing videos and I focused on that. Then it became a huge business because we ended up having five hits in a row with the *Wild America* library, from *Spectacular Showdowns*, to *Dangerous Encounters* to *Precious Moments* to *Fantastic Follies*. This is year after year after year building up a database of 1.5 million customers in three years. Tens of millions of dollars in revenue. It was a very successful business.

*SD:* Which tape did the best?

*BH:* *Dangerous Encounters. Dangerous Encounters* sold 430,000. That was off of TV only. None of the tapes were ever in retail.

*SD:* Why do you think that one did better?

*BH:* I'll tell you why. I came up with the idea because every year, at a certain time of the year, you watch the news and animals come into people's backyards, down from the hills. There is this intrigue, this fascination, that humans have with animals. Especially, the dangerous part of it. I figured that anything that's on the news, that's worthy enough to be put on the news, the most important show for a local station because of media dollars and ratings dollars—that's of interest. If you look at all these shows now, these cop shows and real video shows, all that kind of stuff, that stuff is on the news all the time, too. The car chases and all that.

At that time I saw that, and I thought there is just a great fascination for it. So we did was a commercial for *Dangerous Encounters,* and it just hit a nerve of fear. I mean what emotion are you working on for that one? You're working on fear. What I was doing with *Great Escapes* was the emotion of the underdog. There's fear but at the same time you're safe at home watching it. People love this stuff. Look at wrestling now. Look at violent stuff. People like to watch and not be hurt. It was the way the commercial was cut and the intrigue and the fascination of it. It was something where they just had to have it. Again, that thing of "Not Sold In Stores," and by this time I had already sold *Great Escapes* one year, *Spectacular Showdowns* the next year. This was a fourth quarter and first quarter thing. People knew they could only get these on TV, and it just hit a huge nerve, it was a big thing.

That same year, this was I think '95, Marty Stouffer asked me, "Could you do something soft?" I said, "You know, I think the people really want the hard stuff, the violent stuff, that we make approachable. But you know something, soft stuff has emotions, too. Cuddly and cute and whatever. I could do one. Do you have any baby animal footage?" He said he had tons of it. So, I came up with this concept of *Precious Moments*, and I would just do babies. Baby animals and the "ah" factor. Do that for women. More of the female demos. Buy different media than I bought for *Dangerous Encounters*. Since we were making so much money and were so successful, I just did it, quite frankly, as a test. That's what I learned from Joe and other people, this whole business is just testing. We really don't know what is going to work until you try it. I put out the concept, *Precious Moments*, and it was just "oohs" and "ahs" of baby animals. Our premium tape was *The Beauty of Butterflies*, another one of his half-hour shows that was already completed. That tape did the same fourth quarter…and first quarter ended up selling 300,000.

*SD: Precious Moments* sold 300,000?

*BH:* Yeah, on TV.

*SD:* That's amazing.

*BH:* It is amazing. We sold 730,000 tapes in the fourth and first quarter of '95-'96 on television, just in the United States. That's not including foreign where the stuff worked also. Where Interwood did a wonderful job selling these tapes from day one. They ended up having these tapes, I think, in close to 80 to 90 countries. We are selling still to this day. That's how that business started. Now did I answer your question?

*SD:* Yeah.

*BH:* How I got started, okay.

*SD:* Why don't you tell what you did and what you learned as far as putting the back-end together, because the front-end just had to be a penny business?

*BH:* It was a penny business, but it was a lot of pennies because of the volume. As I mentioned, I had 1.5 million customers in the *Wild America* database. I had learned a lot of it just from talking to experts and reading, and just my own business intuition, that you just can't stop there. You've got to make money on it.

*SD:* Tell me some specifics about what offers worked and what offers didn't work.

*BH:* Well, with the animal tapes, continuity didn't work. At the time I had also made deals with, and worked for, National Geographic Video and Discovery Network. I had some successes with them, but not to the level of *Wild America*'s success. This is an interesting thing about back-end. With the *Wild America* database, I figured what you've got to sell people on outbound telemarketing is something similar to what they bought on the front-end. That's just common sense. So if they bought a *Dangerous Encounters*, they want action, they want violence, whatever. Quite frankly, the *Wild America* library is family oriented. I made up these strong concepts but it's a family show, PBS show. What we did was, I had to look for something that was a harder edge. One of the series that I had tried on the front-end that didn't work, with Discovery Networks, was called *Hunters*. It was a series on Discovery Channel. I loved the title, *Hunters*. It was a very high quality production and a great show, but it didn't work front-end. It didn't work on the front-end as either a one-shot or a continuity. But I had the property, these ten tapes. What we did was we took the *Hunters* tapes and did a test to sell them to the *Dangerous Encounters* and *Spectacular Showdowns* audience and it turned out to be a huge success. Much more successful than selling the *Wild America* catalog to the *Wild America* customers because it was related to the concepts that the people bought.

So I had a deal with Discovery for *Hunters*. It didn't work on the front-end, but whenever I make a deal with somebody I like to try whatever we can, because I hate to lose, to see if we can make some money for them and for us. The test I did of selling the *Hunters* 10-pack to the *Wild America* customers was very successful. Of course, it didn't work to a *Precious Moments* or *Fantastic Follies,* customer but it did work to the *Great Escapes, Spectacular Showdowns* and *Dangerous Encounters* customer. We did millions of dollars of outbound telemarketing selling *Hunters*, which meant a lot of royalties to Discovery Networks. They told us they had never made a deal with anybody—and they had worked with Time/Life, etc.—they had never made a deal with anybody where the company did a front-end offer on television that didn't work and they still got royalties. Big royalties, from the back-end working. What I learned from that was the fact that you can make money on properties on back-end that don't necessarily work on the front-end. I also learned you make much bigger margins on the outbound than you can from, like you said, pennies on the front-end.

You asked about what kind of offers we did. The best offers for the animal tapes were where you would give people four tapes and give them one free, or three tapes and one free—you test different combinations. Then go back to those people at a later date and sell them the completion to the 10-pack. We tried continuity but it didn't really work strong enough for that type of thing. That was basically the type of offer that worked out.

I'm not saying we didn't sell the *Wild America* library to the *Wild America* people, because we did. We created a 12-pack of *Wild America* programs where we took three half-hour episodes and made them thematic, as close as we could. We put titles on the show. That took up 36 episodes. We sold a lot of those to people. We tried to make that a harder edge thing like *Predator & Prey* and things like that. Then we realized when we had the *Precious Moments* audience that the harder 12-pack wasn't going to work. I made eight more shows, three in a tape, because of the perceived value in a tape for $19.95. And people will pay more on the back-end for something than they will on the front-end, if you get the right customer. So, we put three tapes on there for $19.95 and we put an 8-pack together.

**SD:** Wait, let me clarify that statement. So they'll not only pay more for a tape on the back-end, but they'll buy more tapes on the back-end as well?

**BH:** Yes, I'm saying both.

**SD:** That's so interesting that the perceived value of the a tape goes up in the back-end.

**BH:** Well, for $19.95, you can charge perceived value for a 90-minute tape, on the back-end. People will pay that if on the front-end they bought two tapes for $19.95, if you got their interest. Because remember on the front-end, we charged $19.95 for *Dangerous Encounters*. I believe the premium there was *Watching Wild Life*. My pitch on that one was, when the premium came up, and if you want to learn how to watch wild life safely you can get *Watching Wild Life* or something like that. What I'm saying is *Dangerous Encounters* for $19.95 was a one-hour tape. On the back-end I can put three existing episodes of the *Wild America* series and call that particular tape *Predator & Prey*. That would be relative to the people who bought *Dangerous Encounters*, the same audience. They would pay more for it. But what we did on the back-end was rather than just sell them four tapes for $80, you sell them three for $60, and you give them the fourth tape free if they buy the first three. So basically, what you are giving them is four tapes for $60 which is $15 a tape and it's a $20 savings. Sometimes even when we did the Christmas times and holiday times, we'd do three and two free. You know, one for you and one other free. So you give them five tapes for $60, a $12 dollar value.

I learned there about back-end, outbound telemarketing, the foreign. We tested direct mail, print, inserts and different things with *Wild America,* but they didn't work. The only things that worked were international and outbound telemarketing on the back-end. But they were enough to be successful.

With the business I'm in now—I'm doing intellectual properties—I'm finding many, many additional back-end revenue streams that didn't work for animal products are working for my comedy things. So, you have to look at everything separately as a business. Just because *Wild America* only worked foreign and outbound telemarketing…of course, list rental too we made money on, so there is another avenue. You can't look at everything as the same. You have to take every project as a separate business. It can be a lot of work.

**SD:** Tell me the projects you had that didn't work at King World?

*BH:* The first thing that I did was a coin. I remember walking through my fulfillment house when I was doing the *Wheel of Fortune* promotion, I used Motivational Fulfillment. Hal Altman. He had a ton of coins that he was fulfilling through, primarily, catalogs. I asked, "Why can't these coins work on television? Let me try television." We put together a couple of coin offers. A $19.95 offer and a $29.99 offer. That did not work. That was one of the first things I tried that didn't work.

We also tried something that was marginal, but again I learned from it. That was a tape called *Paula Abdul's Get Up And Dance.* Actually, it's now being sold in retail for $9.95. But at that point Vestron, who had gone out of business, had paid a fortune, I think $1 million, for the rights and Live Entertainment, at the time, got the rights to it. I went in and made a deal with Roger Burledge, who was the president of the company at the time, and I said, "Let's do a TV offer." The problem was that there was no upsell and no back-end product. There was just the one videotape, and we created hats and t-shirts and stuff. But I learned that people want to buy the same type of product on the upsell or back-end.

When you talk about back-end, as you know, the upsells are more than vital. They are crucial to the success of any project. If you don't have a upsell on the phone that is going to work, you can't make money. Because as you mentioned on the animal tapes, their worth was pennies on the front-end of the $19.95 offer. Where the profits on the front-end were upsells that we created—good upsells, related upsells—that's where the profits come in. We did very good upsell percentages.

So now I'm doing *Paula Abdul* and I didn't really have the relative upsells but I did the best I could and I thought with her name, give it a shot. We did a very good commercial, I feel. We put it out there and it came in at about a $20 cost per order. Well, you can make money on a $20 cost per order, on a $20 offer, if you have a major upsell and you have a back-end business you can deliver. In this case the hats and the t-shirts did not work as upsells. So, there was really no revenue of an upsell. And if our media came in at $20 and our break-even was $19 or $18 that was based on a good upsell. We didn't have the upsell so our allowable was say, $15 or $14. We couldn't do it.

Now I have offers that come in over $20 that I'm making a lot of money on, because of the upsells and the back-end business. Again, I learned with a failure, that you have to have a back-end for everything, or I don't take on a project.

Also looking at things that didn't work, I did a water cooler. Called The Mini. I thought that was a neat concept. It held eight glasses of water and you put it on your desk. We did a great commercial. Jim McNamara actually did the commercial. We had Nancy Nelson in the commercial. This is all short-form stuff. Picture little Sparklets or Arrowhead coolers that fits on you desk that holds exactly eight glasses of water. The whole pitch there was drink your water. That was a good commercial, the whole thing. Didn't work.

I did some offers for, like I mentioned, the *Hunters*. Didn't work on television but worked on the back-end for Discovery Networks. I did some things for National Geographic, some worked, some didn't work. I was fortunate enough that I was very selective. That I had a very high percentage of things work because I didn't try that many things. But I had plenty of things that didn't work. We tried a police chase thing that didn't work.

As you know in this business, you don't have to have many things that work, you just have to have enough that work. That becomes businesses for you. That's always been my philosophy, and I've learned this, you have to only do things if they work, that have the potential to become businesses and just work those businesses to maximize it. Quite frankly, I had heard when I got into this business, that 1 out of 10 short-forms work, or 1 out of 20. I have had higher luck than that, but the point is even if it was 1 out of 10, you could make money if the one you have is a good business. Because the nine that don't work are small investments compared to the up-side potential of the one that does work.

*SD:* So, what happened, why did you leave King World?

*BH:* What happened was, I was very successful with *Dangerous Encounters* and *Precious Moments*. Success with *Fantastic Follies* had built up. I'm a big believer of diversification of risk. I had built up two businesses there. Not only my intellectual property business but a retail hybrid business with Sears. Joe Batogowski, who was a 22-year veteran of Sears and worked his way to be the top executive vice president of merchandise, and I formed a deal. He was overseeing all merchandise for all divisions and all marketing before they put in a new system where they have different presidents for different lines and different marketing people. When he was there, in the '70s and '80s, he handled everything. I met him and came together with this retail hybrid concept where you sell one product at one retailer while simultaneously advertising on TV. Until that point the whole philosophy of direct response television was, you sell on TV first, create a demand, then go to retail everywhere. But Joe's philosophy was that will just blow you out at retail and eventually it gets to Wal-Mart. Then you're out of business because of the low prices. So he came up with this concept. He learned when he saw a product called the Crosswalk—how it sold at retail and television simultaneously and there never was a mention of Sears. It just sold because Sears had such a high percentage of the retail exercise business.

So he came up with this concept, and I made the deal with him. Then we made a deal with Sears to do that and our first product was the Robo Grip.

*SD:* It was huge!

*BH:* Huge.

*SD:* Huge!

**BH:** How about it's still on the air six years later and it's the biggest selling hand tool in the history of Craftsman. The company has been in business 120 years. We took that product off a back shelf. What we did was, we raised the price from $15.99 to $19.99, took the marketing dollars and used it to market the product. It became a monster. Within the first year, they were selling 1 million of them when they had projected to sell, hopefully, 200,000. That was '94. In '96, and this is all published stuff that I've read, they sold over 3 million Robo Grips. Did over $85 million dollars on that one product line. That was a thing that they had hoped to sell 200,000 two years before.

**SD:** When you first saw this product, how did you ever know that people would buy this thing?

**BH:** It was all about demonstration and showing the uses. Look, Sears has 90,000 products on their shelves, as a lot of the major retailers do. The only way they advertise products is a 1" x 2" thing in the Sunday circular and price discounts. What we did here was, we raised the price, put the money into marketing and blew it out, because people want to buy things that are described to them.

That's the whole thing with direct marketing, you get to do demonstrations, create demand, cause an urgency, working in conjunction with TV and retail, where your real design is to sell retail. Because the retailers could care less about direct response. All they like about direct response is it drives retail. But what they don't like is it drives retail to all the retailers, all their competitors. Here when you're dealing with a branded product or a specific product that's only available at one retailer, it's a huge thing to drive people into their stores and to buy that product.

Robo Grip started a thing where we ended up with, I think, 12 products in the couple of years that we did. All of them were successful except one. We had 11 out of 12 successes. The Pocket Socket, the second one we did, was even a bigger success story. They had a projection to sell 30,000 units in a year. That was just an adjustable wrench on a hook. Well, we made it a special adjustable wrench on a hook and showed all the things it could do and gave it a name and packaging. That went up from 30,000 units in a year-and-a-half to 1 million units a year.

We had a lot of stories like that. With the glue gun. We make it into a special glue gun. That's just what marketing is. Basically, it was a huge business.

We were at the end of the contract with Sears and Sears wanted to change the deal. The way it was, was that we were exclusive to Sears in this business. Now I had two businesses going. I had the retail hybrid going with Sears, making a lot of money for King World and I had the intellectual property business, primarily *Wild America*, making a lot of money. I was coming to the end of a three year contract I had with King World and the Sears contract was coming up. I renegotiated the Sears contract because we were in an entrepreneurial situation with them and any major company, especially retail, they don't mind you making money but not to the levels that we were making. Because we got involved with something that was brand new and the profits were huge. Sears wanted to adjust the deal to make it into more of an agency type of deal. More than that, the exclusivity stopped me from doing that formula with other retailers and I knew it would work with other retailers.

So I'm renegotiating a new contract with King World and I couldn't come to terms. I was having lunch, this was in February of '97, with Rick Hersh. He and I started in the mail room at William Morris and we've been friends ever since and I told Rick, I said, "Rick, I'm having trouble coming to new terms with King World. I might have to get outside financing." He said, "Would you be interested in Guthy-Renker?" I said, "Yeah, but aren't they a competitor?" He said, "No. They've tried short-form and they haven't been able to do it and I think they would like your retail business because they don't do that and they're very hot now." This was '96, with their PowerRider, and other exercise stuff. "They're investing a lot of money into a lot of new businesses. Would you be interested?" I said, "Sure, see if you can get a meeting together."

Well, by the time I got back to my office from his at William Morris, he had a call into me saying he had talked to Greg and that Greg and Bill would like to meet me the next day. I met with them the next day. I explained the business. They asked if I could reconstruct what I did at King World, meaning an intellectual property business and a retail hybrid business, with various retailers. I said, "Yeah." Thirty days later we had a deal. April 1st, 1997, I formed Guthy-Renker Direct. Decided to keep it with their name because they had built a big name value of over 10 years of marketing with infomercials. That's why and how I left King World and started Guthy-Renker Direct.

*SD:* Did it ever concern you that started this new entity on April Fool's Day?

*BH:* Not really, because it's my wife's birthday and we've been married 29 years and that's working out. So, I figured, that's a good day to start it.

*SD:* Bill Guthy and Greg Renker didn't get suspicious when you wanted to meet in a bathroom?

*BH:* I told them that's part of my deal. I'll only have meetings in bathrooms. To this day that's where I have most of my meetings with them because we just happen to meet in the bathroom.

*SD:* Oh, really.

*BH:* At Guthy-Renker, yeah. With all this e-mail and voice mail and stuff like that, it's hard to communicate with people in person anymore unless you just bump into them somewhere.

*SD:* So you have Mark waiting outside the bathroom and he calls you on his cell phone when they're there.

*BH:* Then I run down and get in there and say, "How you guys doin'?"

*SD:* [Laughter] It's good. It's a strategy that I'm sure will be picked up in several business books.

*BH:* It's the bathroom strategy. It works!

*SD:* What was the first thing you ever did at Guthy-Renker?

*BH:* The first thing we brought in was through William Morris. We got the Bob Hope television library of 256 hours of shows. That happened in a similar way to *Wild America*. William Morris, who was representing the property, had taken a trade ad out because they were trying to sell the show to cable or syndication. Nicole picked up on it and asked me if I'd be interested in it and I said, "Yeah, let me call Rick up and let's have a meeting." So we did and we got together with the Hope Enterprises people. We made a deal for direct marketing and retail of the property. The first thing we got was the Bob Hope television library.

In the retail hybrid area, now that I could work with multiple retailers, Joe Batagowski joined me, left King World. Became an exclusive retail consultant to me. Our goal was to reconstruct the business. We started April 1st, 1997, and in the fall of '97 we were fortunate enough to have two projects going with two different retailers, the Home Depot and Kmart. That was how '97 started out with Home Depot, Kmart and *Bob Hope Christmas* on television.

*SD:* What happened with the retail?

*BH:* The retail was successful. The Home Depot was successful and we did another project with them. Kmart was successful enough where in '98 we ended up doing around ten projects with them. Again, it was a successful formula, a successful business, and we expanded in '98 by adding more retailers. The good news is that the company was in the black in our first full year of operation. In '99, this year we're going to be even more successful. So, we built the company.

But I've expanded it to a third area now. We have the intellectual properties area, which in '97 was Bob Hope. In '98 what we did was, and this was with Nicole Ericson with the help of Howard West, our consultant in intellectual properties area, we brought in the *Dean Martin Celebrity Roast* library. And, that has been a huge success for us in '98 and now in '99. The interesting thing about the *Dean Martin* library was that we came out with short-form and then after the short-form worked we did an infomercial. Usually, it works the other way. And the infomercial was a big hit in '98. Also in '98, we tested a continuity program in July, short-form, which was very successful and now we're rolling that out. We're rolling that out now because we wanted to see the stick rate, be conservative.

So in '98 we had the intellectual properties, and the retailers and the third thing, which I call vast market consumer products. Not every product we find for retail fits into the formula of one retailer and television. Sometimes they're just good products that you want to make money on. In that case we developed in '98, a brand of magnetic products starting with the Chi Chi Rodriquez energy band, which is a $19.95 magnetic and copper bracelet. It was patent pending, which the patent has been granted on in about the last two, three weeks. Had a very successful fourth quarter selling this. Now, talking about businesses, that has developed into five product lines. Not only the energy band but we had a back wrap, and insoles and ten-piece system and a wrist wrap. It's a business. You'll see it, third and fourth quarter into all the major catalogs. It's in major retailers right now, WalGreens and Target. So that's the third business, mass market consumer products.

The reason I do that is to diversify risk. Because when one business is doing great another one may not be doing as great but overall the whole company is doing well. And, that's the idea. To be profitable and to grow the company as a business. That's what I'm doing right now.

*SD:* So why is the company for sale?

*BH:* Well, I can only tell you my take from what I know and what I hear and what I see. As I said, in '96, when they financed me, and we made a five year deal, Guthy-Renker was forming a lot of businesses—a radio business, a foreign business with David Carmen, their Internet business, a dating business, a select service, GRTV, and my business. They were looking to take their profits from the exercise stuff and things they were doing and diversify. Well, in the couple years, Bill and Greg had decided that they wanted to go back to their core business of long-form infomercials with continuity. Such as Pro-Active Solution and other cosmetics and vitamins, things like that. Now we have a deal, and they asked me if would I be open to them finding a partner, a financial investor to take them out of the risk business. I'm in the black, it's not a question of making money—it is something where they want to go the other way. They want to go back to just to their businesses. The facts are they are selling off or closing down all of these other businesses they started up right before me or right after me. I am pretty much the only one there that's left, and the reason I'm the only one left is because we're making money. So they asked me if would I be open to it, and I said, "Yeah." So together we're jointly looking to find investors.

*SD:* So it's all up in the air again for you.

*BH:* Yes. That's why I'm telling the people I work with we just have to put blinders on. I don't. I have to be dealing with the investment bankers and people that are interested in investing in me and talking, see what's real and all that kind of stuff. That's a full-time job. On the other hand in order to keep our profits going and make our money this year I tell the people I work with we have to have blinders on and keep building our three businesses because: 1) we want to continue to be profitable; 2) it will make our company worth even that much more; and 3) it's not fun trying to run a business without making money.

It is up in the air as to who my financial partner is going to be in the future. There's always a possibility that I play out the next three years with Guthy-Renker because we have the contract. But since they're wanting to divest, I believe the situation will come up with the right party that they'll want and that I'll agree to, and we'll do it. As of this moment nothing is set. But as long as I'm building long-term profits, it's going to be more and more attractive to the right investor.

**SD:** There have been a lot of rumors floating around lately that you have been asked to come back to manage Jose Feliciano.

**BH:** Even though Jose and I are friends now. That's a part of my past, the personal management. I really like this direct marketing business because it was something that Willie Amos said—Famous Amos—he was actually a music agent with William Morris in the '70s, and I'll never forget this: He came into a conference room, all the music agents are sitting there and he brought a bag of cookies. This was right before he launched the cookies. He said to us, "Guys, I've had it managing artists, and people, the emotions and the craziness. I'm now managing a cookie. And the great thing about managing a cookie is it doesn't talk back, it listens to you, it shows up on time, it does what it's supposed to do, and you can control your own destiny of success and failure without all the emotional entanglements of dealing with artists."

I'll never forget that because it's true. In the direct marketing business, there's a lot of truth to that. With product. Once you own a product, and that's the key, owning a product, owning the rights to it. How far you can go is all up to your own abilities and the people you work with, their abilities. It's not as emotional as dealing with talent. I like products that way. The thrill of being able to find a Robo Grip again—That I could own, rather than just a product that I market and help someone else make millions of dollars on. That's always there. Limit your risk to the point where you're making money in business. That's why I like to have three different business going at the same time. The home run potential is to find a product that can become a world-wide product that you own.

Because as you are talking to investors, they all say, what is your past? They want to see cash flows. There is no better way to do that than with continuity products or owning properties that can sell around the world and have line extension possibilities. That's what I'm looking to do, because it's fun and there's no upsell limit.

# COLLEEN SZOT

*As* with the motion picture industry, writers are the unsung heroes of the infomercial industry. Creating a demand and desire for a product or service is an amazing skill. Colleen Szot has quietly been responsible for some of the most successful campaigns in the direct response television industry. In this interview, she reveals a lot of hard-learned secrets about what really generates sales, and what to avoid.

**Steve Dworman:** Colleen, when did you start writing?

**Colleen Szot:** Well, I actually started writing as a kid, and sold my first article for $1 at the age of nine. I then wrote for a lot of teen publications, interviewing local bands who came to my city and the like. I got into advertising in 1976, after I graduated from college. And I've been in the business ever since.

**SD:** Didn't you work for some big ad agencies?

**CS:** Yes, I've worked at J. Walter Thompson and Foote, Cone & Belding in Chicago, and Campbell, Mithun Esty here in Minneapolis. I've been fortunate to work with some of the biggest advertisers in the country, including Kraft Foods, Coors beer, Wendy's, Oscar Mayer, Coca-Cola, VISA and tons more.

**SD:** When did you start writing direct response?

**CS:** Well, believe it or not, I actually got my start in the 1970s, writing for the Oral Roberts ministries. You know, Christian ministries have been using direct response almost longer than anyone else. "Call this number and get your free book," is what helped a lot of ministries get on their feet.

Back then, we used more of a soft-sell approach, weaving true-to-life stories in with our messages. But I had the opportunity to work with some pretty heavy directors, like Sid and Marty Krofft and Phil Cooke, and learned a lot.

I've always liked the whole idea of direct response because it's measurable—you can run a bank image spot one weekend and not know if that customer opening a new account is here because he saw your commercial or because your bank happens to be around the corner from where he works. But with direct response, you run a half-hour show or a one-minute spot over a weekend, and you can see exactly how many people are responding directly to what they saw. I like that. Too often, creative people aren't accountable for their work. With direct response, even though many other factors, like the direction and talent and certainly the offer come into play, you can actually see the impact your words have on people. That's very powerful.

*SD:* So you were in Los Angeles, working and being very successful at it, in the early '90s and then you upped and decided to move to Minneapolis in 1992. Why?

*CS:* I lived in Chicago for many years, and always felt like a Mid-Western gal. I love Los Angeles, and the thrill and excitement of being there, but really wanted to move my family closer to what I consider my roots. Plus, when we made the move, Minneapolis was a hotbed for direct response, with NordicTrack, American Harvest and K-Tel headquartered here. While some of those companies are no longer here, this is still a great place to be. I'm equal distance from each coast, and with e-mail and faxes, I'm able to work where I want to live. And the work has followed me, which has been great.

*SD:* You sort of cut your teeth on NordicTrack, isn't that right?

*CS:* You know, I was really fortunate to work for NordicTrack at a time when some great creative minds were there, people like Barbara Thomas and Marshall Masko. I was on retainer with NordicTrack for almost three years and it was a great learning experience, as well as a highly successful time to be selling the ultimate in fitness equipment, a NordicTrack machine.

I didn't renew my retainer contract in 1996, because I had a non-compete with NordicTrack, and was getting inquiries from places like FitnessQuest and Tony Little and really wanted to flex my creative muscles. Shortly thereafter, of course, NordicTrack went under. I'm not saying my leaving had anything to do with it [laughs out loud] because I know it didn't, but the timing is certainly suspicious—ha!

Actually, I learned so much from the folks at NordicTrack. During the time I was there I saw them go from all lead-generation to more direct sales, and that was very exciting.

*SD:* You had a front-row seat at NordicTrack and American Harvest. Give us your perception of what happened to these great companies.

*CS:* First, NordicTrack…you know, Jim Bostic, who was the president when I was there, was really the heart and soul of NordicTrack. This was a man who took the company from a small mom-and-pop operation to $400 million in sales. And although he was a bit of a tyrant, and many people referred to his time there as "the reign of terror," he was an unbelievably intelligent and intuitive man, and frankly, I liked him. We would have creative meetings in which we would pitch the work we were doing, and in a matter of minutes he would be able to tell you what to change to make it better, or whether or not it would work at all. And lots of times, that would come across in a mean-spirited fashion, but you know, he knew what he was talking about. Well, in 1995-96, the fitness market was really saturated, and NordicTrack was no longer the only machine on the block. I think one of the big mistakes NordicTrack made was not making "affordable" fitness machines soon enough. It did develop its All-American line, with treadmills and cross-country trainers that anyone could buy, but too late. There were too many other exercisers to choose from at that point. But I think the critical mistake NordicTrack made was ousting Bostic in 1996-97. The parent company, CML, was operating out of fear—fear that they would not continue to enjoy the growth they already had and that was a huge mistake. There was no way they were going to duplicate that kind of growth. It was fiscally impossible, and yet they thought they could do it by bringing in new management. Over a two-year period, they let 300 people go—good, bright, innovative people and that was a mistake, too. The irony is that shortly after Jim Bostic left, he was tragically killed in a car accident, and so they couldn't even bring him back if they wanted to. Very sad, very distressing.

Today, NordicTrack is still a very viable and even memorable name in fitness. It's funny, the company hasn't been on the air for three years now, and yet the other night on NBC's *Will & Grace* I heard Will refer to a NordicTrack like it was still number one. And in many ways it is—it's the ultimate and nothing has taken its place. NordicTrack machines are now made overseas, and you can buy them through their stores and through Sears, but they certainly don't command the presence they once had. But they still command the respect.

As for American Harvest, I knew David Dornbush, one of the founders and CEOs of American Harvest, quite well. He would come over to my house and we would write shows together. He was and is an extremely brilliant man, with the kind of rare insight into what consumers wanted, at the precise time they wanted it. Just like Jim Bostic was NordicTrack, Dave Dornbush was American Harvest, and while he was one of the most innovative thinkers I've ever met, he left some of the other day-to-day decisions to others, and they weren't always right. When American Harvest went under, Dave had patents pending on more than 60 new products, but he lost the backing and the name of American Harvest to fund those products. He's still in the business, still as brilliant and loved as ever. He still has people stop him on the street and ask him for his autograph. And a more personable CEO you'll never meet. I loved him, and still do, and wish we could work together again.

*SD:* Let's fast-forward. In the last couple of years, you've scored big with hits like the Orlimar Trimetal, Tony Little and Toma's Tan Perfect, which was HSN's biggest hit in 1999. How has direct response, and in particular, direct response writing, changed over the years?

*CS:* Ten years ago, a lot of direct response was hard sell. "Operators standing by, call now, call in the next 30 seconds, etc." and while I think an element of that can still be found today, and is applicable for some products, the direction today seems to be less knock-'em-over-the-head, and more of a softer sell. I think DR writing changes, in some way or another, every six months or so, with the introduction of a new way to position products, or a new type of offer. I think on the whole, shows today are much more polished, much more stylized. Infomercials today look more like traditional advertising or even TV programming. Everyone uses animation, and so you have to have some degree of that, everyone uses music, and so you have to use that. Are they artistic? Well, I'd put CNN's "The Cold War" infomercial or the new David Dikeman show up against programming today—they're that good. I think the bottom line, however, is that the same old direct response principles that worked 10, 15 years ago, still work today. You tell 'em, you tell 'em, and you sell 'em. Sometimes it's just that easy.

*SD:* What new techniques have you introduced in your shows?

*CS:* Well, for example, for the new DishPlayer 500 show, that I wrote for The Direct Network, we used a menu to tell the viewers what was coming up. The same technique has been used very successfully on local news shows, and my thinking was that if we tell viewers that we're going to hear from a kid reporter, or find out the answers to your most frequently-asked questions in the next few minutes, then maybe we can hold the viewer for a little longer, and get them to pick up the phone.

In the past, I've had amazing success just using little call-to-action lines like, "If operators are busy, please call again..." That tells the viewer that our product is so hot, we can hardly handle all the calls, so you better be among the first to call now!

I also like to think "outside the box," and would love to see marketers take more risks. Of course, it's not my money, so that's easy for me to say. But I can't tell you how many people call me up and say, "I have this product but I want to do a Victoria Principal show...or a TaeBo show." And I tell them, then hire their writer. Yes, they've enjoyed some tremendous success, and I admire greatly what they do, but how about doing something new and different? Why not position testimonials a whole new way? Or why not borrow a page from daytime talk shows and have the person who lost a ton of weight with your fitness or diet product confront the bullies who teased them in high school? Borrow a *Seinfeld* concept and do a show backwards, or go to a new, exciting background, using new, credible talent. I'm tired of seeing the Santa Monica Third Street Promenade, the Venice Beach area, and if I'm tired of it, what do you think consumers are?

*SD:* Tell me about some of the shows you've written that, after testing, didn't perform and you had to make changes to it—and what kind of changes you made.

*CS:* Well, I'll give you a great example from a recent fitness show I did. I can't get into specifics, but it was a great product, and I had talked the client into offering a charity overlay. He wasn't quite sure of that aspect, but his wife thought it was a great idea, and so we did it. Well, the show in testing pulled about a 2.6, so we made some changes, took out the charity overlay that he thought was holding it back, and tested it again—and you know, it got the exact same numbers. What was the problem? A couple of things, in my opinion. The first was timing. I'm a firm believer in the right timing. You don't run a weight loss product during the Christmas holidays and you don't sell a suntan lotion in the dead of winter. I think if the show had gotten on the air earlier in January, it would have done well. But by the time mid-February or March comes around, the people whose New Year's resolution was to lose weight, have already bought an exerciser, or they've discovered some new weight loss pill or liquid or other regimen, and they're just not interested in your product, no matter how great it is.

I recently rewrote a show that had started at Tyee and then went to a couple of other production companies before it landed in my lap, and that was for a tool show. Absolutely phenomenal product, just the most amazing set of tools in the world, honestly, but the people involved, namely the president and others, were simply too close to it and couldn't divorce themselves from the production. I wrote a script, a great script, too, and everyone loved it, and they shot some new footage with ShadowBox Pictures. But then the president himself decided to edit the show. I don't understand why people hire experts to do a job for them, and then don't let them do it. He tried to do a kitchen sink type of show, putting way too much into it, and while the testimonials were incredibly impactful, there were too many of them. He would have done better to error on the side of keeping it simple and saving some of the great footage for the next great show. But he didn't and the show didn't work.

I think another mistake marketers make is in not pricing the product correctly. They either under or over price it, and the consumer doesn't see it as a value. I worked on a weight loss show awhile back and they tested it at two price points: one for $59.95 and one for $39.95. Now that's a huge difference, and the $59.95 did better. That's because we were able to say, "For just $2 a day, you get one month's supply of all this," and that hit a button with the consumer, like I knew it would. I always tell my clients, you always have the chance to lower your price—you never have the chance to raise it. So start at the higher price, and give consumers value for their money, and see what happens. If it doesn't work, you can always lower the price.

*SD:* What 10 things can marketers do today—that they're not doing—to make their shows work harder?

*CS:* Number 1, coordinating a company's marketing efforts with their Web site. I was talking to my friend Elizabeth D'Orazio of IntelliVision the other day. She and I worked on Toma's Tan Perfect. She said marketers are simply not using the Internet to their advantage, especially with short form and lead generation, and I agree 100 percent. The Web site should appear every time the toll-free number appears, both in the show and in the CTA. That allows the consumer, especially the "thinker" who's on the fence about making a purchase, to go there and get more information and even see demonstrations.

Number 2, there are a ton of things that marketers can do to add production value to their show that don't cost an arm and a leg. For example, good lighting. Good lighting can make a world of difference. I just finished a show in Florida and the lighting changes from locale to locale. It's not only obvious, it's distracting. And anytime you're distracting the viewer, they're not paying attention to your product.

Number 3, music. Most people use the same needle-drop music as everyone else, when they can often get a custom music bed just for the cost of royalties. There are a ton of musicians who'd love to create music for your show, for very little, just for the exposure.

Number 4, marketers should watch more regular TV and see what they're doing. You know, today's consumer is very savvy, and if they're channel-surfing and see anything that smacks of a commercial, chances are they're going to zoom right past it. But if you make your show entertaining as well as informative, you're going to stop them in their tracks, and hook 'em.

Number 5, invest in great directors. Direct response is no longer the bastard stepchild of advertising, like it used to be. It is a viable and highly acceptable means for selling products. So get a director who's doing cutting-edge work on brand commercials and hire him or her. The Direct Network is a great example. Here's an agency who's done a lot of name brand TV commercials, as well as direct response, and they give it the respect it deserves. It goes without saying that you don't hire someone who looks down on infomercials or who's out just for the awards. You want someone who wants to make the phone ring as bad as you do, and do it with some of the latest techniques. And you know, you can get a good director for $1000 to $2000 a day. It doesn't have to be expensive.

Number 6, look for some new pitchpersons. I respect Nancy Nelson as much as anyone, but let's see some new faces, hear some new voices, create some new hosts.

Number 7, do something new and exciting with your testimonials. There are just too many talking-head-type testimonials. Invite all your testimonials to a picnic and capture their unedited comments on camera. Put five women who are going to their class reunion on the same weight loss product or exerciser and then ask the bullies who used to tease them what they think about them now. Have the testimonials meet the inventor of the product and tell him what they think. Do something new.

Number 8, invest in good animation, but not necessarily expensive animation. Beth D'Orazio was telling me that she uses 2-D animation with 3-D camera moves. Less expensive and yet it looks fantastic.

Number 9, rethink your CTA. To quote you, Steve, you once wrote, "You should only put in a call to action when you've built up to such a crescendo that your viewer is salivating." That may be 12 minutes into the show or it may be 24 minutes into the show. Then hear those phones ring.

Number 10, it goes without saying, to invest in a great script. Ask about their recent successes, successes they've had in the last six to 12 months, not successes they had three years ago. And pay them what they're worth. The script is the foundation for everything.

Oh, I have one more. Number 11—take some risks. Create a new format, do something daring, do a show backwards from solution to problem, bring people to tears, or make them laugh, just as long as they pick up the phone.

**SD:** Do infomercials, in your opinion, sell as well as they used to?

**CS:** Well, that's a loaded question, because I think consumers today know that whatever they see on television will, more than likely, be in retail stores within six months. And so they may wait and buy it at retail, but then the infomercial has done its job...it's driven sales, just to a retail outlet versus direct from TV.

Yes, I think infomercials sell as well as they used to, they're just selling to a more focused, more discerning viewer. There was a time when marketers had a lot of returns or people called to ask questions, and not necessarily buy the product. I think that's changed. Returns are way down across the board and more people are calling to order than to ask questions. So I think your answer is yes, they do sell as well as they used to, but in a different way.

I also think that anyone shopping in a store today realizes that we have a labor shortage. All the stores are begging for help, and consumers are suffering because there is no one on the sales floor who is knowledgeable enough to serve us the way we deserve to be served. So we're looking for other ways to buy, and direct response has always been one of them.

But like with all things, a well-written script, is just part of the equation. A great-selling show is also dependent on great direction, good talent, super editing, so many different factors.

**SD:** Speaking of that, you used to produce and even edit your own movie trailers, so why don't you produce the shows you write?

*CS:* Well, to be honest, I don't like producing, and yet I have enormous respect for people who do it, and who do it well. But I absolutely love to write. I'm passionate about words, and I do it pretty well, and so why not do what I love to do and get paid for it?

Plus, a lot of my clients are production companies who value the writer and the script a whole lot more than they have before. I still think there are shows where people say, "We're just going to wing it without a script," but that's becoming less frequent. If you really think about it, the script is everything. It's the foundation for everything you do. That's not to say it's carved in stone. I like to work with a hands-on producer/director, someone like Jeff Young of ShadowBox Pictures, Steve Spinner of FitnessQuest, and Joan Renfrow of Onyx Productions. I value their input and when we brainstorm, you can practically see the sparks fly! I don't write in a vacuum, and I don't care who has a good idea. If it's good and it works, let's use it.

But to get back to your question, there are, of course, a lot of full-service production companies who want to do everything, from writing to fulfillment, and I say more power to them. But sometimes when that happens, something gets short shrift, and more often than not, it's the script. It's like going to a general practitioner for cancer surgery. Wouldn't you rather go to someone who's a specialist at what he or she does and does it successfully, every day?

*SD:* The greatest compliment you can receive is when a product beats its sales estimates.

*CS:* The bottom line is and always will be sales. For example, a WalkFit infomercial I wrote moved 360,000 units in 30 days for NordicTrack, when they had projected 90 days. Tony Little's Gazelle Glider broke QVC's 19-year record in 1998, selling $50,000 worth every minute, and on and on. That is what is gratifying.

*SD:* You started your own non-profit group?

*CS:* Well, for years, I've taken on one new pro-bono account a year and in the past, I've written brochures and sales letters and ads for The Humane Society, the AIDS Foundation and recently battered women's shelters. What I found out when I worked for the battered women's shelters, is that they are absolutely at the bottom of the list for donations, because, by their very nature, they can't advertise their addresses for fear that an angry spouse might show up at their door. So they are totally dependent on organizations like United Way for their funding. When a woman shows up at a battered women's shelter, she has the clothes on her back and that's it. She doesn't even have the basic essentials, like soap, shampoo or toothbrushes. So I started saving my travel toiletries—the kind that hotels give away when you stay with them, or even the kind that come free with purchase—and I gave them to the shelters. Most of the women in these shelters have to share conditioners and stuff, but this way, they have their own. It's a small thing, but it's wonderfully gratifying. So I started collecting them from other business women and even men who travel and now three times a year, on Mother's Day, Back-to-School, and Christmas, I get together with a local Girl Scout troop and we put together personal care packages for the women at the shelters. And it's just heart-warming to see the reactions. Last year, I started NEW, Inc. (Necessary Essentials for Women) and I'm starting to spread the word. We're not set up to accept cash donations yet, but I can reimburse any postage costs for people who want to send me their drawers-full of Marriott shampoos.

# MARIANNA MORELLO

---

*Marianna Morello, has forgotten more about direct response print advertising than most of us will ever know. With almost 25 years of experience in buying print advertising of all types, her insights are priceless. Through her company, Manhattan Media, Marianna specializes in making direct response print deals with magazines that can be as much as 80% off standard rates. Her expertise has helped many entrepreneurs get their start, including A.J. Khubani. If anyone has seen what works and what doesn't in print advertising, it's Marianna.*

**Steve Dworman:** Let's start at the beginning.

**Marianna Morello:** I had really two jobs before. I actually worked for David Geller. That was my first job, selling the *National Enquirer*.

**SD:** Explain who David Geller is.

**MM:** I guess he can be called the "King of Mail Order." He really was a legend in his time, and at 86, he's still working. I started with him and worked for him part-time. After him, I went to Steven Geller and I worked for him for 18 years. In 1995, they moved the company up to Connecticut, and I didn't want to move so I opened Manhattan Media.

**SD:** And you started with a one or two person office?

**MM:** I started with nothing. It was two people in my house on my kitchen table.

**SD:** Wow!

*MM:* And then I got an office within a month or so. I went to 535 5th Avenue and took a very small office. Then we became three because I had one girl to answer the phones. Within a year or a year-and-a-half I was up to six people and a substantial billing. Most of it happened once I went to the NIMA show. I went in 1995, and I put up a booth under the encouragement of A.J. Khubani. He had said to me, "You know, you really should be there because no one knows your end of the business." And he, of course, knew print because he had been in print before TV. No one had ever heard of me.

*SD:* That was about the time we did the interview with A.J.?

*MM:* He mentioned me in the interview and that's how I got all the people standing at my booth. It was your newsletter that launched me.

*SD:* Oh my God!

*MM:* Yeah! It was your newsletter because they came up to the booth with the newsletter in their hands and they said, "Are you the lady that helped to start A.J. Khubani in print?" And I said yes, and they had your newsletter in their hands. I actually did not have a good spot at the show. My booth was all the way in the back outside in the tents. Remember? It was at the Mirage. It was a horrible, horrible place. I don't think anyone would have found me if it wasn't for your newsletter. And that's how you and I met because I wanted to thank you because I thought, I don't even know who this man is, Steve Dworman. That's how it happened because the interview with A.J. was in that newsletter of that show in 1995, and he mentions me as the lady who started him in print.

*SD:* I love when good things happen because of this monthly report!

*MM:* I think that's the thing that really catapulted me. At that time, I was dealing with Mike Warren. He had The Psychic Friend's Network. I was also dealing with Quintel Entertainment, and they also had a psychic line. And all the other people that heard I did the print for Telebrands were just flocking around, and that's how my business started. It was really just perfect timing, I think I was very lucky.

*SD:* So at that point, how long had you been working with A.J.?

*MM:* Well, I had been working with A.J. for years because he was a client of mine at Steven Geller. When I left Steven Geller, I guess he was with me already. I've known him probably 15 or 16 years now. No, I met him before my son was born, so it's 17 years.

*SD:* So you ran his first print ad?

*MM:* I ran his first print ad.

*SD:* Let's talk about that a little bit. What was the ad for and what happened? How old was he?

*MM:* Oh God, he was young, maybe 23 or 24. He was right out of college, and he had some money. I think he had $25,000. He was working out of his dad's office on 26th Street. And he came to run this little half-page ad. The name of his company then was called Direct Connections. We ran the first ad. He had a drill bit and then a camera, a few product ads, and we tested them all around and we hit one winner and he just plowed the money back in and kept going. That's how it started. Incredible really. Incredible story. But he was gutsy. A very gutsy kid.

*SD:* Explain that.

*MM:* He literally took the whole amount of money that came in and just plowed it all right back in and didn't even look. He was a gambler. I called it a gamble. He said, "Well, you know, I think I know what I'm doing." He was, you know, very gutsy. He just kept going and going and going. I said to him that he had to get more product. His father was helping him with that, getting product from the Orient. He was projecting, and he had to get more product. And he was learning as he went because he really didn't have a background in that. But he's very bright, and he could see what was coming on the horizon. I told him, "Well, if these are the projections, this is where we are going to go after that," and we just kept going and going and that was it.

*SD:* That was in the '80s?

*MM:* I think A.J. probably came to me in '82 or '83. It was a long time ago. It's almost 20 years.

*SD:* Tell me how print had changed.

*MM:* Well, print has changed in lots of ways. To me, print has changed in a good way. Because I'll be honest with you, some of the remnant situations are better than I've seen even ten years ago. Some of the magazines really need help. You have lots of big advertisers who have pulled their budgets so page counts are down and it's really a big opportunity. Interestingly enough, when the economy is bad, print and direct response do better. At least print does better because the rates normally come down and it makes them more affordable and when the rate is low enough, as everybody knows, anything can work at the right rate. And right now, the climate has been that. We have publishers that are hurting. We have lots of changes going on in the whole industry.

*SD:* What about the changes that you've noticed in the kind of print ads that work?

*MM:* There is really a whole revolution in what I saw 20 years ago when I first started in the business. Back then there were lots of claims, lots of diet ads, and lots and lots of risky ads running. That's back now in a big way. I mean, look at the bust developers. There are four or five different breast enhancers, bust developers. Emson has one. Another client of mine has one called Isis. There are about four or five others that are in all the women's books. We had a whole line of products running like that in the '80s. Between '80 and '85 they were booming, the same types of products. So you actually kind of see the cyclical effect of what's happening in print is that these very strong ads with lots of claims are back. And the diet ads are very, very strong now. The claims are outrageous. You know, lose 20 pounds overnight! Every magazine you pick up has these four or five diet ads.

*SD:* How are they getting away with it?

*MM:* I don't know. I mean, to be honest with you, Steve, I think that what has happened is that there has been a leniency and I think it's going to turn. I think it's going to turn soon, and that's why I tell a lot of the clients that are out there that you are going to have to be careful because now they are going to start to scrutinize those ads again, and once they start doing that, then you are going to see a lot of these ads drop by the wayside because they are not going to be able to run them with the claims that are in there. But there is an awful lot out there. And also if you look at the *National Enquirer* and all of the rag papers and the tabloids, they are chock full of these heavy-duty ads, direct response, and claims. It all happened in the '80s. Then we went through a span where they stopped accepting a lot of it because there was a lot of scrutinizing of the ads and a lot of people got stopped for not being able to substantiate their claims. They had to cease and desist and couldn't run anymore. But now there seems to be a resurgence back in a very, very big way. I just know from being in the business this long that this too will be stopped again.

*SD:* Let's talk a little bit about response rates. Have response rates changed over the last 20 years?

*MM:* Oh yeah, but they always change. They go up and they go down because response rates are based on: 1) How well you buy your media; and 2) How strong your claims are. If you have a really incredible claim like, "lose 15 pounds over the weekend," like the Hollywood Diet and all of that stuff, then those ads are going to have a tremendous response because that's just the way things go. If you run that ad up against another one with a headline that says, "lose 2 pounds"—forget it. It's like night and day. But you also have to buy the cost of your page at a low CPM (cost per thousand). That's the only way it's going to work. We seem to have a rebirth of the '80s now because the rates are very similar. It's really wild because even in the FSIs and even in some of the women's magazines the CPM is really very comparable. An FSI is a Free Standing Insert, like News America, Smart Source, the thing in the Sunday paper with the coupons. That's an FSI. But those are testing grounds for lots of print products. We use those as tests. And the pricing, they have a very low cost-per-thousand for testing. They are almost the same as what we were paying in the '80s. In that respect, you are still going to be able to test something and it's not going to cost you a lot of money. If you hit a product, you test one million, and then there is a 60 million circulation to roll out to. That's huge.

*SD:* Can you be a little more specific about how this works?

*MM:* Well, let's say you test a million circulation. If that ad works for you, and your response comes back and you pay your cost of the ad plus you are making profit, you turn around and take that money and now buy 5, 10, 15, or 25 million circulation. You can project out what you are going to be making. It's almost like money in the bank. I was talking to A.J. about it and he even said the rates now are very close to the rates we paid in the '80s. He said that if you could get an item that's hot and you get it out into the FSIs and get it to work, you are going to make money in print. There's no doubt about it. And that's really what it's all about, finding the right item, testing at that price and seeing if you make it work. But it hasn't been easy. Since November, since before the elections, people have just been a little scared of what the economy is doing, and I think that has had a big effect on TV as well as on print. People have just been a little hesitant to buy or maybe the extra money they would spend on something like this, they just aren't spending. But then you see that there are certain products that are making it. Diets will always make it. Things to improve yourself like wrinkle cream is still selling—and it will continue to sell through good times and bad, especially if it's well priced.

*SD:* What's a good price?

*MM:* Well, you know what? We always used to have the magic number, anything under $19.95 is going to work, and on TV you always try to keep things similarly priced. But now we've seen things that are working that are $600.

*SD:* Like?

*MM:* Isis is a breast enhancer. The system is $600.

*SD:* But they don't print that.

*MM:* No, no, no. We don't put the price. The big thing now that's really been happening, Steve, is that in a lot of the direct response, nobody is showing you a price. So what they are doing is getting you to call a 1-800 number, and the sale is made by the telemarketers on the phone. That's where the closing of the deal comes and they upsell. So that's really what's going on. A lot of the ads that you will see do not have prices and that's the trick. Because now, it's more if you can get them on the phone and close the deal on the phone, that's really how they are making print work.

*SD:* So, do you have your own trained operators fielding the calls?

*MM:* You either have to have one of two things. You either have to have your own telemarketing in-house where you have your own operators that know everything your product can do, or you take on an outside telemarketer like Aftermarket. I know they do a great job on closing. Today, the consumer is very sophisticated, and they ask a lot of questions. If you want to upsell them, you have to be really talented as a telemarketer. A lot of these telemarketers and companies that I know are on commission, so that really drives the sale.

*SD:* Now, let's say that you test something with an FSI and it makes a small profit. How do you know what media to follow that up with besides enlarging your FSI base? Does it translate to other media?

*MM:* It does translate to other media and it will translate across the board based on a CPM. Let's say, for instance, you ran a page ad and it was about $5 or $6 per thousand depending on if you ran it on a remnant or guaranteed basis. Remnant is space that's available but they can't guarantee where you are going to be, and then guaranteed (GMO: Guaranteed Mail Order) is when you can pick the markets you want and you pay a little bit more for that. It's not even that much more, but it might be 10% more than you would pay on remnant.

*SD:* Is it worth doing?

*MM:* Well, it's worthwhile especially for a client that knows there are regions in the country that are going to do better for them. Let's say for a diet or exercise unit, they might want to go to areas like California or Florida where people are all year around wearing bathing suits. Those people are going to be more conscious of what they look like than somebody in Minnesota in the middle of winter. So when they go to test, they would want to test in those areas so that they know their test is viable and that the product is going to work. So let's say come spring or fall when they want to hit everyone, they can test the product in the winter in Florida or California or anywhere where it is warm, and then they know that come spring they can kind of roll it out to the rest of country. To go back to your question, it does translate into women's magazines or tabloids. You get to take it out into other publications like *Parade* and *USA Weekends* that have tremendous circulations. *Parade* has 37 million on Sunday, *USA Weekend* has 23 million, and then you have *TV Guide* with 9 or 10 million. That's a lot of circulation that you can add. You really can do print in a big way. You know, what's interesting is that most of the infomercial companies don't do it in that way. They really don't get involved in it that steep. Somebody like Telebrands is one of the few people that are doing well.

*SD:* Does television normally translate well to print?

*MM:* Well, it should. Let's put it this way. If you are going to retail, it is absolutely necessary to back it up with print because you are going to get the exposure and the branding that you need once it goes to the shelf. And by using DR, you are paying a lot less than you would if you are going to go out there and just say, "Available at GNC," or "Available at whatever stores." So you can use a 1-800 number and sell it off there or when they call the 1-800 number, you can steer them to a store near you, and you get to use the direct response rate, which is the way to go. A lot of people that are on TV really need the print. This is what I always preach to all the people that are doing just TV. Print brings the credibility factor. For instance, I got Sonny Howard—this is unbelievable—the Good Housekeeping Seal of Approval on LaRente Bakeware. That's an infomercial product that ends up with a Seal of Approval from Good Housekeeping, which now makes it ten times more credible then just a half-hour show on a bake pan. So that's why I say to a lot of clients, if you need the credibility factor and you think it's going to help you, especially once you go to retail, to have that on your packaging is tremendous. I did that for a lot of the products for Telebrands. I also got it for him on the Blooming Onion, and on the Safety Can Opener. I mean, he got Seals of Approval on a lot of things.

*SD:* What does that cost?

*MM:* Actually, it's an interesting process. You have to clear the institute, which is a big deal because they do rigorous testing of the product. But you are paying normally two pages. You have to run some advertising. Along with the advertising, then you get the seal. You get the seal for one year and then it has to be renewed again by paying to advertise in *Good Housekeeping*. As far as I'm concerned, I think for many clients that are just marketing TV driven products, they really have a credibility problem. There are a number of people that are going to order off of a 1-800 on TV and there are a lot of people that are not going to. But if they see it in *Better Homes and Gardens*, *Good Housekeeping*, *Women's Day* and some of these magazines that they believe in the editorial, then they feel that if it's running in there then it must be good. Plus print lasts a long time. You are in a magazine for a month. It's a huge difference than just being on the air even for a half-an-hour or even a one- or two-minute spot. Those come and they go and they do well, but the print lasts for a long time, and you usually get a residual on print that can last months.

*SD:* Most people in the industry are aware of what kind of ratios they get off television, which of course used to be a lot higher. People used to get a 3 or 4 to 1 and now sometimes they only get a 1.5 to 1. How does that translate to print?

*MM:* It's very similar. We used to have winners, you know, in the day when I ran some of A.J.'s things, we'd have 3 or 4 or 5 or 6 to 1's in print. Now it's the same thing. If you get a 1.5 to 2, you are happy. The response rates are not what they used to be, but that's across the board on everything—TV, print, just in general, the economic climate, everything.

*SD:* Do you think people really need the bold outrageous claims to even bring in the 1.5 to 2 at this point?

*MM:* Some of them, yes, unless the item is very unique or it's not available anywhere else. That's another big factor. The print ads will do wonderful if you cannot find this item anywhere else. It's the same thing with TV. When they say, "Not available in any store," it's going to cause you to act now and order. It's the same thing on the print ads. When you say this is not available, or a limited edition, or you only have 30 to 60 days to order, the push is on and usually the response is up. Also the claims—because the claims are what makes it—and the testimonials have proven to be true for print and TV, almost the same. When you have a before-and-after testimonial on a diet product or a wrinkle cream, that's what sells it.

*SD:* What kind of offers have you seen that people have gone to lately to boost response? Have you seen free trials?

*MM:* There are some that are two-step. There are free trials where you are sending out something, but those are really hard because those are going to cost you a lot of money to actually close the deal. So if you are going to do a two-step, you have to have deep pockets. That's what I tell people because you know what, you are going to go out there and advertise and get a lot of leads, and then after that you have to close the sale. It takes a lot of time. If you can sell it off the page, you are usually much better off just to try to make the sale off the page.

*SD:* Do beautiful women sell to women? Pictures of beautiful women in ads?

*MM:* Oh, I think so. Absolutely. Women buy *Vogue* magazine basically just to look at the ads and the beautiful women in the ads. That's something that we've all grown up on. It's been around. A very attractive woman in an ad I think will still sell very well. It depends on what you are selling. If you are selling a breast enhancer, you'll have a beautiful woman there and beautiful breasts. That's going to help you sell it. If you just talked about it and said you can gain two inches and there's no picture, no beautiful woman, no nothing, I don't think you are going to do as well.

*SD:* So pictures in print ads make a big difference?

*MM:* Oh, I think so. Before-and-afters are major. It will really get your response rate up!

*SD:* Tell me about some of the things you've seen over the years where ads have been tweaked and you've noticed little or subtle changes that have made a significant difference.

*MM:* Well, sometimes it's the headline, just a headline change, just the way you say it. Also, the very important thing in the headline is that it has to be a positive sell. You're not going to sell something to somebody because they feel without it they have a problem. If you do a negative turn on it—even with Stop Smoking—if you say to stop smoking because it will kill you, that's not the way to go. It should be stop smoking to be healthy. You have to give it a positive spin. Sometimes we look at headlines and we realize that we need to tweak them or get the point across quickly. You only have a few seconds until people turn a magazine page. That's it. You have to grab them right away. You have to just catch them with the headline, the headline or the photo. Some of them will give you an incredible photo that will stop you. And something has got to stop you so they read that ad. That's really what it's all about. If you don't do that and they go to the next page, you've lost a sale.

*SD:* Are people reading less? Is there less copy in ads now?

**MM:** No, it's not that they are reading less. I think it's just that we are bombarded with so much now between the Internet and everything else you have in your life. People say to me, "Do people read newspapers anymore?" They do read the newspapers. There are people who commute and they read the newspapers. A lot of the magazines have lost circulation, because the truth of the matter is how many magazines can you look at? You have your favorites and you are going to go for those, but then how many more can you look at? I don't know how many more people are going to add to their list because you don't have time. I happen to look through thousands every single month, but that's because it is my business. I don't think the average woman is going to subscribe to 15 or 20 magazines. That's why they say you run in a magazine and you are capturing a certain audience. That's very true because if that person is buying that magazine on the newsstand or even subscribing to it, then they are more than likely reading it cover to cover, because they want it. That's very important because magazines that do much better are ones that are picked up, like *Cosmo*. It's a very hot magazine on the newsstand and the reason it does well is because you get a big turnover. Every month it's not the same subscriber that gets it and throws it in the corner. You now have somebody that went to pick up this because they saw something that they liked on the cover and they are going to read that magazine. If they are going to read that magazine, you have a real good chance that they are going to read your ad because advertisements are also read.

**SD:** So that's an awfully important thing to know when you are thinking about direct response vehicles.

**MM:** And the other thing I always tell my clients, "Look in the magazine and see if there are any DR ads. If there are no DR ads then we don't want to be there." Sometimes a client will come in and say, "I really think I should be in this magazine because my product goes toward this type of person." And I say, "Well, okay, open the magazine and look at it. Are there any direct response ads in there?" If there are only one or two ads in there, I'll never put you in that magazine because there's not direct response. Then I'll open a magazine and show them where it looks like a catalog of direct response. And then I say to them, "Now wouldn't you rather be here? All of these people can't be in this magazine if it's not working." And then if you pick up the magazine month after month and realize that there are people running three, six, nine times a year, then that means the ads are working and the magazine pulls.

# GARY MARCOTTE

# TOM BURKE

Gary Marcotte is Manager of Special Markets for Lexus. Tom Burke, is President of Hudson Street Partners.

The Lexus infomercial is the most innovative infomerical to come out from a major automobile manufacturer. The concept and execution is everything it should be for an automobile of its repute. The Lexus infomercial campaign was so successful that it ran for four years. I believe you'll find this interview fascinating and a portal as to what's coming—as more and more *Fortune 500* companies jump into utilizing infomercials.

*Steve Dworman:* Why don't we begin with how all of this started?

*Gary Marcotte:* It really all started in an effort to raise awareness for Lexus Certified—to give the dealers another tool they could use in their marketplace that was a little bit different, that would break through some of the advertising clutter that is out there on TV and radio and newspaper. We wanted to give them something to actually drive traffic into their stores.

*SD:* The project, or the concept, was talked about internally before Tom was brought in?

*Tom Burke:* Team One was Gary's first line of consultation on this. They handle the advertising. They're a division of Saatchi & Saatchi Advertising as well. They had a high level of enthusiasm for the idea of doing this from the outset and basically they called us in and said, why don't you bring us up to speed and help Gary and his people get up to speed on what capabilities exist in this longer format. What might we do? So we showed some examples of what other people have done and some examples of what we thought they could do. It kind of went from there. Team One was the first group to feel like this was a good idea along with Gary's group.

*GM:* That's really true. The genesis of the idea came from the dealer group side of Team One that does more of the retail-oriented-type advertising.

*SD:* Describe briefly the actual Lexus Certified Program.

*GM:* The Lexus Certified Program is a way to create a new used car brand if you will, instead of just selling used cars. We made an attempt a couple of years ago to try to brand them so that the name Lexus Certified actually stands for something. And it means that a car has been through a multi-point quality and maintenance inspection prior to being able to call itself Certified. When it's able to say it's been Certified, then it includes a warranty, roadside assistance, all those things at no charge, and then the customer also qualifies for financing and/or leasing at new car rates and terms. When a pre-owned Lexus is Lexus Certified, it really sort of brings it under the Lexus new car umbrella.

*SD:* I was very interested in what you were able to do with the customization so that when a person calls in they receive a package on the Certified Program. Why don't you tell a little about that?

*GM:* Well, one of the things that we wanted to do was if customers were able to watch this piece and were intrigued, we wanted them to be able to immediately find out that a Lexus Certified car was affordable. And the best way to do that was to give them a list of cars that were available in their marketplace and let them find out for themselves. So, when a customer calls in to the 800 number, they receive an offer that's only made available to them, that includes getting a list of cars that are currently in stock in dealerships in their market. It makes it easier for them to shop and it makes it easier for them to find out that there are cars that they can afford and it takes a lot of the typical hassle out of trying to find a car you might be interested in.

*SD:* You did have a bit of reluctance from the dealers to participate in this?

*GM:* Well, a little bit of reluctance from the dealers to send a very large list out that in some markets, not all of them, includes more than just their dealerships. So I think in a couple of the markets we are sharing a list that includes all of the cars in a market. In other markets, we are only sharing a list of cars in that immediate area. And to see what impact it has.

*SD:* How are you actually handling the fulfillment of those lists? What are the mechanical processes and who's involved?

*GM:* We maintain a national inventory here, so for us it's very simple to just transmit a list of cars every couple of days to a fulfillment house to develop that list. So it's a relatively simple thing.

*SD:* Can I ask, who's doing your inbound 800 and your fulfillment?

*TB:* Matrixx is doing the inbound 800. Hard Hank's is doing the fulfillment.

*SD:* Hard Hank's, where are they located?

*GM:* Iowa I think, somewhere up there.

*SD:* Can you tell me anything this early on about the preliminary results?

*GM:* [Laughter] I can tell you I'm happy. I got some numbers this morning. We had a really great weekend.

*TB:* This is the second weekend we've been on. In Los Angeles, before the 4th, the last weekend of June, the 24th and 25th, we got results that were beyond my hopes. They were trying to reach a fairly upscale audience here and people who are in the market right now for a new car, or a used car or whatever. But you get that demographic and you cross check one against the other and you end up with a pretty small group of people. And we got fabulous response, given the size of the target audience. This weekend we expanded to more markets and it looks like we just got a flood of calls.

*SD:* Tom, I assume you're buying the media for this?

*TB:* We're buying it with TMT.

*SD:* You had some beautiful slots this afternoon, a CBS affiliate in Los Angeles on Saturday morning.

*GM:* The Sunday one was great, too.

*SD:* Have you been able to corroborate any kind of relation yet to people receiving the fulfillment package to going to the dealers?

*GM:* Not yet, no. It's really too early. We will be able to trace it to actual sales. And probably to actual traffic. We had some anecdotal response from the dealers the first weekend in L.A. saying, "Hey, I had people that came into my showroom that said I watched the infomercial, what's this all about?" This is before the consumer even got the package. They didn't wait to get the package. They just went straight to the showroom. There was some anecdotal evidence, but no numbers of any kind.

**SD:** I was very impressed with the show. Who produced the show? Did you produce it yourself Tom?

**TB:** No, we conceived the show and mapped it out and we brought in Maysles Films as a production partner on it. They also did the Tercel show. It was pretty much the same team that worked on the Tercel show.

**SD:** They're not the same Maysles that did Woodstock are they?

**TB:** Yeah.

**GM:** Interesting on the demographics that Tom mentioned, the target market. I did some noodling around with the numbers this weekend and about 60% of the people who called in, their last purchase was a new car. And if you look at the piece, the piece clearly says, "For the price of some other new car, you could be driving a Lexus." I think the fact that 60% of the people that called were doing that is certainly a good thing. It certainly tells us that the message is right on target and the piece is delivering what it's supposed to be delivering.

**TB:** It really is kind of a mind change show. You look at what you're trying to accomplish with it and that's certainly one of the things. To get people who never would have thought of spending 20, 25, 30, 35 thousand dollars on a car that's been owned before. There's kind of a built-in reluctance to do that I think. After you watch the show, I think that reluctance pretty much disappears. And it comes in large part because the owners of Certified pre-owned were in the same boat. A lot of them say, "I never would have thought about doing this." Then they walk into the dealership and five minutes later say, "I've bought one." It's a pretty powerful show from that standpoint I think. It's going to change a lot of people's minds about that whole idea.

**SD:** I think the only automobile that this would have ever worked on is a Lexus.

**TB:** I hope you're right. [laughs] It was a great project for us from that standpoint. It was one of those things you get really excited about in a hurry.

**GM:** Us too. I think when we originally started talking about this, people have an expectation for what the word infomercial means. Let's face it, their expectation is not that high. The response from all of our executives and people around here that watched it was, "Wow, I didn't realize it was going to be this good." They had a picture of some of the things that had been out there in the past, and they wondered how our luxury customer is going to respond to something like this. When they see the piece they think, "This is alright." I think it changed a lot of people's minds on how you can market an upscale market using a medium that has traditionally been used for a lot of lower priced products.

**SD:** And the fascinating thing about this is you're dealing with such an expensive product that if you whittled everything down and you only had one car sold per two or three airings you're still way ahead of the game. You can't say that about really anything else that's being sold this way.

*GM:* That's another nice thing about having big margins. If this were Gillette razor blades, it would be awfully hard to do. Big margins give you the flexibility to do some innovative type of things. Our dealers are extremely positive. And this was really done in partnership with our dealers. And they're really pleased about it—both on generating new car business for them, as well as generating business for Lexus Certified. That's always a good bonus.

*SD:* Was there any reluctance whatsoever in instigating a program like this since it potentially could take from new car sales?

*GM:* There was reluctance, not on the infomercial itself, but on the new car side when we began to put Lexus Certified pre-owned cars together. There was the potential to cannibalize yourself. And we did a lot of research with a lot of people, a lot of focus groups, a lot of studies up front to try to get a handle on how big that was and how to market it so that you didn't do it. Then we surveyed each one of our customers after they buy one of these cars, just like we do the new car, and we clearly track what their first and second choice was and our cannibalization level is two to three percent. So it's really been a pleasant surprise on how little it really is. The research told us that was probably going to be the case. I was looking at the numbers this morning of people who called in from the infomercial who previously owned a Lexus. It's like 3%. I think when you get down to some of the lower end products, you run that risk. But I think with a luxury car, we're going to cannibalize some other new car brands. We're not going to really get ourselves. People that want to buy a new car and have $50,000 to spend are going to do it.

*SD:* Part of the reason I would think that this works so well is the price of a Lexus has escalated. It makes them unaffordable for a large portion of the consumer audience.

*GM:* That's exactly right. As that has happened, that has caused some people who can't afford a Lexus to perceive that perhaps one is more expensive than it actually is. So what this whole Lexus Certified thing and the infomercial allow us to do is to go to a segment of people who think they can't afford a Lexus and tell them they can. And tell them here's a way to do it. Some of them will come in and buy a pre-owned car. Some of them will come in and find out a new car was a lot more affordable than they thought it was and they'll walk out in a new car.

*SD:* Really?

*GM:* That happens. That's been happening a lot. We're saying, hey folks, you're going out looking at a Buick or you're looking at a Lincoln or you're looking at a Taurus—wouldn't you really rather have a Lexus? A lot of people say yeah. It's an inspirational product, so that makes it a lot easier to do that.

**SD:** What did the show end up costing Tom?

**TB:** It was less than the budget and less than you would ever expect looking at the show. As a point of interest, one of the concerns we had going in was, "Are we really going to be able to get owners of the cars to speak to us on camera?" It's a fairly affluent group, they don't need to do this and also, there's a mystique about their cars. They're used, but they believe they're new. And their friends and family and neighbors believe they're new. Do they really want to participate in this kind of thing? Once we started recruiting, it was really, really interesting. These people not only wanted to, but they insisted on it. Just a tremendous amount of enthusiasm to do it. There's passion for this project and this product. People just came out of the woodwork to talk about it.

**SD:** How did you track the people down for the show?

**TB:** Through dealers basically. Gary's folks gave us names of people who owned them and we just went at them randomly.

**GM:** We maintain a file of everyone who bought one. These people are then included in all of our owner retention activities. Once a person buys a Lexus Certified car, they're just like a regular Lexus owner. So it's very easy for us to print out a list and give it to Tom and let him start talking to people.

**SD:** If this program is as successful as it appears to be, does that in any way contribute to them not changing body styles as often as they might?

**GM:** I don't think it changes their plans. Toyota is a smart enough company that they have already factored this into the equation from the beginning. Luxury buyers don't like to have their product obsoleted every three or four years. They like evolutionary types of changes so that the person driving a new Lexus knows they're driving a new one, knows what it is that makes their car newer than somebody else's. But the person that's driving a two or three year old one doesn't feel inadequate. And I think that's been part of the product planning process from the beginning. Certainly the impact that has on resale value has always been something that Toyota has considered. We have been planning and thinking and strategizing about maintaining industry leading resale values since the day this company was launched. It was launched in 1989 and all of the decisions we make take those kinds of factors into consideration. We don't think it's fair for somebody to buy a car and a year later have that thing lose 30 % of its value. In an effort to maintain lifetime loyalty and lifetime satisfaction, there's a lot of care and a lot of energy to make sure that when that customer comes in to trade for a new Lexus, their vehicle is still worth something. And we have spent countless hours and done a lot of things to make sure that's possible.

**SD:** Is there still a lot of resale value left after they're being sold for a third time? After going through the program? They've got a lot of mileage on them I would think.

*GM:* Oh yeah. But you're moving to a different type of customer at that point. You're moving to, "For $18,000 you could be driving an LS400. Do you really care that is has 75,000 miles on it?" A lot of people don't. The one thing about Toyota products and all the accolades from JD Power, and long term reliability, and durability, is they last. They don't explode after 75,000 miles. That gives the customer a lot of confidence.

*SD:* How many markets are you going to roll this out to?

*TB:* It's going to depend on the dealers themselves. They're the ones who decide to take it or not take it and when to take it.

*SD:* Let's talk about how that works. You're basically approaching the dealer association in each major city and showing them the program and what it's going to cost them and then they make the decision?

*TB:* Correct.

*GM:* A lot of our pre-owned advertising is really executed by our dealer associations. We do the production and we come up with the ideas together with them and bear the burden of producing them and bringing them the tools. It's up to them in each one of their markets what they choose to run, how they choose to run it and when they choose to run it. We're doing the test in the four markets, but beyond that it will be up to the local associations.

*SD:* Tell me the four markets you're in initially.

*TB:* L.A., Phoenix, Dallas and New York.

*SD:* Can you give me an idea in each city what the media budget is?

*TB:* The best way to say it is covering three weekends, three to four weeks of activity, pretty heavy in multiple day parts. We're running some overnight stuff as well. I don't think any market has a budget of any more than a $100,000 or a little more than that.

*SD:* For the total test?

*TB:* Yeah. It might be a little more than that in the L.A. and New York markets.

*GM:* Not a lot more.

*SD:* That's impressive, because one spot on KCOP out here, on a Saturday morning, can run you 15 grand alone.

**GM:** The idea here is cost per lead. By making this a dealer program, it really has to stand up to their standard on how much money does it cost them to generate a customer through the door. And if it's too expensive, they're not going to run it. The only way it's going to work for them is if it's an economical thing. We spent a lot of time making sure it does that.

**SD:** Assuming that this is going to be as successful as you anticipate it being, can you see Toyota doing some others?

**GM:** I think it's opened some people's eyes about the fact that this medium can work. I have not seen any concrete proposals that said let's extend this to these following five projects. I certainly think there is a better chance of that happening as a result of this than there ever was before.

**TB:** The same read came out of the Tercel thing. Steve, remember when Irv Miller was speaking at your conference, he kind of expected another one to be following the lines of the Tercel show. That experience is still viewed very positively within the company and this is now a second one that looks like it's headed that way. I think I would be surprised if they don't do more at some point. To quote Irv, he doesn't want to get into the infomercial business. It's not going to be something that they try to do in every particular case. I think they're going to look for the situations where it calls for something extraordinary, where there's really a story to tell. They really want to break through and have the dealers get an extra level of excitement out of what's coming. So I think it will be selective use. But I would expect more, hope for more from where we sit.

**SD:** Some of the show was shot on film, right Tom?

**TB:** It was all shot on film.

**SD:** How much footage were you able to incorporate from existing commercials?

**TB:** Quite a bit. We have three full commercials in the body of the show, so those are free standing commercials that are running currently in local markets. We've built those into the show, which is a nice integration of a short-length campaign along with a longer format. We also then selectively picked footage from years of advertising that they've had available. So we used a lot of it. What percentage of the show would be hard to say, but they have the best looking advertising footage of anybody in the car business. It is really excellent stuff. It's really fun to look at. It really adds excitement. It speaks well for the car. It was always a plan to try to use that wherever we could. We were all really excited about how we were able to blend the two together.

**SD:** From a mechanical point of view, how did that actually work? Did everyone sit down and take a look at the footage that was there and then build a show around it?

*TB:* No, we built the show. We had the expert interviews and the consumer interviews and the technicians and the basic body of the show was there. We edited that first. Then we put the commercials, the three free standing commercials, in. Built the pods around those, the special offer pods. Then as we were doing that, we took from the world of footage that they had available and just built that in where we could.

*SD:* When I saw the show I got very excited. I think it just continues the steps you took on the Tercel show.

*TB:* Thank you. To hear you're excited about it is very pleasing.

*SD:* I thought that this was a legitimate, very excellent use of an infomercial, especially with what you incorporated in the back-end with the cars for sale and getting them to the dealers. I think you're going to see a lot of positive results.

*TB:* I think you were right to pick up on that. The customization of the kit that people get really is a breakthrough. It's really something we wanted to have. We wanted to make sure that whatever the person called for was more than just a brochure, that it was going to move the sale forward. And something they would instantly want. I think that's going to prove to be the case.

*SD:* And the other thing that I heard was the fact that you were promising the fulfillment kit within 7 to 14 days.

*TB:* Yeah.

*SD:* That's kind of sticking yourself out on the line.

*TB:* Yes it is.

*SD:* There was a heavy sigh there.

*GM:* And another one here. I think that down the road we have some other ideas on fulfillment that will even make that particular part of it even more exciting for the customers and more customizable.

*SD:* What was the whole time frame from the time your first started talking about it to the time the show first tested?

*TB:* When the production budget was agreed to and the production company was appointed on March 30th. So we were on the air June 24th. We wanted to be in L.A. on that weekend because there was a sales event going on and that was really our impetus for not missing this date. It was a little less than three months that the whole production process happened.

**GM:** I think the first time we presented it to our dealers was the second week of February, when we sort of had in our mind that we think it's going to be a good thing to do and we wanted to see if they would be interested in it and if it turned out as well as we thought, would they consider running it in the future.

**TB:** The production process was about three months.

**SD:** That's very fast. When you work in a major corporation, there's whole decision-making processes and a lot of people have to be involved and it's usually very slow. This seems to have proceeded very quickly.

**TB:** This was very similar to Tercel. They really seem to have autonomy. This was Gary's baby, he was in support of it. I don't know how much work went on behind the scenes, but I only saw one other guy that he really had to persuade. One meeting and the guy was on board before the meeting. From there on, there was absolutely no red tape. Even in the approval process, we had extremely tight timing for approvals. We basically said, "Gary, you're getting a show this morning, we've got to know by this afternoon." Somehow he pulled that off. I was very impressed with the quickness that they can move. And there's a whole dealer group out there that's more than a little bit interested in what's going on and they were on board, kept informed, but never slowed the process down at all.

**GM:** There's a dealer advisory board of some 8 to 12 dealers that are in the consent process once a piece is produced. It's sent to them for their review and sort of approval of the thing. We're not a bureaucratic company. We get together and we talk about an idea and everyone is involved in whether it's a good thing. And once everybody agrees it's a good thing, we've been working together long enough to trust each other to know it's going to turn out okay. It's about make it look right, make it work and keep it under budget. There were I think three versions in rough cuts that we looked at and everyone in a room saying what we should change and what we should not and it was done. There wasn't a lot of typical corporate bureaucracy that goes into this thing. I think the other thing is that Team One has worked with us so well over the last six years that they really understand what we're trying to communicate and what's going to work and what's not. So when we see a piece, it's about 98% there. When you can trust your agency to make the decisions that you make, it smoothes the process. It makes it so much more exciting to work on. You know you don't have to second guess and nitpick everything, because you know your agency has already done that work for you.

**SD:** The dealer association was involved even in viewing the rough cuts, making suggestions. They must have looked like real heroes when the powers that be locally saw what they came back with.

**GM:** I don't think they reviewed too many of the roughs, they reviewed the final. It's hard to get dealers to imagine what roughs will look like so we only let them look at the final.

*TB:* They were well aware of what the show was, the concept and...

*GM:* Some of them are in it. You have two or three guys from the advisory board that are actually speaking in a piece, that helps to communicate to the other people what's going on and get them involved up front, saying, "Hey this is an idea we have." And spend an hour kicking it around. What should be in it, how should we present this? It certainly makes it a lot simpler when it's done.

*SD:* That's all the questions I have, except that when I'm ready to get a Lexus can I call you?

*GM:* Sure.

*TB:* If you've seen the show, you're ready to get one.

# BILL GUTHY

# GREG RENKER

This is the final interview we published in the *Infomercial Marketing Report*. Appropriately, it is our second interview with Guthy-Renker. At the start of this industry in the late '80s, many companies had the potential to become the industry leader. After 15 years, only two of those companies remain: Guthy-Renker and American Telecast. As an observer of the industry, it's been fascinating watching the ups and downs, twists and turns, these companies have made through the years. The end result being that Guthy-Renker is the sole leader in the industry by as much as three times over their closest competitor. Their earnings this year will be over $1 billion in sales. That's a startling figure and everyone in their organization should be deeply proud of their accomplishments.

How they did it, what they learned, and where they're headed are all topics covered in this exclusive interview. This is the first time Bill Guthy and Greg Renker have touched on these topics in print. This interview is essentially a look back on the lessons learned over the past 15 years on growing a company to this size, and uncovering what really works over the long haul in the direct response television field. I am deeply honored that they consented to share this information with all of us.

*Steve Dworman:* When did you two start Guthy-Renker?

*Bill Guthy:* October 1988 is the official year.

*SD:* Was that the year of *Think and Grow Rich* and the *Mental Bank*?

*BG:* I'd forgotten all about the *Mental Bank.*

*SD:* Did you?

*BG:* Yeah. You're absolutely right. We did the *Mental Bank.* That was the second one we did. We have them all listed somewhere. We have an archivist.

*SD:* You actually have an archivist at this point?

*BG:* Yeah, it's a full-time position. She keeps track of all the shows and masters, all that stuff.

*SD:* Give me a paragraph on how you two met and why you started the company.

*Greg Renker:* Bill and I had a mutual love and affection for motivational materials and tapes. We really were listening to Earl Nightingale and a lot of products coming out of Nightingale. Bill and I were friends in Indian Wells and we had mutual friends in Indian Wells so, in effect, we were partying and playing together. The business was really started out of those shared interests, but Bill was already a very successful entrepreneur, particularly at such a young age. Everyone who was friends with him admired him for what he had already accomplished and so, in some ways, Bill was a mentor to me as well. He was part of the inspiration that made me want to explore new business opportunities. At the same time, we were discovering that the television direct marketing world was beginning to expand and, individually and laterally, we were both watching that stuff. Curiously, it's kind of like the people who first started playing around with the Internet in its early stage. Bill and I were watching the fledgling shopping channels and we were watching Tony Hoffman—and I am not kidding when I tell you I was watching Tony Hoffman a lot.

*BG:* It was called National Superstars, right?

*SD:* Yeah, I think so.

*BG:* It was like two hours long and a Johnny Carson-type format.

*GR:* It is hard for me to explain to you what the fascination was. I was not looking at it saying, "I can do this or I want to do this." I don't think Bill was either. I think Bill was looking at it saying there should be some duplication clients here and I can make money off these people.

*BG:* And there was a lot of it.

*GR:* And I was looking at it saying, something is happening here.

**SD:** At that point, your background was in real estate, wasn't it Greg?

**GR:** I did have a broker's license but I wasn't very passionate about it. My background was really more in marketing at the family resort, which my brother, father and I owned in the '80s in Indian Wells.

**SD:** So then you came up with the idea of starting a company to actually go on television?

**GR:** We both loved being in the desert and I recall a conversation about wanting to get into the mail-order business. You know, the benefits of mail order were that customers came to you and we would be able to build a business wherever we wanted and work on our own time. There is a little bit of Joe Cossman in that. Bill was intrigued by television and his company had acquired the rights to Napoleon Hill and *Think and Grow Rich*. You might say I helped understand what was going on in the television marketplace. I just started by calling the toll-free numbers and asking the operators who they were, where they were, who they were answering for. And one thing led to another. Bill and I would meet every week and I would say, "You won't believe what I found out this week." And he would say, "Well then, I think this is what we ought to do next." We spent a year researching how we could get into the television marketing business. We were talking to people ranging from Richard Sutter to Don Lewis and Gene Williams. We were listening to a lot of direct marketing tapes, reading direct marketing literature, and there was no information at the time about television direct marketing. Nothing.

**BG:** What about the Financial News Network?

**GR:** Stan Jacobs, Rod Buscher and Jon Schulberg were all early partners and also mentors. I mean we were all learning from each other. Schulberg had a very interesting TV background because of his father and his uncle, and Stan had been doing Financial News Network and Stan was doing infomercials. Stan really understood the construct and Rod Buscher had a sense of the big picture, because he was one of the co-founders of FNN. Bill and I had some good people to talk to, get started with and brainstorm with.

**BG:** At least half my motivation—through whatever Greg and I were going to do together in the mail order thing—was to really find a way to become a controllable large client for the manufacturing business I had started. I was looking for my own marketing business that could feed manufacturing and fulfillment. That way, if I was slow one month or one week in the business when my clients were slow, I could always throw something on the machine to keep my people busy building up an inventory ahead of what I needed on the marketing side. The other half was the desire to have a second business, to have more time in the desert, to have a product business as opposed to being in the service side, which is a totally different kind of business. That's kind of how we got started in the early days.

**SD:** What finally led you to push the button on *Think and Grow Rich*?

*GR:* We asked people who seemed reasonably experienced if they thought it would work and we asked it a lot and asked it often. And we got pretty good responses.

*BG:* I think that was the biggest motivation for us. One weekend we were talking about this business and what we could and what we couldn't do. Neither one of us were speakers. Neither one of us were interested in creating an expertise that we would then start turning into tapes or training materials, but we both loved *Think and Grow Rich*. We really had a passion for selling something we believed in, and what we didn't want was to just sell something that would work. We wanted something to work, yes, but we also wanted it to be something that we were passionate about and had a strong belief in so that it was congruent. That product's title hadn't been produced before in any form other than a book. So the idea was let's go to Chicago and see if we can line up the rights and see what rights are available that could be turned into an audio-video product that could be sold via television.

*GR:* What Bill is also saying is that it was a category we understood, that we were passionate about and believed in. We also knew what other products were out there. So we knew the differentiation between *Think and Grow Rich* and the other motivational products because we listened to them and we bought them.

*BG:* A lot of the products that were being sold then were subliminal tapes. I know because I manufactured most of them—and the "how to make money" tapes. On the motivational side, I can't say that I was a big believer in the subliminal stuff, but I did have a real passion for Earl Nightingale's material. That was something that was really in sync with my philosophy and Greg's as well.

*GR:* Bill understood the subliminal technology well enough that to this day he has embedded a command in our infomercials on television that says, "You will buy now." We have tested subliminal and no subliminal and it definitely works. There is no ERA guideline that says we can't do it.

*SD:* Are you still using the naked women as well?

*BG:* We just splash pictures of phones and credit cards. We just want people to go to the phone and get out the credit card.

*SD:* Well, everybody knows you have really mastered that.

When I first talked about that *Think and Grow Rich* show, the one hesitation I had from a marketing point of view was that I thought the show got the interest up for the product, but it was forcing a lot of people to the bookstore to buy a $3 or $4 book in comparison with the $80 tape package.

*BG:* And that probably happened. We have no way of gauging, no way of knowing. I guess if we were able to find the book sales figures and compared them before and after we might have seen a jump there, I don't know. To this day, we still own the rights to *Think and Grow Rich* material. Actually it's a different entity. We still market quite a bit of it at retail to the bookstores. But back then we had no idea of whether we were driving people and we totally assumed we did. But the real key was no one had ever put it out on tape so one could listen to it many times. That was kind of the hook that we tried to get across. You read a book once and remember very little of it a month later, but if you have something that you could listen to over and over again, because it is easy and in your car, maybe it will sink in better and you will be able to use it more.

*SD:* You got excited. Didn't *Mental Bank* come next, and one other one, before Tony Robbins came along?

*BG:* Tony was a testimonial in *Think and Grow Rich* because while we were putting together the show, Greg remembered that he had read a book the year before called *Unlimited Power* by Tony Robbins (who was not then a household name). He was a motivational speaker, traveling the country. He was an author and, in that book, Tony praised and made reference to *Think and Grow Rich* and Napoleon Hill. It is a good thing Greg remembered that because when he called Tony to see if he would be a testimonial to *Think and Grow Rich*, Tony said yes. and it became the best part of that show.

*SD:* How long did it take you to put the first Tony show together?

*BG:* It took less time to put the show together than it did the contract. I think we spent a year-and-a-half trying to nail down that contract with Tony.

*GR:* That, and we went through several of Tony's advisors. And it was a new experience for us in doing a contract like that.

*BG:* It took a long time to do, to get the rights. And then we had to create the product from scratch. The product of Personal Power did not exist. That had to be created from scratch. The show was created from scratch. My guess is that both of those together in parallel took about a year, something in that range.

*SD:* Was it probably the shortest Tony show you've ever done?

*BG:* I don't know about that, but I would say that they take their time. Everyone involved is a perfectionist and would like to put it out the right way.

*SD:* Didn't that show come out in '89?

*BG:* April 15th, tax weekend.

*SD:* The worst weekend you could come out.

*BG:* That's when we came out.

*SD:* And was it successful right out?

*BG:* You know we had *Think and Grow Rich* numbers to compare to so we knew when we ran it that it would be a big hit for us.

*SD:* And then it was. I guess the other show that was huge at that time and set some landmarks was Victoria Jackson's first show.

*BG:* I don't know exactly when it came out, whether it was prior to April '89. I think it was '89.

*SD:* It was '89.

*BG:* I am not sure if it was before April or after April. I know it was certainly in that time frame.

*SD:* What do you remember about that time frame? That was like your first big success, and media rates were still good.

*BG:* I remember being very thrilled, very excited for two reasons. One, it was going to create a lot of business for CPU and for the manufacturing and fulfillment business. But more importantly it was going to really kick our business off to a much bigger head start than *Think and Grow Rich* was able to do for us. I guess that first huge show is always certainly equal to, if not your most, exciting surprise.

*GR:* I would say that it was never really easy but it was always a lot of fun. There were a lot of challenges going on and we didn't have a lot of depth in our staffing. Bill and I really had to make a lot of day-to-day decisions and we made mistakes.

*SD:* What kind of decisions, Greg?

*GR:* Well a lot of things were new to us. For example, when we originally started with Victoria Principal on the skin care line, it was at a very risky time. If you recall, the winter of 1991 is when the Gulf War hit. We talked to you about this before and that was the same time that Quantum went bankrupt.

*BG:* And we had a joint venture with them and we didn't recoup the funds we put into that.

*GR:* Which at the time was a tremendous amount of money to us and we were left holding the bag on a large bankruptcy, which was not the brightest thing we ever did. We owned media that wasn't performing, our returns were going up, and we were dealing with issues and unknowns that were difficult. We were in unknown territory often in those early periods and having Bill as a partner was an extraordinary experience. He is a very straight thinking, logical, practical person who doesn't get overly emotional about challenges and tries to think them through carefully. That helped us through some of the difficult periods and it also helped us through some of the challenges we had with our partners who were talent, if you will. Talent doesn't always think the way a businessperson does. They mostly do, but they don't always because they have different needs and requirements and visions. One day Bill and I would be looking at a kitchen product, and the next day we would be looking at motivation, and the next day we are looking at skin care. You are supposed to be an expert on all of those and also understand how to compete against people who are not in direct marketing and have your pricing right. Then you hear that fitness is hot, so suddenly you're spending weeks working on fitness products. It was a fascinating time, because at the same time you are watching the shopping channels grow, grow, grow—you're hearing of great numbers and you think maybe that's what you should be doing. So there were a lot of young people, young entrepreneurs, hard working, dreaming, trying, experimenting, and if we hadn't done as many wild things as we did we wouldn't be where we are today. We learned a ton but we made a variety of different mistakes that we still make, but I don't think we make them as seriously as we used to. If we hadn't tried things, we wouldn't have gotten the knowledge and the base that we have today, but that isn't to suggest that tomorrow we won't make the biggest mistake ever. It may come as a big surprise.

*SD:* Did that period of time, where everybody was throwing one product category after another against the wall to find one that worked, last through the majority of the '90's?

*GR:* Yeah and we were right in there. Not always. I like to think we were a little more focused. But it was an interesting time in that regard.

*BG:* Well, I think we definitely went through our phase of not being as focused in the early-to-mid '90's as we were in the later '90's to this period. I do think there was a lot more, maybe even industry wide. Certainly speaking just for our company, we did a lot more of that, a lot more experimentation. We got spread way too thin in the mid '90's and got into many categories and too many subsidiaries and too many businesses and just made some decisions that were ultimately not smart for the growth and profitability of the company. You talked about what decisions we made early on. One of the decisions we made was to stay variable and I think most companies followed suit. There are very few companies in our industry that are vertical. That decision early on was probably a good one. The bigger we get—we'll do just over $700,000,000 this year—we could say, "We could save a lot of money if we just did this in house," but you know to this point we have resisted the temptation to get too vertical and we have kept our payroll below 150 people. We use a lot of really smart, talented companies and individuals and many of them have been with us from the beginning. I mean Lenny Lieberman has been with us since really the finishing up of that very first *Personal Power* show. He was brought on as we were into the production of *Personal Power I.* We've got CPU for fulfillment and customer service, and manufacturing of audio video/DVD/CDs. We've been with Mercury Media since pretty much day one even before the current ownership. A lot of folks have been with us for a long time, both internally and externally, that have really helped shape our success.

*SD:* One vendor group you didn't mention was telemarketing.

*BG:* You're right. We have been with Convergys since '89 as well. They were Matrix at the time, and they've gone through a name change. But you are exactly right, we've had really strong relationships with both the telemarketers and the fulfillment companies and the media companies we have used and the production company in Lenny Lieberman have just been fantastic.

*GR:* The biggest blessings we've gotten have come from people like Ben Van de Bunt and Kevin Knee, and Jeff Engler, Al Kushner, and Charlotte Spielberger, who's been with us since day one. All of our team...

*BG:* She was our first employee.

*GR:* When we tested our new *Youthful Essence* show, she came in Saturday morning to read those numbers and call Bill and to tell us what we've got. She has been doing that since day one.

*BG:* By the way did you see that show, Steve? What did you think?

*SD:* I gotta tell you, when I first saw it I really thought you did a great job with the show. I mean, I thought the first five or six minutes of that show and building up the promise was phenomenal. And then the comparison to what's professionally available and the offer where you are giving away the electronics for free, it was just kick ass. The offer was superb.

*BG:* We'll know tomorrow.

*SD:* I give you two so much credit and also the people that you work with because you studied everyone so well and learned from their successes and learned from their mistakes. The case in point was when I got on your case years ago when Aida Thibiant was dropped from Victoria Principal's show and all of a sudden Victoria Principal was a skin care expert. Now that's worked out extremely well, but I've never seen you do another show in which the celebrity is the expert. I think that's very, very important and American Telecast just did two beauty shows in which Christie Brinkley was the expert and I think it suffered as a result.

*GR:* Victoria Principal is a very unique personality. Not only is she a big star and very well known, with a high Q rating, and high likeability, and high recognition, she really does work hard. She really does know her stuff. She really does study and you know she has been at this with us going on 12 years. And prior to that, she had written three beauty books. So she does her research. She's not a paid spokesperson. She really is and has become the expert for The Principal Secret.

*SD:* I've heard that. I mean she really has taken it on to be her company.

*BG:* She is the one who is thinking of new products. We have a staff of people who work within Principal Secret that are employed by Guthy/Renker. She utilizes that team. She comes up with ideas and together they create and package new products that are launched on QVC and in our catalog. My guess is that there is a new product created every month.

*GR:* Hey Steve, that's one of the reasons we have been so blessed. It's because we've had Victoria Principal at such an early stage and having her be so phenomenal. The same thing is true with Tony Robbins. We have been gifted with some phenomenal, hard-working, visionary talent from day one, including some of the people who are integral to us, such as Ben and Kevin. When you get that early, that's a gift. It's made a difference. Had we started a skin care line with someone else who didn't have the passion, the vision, and the understanding of the category, we might have failed and we might have never gone there again.

*BG:* It is a very tough category, and I think it takes some very unique pieces of a puzzle to come together and make a beautiful thing.

*SD:* Bill, expand on that a little bit. Why is it a category as tough as you're claiming? There are a million of them out there.

*BG:* A daily regimen skin care like Principal Secret is competing at the retail level with many dozens, if not hundreds, of brands. You are limited in terms of what you can claim and can show. Doing it legally and legitimately and making it seem real and valuable and something they have to have right now is not easy with this category. It's not like other categories that are easily demonstrated. Skin care does not sell like a kitchen gadget that you can show and demonstrate how it works and create a lot of excitement around it. It really depends on the credibility of the person, the story you tell, the offer, and ultimately the product they receive and love. If you don't have that big chunk going for you, then they're not going to go through the trouble of buying over and over again. Really, we try to make the trouble very light by giving people the ability to just have it arrive at their door, hopefully at the time they are running out of their old shipment.

*GR:* Our primary drive with celebrities is to make absolutely certain they are passionate about the products they are selling and stand behind them 110 percent and, in fact, have a direct link to that product so that there is no doubt in the consumer's mind, regarding the celebrity's intentions for being involved. Otherwise, they are a hired hand. Victoria Principal is working harder today on this product than she was 10 years ago.

*SD:*   As an adjunct to that, let's talk about how much more competitive the entry level pricing has gotten for products. You used to be able to charge three payments of whatever at the front end. Now, in a lot of cases, it's down to try it for $9.95 isn't it?

*BG:* Well, in very rare cases it is that low. I was thinking you were going to say $29.95, but there are a few, including Natural Advantage, which really isn't $9.95, it's $9.95 for the first payment. Since it's a two month supply, they are really paying $35, where as the Principal Secret it may not seem lower but in reality you're getting a one month's supply for $29. So you are able to get started for $29 and not $35, although it's a one month supply and not a two month supply.

*GR:* You know Bill watches offers very closely and pays a lot of attention to what the ultimate outcome will be, so we are a little skeptical about his new plan, which is to pay the consumer to take the product from us. [Laughter]

*SD:*   Getting back to the pricing issues, even at $29.95, it's a much more expensive proposition because all of a sudden you have a whole other set of SKUs for the front-end products.

*BG:* That's the downside. You do have to maintain inventory levels and different SKUs, which you didn't have to in the past. Obviously the easier you make it for the customer to make a decision the better. Free is always good, but since we can't give it away for free, we have tried going to a lower barrier to get people to give it a try. You don't make a profit early in the process. It takes a while to build up. It all depends on your systems and your product.

*SD:* I've heard, Bill, that it takes an average of three go-arounds to break even or be profitable.

*BG:* You know I couldn't give you a blanket answer because every product truly and realistically is different. Some shows just create a higher response and some shows might do it in less; some shows create a poorer response that might take more. Obviously the poorer the response, the higher your CPO, the longer it's going to take, and in some cases, it's just not worth it because of the cost of money. You're just hanging out there way too long, and you just have to say, you know, this one is not working and we've got to get rid of it.

*SD:* And that brings up another issue. With these offers being so competitive and it taking so long to break even, you're eliminating essentially start-up competition that doesn't have big pockets. They can't afford to enter the marketplace.

**BG:** There's no question it's not for the faint of heart. It does take a lot of capital and a lot of know-how. If you have the capital, you better have the know-how, because you could be wasting a lot of money just by not understanding what you really have and thinking you have something that you don't. Then when you look at it two years later, you realize that it wasn't such a good move. I lost a lot of dough.

**GR:** Hey Steve, don't think we haven't dumped a couple million here and a couple mil there, thinking we had it when we didn't. I am talking even recently.

**SD:** That's such a cryptic message. I wish people could hear what your voice sounds like. You've got at least a handful of beauty lines in development, including one for Cindy Crawford that we've talked about, and that's a long-term project. So, speaking of Cindy Crawford, let's talk a little bit in generalities about what the cost of a celebrity is and how that has risen over the years. It sure seems like a lot more money for rollout than it used to be. Can you take a top-level celebrity and make it work outside of something that doesn't have the continuity of a back-end to it?

**BG:** In which category? In any category?

**SD:** In any category.

**BG:** I would think so. Look at what you discovered. Wasn't it you who found the Total Gym and got that going with American Telecast?

**SD:** Yeah. I recommended that the Total Gym people go with ATC when they had two offers.

**BG:** Yes, in one of your showcase seminars. There you go, Chuck Norris and Christy Brinkley, and it's been going, what, five or six years?

**SD:** At the time of this interview.

**BG:** So it can be done with high-paid talent, sure.

**SD:** The exception to that though, Bill, is that you're talking about a product that is over $500. You know there was a time when you used to say, even on Victoria Jackson's product line, you didn't know if you could do that deal today.

**BG:** Yeah, you're right. When you think about it...

*SD:* It's very nice of you to know about the Total Gym. I've never received even a thank you letter on that one.

*BG:* I am groping for an example of a one-shot product with a big name celebrity that has done very well.

*GR:* How about Jane Fonda? That goes back 10 years.

*BG:* I am trying to think of a more recent example. If you think about it, Tae-Bo was huge, with no major celeb. Carleton Sheets continues to be huge with no celeb. Superblue is the current phenom. No celeb. No big name. The Firm really had no big name. You're asking the question, can it be done? Can you have a big celeb? With the current rollout of fee demands, percentage demands and making profit, my guess the answer to that is a yes. But it's probably unnecessary for most products because there is too much evidence things are working out there without it in big ways. I think certain categories might need it more than others.

*SD:* I have dabbled in the skin care area a little bit myself and know it's a very tough area. You're right about the claims, and then to develop products and then you have to go through testing and all of that. You're talking a year, year-and-a-half, aren't you?

*BG:* At least, maybe two, to do it right. Greg keeps reminding me it takes time to get it right. And usually when we take time and get it right, we mix it with the right person, with the right testing and formulation and we end up with something that lasts a long time.

*GR:* Steve, the *Youthful Essence* show we tested this weekend, we had the product done almost two years ago.

*SD:* So what took so long if you had the product already?

*GR:* The quest to do it right.

*BG:* Getting the deal done with Susan Lucci took a long time.

*GR:* But we were patient and are patient. We have a project coming out—I am not even sure when it is coming out—that started over two years ago. By the time we've done all the clinicals, all the testimonial groups, more clinicals, getting doctors involved…it's a stair-step process that we could have done in nine months, and it definitely could have been on the air. The product was ready almost a year-and-a-half ago.

*BG:* It's in the beauty area, but it's not a skin care product.

**GR:** Just to give you an example, Steve—and I am not saying this is a magic formula because I don't know what any magic formulas are, we only know how to do what we know how to do—in general we are finding that if we commit to quality and commit to excellence and we don't back down, we at least get something we believe we did the best job we could with. And if it doesn't work, we could look at each other and say, hey we really tried very hard and we did the best we could. That feels a lot better than failure and "boy we did nine things wrong and why did we rush it?"

**SD:** Rushing can be really detrimental. I see that over and over again.

**BG:** The Pilates product that is out now, which you may have seen on TV, that was in development for quite a while, for that kind of a product, for a book and video kind of a product, it definitely was in development for quite a while.

**GR:** Well, Bill, I could be wrong about this, but wouldn't you agree that we signed Mari Winsor, of Winsor Pilates, over two years ago and that show didn't go on the air until two months ago. So it was about two years from signing and committing to delivery.

**BG:** Looking back, were there shortcuts we could have taken on that one to make it quicker without sacrificing what we ended up with? I think so. Creating the product was on our own calendar, our own internal scheduling and conflicts, but there is no doubt we could have pushed it faster. But things for us are in production longer; the process of birthing a new brand or new product is just longer.

**GR:** Let me give you an example, Steve, on what Bill just said about how we could have sped up Pilates and why we chose excellence rather than speed. Bill partially drove this process. We completed the video shoot in its entirety and agreed that unless the product was excellent we were not going to start the infomercial. So when we signed the talent and agreed on the concept, we said we will do the product in its entirety first and—if we will love it—we will go into production of the infomercial, not simultaneously. *Personal Power*, 12 years ago, was a simultaneous development. You can really speed it up if you did both at once.

**BG:** My belief is that if you've got a really great product and really incredible people behind it your odds go up. I just didn't want to have a product that was kind of "me too," like all the other Pilates tapes, which were not very well done, and then try to sell a bunch of them.

**SD:** You know I understand the rationale for doing that, especially the product categories you are involved in, but do you ever worry or get concerned that you are losing a big opportunity by not being out faster in some cases?

**BG:** I say that we worry about that all the time. You question and worry about it, sure. In business you have to make adjustments, not the kind of adjustments that would cause you to want to sell something that was a piece of crap but certainly you question and ask yourself if there's a faster way of creating the right product, with the right talent, on a more speedy basis.

**GR:** Steve I will give you my favorite example. Bill and I and Ben and Kevin and others were involved, as you know with Ron Perelman, who was part owner of our business in 1993. He owned Marvel and they owned Spider Man. And Spider Man was in development as a movie. James Cameron was going to direct it, and they thought it was going to be huge. They knew in 1993 that it was going to be the biggest thing they had. Bill and I were meeting with Ave Arid and Ike Perlmutter and the people who own Toy Biz, who now own Spider Man. If that movie had come out in '93, '94 or '95 it wouldn't be the same movie. That movie today is a result of digital technology and the passion that Ave Arid had for it, to deliver it the way he wanted it, and to fulfill his vision and is the reason, in my opinion, as to why it is the blockbuster it is. He committed to excellence and patience helped him, it didn't hurt him.

**SD:** Yes, that's very true. I think they based that movie on the Cameron outline, if I am not mistaken. They didn't use the script but they used the outline.

**GR:** Well, let me give you another example about serendipity, timing, and everything coming together in a way you never anticipated, but being committed. When I first saw the front-page article about you and your film in *The Los Angeles Times,* I said to my wife, the thing that I really admire about this is that Steve abandoned everything to commit to this project and he said I am going to bring it in no matter what it takes. Not only did that end up being a front page article in *The Los Angeles Times,* which I thought was huge, but it also was on CNN Headline News, and a variety of other places and the timing of that and the way that it worked out was serendipitous, but it was a result of a full commitment as opposed to you having rushed it or cut corners in the process.

**SD:** That's true and the jury is still out as to where it's all going to end up, but it's been a roller coaster ride. Bill, if you were starting out in this business today and you didn't have significant financial resource, do you see any opportunities where an entrepreneur can still get in? Where do you think the opportunities are?

**BG:** You are talking about an entrepreneur who has how much money?

**SD:** Not a lot. I mean a hundred thousand, fifty thousand dollars.

**BG:** Well for that kind of money, you'd have to be very smart and very creative. There's definitely an opportunity. I would probably say it is not in categories that require a lot of money or time for development. If you're a savvy person who can license a product or if you are an expert in a category like real estate, could you go to someone like a Kevin Trudeau and produce a show for a very low amount of money and try something? Sure. Another great way to start could be if you have the right product in the right category, it would be going onto QVC or the Home Shopping Network and leveraging your way into an infomercial through the profits you made that way. That's in addition to trying to do your own show. There is also the service sector. Fulfillment, customer service, telemarketing, I mean if you are in those kinds of businesses already you could learn a lot about the industry in that way and then invest profits accordingly. Greg's point was find a partner! Look at Carl Daikler. Raise the money with partners and create the Power 90 show. There is a guy starting from scratch with a couple of partners and creating a nice little business, growing into a larger business. I think it could definitely be done especially in that weight loss and fitness category, kitchen category, books and tapes.

**SD:** As far as starting out goes, let's talk a little about the difference in media cost and orders now versus when you started. With audience degradation, I know that when Tony Robbins went on in '89, the average person had eight or nine channels on their television. The day after the show aired for the first weekend everybody was talking about it.

**BG:** You had lower rates and bigger audiences, which was a nice combination.

**SD:** It's not happening now. You don't have that word of mouth that you used to, and you have to air a lot more places.

**BG:** It means you have to have that much more firepower in your show, in your offer and your product. I think it's forced all of us to get better at what we do. We would love the rates and the viewership of ten years ago, sure. With our current line-up it would be unbelievable, but I just think you have to be smarter, more effective, maybe a little more patient. You've got a lot more firepower both in the product and the offer and the creative and the talent, and I know you can be very effective and have a very large and profitable business even in the environment today, but you've got to be better at what you do and have to use a mixed media. You can't just rely on television.

**SD:** Would you say that you spend more money on media or about the same?

**BG:** We spend more money on shows now than we did then. It's because it's a bigger business. We are more successful, and we are just not relying on television.

**SD:** When you say you are not just relying on television, outside of QVC, what else are you talking about?

**BG:** Direct mail, space advertising, package inserts, Internet, catalogs.

**SD:** Is Internet accounting for many sales at this point?

*BG:* For a lot of our products, it's very significant.

*SD:* And is that something where people find you once they have seen the show?

*BG:* We promote the Web address for each product and each product has its own Web address, and we promote that Web address within the CTA. We also do some marketing on the Web itself, but I have to assume that the majority of our traffic flows from the promotion we are doing elsewhere. The Web address appears in every print ad we put out, it appears on virtually every product we send out, and all the literature we send out.

*SD:* Do the people order right on the Web, or do they get an 800 number?

*BG:* Both, but we get a significant amount of business on the Web avoiding the telephone call and the expense of that all together.

*SD:* How extensive now is your outbound telemarketing programs?

*BG:* Almost non-existent. That's why I didn't mention outbound in the mix of media. There's really only one program where we continually do outbound. None of us like getting calls at home and so we try to minimize what we subject our customers to.

*SD:* Is it just that with all the testing you found that it just wasn't that profitable?

*BG:* It starts with none of us liking to be called at home at dinner. If I don't have to I'd rather not. Ultimately, it just did not fit the personality of our business, and it wasn't as effective as other things could be so we just opted not to do very much of it. Let's put it this way, it amounts to less than 1% of our sales.

*SD:* Do you do direct mail to your customers outside of their usual orders?

*BG:* Yes, we direct mail to our list and to other people's lists and we do a fair amount of that and it's growing.

*GR:* I think the one thing that Bill and I wish for the most often, and I won't go on the soapbox I promise, is that I wish everyone would play on the same playing field in terms of claims and representations—the same rule book. We've been appreciative of the advice we have gotten over the years from the lawyers who told us where not to go and they have always kept us inside the box. It's made a difference because we have never had a problem, we've always stayed in the box. It has cost us money but it has also helped us create a sustainable business that is fair. Bill and I and our partners are sleeping well.

*SD:* You've done very well. I know there were a couple of instances where there was a little bit of heat on but you have always come through extremely well.

*GR:* We try to play by the rules, wish all others would do the same, most do, and in fact the bigger they get the more they start to commit to playing by the rules, which is always interesting because they realize what the downside is if they don't.

*SD:* You think ERA (Electronic Retailing Association) is important at this time Greg?

*GR:* It seems to be doing very well, I mean I am not as privy to the numbers as I used to be, but my understanding is that the cash flow is better than ever and the membership basis is solid.

*SD:* But is there a need?

*GR:* We just had a fascinating and fully attended strategic planning session with a facilitator and there were probably 20 top industry executives, and I thought it was quite stimulating but most importantly it was a deal-making scenario.

*SD:* I heard that your new *Youthful Essence* show tested well.

*GR:* Yes it did, but we have no idea what the long-term prospects will be. You originally predicted that the Victoria Jackson show would be a home run and it appeared that it would be a home run, but things didn't quite turn out that way.

In a presentation at one of your seminars, Steve Scott said, "I don't measure the success of a campaign at the beginning or the middle. I measure success when the campaign is all over and the books are closed, because so many things can happen in the process that you can never truly know in advance of the final outcome." So yes, a show might test well, but that doesn't guarantee a great ultimate outcome. GRC experienced that on the *Fitness Flyer*.

*BG:* We've also experienced situations where we thought we had a good response, and then after the test period, due to circumstances we hadn't anticipated, the response dwindled and we started getting into a more costly media area.

*SD:* The offer on your new *Youthful Essence* show is so good that it appears you are not making any profit at all on the front end. It appears that you'll make a profit only from the product's continuity program. If that's so, you won't be able to gauge the campaign's success until you see how many re-orders come in.

*BG:* That's the theory. It will take a while to grow out the product. Unfortunately, you can't just test the show on the weekend and on Monday fill your inventory and immediately roll. We will have to be patient.

*SD:* Very patient…Looking over your history, I think Guthy-Renker has an absolutely fascinating story. Your company is the only one that has successfully transitioned its operations from a one-product factory to an ongoing continuity business.

*BG:* First of all, it hasn't been a complete transformation. We still are and will continue to be involved in a lot of products that don't have a continuity element. The Winsor Pilates show is a one-shot. The Tony Robbins show is a one-shot. And we have other similar shows coming.

We want a good mix of products. Some of them will be more brand-oriented and long-term, building slowly and requiring patience. Other products will produce more immediate results. We believe we need both kinds of products.

*SD:* Why do you believe you need both kinds of products?

*GR:* We look for long-term and brandable—but not necessarily long-term continuity—products because they are durable and difficult to compete against. And if we can own a position with a brand that can last and be difficult to compete against, that definitely appeals to us. We do not operate very well in a world of urgency. We are slow. We take pride in being focused on excellence and we are willing to put in the time necessary to achieve excellence.

We do not like to chase things or have things chase us. We have been down that road. We've rushed. We've been caught up in, for instance, the fitness mania. We've learned that rushing usually causes problems and doesn't facilitate the best use of our resources. We think it's better to focus on creating long-term brands that can potentially generate sequels. That way, we believe, with good blessing, we'll sometimes get the long-term outcome we've hoped for.

*SD:* One way to build a unique long-term brand is by using a celebrity spokesperson. Nobody can knock off the celebrity, even though they might knock off the product.

*GR:* Well, the use of celebrities has its pros and cons. We are really in the product business, not the celebrity business.

There was an article about Nike in a recent issue of *The New Yorker* that basically said that in the golf world, Nike has been selling brand and Callaway has been selling product. The article seemed to suggest that Callaway will continue to prevail because it is focused on product.

So yes, celebrities can enhance the sale of a product, sometimes greatly. But for a long list of reasons, that strategy can also be dangerous.

**SD:** To revise my original question then, Guthy-Renker has transitioned from operations spread across a lot of different product categories to a leaner, more efficient, more focused business structure. You have certainly pared down the number of your employees while simultaneously investing an awful lot of time and money to put your systems in place.

**BG:** Essentially, we have focused the organization and the structure. I don't know if we have added as many capabilities as you might think.

From 1996 through 1998, we went through a fairly large growth period. We did very well in the middle 1990's. We made a lot of money and decided to reinvest in a broad spectrum of activities, from telemarketing centers to the GRTV Network to international growth to Internet growth, etc. We experimented across a very broad range of product categories, including hard goods, fitness, information, beauty and psychic. But we realized at the close of the books that many products were not working. We realized we couldn't be good at everything.

Ultimately, we found out that we are best and most profitable—and that we have a more enjoyable business—when we focus on a smaller range of products. So we had to pick and choose those products we enjoyed the most, and then we pointed our operations toward those selected areas.

**GR:** But we are smarter for having tried that broader range of products. And we are going to continue to try to be adventuresome and experimental in order to learn still more.

**SD:** Can you offer any tips for getting systems and procedures in place in a direct marketing company so that leaders don't have to be involved in every decision?

**BG:** I don't know that there is any secret or magic formula. For every company, I think the answer is probably different. Generally, it is important to pick a strategy and a focus. Then you have to get the best people and the best outside support from vendors. You also have to build good long-term relationships with outsiders and also, obviously, with your internal team. Most importantly, you have to know what you are good at and what you enjoy the most.

**GR:** If there is a secret to our current operational success, I think it's directly related to the outstanding quality of teammates and partners that we've assembled. One of the things that makes our company different, and I think QVC has this going for it also, is that our employees, particularly those at the highest levels, have been here for a long time. They are committed and we are committed to them. We understand each other.

Our ability to retain good employees has been crucial. If you look at some of the companies that tanked, including e4L and National Media, they always had a lot of turnover. It's easy to compete against turnover. It's easy to grow beyond those businesses. But you have to work to minimize turnover. You can't achieve stability and loyalty and commitment from your partners and teammates just by showing up. It takes work, and it takes flexibility and open-mindedness.

**BG:** You have to have the right talent. They have to be creative, smart and experienced.

**GR:** So you have to pick your teammates and partners well and you have to have luck. And they have to have some respect at the end of the day for the company, for each other, and for top management. I think that is probably the number one factor that has worked in our favor.

**SD:** How do you two divide your daily responsibilities? Does each of you focus on specific areas?

**GR:** There are a couple of analogies I can give you, and then Bill will change everything I said…just kidding. [Laughter]

First, both Bill and I, along with Ben and Kevin, are responsible for the day-to-day overall management and global top line of the entire company. The Board, if you will, is Bill, Ben, Greg and Kevin. So management responsibilities are divided up among the four of us, not just between Bill and me.

Ben is primarily responsible for business affairs and legal affairs. Kevin looks after administration, finance and operations. You might say Ben and Kevin "run" the company. Bill is responsible for all marketing on the back-end and for all ultimate roles of all products all the time. But again, we have management/board oversight over all processes, including firefighting.

My primary responsibility is on the front-end, and I have an excellent team. My team basically runs R & D and production. We bring in new products, get them produced, and deliver them. I'll give you an analogy: We are like a group of producers who deliver movies into a studio. Bill and his team run the studio. They are the suits, for lack of a better way of putting it, and we are the creative team. It's not exactly that way, but it's a fun way to think about it. Bill, Ben and Kevin, of course, approve every movie that gets done before it gets done. You might say that the studio is paying the money and we go out and get it done. Some projects work, some don't, and then some get sequels. I know that's an oversimplification. Bill, let's talk about what I said wrong and what I left out. [Laughter]

**BG:** Greg, I agree 100 percent with your point of view. [Laughter] Actually, it is pretty accurate. Ben also handles human resources and risk management. Kevin's domain is finance and operations. I wait for the shows to work and then I manage successful brands and products.

**SD:** Bill, do you still plug numbers into the Excel spreadsheet yourself?

*BG:* That I am not doing. I am very good at reading those sheets and analyzing, asking questions, probing and altering the assumptions. The actual manipulation of the model is not my forte. For that, we have very good analysts.

*SD:* You have another big make-up show in the works. Is the Victoria Jackson show basically dead as an infomercial?

*BG:* You are treading on thin ice here. [Laughter]

[Editor's note: Guthy is married to Victoria Jackson.]

Selling cosmetics has not been the easiest enterprise for us because it's a fashion-oriented activity. Women want more choices. They don't want to be force-fed a regular supply of the product. They want to experiment, to pick and choose, and they are not especially brand loyal. It's not hard to get customers in the door, but it's hard to get them to stay so that the business is economical and profitable.

But it wasn't a bad experiment. We just didn't achieve the level of success we wanted. As a result, we decided for the good of Victoria and of GRC, we would let her take back over the Victoria Jackson brand and move into some other areas with it. I am not sure yet where the brand is going—that will be Victoria's decision. She'll also manage the new Lola brand.

*SD:* Was that disappointment stressful to your marriage, Bill?

*BG:* We try to keep things very separate.

*SD:* How do you see the future of the infomercial industry?

*GR:* There are a few points I'd like to make. First, the Internet is a gift, an unexpected windfall gift, and it's only going to get better. Second, TiVo digital recorders could be dangerous. Third, there are still infomercial companies that make false claims and misrepresentations that taint the entire industry and cause people to not trust us. That situation does not seem to have improved. But there continues to be ethical and experienced business people and entrepreneurs who understand the industry and its nuances.

More broadly, I still think television is a profound distribution medium and it amazes me to this day how staggeringly effective a good campaign can be in creating a huge database instantly. That kind of success can be very challenging to the operations and management of an inexperienced company—but boy, it can also take you for a great ride if you hit the market at the right time with the right product.

Looking ahead, we are as optimistic now as we have ever been. I am a little bit concerned with economic factors associated with what I would call a potential wartime mentality now and in the future. But I'm more concerned about the future than I am about the situation right now. I'm concerned because the Gulf War crisis in 1991 seriously damaged our business. We were lucky to have survived. I think that with all the heat going on around the world right now, a similar event could impact our industry. Maybe not. I hope not.

**SD:**  In this kind of fearful economy, do some product categories tend to suffer more than others?

**GR:**  I don't know.

**SD:**  What about during an economic downturn?

**BG:**  That affects viewership, for sure, but I don't think it discriminates among products.

**SD:**  I would think that, for instance, a fitness product would be affected much more than an acne product.

**GR:**  That's a fair assessment.

**BG:**  Luxury products could be affected more than perceived necessities.

**SD:**  You own blocks of time on cable systems. How much has that contributed to your success?

**BG:**  We used to have our own media company, but we sold it about three years ago to TVN. We learned a lot and I'm glad we were in that business. But right now, basically like everybody else, we buy media time as we need it. There are some packages on various big cable systems that we try to maintain, but we don't own those packages. We try to maintain them by paying the money for them and by maintaining relationships with the cable companies.

**SD:**  On the average, what percentages of cable vs. broadcast time do you buy?

**GR:**  If I give you the numbers off the top of my head, probably four people in our company will send us an e-mail saying that we are nuts and out of touch. It would be an embarrassing estimate to make. But do you want me to make a guess?

**SD:**  Sure.

**GR:**  Fifty to sixty percent cable.

*BG:*  I think it is either 50-50 or 60-40, in favor of cable. I doubt that our numbers are much different from those of other infomercial companies.

*SD:*  You said earlier that you have been with Mercury Media from the beginning. I thought you did a lot of your media buying internally.

*BG:*  We buy most of our cable time internally and most of our broadcast time through Mercury. It is not 100 percent either way. Those are just the general directions.

*SD:*  What about the spot business? Is that something you are continuing after the business that Burl Hechtman started for you?

*BG:*  We don't have a separate business unit focusing on spots or a whole different product mix for retail deals. We have worked with retailers, including Kmart, Target and Home Depot, on products that were basically exclusive to those stores. We would create the spot, run the media and participate in the retail sales on a hybrid-marketing basis. We also created spots and bought time for them as an additional marketing channel for our existing products. This hasn't been a huge part of our business, but it is a marketing channel we use.

*SD:*  Are there any other important points that you'd like to make?

*GR:*  The direct response business—whether through infomercials, the Internet, print or spot ads—continues to hold the promise of the American dream. If you have a really good product that can help people and if you have a true service orientation, direct response is a fabulous way to get started as an entrepreneur. It offers an opportunity to start small, create word of mouth, and then begin to build a business by leveraging off your cash flow.

Bill and I began as a simple start-up in direct marketing. Initially, we only had a limited amount of capital. But we were willing to invest a lot of time into our business and into learning about the fundamentals of direct marketing, so we succeeded. Direct marketing works! With limited capital and a really good product, you can go to the moon. I think that's inspiring. And people are still doing it today. We are constantly looking over our shoulder to see who's coming next with what product in which categories. We love this business because it is as stimulating today as it was in the beginning. With some programs that we put out today, people respond as though they were Spider Man. That's fun!

Our company—not just Bill and I, but most of the people here—are having a lot of fun. We are having fun because we have redirected our vision toward quality products. I am not saying that we didn't offer quality products before, but primarily we focused on products that we knew we could sell and we were excited about being able to sell them. But since we've decided to focus on putting out only those products that we consider to be the best, the atmosphere here has changed. I think we've sent a "dynamic" out to the universe, and that because customers really believe in our products, we get rewarded. That is the accomplishment I am most pleased about.

*BG:* We are trying to find the best products in a limited number of categories. I think it is hard to be really good at a broad range of activities. As a company, we need to focus.

On the flip side, we are not totally focused on television or the infomercial format, although that is our lead strategy. You have asked where the future is heading. I am very optimistic for our company and for the direct marketing industry. I think as long as you remain focused on the right strategy and choose wisely—your product and business model—you'll have a good chance for success. You have to be good at a multitude of channels: infomercial, spot, print, direct mail, radio, Internet, home shopping, international, domestic, etc. You have to have a finely tuned machine to take advantage of all the available channels. Even as the television world changes with devices such as TiVo, if you develop expertise in other media channels, you will be able to continue to grow and prosper.

*SD:* Aside from television, which media channels do you think represent the most exciting avenues for growth? What markets or operational strategies hold promise for the future?

*BG:* I think we have only started to tap into the huge international market. Regarding other marketing channels, I think print and the Internet are the leading media, with radio, spot and other kinds of media trailing behind. Print offers a broad range of options, from space advertising to direct mail to package inserts. But I think the Internet is racing up the line quickly.

*SD:* Do you still need some other medium to drive business to the Internet?

*BG:* Of course. At least, so far we haven't figured out how to create a large enterprise using just the Internet by itself. Like I said, television remains the lead medium. It reaches a wide audience and creates a buzz for the brand. Other media channels supplement television, making the whole campaign more profitable. There is nothing really new with that.

*SD:* In a previous interview, you talked about motivational audio tapes that you listened to regularly. Do you still do that?

*BG:* No. There isn't any tape or tape series that I use repetitively. I do occasionally go back to some of the tapes I've used in the past, but there is nothing that is sitting in my car that I play weekly, if that's what you mean.

*SD:* The jet doesn't have a tape deck, Bill?

*BG:* You know it doesn't. We have to change that. It has a portable CD/DVD player, but it doesn't have a cassette deck.

*GR:* Steve, we only work on the plane. [Laughter]

*SD:* Now that your company's success is so firmly established, can you take more time off?

*BG:* Yes.

*SD:* So you can enjoy life outside of work?

*BG:* Yes. I am sure Greg will say the same thing. At this stage, we have a very stable business with stable brands and we have really good people in place. That allows us to keep our eye on the ball. This is so much fun, and we enjoy it so much. It is still very exciting to select and launch new brands and new products. It is still as thrilling as when we first got started.

What's great about our company's success is that it lets us strike the right balance between professional and personal life. What would be the point of having all of this if we had to work 70 hours a week like we did when we started? The ideal is to have a successful enterprise without the demands of a 70-hour work week. You need time for your kids and your personal life.

*SD:* Do you have an exit strategy?

*BG:* No…at least I don't. If our business becomes boring or if we are overly stressed, then I guess we might think about it. But we have a really fun, exciting business that occupies the time we allocate to it and we also have a flexible schedule that allows enough time off for our families and personal activities. So why think about leaving? The idea of selling or merging our company doesn't interest us because what would we do once it was gone? What could we do that would be more creative or more fun than this?

*GR:* I am sure the good Lord has his own exit strategy for us, but we are not sure what it is or when it will occur. [Laughter]

To add to Bill's point, we have seen other ways of doing business. Some years ago, we were given the gift of an opportunity to have a minority partner, a very wealthy man, who contributed capital, and we were later given the gift of an opportunity to join forces with a major media organization, i.e. Fox. We are now blessed with having been there and seen that, and we realized that wasn't exactly what we wanted.

We are grateful now that we were able to regain 100% control. We did not enter an irrevocable situation because we had very good advisors on those deals. Some people wonder what it would be like to take their company public, or to sell for a lot of money and then have partners. We've taken a look inside that house and we don't want to live there. We like where we are living now.

*BG:* Specifically, we sold a little over a third of our business to Ron Perelman's company, New World Entertainment, in 1993. He sold that entire operation to Fox, in 1996 I think. Two years later, we bought back the piece of our company that Fox then controlled.

*SD:* Was it difficult to do that?

*GR:* Yes, it was a risk. A big risk!

*BG:* Obviously, we had to come up with the cash to buy it back. So we had to believe in ourselves and in our company's future to justify the cost of buying back the stock.

*GR:* We did that by taking in orders for about six months, but we never shipped product. We just took the credit card cash and used it to buy back stock from Fox. Customers never got the product, so that helped a lot. [A big laugh]

*SD:* Your business is very stable now. You have product lines that yield steady and consistent profits, whereas in your early days, you were only as good as your last product.

*BG:* Exactly. Yet we also have some products—some currently offered and some in the pipeline—that don't fit that model. These are more one-shot oriented.

*SD:* From those partnerships you talked about, you got an inside view of some of the biggest companies in America, and how they work and how they don't work.

*GR:* By the way, those relationships weren't bad. We enjoyed them. We learned a lot.

*BG:* And we had some luck along the way. We got to see the inside of two large companies. We worked with great people, we had a bright future, we liked what we were seeing and liked our new focus and wanted to go a different way. Most large companies want you just to grow, and grow fast. We really wanted to focus on a slower growth strategy and to have more control over operations.

*SD:* Was there no real synergy between Fox and your company?

*BG:* I am sure there was potential, but I think the synergy factor is overrated. Look at the supposed synergy between AOL and Time Warner. That was touted greatly but I don't think it is materializing.

One of the challenges that a company like ours will face in the future is to remain entrepreneurial without becoming overly bureaucratic. The bigger you get, the more systems you must put in place, the more employees you acquire, and the more you have to follow various policies and procedures that may inhibit entrepreneurial, quick-footed action. One of the things we learned, particularly from Fox because Fox was so big, was that if we became fully owned by Fox, we might have to wait a year to get a green light on a show. The whole market could have come and gone before we'd even gotten started.

*GR:* That was one stage in our company's evolution, and we're glad we went through it. To keep growing, you have to keep changing. But I strongly believe there has never a better time in America to have a private company and the direct response industry opens the door for many small entrepreneurs. Again, all you need is a good product, a true service orientation, and the willingness to work hard. That's how we did it. That's how we made our dream come true.

*Bonus!*

# SPECIAL REPORT:

# MY PERSONAL FORMULA FOR WEALTH

By *Steven Dworman*

**Publisher**

**Infomercial Marketing Report**

# INTRODUCTION

n 1989, I began consulting for a number of companies in the infomercial industry. I had a fairly extensive background in both direct response marketing and the entertainment industry. Both were very essential elements utilized in my new consulting role. I immersed myself in every aspect of the business—from show creation to creating product, telemarketing scripts, back-end programs, and additional marketing avenues. This early information that I learned was essential in my education. But it wasn't until I created my own product (a perfume called Curiosity) produced my own infomercial, purchased the media time, and created my own back-end marketing programs that I really learned all aspects of the business from the trenches.

The following report is a compilation of what I learned from my hands-on experience, and the experience of others in the business who shared their startling insights with me confidentially. You'll notice I don't talk about any of their actual campaigns, just the lessons learned.

This report contains the most important information I've learned over the past 15 years in this business. It's never been printed in any book, report, or literature previously. In fact, fewer than 10 people in the world probably know it. This isn't an exaggeration. When I printed this information in the final issue of *The Infomercial Marketing Report*, the most successful company in the industry, The Guthy-Renker Corporation, made this mandatory reading for all of their employees.

Everything in this report is based solely on what has been proven to work in the real world. Companies have literally spent millions of dollars discovering the secrets I lay before you.

Properly applied, this inside information will be a gold mine to your marketing efforts.

Enjoy!

Steven Dworman

# THE INFOMERCIAL

❭ No one can predict a hit. It's very much like the movie business. You can put all the elements together, but until you test your show, there's no way to know exactly what you've got.

❭ The only exception to the first point occurs if you find a product that's already selling like hot cakes in a county fair-type venue and hasn't yet found widespread exposure. Then, it's just a matter of not screwing up a successful pitch that's been perfected over time. Examples of this include The Smart Mop and The Miracle Blade.

❭ Successful products on QVC or the Home Shopping Network do not necessarily translate to good spot or infomercial products. If this were true, these networks' DRTV divisions would be the most successful in the industry. This situation really is a mystery. My guess is that none of these companies have a DRTV genius who can pull this off.

These networks are such an incredible testing ground. For example, companies that present a product in multiple appearances during just one weekend can often double or triple their sales from their first to their last appearance simply by paying careful attention to the sales impact of specific on-air comments and then incorporating more of these revenue generating claims and statements.

❭ There are only a handful of true DR geniuses with whom I would trust my own money to produce a winning show. Who are they? Steve Scott and Frank Kovacs, who produce for American Telecast; Eric Stilson, the marketing genius behind HealthRider; Lenny Lieberman of ProActive; Tony Robbins; Victoria Principal; Ron Popeil, who produces for himself with incredible results; and Mike Levy, creator of *Amazing Discoveries*. I also take my hat off to the people at American Marketing

Systems for making Carlton Sheets such a success as it enters its second decade.

❯ A successful infomercial is a miraculous science of entertainment and sales. It's a high-wire balancing act: too much of one element at the expense of the other and you've lost the sale. Entertainment gets people to stop and watch what you're doing and it keeps their eyeballs glued to the program. But too much entertainment undercuts the sales message. Direct marketing copywriters learned this long ago. That's one of the reasons that cute headlines seldom work.

❯ During the early 1990s, many supposed experts recommended repeating your infomercial message every seven minutes in a "pod" format. This has never been proven effective, and I don't believe it works. Studies show that 90% of all orders come in at the end of the show. Logically, the more you repeat yourself, the more people will feel they've already seen your entire message and the more they'll tune out early. These people won't be around to participate in that golden 90% sales window.

❯ Direct response TV is a mass medium. Small changes made in a show can, over a period of time, significantly impact profitability. A new word in your offer, a different bonus, different placement of your commercials—any such adjustment can generate a 1% to 2% increase in orders that will mean a $1 to $2 million increase to your bottom line on a $100 million campaign.

❯ Having watched infomercials for 15 years, the public has become very sophisticated. Most of the shows on the air now are old, tired and formula-driven. I haven't seen anything really new and exciting in quite a while. Neither has the public.

Think outside the box. What will capture the public's attention, startle them, and get them talking the next day?

❯ Never make your celebrity the expert. Always have your celebrity play the role of the satisfied customer.

❯ Make your before-and-after examples as realistic as possible. The public is sophisticated. Don't change filters or lighting…customers will see it in the eyes and know that what you're promising is not true.

❯ Many successful shows have a certain magic about them that works, regardless of the technical polish of the presentation. I always remember a lesson that Tony Hoffman taught at one of my seminars. He showed an infomercial he had produced for a kitchen product. The show wasn't well produced, but the product was selling extremely well. Tony figured that if he went back and reshot the show with higher production values, sales would climb even higher. He used the same script and talent as for the first show. But when he tested the new version, it bombed. Tony went back to the old, poorly produced show immediately. Maybe it was the spontaneity of the first version, maybe just voodoo.

❱ American Telecast always has an announcer read the 800 phone number over the air, in addition to supering it onscreen. I have no doubt they've tested this and it obviously makes a difference, or the company wouldn't consistently spend the additional time and money.

❱ Original music may be the most important element missing from most infomercials. Filmmakers learned the importance of music years ago. Music can make a good scene great. It tugs on the heartstrings and stirs emotion and desire.

❱ To increase your credibility 100-fold, have a member of your talent stand in for the home audience and express doubts or disbelief about the product. In his most effective shows, Mike Levy proved a master at this. He played skeptical, asked hard questions, and then presented knockout answers.

❱ Want to really gain tremendous credibility? Show something go wrong during a demonstration and acknowledge the problem. The audience will believe you have nothing to hide.

❱ Television buyers, as a general rule, are not as faithful or as long-term as print buyers.

❱ Most shows use too many call-to-actions and the first one usually occurs much too early. When I ran my infomercial for Curiosity Perfume, five different women told us that they were ready to order the product about seven minutes into the show. We then put a commercial in that exact spot and re-tested the show on the stations where it had previously run. Sales dropped in half. Why? I think it was because although their heads said they were ready emotionally, the women hadn't been whipped up into enough of an emotional frenzy to pick up the phone and dial.

Unfortunately, most call-to-actions appear before the viewer is sold. But once the offer has been revealed, the viewer has no reason to keep watching.

❱ Expert opinion on your show can add tremendous credibility. The more authoritative your source, the more impact he or she will have.

❱ What can you do to create excitement during your show? Ron Popeil generates excitement in a kitchen by having multiple activities going on simultaneously. Eric Stilson produced an avalanche of excitement in the HealthRider infomercial by having a troop of attractive women perform dance movements on the machine in different settings. Mike Levy set the hood of a car on fire to demonstrate a car wax. Ask yourself: How can you get people to stop flipping channels and become mesmerized by your product?

❯ American Telecast claimed for years that celebrities make a huge difference in response rates. Guthy-Renker has obviously tested this and is using bigger and bigger celebrities in their upcoming shows. They wouldn't be paying substantial pieces of the gross unless the celebrity was elevating response by a rate significantly higher than the celebrity's cut.

❯ You're not selling a product…you're selling a solution to a problem that the viewer has. Your product is a magic elixir that will greatly improve the customer's life. Logic is the ammunition, but emotion is the power that compels the sale.

❯ What demonstration will show that your product is better than anything else on the market? Can you add some entertainment value to the demonstration? Does your product have a flaw or weakness? By revealing the one flaw, the viewer will view you as honest and trustworthy. Your claims will have much more believability.

❯ Selling multiple products in a 30-minute show never works. I've seen it tried, always unsuccessfully, with fitness equipment, African artifacts, new products, and on a syndicated show featuring Joan Rivers as host. There are several reasons that multiple product shows fail.

At one of my seminars, Joe Sugarman told a story about a print ad for a watch that he ran in *The Wall Street Journal*. The ad pulled in a lot of business, but the watch manufacturer was upset that the ad didn't feature the eight other models in which the watch was available (e.g., children's styles, woman's styles, different colors). To placate the manufacturer, Joe created a new multiple selection ad and ran it and his original ad as an A-B split in *The Wall Street Journal*. The new multiple selection ad achieved a response rate that was only one-third that of Joe's first ad.

Anytime you try to sell more than one product in a single ad, you dissipate the emotional intensity you've carefully built up for the main product. The only exception I've seen to this rule was a brilliant 30-minute show created and produced by Eric Stilson. With a male and female host showcasing four or five various new products, the show was designed to identify which product—if any—might generate a high enough response rate to justify its own infomercial. As a benchmark, Stilson inserted into the new show a successful direct response ad that he had run repeatedly during the previous year. By comparing the new products' sales performance against the known commodity's results, Stilson was able to identify one of his most successful products ever…a product he didn't think had a chance in hell before testing.

# TESTIMONIALS

❯ Most testimonials are dull and unexciting. In your show, question your testimonial subjects. Play devil's advocate. If these people really love your product, make them convince us. The public is smart. They know that when you jump-cut, something is getting cut out.

❯ This may be the most important subtlety I've ever learned about testimonials: Instead of focusing on the affect that a product has had on a person's own life, emphasize the affect that the person testifying thinks the product will have on the *home viewer's* life.

❯ Testimonials should always reflect as closely as possible the age range and ethnic makeup of the group you are targeting as customers. Of course, you want your testimonials to be as broad-based as possible, so that your target audience will be as large as possible.

❯ Testimonial style of dress should be similar to that of the customer you're trying to reach. An authority should dress up to reflect his or her stature.

❯ Before-and-after shots should be as real and unaltered as possible. The public is smart. They've been looking at these shows for 15 years. They can tell when an image seems altered. Keep your lighting, lenses, and filters consistent from one picture to the next. Guthy-Renker does a superb job of this in their skin care shows.

# OFFERS

⟩  Offer viewers the products at half the price of retail, and then add other items to double the value.

⟩  The lower your entrée price on a continuity program, the less qualified your lead will probably be.

⟩  A lower price doesn't always guarantee more orders. There are many instances when raising the price increases perceived worth of the product and therefore increases orders. The only way to know is to price-test.

⟩  An infomercial pulls more leads on an expensive product if the full price isn't quoted on the show. However, to make this work effectively, you need a trained team of inbound operators who receive a commission on sales.

⟩  "Get a second one free" almost always tests as the best offer.

⟩  It helps to put a face to your company. Try showing one of your operators standing by—that always seems to increase response.

⟩  To further boost response, have a clock onscreen counting down the seconds left in which people can place an order.

❱ Make your offer so irresistible that it appears that you have to be losing money on every sale.

❱ Begin showing the value of your product at an extremely high price so that by the time you reach the real sales price, it seems dirt cheap in comparison.

❱ "But wait—there's more" gets repeated over and over again for a reason. It works.

❱ Multi-pay generates more orders than single pay. You can generally convert over 60% of multi-pay callers into single pay with the right incentive. If you do this, it will diminish the response rate to your subsequently read upsells.

# TELEMARKETING

▶ 90% of your phone calls come in at the end of your show.

▶ When a customer calls into your telemarketing center to order your product and you ask them a question about buying an upsell or additional product, a certain percentage of people will always say yes. The trick is to discover the right question at the right time so that the majority of them will say yes.

▶ Spend time and make the effort to learn the sequence in which your telemarketers' order screens appear. These screens are usually programmed to act in a certain way. For example, if the customer answers, "Yes," we go to computer screen B. After spending time uncovering this for my own infomercial, I discovered a different order for the screens that resulted in 10% more orders. Don't assume that the way your telemarketer traditionally operates is the way that's most profitable way for you.

▶ Have your telemarketing company record an assortment of your incoming telephone calls. You can learn a tremendous amount by listening to the questions that come up during calls. Use this information to rewrite your telemarketing scripts. It's a sure bet that many more people have the same questions, but just aren't asking. If you address the issues you hear in phone calls, viewers will be more likely to order your product.

▶ The most amazing, profitable, yet underused tool in the direct response television business is the A–B split on incoming telemarketing calls. Here's how the A–B split works: You create two scripts. Each script is read with every alternate call. You can test different price points, different upsells, the order in which the upsells are read, and almost anything else you can think of. You can even test whether a certain shipping and handling cost makes a difference.

I used this constantly for my Curiosity Perfume infomercial and as a result, was able to boost my upsell rate as high as 65%. I also got check debit to work (the only time in West's history up to that point). If you're able to increase upsell rates by even a few percentage points, that can easily represent millions of dollars to you over the life of a campaign. And the amazing thing is, this costs next to nothing to use. It's the most profitable industry tool—bar none!

❱ It is not generally profitable to have dedicated operators on your inbound phone calls. However, it is profitable on back-end and customer service calls if you are selling: a continuity program, a product costing more than $400, or costly upsell items (as are often found in business opportunities). Guthy-Renker has 300 dedicated operators handling its three million ProActive customers. This is an expense you need to figure on when dealing with large-scale programs.

❱ At a telemarketing center like West, an average of 50% of incoming calls are for information. You pay for all those calls without seeing any return.

When you test your show, have your telemarketer record these calls. You'll find out what information people didn't hear—or didn't hear often enough—during the show. Then, before rolling out your show, go back to post production and insert answers to the most frequently asked questions. You'll save a fortune in customer service calls over the course of your campaign.

❱ The highest positive response you'll receive is for the first upsell you pitch to your customer. Each additional upsell will yield a diminishing response rate.

❱ If a customer says no to your first upsell, be prepared with a fallback, a less expensive upsell. Even if a customer refuses your first upsell offer, he or she will often say yes to a second upsell if you make it easy for them.

❱ For an ongoing campaign, such as for continuity products, customer service operators should all be trained and using your products. They are the spokespeople and representatives of your company. Take good care of them. Make them feel like they are part of your company. Keep them informed, and bring them into your company's decision-making and direction-setting processes. Encourage your customer service operators to feel pride in your company and the products that you are selling together. They'll transmit their positive attitude during sales calls, and your customers will begin to feel the same way.

# OUTBOUND TELEMARKETING

❱ Outbound campaigns are usually much more effective if the customer first receives a mailed offer, then a follow-up phone call.

❱ Outbound telemarketers produce better results if they receive a commission on each sale. However, a commission pay structure can backfire by making telemarketers more aggressive and consequently more likely to alienate customers.

❱ If customers are thrilled with your product, they will want to hear from you. If your product isn't everything they expected, you'll spend a fortune on customer service calls rather than sales calls.

❱ I once knew I was going to have a shortage of product. I implemented an outbound campaign to my best customers to inform them that we were going to be out of product for 90 days. Over 75% of the customers contacted placed an order so they wouldn't run out of product. If you can turn a sales call into a call where you're giving customers true inside information, they'll not only feel appreciated and cared about, but they'll reward you.

❱ Limit the number of times per year you call a customer. You are intruding on their private time at home and with their families. One call too many and you'll no longer be welcome.

❱ From your customer's point of view, make sure you have a good enough reason to call. Make sure your offer is truly special.

# PRODUCT

❱ Product is king. A gorgeous show won't sell a lousy product, but a poorly produced show will sell a great product.

❱ Television is a mass-market medium. For your product to really succeed, it needs to appeal to the largest number of people. As popular as golf is, it's not a mass-market sport and consequently few golf shows have ever been very profitable.

❱ A successful product should do two things: solve a major problem for the customer and hold the promise of tremendously enhancing one's life.

❱ A product needs to sell at four to six times its cost. The more expensive the product, the lower the acceptable margin.

❱ Prevention-oriented products never seem to sell. I've seen some amazingly produced shows that have tried to do this and failed miserably.

❱ A product should exceed a customer's expectations. Many a company has been pushed to the brink of ruin by an avalanche of returns.

❱ Every product should have a unique selling proposition. What makes this product superior to everything else on the market? How can you best demonstrate that?

❱ A product that is exclusive and covered by patents is certainly preferable to one that isn't. However, if your product succeeds, you'll probably be forced to spend a fortune in legal fees defending your patent against knock-offs.

❱ The most difficult thing in the infomercial business is to be an entrepreneur who takes a chance on a new and innovative product. It's impossible to know whether a new product will work until it's tested. The easiest thing in the infomercial business is to be the person who knocks off a successful product and settles in court later.

❱ Most audio and video programs that are sold never get listened to. They sit on customers' shelves unopened.

❱ The higher priced your product is, or the more payments it requires, the better your chances are of getting it back as a return.

❱ If you see an infomercial selling a $39.95 product, understand that it's impossible for the seller to make money at that price. The seller plans to make money via much higher-priced back-end products or services

# MEDIA

❱ If a product can easily be demonstrated in a 2-minute spot, don't even think about using an infomercial. You don't need to spend the money on the extra 26.5 minutes.

❱ In general, cable customers are wealthier and more likely to have access to credit cards than broadcast buyers who receive their TV signal for free.

❱ Media buyers make their money by selling media time. Set a minimum response rate that they must meet. It's the only way to hold them accountable.

❱ Yank your show off at the beginning of April to avoid the bottomless response pit of April 15th.

❱ The more media you purchase on a weekly basis, the faster your show will burn out.

❱ In broadcast, keep in mind that compelling local events can put a huge dent in response rates. You don't want to run opposite a big local sporting event. You want to run before or after. Likewise, a big news event will keep eyeballs away from your show.

❱ When a disaster occurs—a war, stock market crash, or major international incident—and all eyes turn to CNN and other news channels, get off the air. No one will watch your show.

❱ Make sure your media buyer gets station affidavits showing that your spot aired. Every once in a while, a show doesn't run and the telemarketer assigns calls to the station by mistake. You may assume incorrectly that your show ran and pay for it.

❱ Nothing beats asking a media buyer who grew up in a local market for his or her recommendations about when to run your show in that area.

❱ An average of 50% of all 2-minute DR spots don't run.

❱ Compared to 10 years ago, it now takes a lot more media to reach the same number of eyeballs. Cable and satellite systems offer hundreds of stations. But even though fewer eyes are watching, the cost of the media has continued to rise, as much as 500% during the past decade.

❱ First and fourth quarters are traditionally the best times for higher direct response rates. Summer is usually the worst.

❱ Every year, everyone gets shocked by the proposed third quarter rates.

❱ Traditionally, a media buyer should look at four categories in a media test: major metropolitan areas, rural, broadcast, and cable.

❱ Cable is pricing itself out of the market. Cable companies keep raising their prices while their audience dwindles or gets overlaid by local cable operators. Less cable time is available now compared to five years ago. At current cable rates, most infomercial companies are finding it extremely difficult to turn a front-end profit. The situation is only going to get worse.

❱ An average infomercial campaign in today's market consists of 60% broadcast time and 40% cable time. Cable is becoming less and less efficient because of increased rates and overlays.

❱ The biggest danger to the infomercial industry arises from TiVo and similar digital recording devices about to be launched. These machines eliminate the need for viewers to scan channels and thereby reduces the likelihood of them finding your show by accident.

❱ QVC and HSN are the greatest partners a direct response television company can have. The difficulty at times is that the margins don't work, especially with products costing less than $19.95. With some of the aggressive offers taking place, it's nearly impossible to sell product to these networks at a wholesale price of 50% or less and the networks insist on offering their customers the best prices being advertised.

# BACK-END

> Without any doubt, the back-end is where 96% of the money is made.

> Your back-end program should be thoroughly thought out before you spend a dime to produce your show. The entire show should not only sell your initial product—it should also build anticipation and desire for subsequent products.

> One of the best investments you can ever make is a 37¢ stamp on a piece of mail making your customer feel important and special, instead of trying to sell them something.

> In today's market, it's essential to gather your customers' e-mail addresses. Once you've built up your list, it costs nothing to inform your customers of the latest special, product update or new product introduction.

> The greatest sales I've ever generated in the back-end resulted from sharing inside information on a personal basis with my customers. I tell them what's going on behind the scenes and how they benefit as a result.

> Most companies tend to send catalogs or printed matter to their customers. Instead, try sending an offer from your spokesperson personally addressed to your customer. This will not only increase sales, but customer loyalty as well.

> Make your customer feel as if they belong to something special. Give them a free gift com-

pletely unexpectedly. Tell them you're doing this strictly because you want them to know how much you appreciate them. Resell your customers on your commitment to them.

❯ When setting up a continuity business, make sure that you have the ability to instantly alter your customer's shipping cycle or alter the products that are normally included. You never want your customers to feel like you're inundating them with products they don't yet need or want. Customers who have this control stay on continuity plans for a longer period of time. There are only a handful of fulfillment companies that can truly offer flexible shipping plans.

❯ If you're running an infomercial promoting real estate purchasing or some other business opportunity, remember this hard-learned lesson: Your back-end programs (which is where your money is) are only as good as the infomercial driving new leads into your business. If your next infomercial bombs, your back-end will dry up shortly thereafter.

❯ American Telecast did something very unique with its continuity programs. They make every 5th kit free. The company tested this idea and found that it kept a majority of customers in the game for a longer period of time. Other companies offer a free gift. People are motivated by personal gain.

❯ Spend a couple of hours every month on the telephone talking to your customers. You'll learn more this way than from any report that lands on your desk. Your customers can be your greatest source of ideas and information.

❯ Test different offers and/or price points for your list before rolling out to your entire customer base. That sounds obvious, but too often companies are in a hurry and don't take the time. Again, a slight change in response can yield a tremendous upsurge in profits.

❯ If a customer returns a product, or opts out of a continuity program, attempt to resell them on another product. For example, if a customer decides to cancel her continuity program from Victoria Principal, send a letter from Victoria Principal stating that she's sorry to see her go, but Victoria's main concern is that the customer gets products that work for her. Victoria then recommends her friend Kathie Lee's products. Enclosed is a free gift certificate worth $25.00. You can then pay Victoria Principal a percentage of sales for every customer who sticks. It's a win-win proposition for everyone.

# BUSINESS PRACTICES WITHIN THE INDUSTRY

❯ The public is skeptical of infomercials to begin with. The moment they see a show making disparaging remarks about a competitive product, the credibility of the entire industry suffers.

❯ The minute a national news program airs a story critical of an infomercial product, response rates drop dramatically for every show airing and every product being sold.

❯ The infomercial industry employs some of the best patent attorneys in the world to uncover ways of getting around the patents of successful products.

❯ When one infomercial company discovers a hot product category, a slew of other companies rush to knock off the product. The philosophy is, "Get while the getting is good and settle later." Unfortunately, in many cases, a company can make tens of millions of dollars knocking off products. Settlements always seem to be for less than the amount gained. As long as this is the case, this practice will continue.

❯ Few companies have explored cooperation. I wrote an editorial about this years ago and I still believe it's a strategy worth pursuing. Let's say that a customer returned a Total Gym. There's no good reason that a letter can't go to the customer expressing the company's regret that the machine didn't work for that person and offering to send a Bowflex at a significantly reduced price as a thank-you for trying the Total Gym. Bowflex and American Telecast would then split profits on the Bowflex sale. It's a big win-win, and entails no marketing cost except for the letter and possible follow-up phone call.

❱   For infomercial campaigns featuring stand-alone products, the net profit before taxes is only 8% to 12%. If you give a celebrity a 4% royalty, he or she will pocket 33% to 50% of your net profits.

❱   Depending on your product category, you can sell an average of four to five times more product in retail than on television. Often, companies run their television campaign on a break-even or loss basis in order to drive their retail campaign.

# Steven M. Dworman
## Author

In the burgeoning field of infomercials, Steve Dworman has emerged as the industry expert. In 1991 he began publishing "The INFOMERCIAL MARKETING REPORT, " a monthly subscription newsletter read in over 20 countries worldwide. He also published with Adweek Magazines, "Adweek's Direct Response Television Sourcebook."

Having produced and run his own direct response television campaigns, Dworman learned all aspects of the industry. He has consulted with *Fortune 500* companies such as Procter & Gamble, Estee Lauder, Mattel, Avon, Apple Computer, Microsoft, and many others.

He's been quoted by over 3,000 news sources including: *Wall Street Journal, Los Angeles Times, The Economist, The New York Times, CNN, The Washington Post, The Chicago Tribune* to name just a few.

He has a key eye for picking products and was responsible for many huge successes in the industry such as Total Gym, which grossed close to $1 billion in sales.

Dworman served on the Board of Directors for Positive Response Television, a public company in the direct response television industry.

He also served as President and Founder of DMMO, the Digital Media Marketing Organization with members such as, Eastman Kodak, Technicolor, Warner Home Media, Sony Digital, and JVC amongst many other leading companies.

In 2001 he wrote, directed and acted in a feature film entitled, *Divorce: the Musical.* The film was featured on CNN, and in a front-page story in The Los Angeles Times.

He is currently consulting within the DRTV industry.

His email address is: steve@itreallyworks.tv

The website for this book is: www.drtvsecrets.com